Live Linux® CDs

D1121079

Your practical, hands-on guides to getting real results with free software

Books in the Negus Live Linux Series encourage and challenge you to advance in the free software world. Boot the live DVD or CD that comes with each book and watch the Linux system, applications, and content described in the book come to life before your eyes.

Start as a novice by trying out examples and finish as a professional, mastering the many topics covered in the series, from building PHP/MySQL sites to customizing live CDs and more. When you are finished, you will know how to use, customize, and rebuild that free and open source software yourself.

Overseeing the series is Christopher Negus, bestselling author of the Red Hat Linux Bible series, Linux Toys series, and the signature book for this series, *Live Linux CDs*.

NEGUS LIVE LINUX SERIES

Live Linux® CDs

Building and Customizing Bootables

Christopher Negus

PRENTICE HALL

An Imprint of Pearson Education

Upper Saddle River, NJ ■ Boston ■ Indianapolis ■ San Francisco

New York ■ Toronto ■ Montreal ■ London ■ Munich ■ Paris ■ Madrid

Cape Town ■ Sydney ■ Tokyo ■ Singapore ■ Mexico City

Many of the designations used by manufacturers and sellers to distinguish their products are claimed as trademarks. Where those designations appear in this book, and the publisher was aware of a trademark claim, the designations have been printed with initial capital letters or in all capitals.

The author and publisher have taken care in the preparation of this book, but make no expressed or implied warranty of any kind and assume no responsibility for errors or omissions. No liability is assumed for incidental or consequential damages in connection with or arising out of the use of the information or programs contained herein.

The publisher offers excellent discounts on this book when ordered in quantity for bulk purchases or special sales, which may include electronic versions and/or custom covers and content particular to your business, training goals, marketing focus, and branding interests. For more information, please contact:

U.S. Corporate and Government Sales
(800) 382-3419
corpsales@pearsontechgroup.com

For sales outside the United States please contact:

International Sales
international@pearsoned.com

 This Book Is Safari Enabled

The Safari® Enabled icon on the cover of your favorite technology book means the book is available through Safari Bookshelf. When you buy this book, you get free access to the online edition for 45 days. Safari Bookshelf is an electronic reference library that lets you easily search thousands of technical books, find code samples, download chapters, and access technical information whenever and wherever you need it.

To gain 45-day Safari Enabled access to this book:

- Go to http://www.prenhallprofessional.com/safarienabled
- Complete the brief registration form
- Enter the coupon code CNF9-3FRE-N1I7-N2E3-1965

If you have difficulty registering on Safari Bookshelf or accessing the online edition, please e-mail customer-service@safaribooksonline.com.

Visit us on the Web: www.prenhallprofessional.com

ISBN 0-13-243274-9
Text printed in the United States on recycled paper at R.R. Donnelley and Sons in Crawfordsville, Indiana.
First printing, November 2006

Library of Congress Cataloging-in-Publication Data

Negus, Chris, 1957-

Live Linux CDs : building and customizing bootables / Christopher Negus.

p. cm.

ISBN 0-13-243274-9 (pbk. : alk. paper) 1. Linux. 2. Operating systems (Computers) 3. CD-Rs. I. Title.

QA76.76.O63N4245 2006

005.4'32—dc22

2006027573

As always, I dedicate this book to my wife, Sheree.

Contents

Acknowledgments

I'd like to acknowledge the work of the thousands of free and open-source software developers around the world who have built, tested, tweaked, and published their software so that everyone can use it freely. Because of their efforts, you and I have literally thousands of unique software packages to choose from as we build the live CDs described in this book.

Thanks to Debra Williams Cauley for encouraging me to do this book and start the *Negus Live Linux Series* with Prentice Hall. Her work has helped me produce the kinds of Linux books I want to write, while still getting me to do them within the time constraints of the publishing world. Others from Prentice Hall who have helped me through this project include Songlin Qiu (development editor), Krista Hansing (copy editor), and Christy Hackerd (project editor).

Direct help in writing and technical editing has come from several sources. Joe "Zonker" Brockmeier came through in a pinch and wrote the Firewall and Cluster live CD chapters. Jasper Hartline, a key developer on the Fedora Kadischi live CD team, tech-edited the entire book. Chris Ginelloni, lead developer of the Gentoo installer (Catalyst), reviewed the chapter on building a Gentoo live CD (with the latest Catalyst software just recently completed). John Kennedy came in to provide last-minute technical review assistance.

Finally, I'd like to thank my family for helping me stay at it for the many months it takes to write a book.

About the Author

Christopher Negus has been one of the world's leading writers of Linux books for nearly a decade. His *Red Hat Linux Bible* series has sold more than a quarter-million copies worldwide. Chris also authored or coauthored the books *Linux Bible* (2005 and 2006 editions), *Linux Toys, Linux Toys II,* and *Linux Troubleshooting Bible* for Wiley Publishing.

Before becoming a full-time author, Chris Negus worked on UNIX operating system development teams at AT&T Bell Labs, UNIX System Labs, and Novell in the 1980s and 1990s. In particular, Chris worked in the areas of UNIX system administration and networking.

Live Linux CDs is Chris's first book in the *Negus Live Linux Series* with Prentice Hall. This book reflects Chris's dedication to getting powerful, free software up and running quickly and securely. Chris is helping Prentice Hall develop other books in the series, which you can expect to follow in the near future.

When not working on computer books, Chris likes to spend time with his family: Sheree, Seth, and Caleb. Chris also enjoys playing soccer, singing opera (when nobody can hear him), and making things out of old computers.

Introduction

A live CD is a complete computer operating system on a single disk. You simply pop it into your PC and reboot. Whether the computer has Windows, Linux, or nothing at all installed on it, the live CD hands you control of that computer, using the operating system, applications, and data on that CD.

That's when the fun begins.

Today dozens of live CDs based on Linux are available for purchase or free download from the Internet. Some of the live CDs are made as general desktop Linux systems (such as Knoppix). Others are built as specialized toolkits, as with the BackTrack Security CD or Dynabolic multimedia production CD. Still others are made to run specialized systems, as with the Devil Linux firewall CD or the ParallelKnoppix cluster live CD.

The goal of this book is to introduce you to the world of Linux live CDs and then take you as far as you want to go with it. You might just want to try out some existing live CDs (we give you some to try). If you like a particular live CD, you might want to save settings and data across reboots. Or, eventually, you might want to build a live CD completely customized to your desires.

This book starts pretty basically with how to use live CDs, but the ultimate goal is to help you make the exact live CD you want. For example, with procedures in this book, you can end up with a Linux live CD that does the following:

- Boots directly to a presentation or slide show (Chapter 10)
- Lets you add software to a running security toolkit (Chapter 9)
- Includes your own movies or music with a player set to play them (Chapter 12)
- Acts as a personal firewall live CD to protect your LAN (Chapter 13)

1

- Can configure cluster computing among a group of computers (Chapter 14)
- Lets you set up a gaming console or server from any available PC (Chapter 11)

If you are partial to a particular Linux distribution, you can probably find a live CD described here that's built on that distribution. For example, in Chapters 6–8, we describe how to build live CDs based on Knoppix (Debian), Fedora, and Gentoo Linux distributions. BackTrack (Chapter 9) is based on SLAX (a slackware CD). The presentation live CD (Chapter 10) is built on Damn Small Linux.

If you want to dig deeper into building your own live CD, the book includes description of core technology. You learn how to work with boot loaders, make compressed file systems, and follow (and adapt) the boot process from the time the machine turns on until you see a working desktop or shell prompt.

AUDIENCE FOR THIS BOOK

If you have never used Linux, live CDs are a great way to try out different types of Linux systems. Chances are, you will be able to follow along quite comfortably for a few chapters, trying out some live CD desktop systems, games, and various applications. You should even be able to learn how to save your desktop files and settings without much trouble.

As you enter the second part of the book, however, some knowledge of Linux is useful (if not necessary). You don't need to be a programmer to remaster a live CD or even build one from scratch. However, a working knowledge of how to use the shell, a text editor, and shell commands are needed as you move into the more technical areas of the book.

ORGANIZATION OF THIS BOOK

This book follows the charter of the new Negus Live Linux Series to get hands-on experience quickly, dig in deeply to key components, and then step through how to get real, specific results. To that end, this book is divided into three major parts:

- **Part I, "Beginning with Bootable Live Linuxes"**—This is the Linux live CD "user" part of the book. It is designed to get your hands on a working live CD within a few minutes. You will tour a few Linux live CDs and then learn some basics about boot options, customizing your desktop, and ways to save your data to hard disk or removable media.

- **Part II, "Creating a Custom Bootable Linux"**—In this part, I get deeper into the inner workings of a live CD. You will learn about boot loaders, file systems used on live CDs, and the `init` process. The last three chapters are dedicated to remastering or customizing live CDs based on Knoppix (Chapter 6), Fedora (Chapter 7), or Gentoo (Chapter 8).

- **Part III, "Making a Specialized Bootable Linux"**—Because creating a Linux live CD involves more than just running a few scripts and burning CDs, this part focuses on specific types of live CDs that might interest you. For different types of live CDs (security, gaming, multimedia, firewall, and so on), one or two live CDs are showcased.

From each live CD category chapter, you can learn about the types of components in that type of live CD so you can begin thinking about what you might put into a live CD of that type. In some cases, you will learn how to use tools from the featured live CD to quickly personalize it. For example, you could learn to add your own presentations or slide shows to the bootable presentation live CD (Chapter 10), add movies to a multimedia player live CD (Chapter 12), or add software to a SLAX live CD (Chapter 9).

The two appendices provide some supporting information. Appendix A, "On the DVD," describes the contents of the DVD. Appendix B, "Building, Testing, and Burning ISOs," goes into some depth about tools touched on throughout the book for making ISO images (`mkisofs` command), testing them (`qemu` emulator), and burning images to disks (`cdrecord` or `K3b`).

ABOUT THE DVD FOR THIS BOOK

The DVD that comes with this book offers a wide array of live CDs. Several of the CDs have been remastered so you can boot to them directly from the DVD's boot prompt. Others are available as complete ISO images that you can copy from the DVD and burn to individual CDs.

If you are just starting out with Live CDs, I recommend that you boot the DVD and select to boot the Knoppix live CD contained on the DVD. For a listing of the software contained on the DVD, refer to Appendix A.

WHAT YOU NEED TO USE THIS BOOK

Linux live CDs are available to run on a range of computer hardware, such as standard PC architecture (i386), PowerPC (ppc), and 64-bit AMD (AMD64). Some Linux live CD tools let you build for the architecture you like (such as the Gentoo Catalyst installer). For the purpose of this book, however, the software we provide and the procedures are geared toward the standard 32-bit PC architecture.

The PC you use to follow along with this book requires a DVD drive or a CD drive (if you can burn your own ISO images to CD). Although each live CD has its own minimum hardware requirements, I suggest starting with at least a Pentium-class PC and at least 128MB of RAM. As noted later in this book, live CDs (by nature) consume a lot of RAM and will run poorly in low-RAM environments.

As for hard-disk requirements, you don't even need to have a hard disk in the computer to run the live CDs included with this book. However, if you are remastering a live CD or building one from scratch, the amount of hard-disk space can range from a few hundred megabytes (to remaster Damn Small Linux) to several gigabytes of disk space. The space you need depends on how much software you are adding to your live CD (or live DVD).

You might consider getting a USB flash drive (also sometimes called a pen drive or thumb drive). Because live CDs are typically run from read-only media, USB flash drives are good to keep handy in case you want to save any of the data you create.

Part I

Beginning with Bootable Live Linuxes

Starting Up with Live Linux CDs

Creating live Linux CDs involves more than just boot files and compression techniques. It's about letting loose your own creativity to make available at all times the exact set of toys and tools you love to use. It's about creating and displaying your presentation, music, video, and image content exactly as you want it.

This book is about live CDs that are built from Linux system technology and that draw on a pool of thousands of open-source software components available today. In this book, you learn how to find, use, customize, and remaster live Linux CDs—and even build them from scratch.

The DVD that comes with this book contains a handful of live Linux CDs that you can use separately from a single boot prompt. It also contains many of the software tools you need to create anything from a lightweight desktop system that would run from a 50MB bootable business-card CD to a multigigabyte DVD containing a dizzying array of desktop, server, and system-administration software.

This book starts with novice tricks for running live Linuxes included with the book's DVD and takes you to guru skills, where you build, customize, and remaster specialized live Linux distributions. When you are finished, you end up with the perfect bootable Linux system for your own use, or even your own Linux distribution to share with the world.

UNDERSTANDING LIVE LINUX CDS

A live CD separates the computer system from the computer. Whereas an operating system is usually permanently installed on the computer's hard disk, a live CD is typically designed to boot and run entirely from a read-only medium (such as a CD-ROM).

With a live CD, you no longer have to be tied to a desktop or even a laptop computer to do your computer work or play. Instead, you can carry an entire operating system, important applications, and even your data (music, documents, video, images, and spreadsheets) on a single CD, DVD, or USB flash drive (about the size of a pack of gum). Your whole computer system can go where you go and run on almost any PC that's handy.

The explosion of high-quality open-source software and the popularity of the Linux operating system have created a fertile landscape for live Linux CDs. As a result, you can find dozens of Linux-based live CDs that are available for you to download and use freely. There are also powerful tools for customizing live CDs or building your own remastered (or from-scratch) live CDs.

In recent years, live Linux development has seen a lot of action, resulting in some sophisticated tools and solid base systems to build from. Low-cost, high-capacity media, such as USB flash memory, CDs, and DVDs, make the concept inexpensive for anyone to create a live Linux distribution. Also, unlike proprietary software, you have great freedom to copy, adapt, and customize most open-source software, without cost.

RUNNING A LIVE LINUX CD

Using a live Linux CD is one of the best ways to start with Linux, whether you want to try Linux for yourself or encourage others to become Linux enthusiasts. With a Linux live CD, you can do the following:

- **Try Linux**—If you are hesitant to mess with your hard disk, a live Linux CD represents a way to try a functional Linux system without disturbing your hard disk's contents.

- **Test hardware**—Before committing to a hard-disk install, you can use a live CD to check that the hardware will work with Linux. Live CDs such as Knoppix even provide tools for getting some of the trickier PC hardware elements working (such as sound cards and wireless-networking cards).

- **Take Linux on the road**—When you become comfortable with Linux and your favorite open-source applications, a live CD is a great way to take the whole system on the road without carrying a computer. Boot up the live CD on an available PC (especially if you've included your own settings and customizations with the CD), and you can be up in minutes with all your favorite applications.

- **Do something special**—You can set up a live CD to do special tasks. For example, you can use a distribution such as GeeXboX or MoviX to boot up to a movie and music player. Or you can use a Linux security-oriented live CD as a toolbox for monitoring and checking the security of systems on your LAN.

- **Harness a cluster of computers**—Using a cluster-type live CD in multiple computers on a network, you can share those computers' processing resources. This enables you to provide high availability (if one system fails, the other can take over), load balancing (so demand for a server can be spread across multiple machines), and high performance computing (to divide computation-intensive applications across many systems).

- **Install Linux permanently**—Linux systems such as Ubuntu, Gentoo, and PCLinuxOS offer a live CD that can double as an install CD. That way, if you are comfortable with how the live CD works, you can install that Linux system permanently right from the running live CD environment.

Starting up a live CD or DVD is often as simple as inserting the CD or DVD into the computer and rebooting. You can use options you pass on the boot screen to enable or disable various services associated with the live CD when it is running. Then it is up to you to do any special configuration that's needed (set up printers, desktop settings, network connections, and so on).

OVERCOMING THE FIRST HURDLES TO LINUX

Although installing Linux is not that hard if you are used to it, installing can be a showstopper if it is your first Linux experience. Using a live CD can make the first brush with Linux much more pleasant by avoiding common problems that first-time users have with Linux installation.

Here is a common scenario when installing Linux for the first time on a PC with a hard disk that is completely consumed by Windows.

- **Freeing disk space**—Because all disk space is assigned to a Windows (NTFS) partition, the first task is to free up some disk space from Windows to make room for Linux. Because of patent issues, some Linux distributions don't even include the capability to resize Windows (NTFS) partitions; you might have to find a separate partitioning tool.

- **Partitioning**—Before Linux can be installed to the disk, the free disk space must be divided (partitioned) and formatted in particular file system types. In some cases, the Linux installer handles the partitioning; in others, you must understand issues such as swap space, file system types, and whether a separate, small /boot partition is needed.

- **Hardware configuration**—During the install process, you might be asked to configure your video card, monitor, network card, or other hardware. Some Linux systems are better than others at detecting and automatically configuring your hardware; most ask you to provide some level of information to configure hardware during the installation process.

A live Linux CD such as Knoppix is designed to start up without prompting you for any information. It doesn't care if Windows consumes your hard disk because it doesn't need to touch your hard disk to run. It is designed particularly to detect and configure (at least, to a workable minimum configuration) your video card, network hardware, sound card, and other available hardware. If any of those features isn't working, you have an opportunity to pass options at the boot screen to have the live CD enable or disable selected features.

With a booted live CD acting as the proof that Linux will run on your PC, moving to a permanent install is a less daunting prospect. In fact, Knoppix includes the tools you need to resize your disk partitions and further configure hardware (such as printers, TV cards, and other hardware). You can write down the drivers and configuration information from your Knoppix system and use that information to reconfigure Linux if problems arise when you later permanently install Linux.

USING DIFFERENT TYPES OF LIVE CDS

When creating a live CD, you can choose which applications and other components to include in it; the live CD can be a generic or a highly tuned system. The Linux CD can contain a complete computer system, loaded with nearly every application imaginable. Or it can be a special-purpose system.

Special uses for a live Linux CD are limited only by your imagination. By making your own live Linux CD, you can go beyond what many popular Linux distributions can do. As an individual, you can obtain or purchase all sorts of applications or content for a personal live CD that aren't available for a Linux distribution to distribute freely.

Chapters 9-14 describe different types of live Linux CDs that you might be interested in using or creating. The following subsections describe some examples of specialized live Linux systems that other people have created.

Desktop Live CDs

With a live Linux CD that's tuned to be a desktop system, you can work on the road as you do from home. A typical desktop live CD contains word processing, spreadsheet, gaming, e-mail, and Web browsing applications, as well as any other type of software available from a typical home or work desktop computer. With live CDs that offer *persistent desktop* features, you can store your own Web bookmarks, e-mail settings, buddy lists, or other personal features you need on a USB flash drive or other writeable medium.

As I noted earlier, Knoppix is the most popular live CD and is one of the best ones to start with. Its excellent hardware detection and configuration make it easy for beginning Linux users. Although Knoppix boots up to a KDE desktop, custom versions of Knoppix offer other desktop environments and window managers.

Chapter 2, "Playing with Live Linux CDs," and Chapter 3, "Customizing a Live CD," contain descriptions of how to use Knoppix. Chapter 6, "Building a Custom Knoppix Live CD," includes information on remastering Knoppix. Figure 1-1 shows an example of the Knoppix desktop:

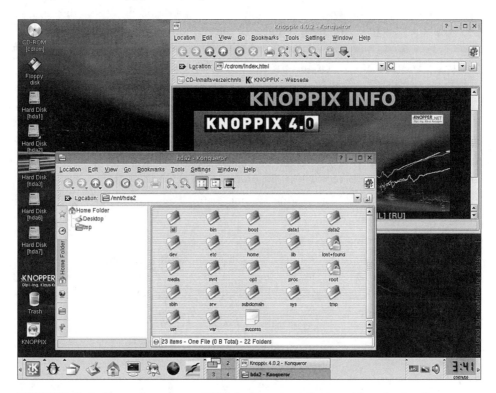

FIGURE 1-1 Knoppix sports a KDE desktop interface and hundreds of applications.

To try out a live CD that offers a GNOME desktop, you can get the GNOME version of Knoppix called Gnoppix (www.gnoppix.org). Another live CD that offers the GNOME interface is the GNOME LiveCD, which comes directly from the GNOME project (http://live.gnome.org).

For a more lightweight desktop system (fitting on a medium of less than 50MB), try Damn Small Linux (www.damnsmalllinux.org). Other live CDs in the lightweight desktop category include Puppy Linux (www.puppyos.com) and Feather Linux (http://featherlinux.berlios.de). These mini desktop live CDs usually work better on older machines that have a smaller amount of RAM and slower CPU.

Gaming Live CDs

Hundreds of open-source games are available today. Demo versions of commercial games for Linux also can be redistributed. Live CDs and DVDs tuned specifically for gaming can make your transition to Linux gaming much easier than if you were to try to do a fresh Linux install and put together a gaming system yourself.

The PCLOS SuperGamer live DVD, for example, is based on the PCLinuxOS distribution. It contains about 3.6GB of gaming software, including demos of popular 3D games such as Wesnoth, Quake 4, and America's Army. It also includes a bunch of arcade games, card games, and strategy games. The Live Linux Game Project live CD (http://tuxgamers.altervista.org) is a nearly 700MB live CD containing hundreds of free and open source games.

SuperGamer and other live CD/DVDs differ from other live Linux systems because they can be optimized for gaming. For example, SuperGamer-1 includes a kernel that is tuned for gaming, a special desktop theme, and drivers for video cards capable of doing 3D video in Linux. (NVIDIA video drivers currently are included, and a version of the distro is being developed with ATI video drivers as well.)

You can read more about SuperGamer at the PCLinuxOS forum: www.pclinuxos.com/forum/index.php?board=31.0. Figure 1-2 shows an example of the PCLinuxOS SuperGamer desktop.

Another example of a gaming live CD is Games Knoppix (http://games-knoppix.unix-ag.uni-kl.de); both German and English versions are available. Features in Games Knoppix include hardware acceleration that is on by default and NVIDIA video drivers.

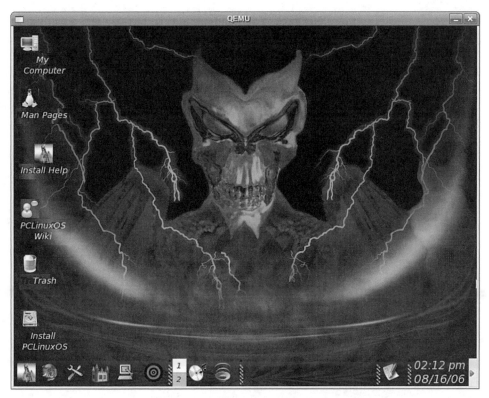

FIGURE 1-2 SuperGamer is tuned to play dozens of 3D and arcade games.

Clustering Live CDs

Take a clustering live CD and boot copies of it on many computers in a lab environment or a school. Using Autodiscovery of nodes running the live CDs, the clustering live CD will produce a supercomputing environment. With this arrangement, you can process loads of similar data over many processors.

A clustering live CD example is ParallelKnoppix (http://pareto.uab.es/mcreel/ ParallelKnoppix). As its name implies, ParallelKnoppix is a Knoppix remaster used to configure a cluster of cooperating computers.

Multimedia Player Live CDs

Some live Linux CDs are devoted to music, video, images, and other types of multimedia. Using these live CDs, you can often play content from your local system (hard drive, flash drive, CD, DVD, or other storage devices) or from a network server (using NFS, Samba, or a streaming media server).

GeeXboX (www.geexbox.org), Limp (http://limp-vkk-ver1.sourceforge.net), and MoviX (http:/sourceforge.net/projects/movix) are live CDs that are dedicated to playing multimedia. All three boot up directly to the mplayer media player and are compact enough to run in RAM. Using GeeXboX Generator or MoviX's related eMoviX project, you can add your own content to a multimedia CD to create a personal, bootable movie. Figure 1-3 shows an example of the Limp multimedia player live CD as it boots up.

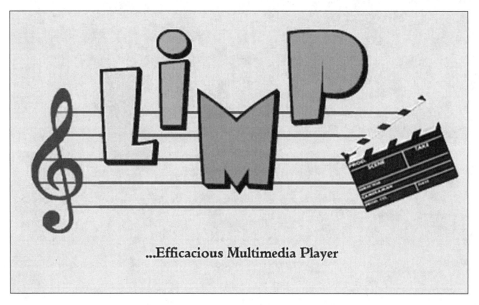

FIGURE 1-3 Run Limp in RAM to play CDs and DVDs.

MythTV is probably the most popular open-source entertainment center software. A live CD called KnopMyth (www.mysettopbox.tv/knoppmyth.html) was designed to help simplify what can be a complex installation process for MythTV.

amaroK Live is a live CD designed to display the features of the popular amaroK music player. This live CD not only boots up to a KDE desktop with amaroK ready to play, but also includes free music, much of which Magnatune (www.magnatune.com) provides. By adding desktop links to amaroK resources, this live CD acts not only as a fun music player, but also as a promotional tool for the project itself.

Multimedia Production Live CDs

Several Linux live CDs for producing music, video, graphics, and Web content are available. Dynebolic (www.dynebolic.org) refers to itself as a "free multimedia studio in a GNU/Linux live CD." Software on this live CD can be used for video production (using Kino, Cinelerra, or LiVES), audio production (Audacity and ReZound), 3D modeling (Blender), and image manipulation (GIMP).

Dynebolic can be used as a pervasive desktop. With a feature called a "Nest," you store data and settings on a hard disk or USB flash drive, yet you run the operating system from CD. The desktop is represented by the WindowMaker window manager instead of GNOME or KDE, to keep the system requirements for running Dynebolic lower. Figure 1-4 shows the Dynebolic desktop.

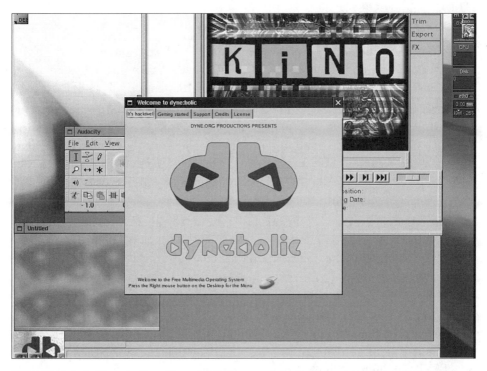

FIGURE 1-4 Dynebolic offers a full-featured desktop multimedia production live CD.

Recovery and Security Live CDs

One of the first (and still one of the best) uses of a live CD is to recover and/or secure a computer or network of computers. Several recovery types of CDs, such as System Rescue CD (www.sysresccd.org) and INSERT (www.inside-security.de/insert_en.html), fit on a mini CD. Full-size security live CDs can include hundreds of additional tools for repairs, forensics, monitoring, and other security features.

Security live CDs tend to offer simple graphical desktop environments, for the greatest flexibility in the types of systems they can run on. Some of the smaller security live CDs offer no graphical interface but still make hundreds of Linux commands available to use (while consuming only a few megabytes of disk space).

Knoppix-STD (http://s-t-d.org) contains hundreds of applications for tracking down problems and repairing systems and networks. It contains forensics tools such as autopsy and sluthkit. It also includes honeypots (such as `honeyd`) for catching intruders and a range of network-monitoring and sniffing utilities (such as `ethereal` and `tcpdump`). Vulnerability-assessment tools include `nessus`, `nmap`, and several CGI scanners.

Firewall Live CDs

You can run a dedicated firewall system from a live CD. Along with basic firewall features (such as those included in iptables), a live Linux firewall typically also includes server features for your LAN, such as DHCP and DNS.

Firewall live CDs often fit in less than 100MB of space and are built to run on low-end computers (so you can use an old Pentium in your closet as a dedicated firewall). If there is a GUI at all, it typically is lightweight. However, more often the firewall is configurable by commands or a simple menu system. In other cases, a basic Web server runs on the live CD so you can configure the firewall from a Web browser on another machine on the LAN.

Devil-Linux (www.devil-linux.org) is a firewall live CD that can be configured to match the network environment you are using. With Devil-Linux, you can run a firewall on a computer that has no hard disk at all.

The Sentry Firewall CD is an example of a live Linux firewall CD that can run on minimal hardware (a minimum of only 32MB of RAM is required). The kernel is a 2.4 Linux that is enhanced to include several security patches from projects such as OpenWall, strongSwan, and ebtables. Sentry Firewall includes Snort (www.snort.org) for intrusion prevention and detection and Bind (www.isc.org/products/BIND) so the firewall can act as a DNS server.

Live CDs for Developing, Testing, and Showcasing Applications

For software developers, having to install a new operating system to test a software project they are working on can be a bother. A live CD containing a particular operating system version, desktop environment, or server configuration can provide the platform a software developer needs to test software without having to install a new operating system.

The GNOME project offers the GNOME LiveCD (http://live.gnome.org/Gnome-LiveCd). Although the GNOME LiveCD is intended primarily to demo GNOME for people such as Linux user group members and journalists, the GNOME project encourages other software projects to use this CD as a base for doing demos of their projects.

Monoppix is a Knoppix-based live CD that helps developers start using tools to develop Mono applications. The CD includes tutorials to help developers learn to use the Mono runtime environment, compiler, and class libraries. Sample applications let developers see how to begin writing text-based and graphical applications, as well as applications for accessing MySQL databases.

One version of the Slax live CD (http://slax.linux-live.org), called KillBill, is specifically geared toward testing Windows applications to see whether they can run in Linux. Tools included on the disk to help people try Windows applications include WINE, dosbox, and Qemu.

Specialty Presentation Live CDs

You can create a live CD that launches into a special presentation or application. For example, you can boot up to a slide show or an OpenOffice.org Impress presentation. Using a variety of methods, you can configure your selected application to start up at boot time, without requiring the user to log in.

Add custom backgrounds, icons, screensavers, and menus to have the entire desktop present the look and feel representing your presentation. Alternatively, you can run an application, such as a Web browser, in full screen mode so that the person using your CD doesn't even see anything but your presentation.

Disaster Center Live CD

When someone says that necessity is the mother of invention, that person might be referring to some live CDs created during the 2005 hurricane season in Louisiana. One disaster center in Lake Charles, Louisiana, started with some used (even diskless) PCs and a single Internet connection. They created both Linux and Windows live CDs that included a secure operating system to let people browse the Web, send and receive e-mail, make phone calls (VoIP), and complete other critical communications during the aftermath of the disaster.

SELECTING BOOTABLE MEDIA

The term **live CD** is used generically to describe a bootable operating system that sits on a removable medium outside of your computer's hard disk. This term is widely used because some of the first popular full-featured live bootables (in particular, Knoppix) were made specifically to fit on a CD. Now, however, you can consider many different media types for holding your bootable live Linux. Table 1-1 describes some examples of media you can use to hold your Live Linux (shown in Figures 1-5, 1-6, 1-7, and 1-8).

Although CDs, DVDs, and USB flash drives are the most popular bootable media, you can actually put a bootable Linux on any device that the PC's BIOS can recognize as a boot device. For example, PCs can also boot from Zip drives and floppy drives (although the Linux 2.6 kernel has become too large to fit on a floppy drive). You can even launch your bootable Linux from some local medium on the computer (such as a floppy or PXE-enabled Ethernet card) and run your bootable Linux from a device available on your network.

If you have an ISO image of a CD in a directory on your hard disk because you just downloaded it or are in the process of testing one that you created, you can often try out that image using some sort of virtualization software. For example, you can use VMware or Qemu and run the bootable image so that it appears in a window right on your desktop screen. This lets you try out your live CD before you burn up your media.

Getting the Most from a Live CD

When using a live CD, you can use some tips and tricks to get the most of your experience running live Linux systems. When trying out a live CD, many people find the whole concept quite cool. When you start using a live CD, however, you will likely want to do more:

- **Run faster**—Accessing from a CD or DVD drive is generally slower than accessing data from a hard disk. Add to that the fact that data on the CD is usually compressed (to fit on as much software as possible), so decompression adds another performance hit. Some live Linux distributions include a feature that lets you write the entire distribution to memory (provided your PC has enough available). As a result, the live Linux system might actually run faster than one installed to your hard disk.

  If you are building your own live CD, you also can build it to run in low-RAM or slow CPU environments. For example, you might choose simple applications and window managers for your live CD.

TABLE 1-1 Popular Bootable Media

MEDIUM	DESCRIPTION	IMAGE
Compact disc (CD)	Many available live Linux bootables are made to fit on a standard CD (about 650MB to 700MB). Actual size is 122mm.	**FIGURE 1-5** A standard 122mm CD
Mini CD (bootable business cards)	Mini CDs, measuring 80mm, can hold up to 180MB of data. Cut down to a size of a business card (referred to as bootable business cards), the mini CD can hold about 50MB of data. (The Damn Small Linux distribution fits on a bootable business card.)	**FIGURE 1-6** A mini CD and bootable business card CD.
Digital versatile disc (DVD)	DVDs are the same proportions as CDs but can hold about 4.7GB (single layer) or 8.4GB (dual layer) of data. Dual-layer CDs are much more expensive than single-layer CDs. Drives for writing to dual-layer DVDs are more expensive as well.	**FIGURE 1-7** Digital versatile disc (DVD)
USB flash drive (also referred to as a pen drive, key drive, USB key, or thumb drive)	Flash drives come in a variety of shapes and sizes, with popular sizes being about the size and shape of a pack of gum. Storage capacities range from 16MB to 64GB. Most PCs can boot from a USB flash drive. And because they are rewriteable, you can add and change data and applications as you use your flash drive. You can also use a USB flash drive in tandem with a read-only medium to store data and persistent desktop features.	**FIGURE 1-8** USB flash drive

- **Access hard disks**—A live Linux system doesn't need to access your hard drive. However, sometimes you will want to use the data on your hard drives to perhaps play music, open a document, or view images using your favorite Linux application. Or you might want to save data that you gather or create from your live CD to a more permanent hard disk.

  Some bootable Linux systems provide icons right on the desktop representing all the hard-disk partitions on your computer. Accessing data on those partitions is often as simple as opening those icons. Writing to those partitions often requires a special request (to prevent you from writing to hard-disk partitions unintentionally).

- **Access the CD drive**—Because the operating system is, by default, running from your boot medium (CD or DVD), if you then want to play a music CD or a video file from DVD, you can't just eject the medium from its drive. If you have two CD drives you can use one for the live CD and one for the content you want to play.

  If you have only one CD/DVD drive, however, a way around this problem is the same technique used to improve performance. With enough available memory, run the live Linux from RAM; you can eject the bootable medium Ito insert the CD or DVD you want to play. Some specialty movie player live CDs are, by design, stripped down to the minimum you need to play multimedia content, so they automatically load into RAM and let you eject the CD.

- **Access networks**—Most bootable Linux systems are configured to automatically detect the availability of a DHCP server on most supported wired Ethernet cards. This immediately provides you with a working Internet or other network connection. Tools for configuring static IP addresses or connecting with wireless cards are also available with many bootable Linux systems.

- **Add applications**—You might have an almost-perfect live CD but find that it lacks an application or two that you want. Some live Linux systems enable you to install applications to a running, live Linux system (usually with downloadable packages that are preconfigured for the particular live Linux distribution you are using).

- **Save custom features**—With a read-only medium, such as a CD-ROM, you might be able to change your desktop background, write a document, or save some Web bookmarks. But as soon as you reboot (by default), all that stuff just goes away. As already mentioned, you can access the local hard disk or network for saving data, but you might want to keep custom settings and applications with your live Linux so that every time you reboot the CD, those settings just reappear.

Some live Linux systems include features for gathering your custom settings, saving them somewhere (such as a hard disk, USB flash drive or floppy), and having them restored the next time you reboot. They might do this by backing up all the files in your home directory and your /opt directory into a single file (called a tarball), storing it somewhere (such as a floppy or disk on the network), and restoring it when you reboot.

- **Install to hard disk**—Even though most bootable Linux systems weren't made to be installed on hard disk, some people love their bootable Linux so much that they want to add it permanently to disk. Some live Linux distributions offer a feature for installing to hard disk. (Keep in mind, however, that many live CDs are made for temporary use and may not offer the level of security you would like on a permanent desktop system, unless you do some extra configuration.)

- **Install to USB flash drive**—If you love your live Linux on a CD, you might love it more on a flash drive. After booting your live Linux from a USB flash drive, you can modify your data and add more as you go along.

You can do a lot to customize an existing live Linux. However, you can do even more by putting together your own live Linux that includes exactly the components you want. After you have played with the live CDs out there, you might want to create one yourself.

BUILDING A LIVE LINUX CD

You might be perfectly happy using the exact versions of a bootable Linux live CD you download from the Internet or use from the DVD that comes with this book. However, to make the CD fit your needs more specifically, you will almost surely want to add more software or data to the CD or change the look and feel so it better suits your needs.

You can make changes to a live CD so that it includes (and keeps) the personal data and applications you want it to include. In this book, we describe several different ways you can go about changing, or even starting from scratch, so that you end up with the exact live CD that suits your needs. These basic approaches to producing the live CD that you want are described in this book:

- **Customization**—You don't need to know about the inner workings of Linux or live CDs to be able to change and save customized settings for live Linux distributions such as Knoppix or Damn Small Linux. Using persistent desktop features in those two distributions, you can save your desktop settings, applications, and data to an alternate medium (such as a USB flash drive or hard disk). The next time you boot your live CD, with that backed-up information available, all your saved settings and data are restored. For casual live CD users, this is the best way to personalize the live CD. Chapter 3 contains descriptions of this approach.

- **Remastering**—To remaster a live CD requires a fair amount of Linux expertise. Instead of just adding your own settings to an existing CD, you unpack it to a directory on your hard disk. Then you often work from this contained area of the hard disk (in what is called a chroot environment) so that you can run commands to add and remove software and data as you please.

  The advantage of remastering is that, by starting with a working CD, it's easier to end up with a working CD. You simply change the parts you want to be different. Then you recompress the file system and rebuild the live CD (using the mkisofs command). This approach is described in Chapter 6, where you learn how to remaster Knoppix.

- **Fresh install**—Several Linux distributions have (or are working on) tools that let you build a live CD from scratch from their software repositories. Essentially, you are running a fresh install of the Linux distribution that results in a single ISO image instead of a permanent install to hard disk. The downside of this approach is that more problems can occur in the process (such as missing dependencies and incompatibilities).

  Two Linux distributions that include tools for creating live CDs that are built directly from those projects' software repositories are Fedora and Gentoo Linux. Although these tools are still under development, with some persistence, you should be able to come up with a live CD that contains only the software you want. That software can be drawn from the huge software repositories available for Fedora and Gentoo.

  Fedora uses tools from the Kadischi project, along with the standard anaconda installer (the same tool used to install Fedora permanently to hard disk) to produce the ISO image representing your live CD. Chapter 7, "Building a Basic Fedora Live CD," contains procedures for using Kadischi and Anaconda to produce a Fedora project live CD.

  Likewise, the Gentoo installer, called Catalyst, is being adapted to become a tool for producing live CDs. Using Catalyst, you can actually recompile all your applications for the particular environment you want to run in (instead of simply using prebuilt binary packages, as Fedora/Kadischi does).

Although the Catalyst tools represent the greatest prospect for building and tuning a live CD to your exact specifications, they take a long time to run and require more expertise to make corrections when something goes wrong. For that reason, descriptions for building Gentoo live CDs in Chapter 8, "Building a Basic Gentoo Live CD," start with a remastering approach before getting into how to use Catalyst to build a live CD.

If you decide that just saving a few settings and some data (customization) doesn't meet your needs, you must have (or develop) some expertise in using Linux systems from the command line. You cannot remaster or build a live Linux CD from scratch entirely from a graphical environment (at least, so far); you must work as the root user from the command line, in most cases.

What you will find as you dig in, however, is that Linux is an extraordinarily rich environment for creating your live CD. Linux is the natural platform for custom, bootable operating systems because of these characteristics:

- **Small core**—A minimal kernel and a few applications can run in only a few megabytes of memory. So your live CD can be tuned to run efficiently from the live CD or even loaded completely into memory (making it blazing fast to use).

- **Building-block nature**—Unlike developers of some proprietary operating systems, most open-source developers strive to interoperate with existing components created by other people. This gives you the choice to piece together components that best suit your needs. For example, you can include any of several boot loaders (ISOLINUX, GRUB, or LILO) to start your live CD, or choose a desktop that is either full-featured (such as GNOME or KDE) or lightweight (such as Fluxbox or WindowMaker).

- **Vast amount of available software**—You can draw on literally thousands of open-source software projects for your live CD. By starting with an established Linux distribution (such as Debian, Fedora, and Gentoo, as were chosen for this book) you begin with versions of those software projects that have been packaged and tested for these particular Linux environments. For you, it's usually more like just making a shopping list of software packages than it is like having to make every piece of software work yourself.

If you are already familiar with Debian (including Knoppix), Fedora Core (including Red Hat Enterprise Linux or CentOS systems), Slackware (including SLAX) or Gentoo, you might most naturally want to begin by building a live CD that is based on that distribution.

Choosing a Base Linux System

One of the biggest choices you make before you start is which Linux system to base your live Linux CD on. For this book, three basic Linux distributions were chosen for producing live CDs: Debian/Knoppix, Fedora, and Gentoo. Each of those three Linux distributions has large software repositories for you to draw from and active communities to back you up.

> **NOTE**
>
> If you are a Slackware enthusiast, there are several SLAX live CDs (www.slax.org) you can try out. You can easily customize a running SLAX live CD by adding software modules (www.slax.org/modules.php). That process is described in Chapter 9, "Customizing a Secure Live Linux CD," for customizing the SLAX-based BackTrack security live CD.

Knoppix and Debian-Based Live CDs

Knoppix is the most mature and widely used bootable Linux CD. It's the first live CD you should try. This is probably the best one to use for your first remaster as well. That's because Knoppix was built from the ground up to run as a live CD and has gone through many iterations to get it right. When you begin with Knoppix, you know you are starting with a known, working commodity.

Features in Knoppix include the following:

- **Linux 2.6 kernel**—The Linux 2.6 kernel offers many enhancements over the previous 2.4 kernel, especially in the area of managing devices. Although all major Linux distributions offer the 2.6 kernel, many live CDs available still use the 2.4 kernel.

- **Hardware detection**—Knoppix offers excellent hardware detection and configuration. Most notably, you will almost always get a working X desktop (which you can tune further, if you like) because Knoppix does such a good job detecting and configuring your video card.

- **KDE desktop**—Knoppix uses the KDE desktop by default, although you can select to use a lighter window manager instead (including fluxbox, icewm, twm, larswm, wmaker, or xfce). KDE offers many more custom applications than does GNOME (the other major Linux desktop environment). Many more features are available for customizing KDE as well. If you prefer GNOME, you can try the GNOME version of Knoppix, called Gnoppix (www.gnoppix.org).

- **Office applications**—The OpenOffice.org application suite provides the centerpiece for office productivity applications in Knoppix. Applications also exist for managing address books and personal information (Kontact and KOrganizer), as well as for page layout (Scribus), to round out the offerings.

- **Graphics applications**—GIMP is probably the most popular application for working with digital images, but Knoppix includes more than a dozen applications for manipulating graphics. Software included lets you take screen shots (Ksnapshot), download images from your camera (gqcam, gtkam, and xcam), view images in various formats (KGhostView, Kuickshow, and xpdf), and use a scanner (xscanimage).

- **Internet applications**—Knoppix is well equipped to help you access the Internet. It includes several Web browsers (Firefox, Konqueror, and Lynx), e-mail clients (Thunderbird, Kmail, and Mutt) and messaging clients (Xchat and Gaim). From the command line, you can use dozens of commands for file copy, file transfer, remote login, and other network clients.

- **Multimedia applications**—Sound applications include XMMS (multimedia player) and aumix (audio mixer) graphical applications and a variety of commands for playing, encoding, and working with audio. In the area of video, Knoppix comes with the xine media player and xawtv television viewer.

- **Gaming applications**—Knoppix includes a full range of open-source games, including arcade games, board games, card games, kids' games, puzzles, and strategy games.

- **System-administration tools**—Knoppix offers many system-administration tools with the KDE desktop (K Control Center, KCron, KUser, and KPackage), but it also offers some of its own tools to make it easier to configure difficult hardware and to improve the Knoppix live CD environment. From the KNOPPIX submenu of the K menu, you can configure printers and sound cards. However, you can also save a persistent desktop to a hard disk, create a SWAP area, and back up your settings to a floppy.

- **Servers**—Although most Knoppix features are desktop oriented, you can configure several useful servers to run from a Knoppix live CD. From the KNOPPIX menu, you can start up a remote login server (SSH), logging server (SYSLOG), or Windows file-sharing server (Samba). You can even configure Knoppix as a basic Web server (Apache), mail server (smail), DHCP server (dhcp3), Rsync server (rsync), or proxy server (squid).

More than 1,200 software packages are included in the Knoppix live CD, and more than 2,700 in the live DVD. To see a complete list of packages for the

Knoppix CD or DVD, look for the `packages.txt` and `packages-dvd.txt` files, respectively, on any Knoppix mirror site. For example, those files can be found at www.kernel.org/pub/dist/knoppix/packages.txt and www.kernel.org/pub/dist/knoppix/packages-dvd.txt.

Software packaging brings us to another good reason to use Knoppix as a base for your live CD. Knoppix is built from the Debian GNU/Linux distribution; therefore, you can incorporate software packages from the massive Debian software repositories. Likewise, you can use the same tools for downloading, installing, removing, and otherwise managing those software packages, including apt-get, dpkg, KPackage, and many others.

Software packaging tools have a limited usefulness when you are working in a read-only environment, but if you are remastering Knoppix, you can use those tools to add and delete software as you please. Then when you rebuild the ISO image representing your live CD, it can include exactly the software you need from Debian repositories.

Other live Linux CD distributions based on Debian can also be remastered. For example, you can find a procedure for remastering the Ubuntu live CD from the Ubuntu Wiki that follows the same general procedure: https://wiki.ubuntu.com/LiveCDCustomizationHowTO. Of course, you also can choose a live CD that is derived directly from Knoppix to begin customizing your own Live CD. A list of customized (remastered) Knoppix live CDs is available from the Knoppix Customizations page, www.knoppix.net/wiki/Knoppix_Customizations.

Fedora-Based Live CDs

Fedora Core (www.fedoraproject.org) is the free, community-oriented Linux operating system that is sponsored by Red Hat, Inc. Projects under the Fedora umbrella include Fedora Extras (repositories of software packages outside the scope of Fedora Core), Ambassadors & Marketing (to spread the word about Fedora), Documentation, and Kadischi. The Kadischi project is where the tools are created to build live CDs from Fedora.

The Fedora project comes from the legacy of Red Hat Linux, a general-purpose Linux operating system designed to include a range of desktop and server features that scale well from home and small-office computing up to enterprise-level installations. When Red Hat, Inc., focused its for-profit Linux system-development efforts on Red Hat Enterprise Linux, the Fedora Project was created to allow Red Hat Inc. to still contribute to a Linux system that could be freely distributed.

Despite the fact that Fedora Core comes with no guarantees (then again, what Linux system does?), Fedora Core is developed and maintained primarily by world-class software developers employed by Red Hat. In fact, most of what is developed in Fedora Core (which is released every 6 to 9 months) finds its way into Red Hat Enterprise Linux (scheduled to release approximately every 18 months). So Red Hat, Inc., has a vested interest in making Fedora Core a good distribution.

Fedora and Red Hat Enterprise Linux are among the last major Linux distributions to offer a live CD. The effort started in earnest with the Google 2005 Summer of Code Project by Darko Ilic. Darko created Kadischi, a set of tools for producing live CDs using Fedora software repositories and the anaconda installer.

In the past year, lead developers from Red Hat Inc. have begun picking up development of Kadischi-related tools. Most significantly, some of the features previously built into the kadischi command are now being incorporated directly into the Fedora anaconda installer. In effect, producing a live CD is becoming more like doing a regular Fedora installation to hard disk.

By relying on the anaconda installer, kadischi gives you access to a lot of the different installation features in Fedora when you produce a live CD. Therefore, you not only get the software packages you want, but you also can choose your language, keyboard, network configuration, time zone, and other configuration settings. Kadischi usually launches the anaconda installer to produce a live CD in one of two ways:

- **Graphical installer**—When you launch the kadischi command, you must identify the location of your Fedora software repository and the name of the resulting ISO image. Then, by default, anaconda runs in a window on the desktop. You step through the screens as you would during a normal hard disk. When anaconda is done, kadischi cleans up unnecessary files, compresses the file system, and produces the ISO image.

  Figure 1-9 shows a kadischi command line that starts the process of producing the live CD (upper right corner in the Terminal window). The anaconda installer screens, to step through the install process, appear in a separate window.

- **Kickstart install**—If you are going to run kadischi multiple times to get your live CD just right (which is normally what happens), the better approach is to create a kickstart file that includes settings that are passed to the anaconda installer.

  Information you add to your kickstart file allows anaconda to bypass graphical installer screens. In fact, the normal way to use a kickstart file is to have it include all information to complete the install so you can bypass the graphical installer altogether.

Using the %packages section of the kickstart, you can indicate exactly which packages and package sets you want to install to your live CD. Simply adding and removing packages from the list lets you adjust the size and feature set of your live CD. Then, after each change, simply run kadischi again to build a new ISO image.

At the end of the kickstart file, you can add commands that are run when anaconda is done (%post section). This is where you can make final modifications to your live CD system, such as add a user or copy data files you want to be on the live CD.

FIGURE 1-9 From the Fedora desktop, run kadischi to create a live CD with anaconda.

To get the best performance, you can copy the whole Fedora Core distribution to your hard disk. After that, you can add any RPM packages you want from Fedora Extras repositories or from third-party repositories, such as rpm.livna.org or atrpms.org. When adding new packages and package groups to the comps.xml file that anaconda uses, anaconda lets you select those packages for installation. As long as you include all dependent packages with the ones you want to add, anaconda will install those dependent packages as well.

Gentoo-Based Live CDs

Creating live CDs from Gentoo software repositories using tools associated with the Catalyst installer (www.gentoo.org/proj/en/releng/catalyst) is probably the most challenging approach to producing live CDs that is covered in this book. However, using Catalyst to build Gentoo live CDs also provides the most promise, in the long run, for producing live CDs that are specifically tuned for the computer architecture and hardware the CD is intended to run on.

Gentoo offers the capability to include cutting-edge software in the systems you install (or build into a live CD). Because packages can be built on the fly using simple commands, the software can be tuned for your specific computer system with only those features you want built into each package. The result is software that is leaner (including only what you need) and faster (because it's tuned to a specific computer architecture).

The Gentoo project produces a live CD that offers a usable GNOME desktop system. That live CD also includes desktop icons that let you launch the recently added installer, in either graphical or text mode, so you can permanently install Gentoo on your hard disk. The advantage is that, from this CD, you can set up the permanent Gentoo system you need to build your Gentoo live CD. Figure 1-10 shows an example of the Gentoo live CD desktop, including icons for launching the Gentoo command-line and graphical installers.

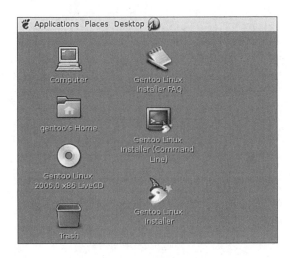

FIGURE 1-10 Install Gentoo from a live CD to create a build environment for Gentoo.

Chapter 8 describes both the Catalyst and remastering approaches to creating a Gentoo live CD. Remastering is similar to the procedure in Chapter 6 for remastering Knoppix.

The packaging system for Gentoo is called Portage and is based on the BSD ports system. Software management is done from the listing of more than 10,000 packages that make up what is referred to as the *portage tree*. Using the portage tree and the emerge command, you can launch commands that request that selected software packages be download, compiled, and installed, while resolving any software dependencies along the way. (Be careful, though, because a single emerge command can result in hours of downloading and compiling.)

TRYING OTHER LIVE CDS

Several live Linux CDs are included on the DVD that comes with this book, and many more are available for free download over the Internet. You can refer to these online lists that contain descriptions of and links to a broad range of live Linux CDs:

- **Wikipedia List of LiveCDs (http://en.wikipedia.org/wiki/List_of_LiveCDs)**—The list of live CDs from Wikipedia arranges live Linux CDs by the distributions they are based upon. Live CDs are listed for Debian, Gentoo, PPC/Mac, RPM-based systems, Slackware, and other Linux systems. You can also find lists of live CDs derived from other operating systems (Microsoft Windows, MS-DOS, BSD, OpenSolaris, and others).

- **FrozenTech's LiveCD List (www.frozentech.com/content/livecd.php)**—Names of live Linux CDs are listed in a table, along with information about the sizes of each CD's ISO image, the live CD's primary function, and links to download sites, home pages, and descriptions from distrowatch.com. You can select a column to view the live CDs by name, size, and primary function (desktop, gaming, rescue, security, and so on). This list is also available from http://livecdlist.com.

- **DistroWatch CD-based Linux Distributions (http://distrowatch.com/dwres.php?resource=cd)**—Several dozen live CDs are listed here, along with descriptions and links to each. Because this list is no longer maintained, readers are also referred to the FrozenTech LiveCD list.

Another place to look is on Web sites for Linux systems that are typically installed to hard disk. Using a live CD from one of those Linux distributions will give you a good idea of whether you will encounter problems before you go to the trouble of installing it. The following list describes where you can get live CDs representing different Linux distributions:

- **Ubuntu Live CD**—You can order or download an Ubuntu live CD that doubles as an install CD from the Ubuntu Web site (www.ubuntu.com/download).

- **Gentoo Live CD**—Currently, the Gentoo Linux project offers only an x86 live CD. However, tools being developed in Gentoo's Catalyst project will eventually allow live CDs to be created for other architectures as well. You can find out how to get the Gentoo LiveCD from the "Where to Get Gentoo Linux" page (www.gentoo.org/main/en/where.xml).

- **Mandriva Live CD**—The Mandriva Linux (formerly Mandrake) distribution produces a live CD version called Mandriva Move. You can find it from the Mandriva download page (www.mandriva.com/en/downloads). The Mandriva project is also developing a new live CD called Mandriva One. That CD, currently in beta testing, combines a live desktop CD and a Mandriva installer.

Although several major Linux distributions don't offer official live CDs, trying out a live CD created from one of those distributions is a good way to get a sense of how it will work after it is installed. The Debian/GNU FAQ recommends using Knoppix as a way to try Debian features. For Fedora, Red Hat Enterprise Linux, or related distributions, I suggest keeping an eye on the Fedora-livecd-list mailing list, where they are getting very close to developing an official live CD. (In the meantime, you can try making one yourself from the descriptions in Chapter 7.)

LEARNING ABOUT LIVE CDS

As you go through this book, you will learn about software technologies that you just don't run into while you are normally using a computer. Likewise, you can look at certain aspects of features that you use daily (such as your KDE desktop environment) in a different way when you create a live CD.

Chapter 4, "Understanding How Live Linux CDs Work," takes you through the components that come into play when you boot a live CD; Chapter 5, "Looking Inside Live CD Components," describes many of those components in greater depth. By way of introduction, the following sections describe some of those components.

Using Boot Loaders

A boot loader is loaded by the computer's BIOS, before any operating system is run, to enable the person booting the computer to select which operating system to run. For a live CD to be bootable, a boot sector must be added to the CD image so that if the computer is set to boot from CD, that image can be loaded and run.

Isolinux is the software from the Syslinux project (http://syslinux.zytor.com/iso.php) that is most commonly used to handle boot loader duties on Linux live CDs. Isolinux contains components that implement the ISO 9660 El Torito specification for booting CD-ROMS.

You identify the location of the El Torito boot image when you build your ISO image. During the initial boot process, using information contained in your /boot or /isolinux directory, the boot image can make use of information you provide to the boot process. For example, you can modify the isolinux.cfg file to do the following:

- Select different operating systems to boot (or select to have the same operating system booted with different options).
- Display different message files. You can create message files and then indicate which message file should be displayed when a particular function key is pressed from the initial boot screen.
- Include your own splash screen. You can use a graphic that can be reduced to 16 colors and will fit on a 640×480-pixel display as your splash screen when the initial boot prompt is displayed.

Although isolinux is by far the most common boot loader used on live CDs, you can also use other boot loaders that are more commonly used to boot from hard disk. Those boot loaders include the GRand Unified Boot loader (www.gnu.org/software/grub), also called GRUB, and the Linux LOader (http://lilo.go.dyndns.org), also called LILO. Although GRUB is a bit more difficult to set up as a live CD than is isolinux, it offers the advantage of letting you choose which operating system to boot from a menu (instead of just typing in a label name).

Choosing Compression Techniques and File System Types

Because disk space is an issue on a live CD, most live CDs incorporate some type of compressed file system for storing the directory structure. As a result, you can get a whole lot more stuff on a live CD than you could if you didn't compress the file system.

Knoppix uses the create_compressed_fs command to compress the KNOPPIX file system. When the file system is used later from the live CD, it is uncompressed on the fly using the cloop driver (that is added to the Linux kernel Knoppix uses). As a result, the Knoppix live CD ISO image that is about 700MB can actually contain about 2GB of compressed applications and data.

To have the compressed Knoppix image behave like an installed Linux system, in which you can write to directories throughout the entire file system, Knoppix incorporates a Unionfs file system (ww.unionfs.org). Unionfs makes it possible to merge the contents of a read-only file system (such as the / directory on the live CD) with a writeable file system (such as the Unionfs file system in memory). As a result, someone using the live CD can save files to a read-only directory from the CD, have those files actually stored on the Unionfs file system (/UNIONFS), but have the entire contents of the two file systems be merged to appear as a single file system.

Some live CDs that don't use Unionfs have many of the directories from the live CD be read-only. Therefore, you can save files only in directories that need to be writeable (such as the /tmp and /home directories). Live CDs built from Fedora Linux, using Kadischi tools, include support for the Squashfs (http://squashfs.sourceforge.net) file system type. Squashfs is a read-only, compressed file system designed particularly for Linux. To help ensure that a /tmp file system doesn't run out of space too easily, some live CDs use the tmpfs file system. tmpfs can grow to consume more memory (RAM plus swap) as needed.

Understanding Hardware Detection

Because live CDs are usually expected to run on many different computers, with a variety of hardware components, good hardware detection is important. The goal is to have the live CD go from the boot screen to a running system with all USB devices, network cards, video cards, monitors, mouse devices, and other hardware components detected, drivers loaded, and necessary configuration done automatically.

Several different hardware-detection features are used on most live CDs to ensure that the live CD will boot up to at least a minimally configured desktop system. Knoppix hardware detection is based on the Kudzu facility (which was originally created for Red Hat Linux and is still used in Fedora Linux). PCLinuxOS uses hwdetect to detect hardware. Other live CDs use udev and hotplug for initial hardware detection, as well as to manage devices that are plugged into a running system.

Configuring System Services

Even if certain services are installed on your live CD, you might need to configure them to start automatically at boot time. For example, if it is a server live CD, you might want to start up the Apache Web server service (httpd) and the remote shell service (sshd). Live CDs based on Fedora Linux are based on the System V init scripts, which enables services to be started and stopped at different run levels.

Choosing Software Packaging

One of the primary features you are choosing when you choose a Linux distribution to base your live CD on is the type of software packaging you want to use. When you are remastering a live CD or building one from scratch, you use the tools associated with the packaging type for your base Linux distribution and draw from that distribution's software repositories.

Software packaging for live CDs described in this book focuses on Debian (.deb) and Red Hat (.rpm) software packaging. Besides the Debian project itself, Debian packaging is used by many live CDs and other installed distributions (such as Ubuntu). Besides the Red Hat–sponsored Fedora project and its own Red Hat Enterprise Linux, distributions such as SuSE, Mandriva, CentOS, and others use RPM packaging as well.

Gentoo takes a different approach to packaging, focusing on the Portage package management system. Portage software is arranged in a hierarchical directory tree consisting of ebuilds (scripts that directs how each software component should be built).

To add and remove software packages for each of the packaging systems just mentioned, a set of tools is available:

- **RPM software tools**—The rpm command is the most basic tool for adding, removing, updating, and querying RPM packages. The yum command is used more often than rpm these days because yum was designed to look at online software repositories to search for, download, and install the latest available RPM file.

- **Debian software tools**—The apt-get command is the most popular command for downloading and installing .deb packages. At the base of the Debian packaging tools is the dpkg command.

- **Gentoo software tools**—The emerge command is the primary command used to download, install, build, remove, and update Gentoo software packages from the portage tree.

The software tools just described are used primarily for the operating system for which they were intended, but some of those tools are available on other operating systems as well. For example, a version of apt-get that can be used to get software for Red Hat systems from online repositories. Likewise, you can use commands with Debian to install RPM packages.

Besides the tools just mentioned, graphical tools are available for working with software packages. Graphical front ends for APT-related tools include aptitude, KPackage, and Synaptic. For Fedora and Red Hat Enterprise Linux systems, there are the Package Manager window (for installing packages from software repositories) and the Package Updater window (for updating existing packages).

NOTE

Keep in mind that, even though different software distributions use the same packaging tools, each draw on software repositories that are specific to that distribution. These days, distributions such as Fedora and Debian are set up automatically to draw on software repositories that match distribution and version. So everything should just work.

Selecting a Desktop Environment

If a nifty desktop system is a priority, you might go with KDE or GNOME desktop environments for your live CD. If you want your desktop to run more efficiently, you might consider just using a simple window manager.

Besides choosing the type of desktop you want, personalizing it for yourself or for the software project you are showcasing on your live CD can do a lot to make that live CD special. You can add a customized login screen, wallpaper, desktop icons, menus, screen savers, or other items to present the look and feel you want to get across with your live CD.

BURNING AND FANCYING UP YOUR LIVE CD

After you have produced your live Linux CD, how you distribute it is the last question you need to answer. You can simply deposit the live CD image to an FTP server (adding an appropriate checksum so downloaders can verify that it's not corrupted) and publish the address to anyone you like. If you want to distribute your live CD, you can have it burned to CD, DVD, or possibly a USB flash drive.

Linux, Windows, and almost every other operating system include applications for burning an ISO image to CD or DVD. In Linux, the most common command-line utility for burning CDs is the `cdrecord` command. You can use the `growisofs` command to burn multisession CDs and DVDs. For a graphical interface, you might consider trying the K3b CD writing application.

To add some final polish to your live CD, consider printing a label for it. Some live CD projects produce their own labels that they give you permission to use (although they might want you to use it only if you are not remastering the CD). Figure 1-11 shows the CD label (left) and jewel case cover (right) that are available with the Dynebolic live CD.

FIGURE 1-11 Use labels and jewel case covers from live CD projects or create your own.

Appendix B, "Building, Testing, and Burning ISOs," contains information on burning your ISO images to the medium of your choice, along with information on how to nicely finish off your CDs.

Summary

Whether you want to just boot up and use a live CD or build your own, this chapter presents the concepts that are covered in this book. As a user, you can find out different methods of booting and using a live CD. As someone who wants to build a live CD, you can learn about ways in which you can create a custom live CD.

This chapter presented some opportunities you will face as you choose the Linux distribution you will build from, the approach you want to take in building it (remastered or from scratch), and the components you want to include in it.

Some different, existing types of live CDs were described. Those types include live CDs oriented toward desktop systems, security/rescue, gaming, multimedia players, and others. You can build those types of live CDs as well, or you can start with one of them and remaster it to suit your needs.

The next chapter is meant for you to get your hands on some live CDs. Using the DVD that is included with this book, Chapter 2 describes many of the ways in which you can boot, use, and configure your live CDs to get the most out of them. It also provides a survey of features in each of the live CDs included on this book's DVD.

Playing with Live Linux CDs

The DVD included with this book contains more than ten Linux live CD distributions. By trying out these different distributions, you can start drawing on the wealth of open-source software that is available today. You can also get a sense of the applications and decisions that went into making these different live CDs, so you'll have a head start when you create or customize one of your own.

Among the mix of live CDs on this book's DVD are CDs meant for general desktop use, gaming, multimedia, and security/recovery. This chapter describes special features of each of those live CDs, as well as some of the applications that come with them. If you don't have a DVD drive available, later sections describe where you can download or purchase the CD versions of those live CDs.

BEFORE BOOTING A LIVE CD

Most Linux live CD developers want you to have the same experience with their live CD as you would using an installed Linux system. To get that to happen, however, they have to do a few tricks. Before you boot up a live CD, you should understand that using live CDs can result in different behavior than you would expect from running an installed Linux system:

- **Longer boot time**—Booting from a live CD typically takes longer than booting from a hard disk. One reason for this is that data access from a CD is slower than hard-disk access. Also, booting up a live CD typically takes more time to autodetect and configure hardware that would have already been configured during a hard-disk installation. Extra time autodetecting such things as your video hardware is needed partly to get a working desktop system without any user input.

■ **File saves**—Because the root file system (/) of the live CD often resides on the live CD or other read-only medium, you can't directly add files to that file system or modify files from that file system. As a result, for example, you could not install new software or change settings in files located in directories on the live CD.

Live CD developers have taken a few different approaches with that issue. On Fedora live CDs, you simply can't install new software or otherwise add new files to directories in read-only file systems. Directories that need to be read/write (such as /tmp and /home directories) are mounted on a writeable file system that is mounted from system memory. In other words, you are just saving your data to temporary, transient work space.

On Knoppix live CDs, using the Unionfs file system, a read/write file system is overlaid on the read-only file system. That way, files that you save to the /bin directory, for example, appear to be in the /bin directory, even though they actually reside on a different physical file system. That writeable file system would, as with Fedora live CDs, be saved in RAM.

■ **Changes you make**—Unless you make some other arrangements, all the files you add and settings you change during a live CD session disappear when you reboot the computer. For any live CD, you can save files during a live CD session by either opening write access to a hard-disk partition or inserting your own writeable medium (such as a USB flash drive).

In some cases, however, just saving files isn't good enough. For example, you might want to save installed software, your desktop background, or other data that has to be in a particular location in the file system to be used automatically. In that case, you need a live CD that supports the capability to put data back where it belongs the next time you reboot. In Knoppix, that feature is referred to as a *persistent desktop;* in Dynebolic, the same feature is called a *Nest.*

■ **Hard-disk access**—Most live CDs are designed to prevent unintentional changes to the hard-disk partitions on the computer. For that reason, those partitions are usually not mounted when the live CD boots up. If a desktop feature is available to let you choose to mount those partitions, it typically does so in read-only mode, by default.

Exceptions to this rule exist, however. By default, the Puppy Linux live CD (www.puppylinux.org) creates a file system, represented by a single 256MB file, on a hard-disk partition in which the data you create is saved. It does this without asking if it's okay. By default, that file (called PUP001) remains on the hard disk after the reboot, so all your settings return the next time you reboot your live CD on that computer.

The bottom line is that, although most Linux live CDs don't write to the hard disk at all by default, at least one (and probably more) does. Be careful about what data you are saving, and be sure to clean up the saved data before you leave the machine.

- **CD/DVD drive access**—If you have only one drive for booting the DVD that comes with this book (or Knoppix CD you've obtained otherwise), you can't just pop it out to insert another CD or DVD to play music or video. Because Knoppix is running from that drive, removing it would be like removing your hard disk from an installed computer system.

  If you want to be able to use the CD/DVD drive from Knoppix, you can either copy the image to hard disk or run it entirely from memory (provided that you have enough memory available to do so). Procedures for running Knoppix from RAM are included in the "Getting a Live CD Working Just Right" section later in this chapter.

Using the DVD that comes with this book, you can boot several different Linux live CDs that have been consolidated on the DVD. Features for booting and using those live CDs are covered in this chapter and in Appendix A, "On the DVD." Chapter 3, "Customizing a Live CD," covers ways of customizing a live CD (without remastering) and saving those customized settings and applications (using persistent desktops).

Starting from the DVD

The DVD that comes with this book represents a consolidation of several popular live Linux CDs. Those live CDs are included in one of the following forms:

- **Directly bootable**—Several live CDs, including Knoppix, BackTrack, and others can be requested and run directly from the DVD's boot prompt. After the selected live CD starts up, it works as it would if running from a stand-alone CD.

- **ISO images**—Some of the live CDs included on the DVD are stored in the form of the exact ISO images that came from the project that created the live CDs. To use those live CD images, you can copy them from the DVD and burn them to blank CDs to use separately.

Use the following procedure to begin trying out live CDs from the DVD that comes with this book:

1. Insert the Live Linux CDs DVD that comes with this book into the DVD drive of your PC and reboot the computer. In a few moments, you will see the boot screen.

2. Type one of the following from the boot prompt to boot the live CD you want to try:

- **knoppix**—To boot the Knoppix live CD; this is the default live CD booted from the DVD, so pressing Enter will work as well
- **gentoo**—To boot a Gentoo live CD
- **slax**—To boot a SLAX live CD
- **backtrack**—To boot the BackTrack security live CD
- **llgp**—To boot the Live Linux Game Project live CD
- **dsl**—To boot the Damn Small Linux live CD

Other live CDs that can be started from the boot prompt are noted on the boot screen and described in Appendix A.

3. Wait as the live CD you selected boots up. In most cases, you are presented with either a running desktop interface or a login prompt.

Instead of booting directly to one of the live CDs directly from the boot prompt, in many cases you have the option to copy a complete ISO image representing a live CD and burn that image to a blank CD. Refer to Appendix A for information on which ISO images are available on the DVD and how to burn those images to CD.

If you have never tried out a live CD before, I recommend you try Knoppix. Information on using Knoppix is contained in the following sections. To get the full effect (Knoppix boot screen and complete boot options), you can burn the Knoppix ISO image to a separate CD to try it out.

RUNNING A DESKTOP LIVE CD (KNOPPIX)

Knoppix is the default Linux live CD on the DVD that comes with this book. Because Knoppix is the standard by which other live CDs are judged, it's used in this section to demonstrate how to use a desktop-oriented live Linux CD. This tour of Knoppix assumes the following:

- **CPU**—Your computer's processor is x86-compatible (at least i486).
- **RAM**—You have at least 32MB of RAM (text-only mode) or 84MB of RAM (graphical mode). To run KDE and OpenOffice.org, you need at least 128MB of RAM to run effectively. (Having or creating a swap area, as described later, will help if you are low on RAM.)

- **Video card**—To run in graphical mode (KDE or other desktop environment), you have an SVGA-compatible graphics card and a mouse (standard serial, PS/2, or IMPS/2-compatible USB mouse).

- **DVD drive**—You have a PC that includes a DVD drive. Also, the computer's BIOS is set to boot from DVD.

- **Hardware detection**—Knoppix can properly detect and configure your computer hardware. (If it can't, refer to the section "Getting a Live CD Working Just Right," on boot options, to learn how to get around hardware-detection problems.)

If you are able to boot up the DVD to Knoppix, follow the next tour to get a feel for the features in Knoppix.

 NOTE

If you want to try Knoppix on a computer that doesn't have a DVD drive, there are two ways to go about that. You can copy the ISO image from the DVD (on a machine with a DVD drive) and burn it to CD (as described in Appendix A). Alternatively, you can download or purchase an ISO image of Knoppix, as described at www.knoppix.net/get.php.

Touring Knoppix

With the computer in front of you and the DVD inserted into the DVD drive, follow this procedure to tour the Knoppix desktop features:

- With the DVD inserted, reboot your computer.

- When the boot screen appears, press Enter. When Knoppix finishes booting and detecting your hardware, the Knoppix desktop should appear as shown in Figure 2-1.

In many ways, Knoppix looks like any other desktop system based on the K Desktop Environment (KDE). If you want to find out more about KDE and the features it contains, refer to the KDE Web site (www.kde.org).

Many of the features that Knoppix adds to the KDE desktop make it easy to overcome those issues that make a live CD different from an installed Linux system. In particular, it displays icons representing hard-disk partitions and other storage devices. It also has a Knoppix icon on the desktop panel that provides access to special configuration features, in case Knoppix doesn't detect and configure every piece of hardware as you would like.

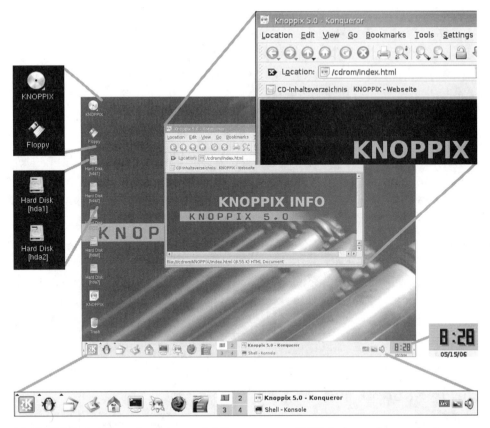

FIGURE 2-1 Knoppix adds special features to a KDE desktop that make it useful for a live CD.

CD, Floppy, and USB Memory Drives

Icons for CD and floppy drives appear on every Knoppix desktop. To work with one of those drives, right-click the mouse on its icon and select Actions from the menu that appears. Keep in mind that you can't remove the Knoppix CD or DVD from the drive unless you ran Knoppix from RAM (using the toram boot option) or from a Knoppix image copied to hard disk. Double-click any of these icons to open the contents in a file manager.

Using the udev facility, Knoppix mounts any USB storage devices it encounters, either at boot time or when one is plugged into a running Knoppix system. Because USB storage media are mounted read-only by default, you need to right-click the USB device icon and select Change Read/Write Mode to be capable of writing to that drive. (Writing to a USB flash drive is a typical way to save custom settings for Knoppix, as described in Chapter 3.)

Hard-Disk Partitions

During boot-up, Knoppix checks your hard disks and adds an icon representing each hard-disk partition it encounters to your desktop. None of those hard-disk partitions is mounted by default. To mount one and open its contents in a file manager, simply select the icon. It will open with read/write permission.

Knoppix offers support for many different file system types. So whether the computer you are running Knoppix on has Linux, Microsoft Windows, BSD, or another operating system type installed, there is a good chance that you will be able to mount its file systems from Linux.

One feature that Knoppix includes that some Linux systems do not is support for the NTFS file system type. Because NTFS is the file system type most often used with Microsoft Windows XP, Knoppix can be very useful for playing, displaying, or otherwise using the data from your Windows XP computer.

Knoppix makes it easy to mount and unmount file systems for your disks and other storage media by adding information about each of your partitions to the /etc/fstab file. Knoppix mounts each partition to directories under the /media directory. Each directory is named based on the device type (IDE or SCSI) and the partition number. For example, the first partition (1) on the first IDE hard disk (hda) is named hda1. It is mounted on the /media/hda1 directory (with a link to /mnt/hda1 for backward compatibility).

For SCSI hard disks, the mount point begins with *sd*. For example, the first partition on the first SCSI disk on your computer is mounted on the /media/sda1 directory. Because USB flash memory drives are mounted as a SCSI device, with no SCSI hard drives, a USB drive would be mounted on /media/sda1.

KDE and Knoppix Menus

As usual on a KDE desktop, you can access most of the graphical applications available from Knoppix from the K menu in the lower-left corner of the panel. Knoppix adds its own menu button to the panel, however, in the form of a small penguin icon.

Although it is not that difficult to use a menu (just click to find the application you want to run), Knoppix menus offer a few nice features:

- **Drag-and-drop**—If you use a certain application often, you can drag-and-drop the menu item to the desktop. Knoppix asks if you want to copy the desktop configuration file representing the application to the desktop or instead create a link to that file.

- **Copy to desktop or panel**—As an alternative to drag-and-drop, you can right-click on a menu item and select from a list of actions to do with that item. You can add the item to the desktop or main panel.

- **Run command with new options**—If you want to modify how the application is run, you can right-click the item, then select Put into Run Dialog, and add options to the command from the pop-up dialog box that appears.

- **KDE Menu Editor**—To edit the command line and associated information for a menu item more permanently, right-click that item and select Edit Item. The KDE Menu Editor opens for that item and lets you change the name, description, comment, and command line associated with the applications run from that menu item. Select File → Save to make the changes permanent.

To change many features of your KDE desktop, select the Control Center from the K menu. More tools you can use for configuring your Knoppix system are available from the Knoppix menu.

The Knoppix menu (small penguin icon next to the K menu), in particular, offers several special configuration tools for configuring your desktop. From the Knoppix menu, select Configure to display a menu where you can configure the following features for your Knoppix system:

- **TV card**—You can find and configure the driver for a TV card, plus configure it to include TV channels for your local broadcast or cable service.

- **Printers**—This launches the KDE Control Module for adding or configuring printers. The CUPS printing service (`cupsd`) is used by default with Knoppix. However, you can print to a variety of locally (parallel, serial, USB) and remotely (CUPS, LPD, Windows/SMB) connected printers.

- **Sound card**—Configure your sound card by running the `sndconfig` utility.

- **Network/Internet**—The default case, in which Knoppix boots up and finds a DHCP server on a wired Ethernet card, works in many cases. However, because Knoppix is meant to be a portable operating system, it includes tools for configuring a wide range of networking hardware. The Network/Internet menu on the Knoppix menu has tools for configuring connections on modems, ADSL, ISDN, and a variety of mobile and wireless hardware.

Other configuration features from the Knoppix menu help you run Knoppix more efficiently. For example, if you are running Knoppix from a computer with Linux installed to hard disk, Knoppix will automatically use any swap partitions that are available. On a computer with only Windows, however, there will probably be no swap partition. In that case, from the Knoppix Configure menu, you can select Swap File Configuration to run the `mkdosswapfile` script to first create a swapfile on a local DOS or NTFS partition and then enable it.

Under Utilities, you can run Harddisk/CD/DVD/DMA Acceleration to have direct memory-access acceleration turned on or off for your hard drive or removable media drives. Having DMA on improves disk performance in most cases. However, you can avoid disk-access errors by turning DMA off for those drives that have defective DMA controllers. In most cases, it's worth a try turning it on, although some say that, in extreme cases, data corruption can occur on a writeable drive that doesn't support DMA.

Panel Buttons

To the right of the KDE and Knoppix menu buttons on the Knoppix KDE desktop are buttons for launching several popular applications. These applications include (from left to right) a window list menu, a desktop-access button (to minimize everything on the desktop), a home button (to open the /home/knoppix directory in Konqueror), Konsole (shell Terminal), Konqueror (file manager and Web browser), Firefox (Web browser), and Open Office (OpenOffice.org Writer).

You can move, remove, or add panel buttons. Right-click an icon and then select Move, Remove, or Configure the application associated with that panel button. To add a new application button to the panel, right-click on the panel (to se the panel menu), and select to add an applet (small application that runs on the panel) or an application (which you can select from the KDE menu that appears).

Desktop Pager and Taskbar

Four workspaces are available by default from the KDE desktop used with Knoppix. The Desktop Pager makes it easy to work among those four desktops or even add more (up to 20). The taskbar shows all the desktop applications that are currently running.

Switch among the four workspaces by clicking on the one you want on the Desktop Pager. Rectangular icons represent the applications that are open on each workspace. You can drag-and-drop an application window between Pager workspaces to have the application move to the new workspace. To see a larger version of the Pager on the desktop, right-click on the Pager and select Launch Pager. Figure 2-2 shows an example of the Desktop Pager window:

FIGURE 2-2
Move between workspaces using the Desktop Pager.

Hover the mouse over applications in the taskbar to see the task's name and which workspace it is in. The taskbar can also interact with the Desktop Pager. You can drag and drop an application from the taskbar to any workspace on which you want it to appear. To have an application appear on every workspace, right-click the application in the taskbar and then select To Desktop → All Desktops.

System Tray

Small icons representing applets appear in the right side of the KDE Knoppix desktop panel in what is called the system tray. Applets provide another means of conveniently changing system settings on a KDE Knoppix desktop.

Applets that appear on the Knoppix KDE desktop include the KDE Keyboard Tool, Screen Size applet, and KMIX applet. You can configure your keyboard, screen resolution, and refresh rate, and adjust the volume on your audio channels.

Select the Panel menu and choose Add Applet to Panel to see a list of available applets. You can add such applets as Konqueror Browser bookmarks, a puzzle game, Klipper (a cut-and-paste utility), network folders, a printer menu, a quick file browser, a control center menu, the weather report, and wireless network information.

Konqueror File Manager

Konqueror is the primary graphical application for viewing content on a KDE desktop. Besides enabling you to view the contents of your local or networked folders, Konqueror is a Web browser and universal document viewer.

When Knoppix starts, the Knoppix Info page is displayed in a Konqueror window. You can open a new Konqueror window at any time by selecting the Home icon from the desktop panel. You can use it to browse a directory (/home/knoppix) or a Web page (www.knoppix.net). But you can use it to browse special features as well, including the following examples:

- about:konqueror—Browse descriptions, specs, and tips related to Konqueror.
- about:plugins—View which Web browser plug-ins are installed for Konqueror.
- applications:/—See the applications on your system represented by folders and icons.
- settings:/—View the icons representing applications for changing system settings.
- remote:/—Use the Add a Network Folder icon to add links to network resources (such as remote shared NFS and Samba files systems from your LAN).

- smb:/—View shared Windows folders available on your network from Samba or other SMB Windows file-sharing servers.

- media:/—View the hard-disk partitions, CD/DVD drives, flash memory, and other storage devices on your system.

Using Web shortcuts, you can use the same syntax to search a variety of search engines on the Internet. For example, google:Knoppix would use the Google search engine to search for the term *Knoppix*. You can select to enable dozens of more search engine Web shortcuts from the KDE Control Center (open the KDE Control Center and search for "Web shortcuts").

A variety of plug-ins also are available for Konqueror, to allow Konqueror to do special features. These plug-ins might be available for your distribution in a kdeaddons package. When available, many of these plug-ins can be selected from the Tools menu (when appropriate for the type of content you are displaying). For example, for a folder containing images, you can run the Create Image Gallery tool to create an HTML page containing thumbnails and links to those images. From an HTML page, you can select the Translate Web Page tool, to translate the contents of the page into a variety of languages. Read about other Konqueror plug-ins in the *Konqueror Handbook:* http://docs.kde.org/stable/en/kdebase/konqueror/konq-plugin.html.

When building a live CD, you should understand that Konqueror has many configurable features. Start by selecting Settings → Configure Konqueror to select dozens of configuration settings. For your live CD, you might want to set the appearance, file manager behavior, Web browser behavior, and many other features to match the look and feel you want with your live CD.

One particular approach you might want to take is to lock down Konqueror to limit what a user can do with your live CD. By configuring KDE in Kiosk mode, you can use Konqueror as the entire desktop interface, allowing users of your live CD to access and play only the data that you want to present. (See Chapter 3 for information Kiosk mode.)

The Shell

As do most Linux distributions, Knoppix uses bash as its default shell. When you select the Terminal icon on the KDE panel, Konsole is the default terminal window used.

When you open the Konsole window, your user ID is the same as the user running the desktop: knoppix. The home directory is /home/knoppix. Standard Linux system permissions apply when it comes to read/write/execute permissions for the Knoppix user. The Knoppix user can change files in /home/knoppix and /tmp, but not in /etc or /bin, for example.

To allow the Knoppix user to use root permission when necessary, you can use the sudo command. The /etc/sudoers file is configured to allow the Knoppix user to run any command as though it were the root user. For example, to edit the /etc/hosts file and change its contents using vi, you could type the following:

```
# sudo vi /etc/hosts
```

Because sudo is configured to let you run any command as the Knoppix user, without typing a password, you can simply begin editing the file. If you want to run a longer session, as the root user, you could type something like **sudo su** - to start a shell session as the root user.

If you know your way around the KDE desktop, understanding how to use live CDs other than Knoppix that provide a KDE desktop mostly means getting used to the different tools that the CD puts together for you to use. The following sections provide brief tours of other live CDs.

RUNNING A GAMING LIVE CD

With literally hundreds, if not thousands, of open-source games available today, putting together a full toy chest of games on a live CD was a natural idea. The Games Knoppix CD contains more than 200 games for you to play, with a DVD version that contains many more games. The SuperGamer live DVD, based on PCLinuxOS, contains more than 3GB of software, including many free 3D games and several demos of popular commercial games. The Linux Live Game Project (LLGP) live CD contains hundreds of freely distributable games (LLGP is described in Chapter 11, "Customizing a Gaming Live Linux CD").

 NOTE

See Appendix A for information on which gaming live CDs are included on the DVD that comes with this book.

Most basic games created originally for Linux or other UNIX-like platforms will run on most any X desktop environment. Some older UNIX games run from the shell. If you are happy with the occasional board game, card game, and simple shooting game, there will be no problem finding stuff to keep you amused on most Linux desktops.

Although some exceptions exist, most commercial video games were made to run on other platforms. Though things are improving, Linux users are still not seen as a major computer gaming market. So the bad news is that you need to use a gaming console (Playstation, Xbox, and so on) to play most of the latest commercial games or run Windows games in some sort of emulator or applications-compatibility mode, to use them in Linux. And in most of those cases, you won't be able to redistribute the games on a live CD.

The good news, however, is that there have been some fun older commercial games released into the public domain. Add to that the fact that a lot of open-source developers think it's fun to write their own gaming console emulators, and you end up with the possibility of a whole new world of games being available to play with on a live CD (or add to your own).

Using Gaming Emulators

Here are some examples of emulator technology that can be incorporated into a Linux live CD that opens up the possibility of playing lots of games from your live CD:

- **MAME (www.mame.net)**—The Multiple Arcade Machine Emulator, or MAME, started out in 1997 as a project for documenting how different arcade game consoles work. It is now capable of playing more than 6,000 different games created originally for game consoles from Atari, Sega, and other hardware manufacturers, mostly from the 1970s, 1980s, and 1990s. MAME (which includes the xmame client that runs in X on Linux) is available on the Knoppix Games CD.

  The problem with using MAME to play these games is that few of the games that run on it can be freely distributed. To play these games in MAME someone needs to rip copies of the game ROMs from the cartridges to be able to play them in Linux. Even if you own original cartridges of these games, it might not be legal to transfer these games to a different medium (such as a CD or hard disk running Linux). See a discussion of this issue in Chapter 11.

- **ScummVM (www.scummvm.org):** Using ScummVM, you can play a variety of games used to create some of the famous LucasArts adventure games of the 1980s and 1990s. It has also been expanded to include virtual machines to play other games from than period, such as *Simon the Sorcerer, Broken Sword 1/2,* and *Inherit the Earth.*

  ScummVM is available under GPL, so it can be freely distributed. It also has some advantages of being capable of playing games originally sold on CD, so you can legally purchase some of these CDs from second-hand stores or online auctions (such as eBay).

  As for including some of these games on live CD, some games that ScummVM will play have been released into the public domain.

These games include *Beneath a Steel Sky* and *Flight of the Amazon Queen,* which are available on the Knoppix Games CD for you to try.

■ **Other gaming emulators**—A variety of other game hardware emulators are also available on Linux gaming CDs, such as Knoppix Games. Few of these emulators come with any games, but if you have legal game ROMs for older Atari, Commodore, or Apple hardware, you can try them with emulators you select from the Emulators list on the K menu.

Besides gaming consoles, emulators and application-compatibility software projects are available to run games intended for computer operating systems. WINE (http://winehq.org) and Bochs (http://bochs.sourceforge.net) can be used to run applications created for PC-compatible (x86) hardware. DOSBox (http://dosbox.sourceforge.net) can run a rage of DOS and Windows applications, but it is particularly developed to run older DOS games that won't run on more modern PCs.

NOTE

A popular way of playing Windows games in Linux is to use a commercial product called Cedega from Transgaming Technologies (www.transgaming.com). Previously called WineX (because it was originally based on WINE), Cedega implements a version Win32 API in Linux. It then supports many Windows multimedia APIs (such DirectX, Direct3D, DirectInput, and DirectSound) that are critical to Windows gaming. It then specifically tests those games that are wanted by their customers so the games will run well in Linux.

Although all the gaming emulators just mentioned are covered under the GPL and, therefore, can be freely distributed, the major issue is finding games that run on those platforms that can be freely distributed as well. Again, the issues of getting games you can play legally and even, in some cases, redistribute freely, are discussed in Chapter 11.

The other limiting factors related to gaming have to do with your video hardware. Games that demand 3D acceleration usually work best with NVIDIA or ATI cards. Although open-source drivers are available for NVIDIA and ATI cards, proprietary Linux drivers available from NVIDIA and ATI simply work better for gamers.

Trying Games in Linux

As a way of trying out some games, the DVD that comes with this book includes the Linux Live Game Project live CD. Another way is to try the Games Knoppix live

CD, which you can get from the Games Knoppix site: http://games-knoppix.unix-ag.uni-kl.de. This section describes the Games Knoppix CD.

Because Knoppix Games is a remastered version of Knoppix, once you can get around on Knoppix, most of what is different here are the games themselves. To get started, just open the Games list from the K menu. Figure 2-3 shows an example of the Knoppix Games screen displaying the games Beneath a Steel Sky (upper right) and Flight of the Amazon Queen (middle), along with a list of games displayed in the Konqueror window (type **programs:/Games/** in the location box to see this list):

FIGURE 2-3 Beneath a Steel Sky and Flight of the Amazon Queen were commercial games that are now free.

NOTE

Intel recently announced that it will release drivers for its video cards in open source. Although Intel video interfaces are not considered to be as good as NVIDIA and ATI cards, Intel's announcement is expected to result in much-improved gaming with open source drivers and could encourage NVIDIA and ATI to release their drivers in open source as well.

Most of the games described here are covered under the GNU Public License (GPL) or similar license and can be freely distributed. You might be free to use some games that run in Linux, covered under other licenses; on the other hand, you might be free to use on your own live CD, but not on one that that is redistributed. For example, demos of some commercial games might fall into this category. You may need permission from the company making the game to redistribute the demo (and that request will likely fall on deaf ears).

You can try a variety of games from the Knoppix Games CD. Some games represent good examples of those that were developed from scratch to be free and those that began as commercial games that were available as freeware. There also were many games created as clones of popular board games and card games. The following sections contain examples of traditional free games, previous commercial games that are now free, and clones of popular board and card games.

Running NetHack and Traditional Free Software Games

Because gaming has always been a popular pastime for free software enthusiasts, some long-existing games were built from scratch to be freely distributed. Many of these games are continuously developed (when the developers have time), have strong followings, and are actively discussed in forums and mailing lists. Others lie dormant until someone has the time and interest to pick them up. Here are examples a few free software games to try:

- **BZFlag 3D tank game (Games → Arcade → bzflag)**—Play capture the flag or other games (with teams or as individuals) in this 3D, multiplayer tank game. By connecting to a BZflag server, you can play against other around the world over the Internet. Read more about it at http://bzflag.org.

- **KQ (Games → Adventure → KQ)**—In this role-playing adventure game, players are asked to help a mysterious old man named Nostik to go on a quest to retrieve his stolen Staff of Xenarum. The staff was broken into two pieces. The player who can return both pieces will gain great fame and fortune.

  Development of KQ was taken over by the Allegro game development community (www.allegro.cc) after being abandoned by its original developer. You can find out more about game play at the KQLives Sourceforge site (http://kqlives.sourceforge.net).

- **GNU chess (Games → Board Games → Xboard)**—You can play chess against the computer or against online opponents. The graphical version of GNU chess is called Xboard. The GNU chess home page is www.gnu.org/software/chess.

In the Dungeons-and-Dragons-like adventure game NetHack, you descend into a dungeon to find the Amulet of Yendor. Along the way, you kill monsters, gather cool stuff, and explore dark and mysterious places.

NetHack (http://nethack.org) is a good representation of games that began as free software, while evolving and spawning new versions over the years. Its early ancestors can be traced to text-only games such as Adventure and, later, the screen-oriented Rogue game. The code base for NetHack came from the game Hack, which ran on character-based terminals on UNIX systems. The evolution of NetHack includes several available user interfaces (both graphical and text based) that run on many different computer systems (including UNIX, Linux, MacOS, DOS, and OS/2).

You can start different versions of NetHack by selecting Games → Adventure from the K Menu, on the Knoppix Games live CD, and then selecting NetHack (no GUI), Nethack, Hack, or Falcon's Eye. Figure 2-4 shows an example of the Falcon's Eye version of NetHack.

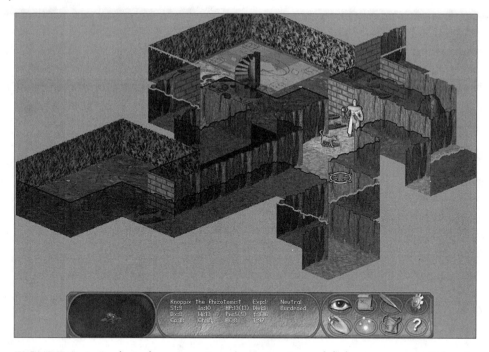

FIGURE 2-4 Explore dungeons, acquire treasure, and fight monsters in Falcon's Eye (NetHack).

In character-based versions of the game, every item in the dungeons is represented by a symbol. The at sign (@) is you, stairs go up (<) or down (>), and items such as a wand (/), ring (=), scroll (?), or a potion (!) might just be lying around to pick up. In Falcon's Eye, however, you can move the mouse over an item to see a description of it. You can also right-click an object or location to act on it or move to it.

Because these NetHack games are based on the same underlying engine, you can use the same keyboard commands in any of these games. Table 2-1 shows a list of keyboard commands and resulting actions from the NetHack help page.

Playing with NetHack connects you to some of the first adventure-type games played on UNIX systems. For more detailed descriptions of options and game play, refer to the *Guidebook for NetHack* (www.nethack.org/v343/Guidebook.html).

Running Beneath a Steel Sky and Now-Free Commercial Games

Although slow and graphically simple by today's standards, Beneath a Steel Sky is an engaging game if you like to solve puzzles in the context of a story. It is an example of games that were released into the public domain when they were no longer being sold as commercial products.

Another example of a game that was released into the public domain that you can run in Linux is Flight of the Amazon Queen (Games → Adventure → Flight of the Amazon Queen). In this adventure game set in the 1940s, you crash into the Amazon jungle as pilot Joe King. You fight a mad scientist and try to save your movie-star passenger and an Amazon tribe. As with Beneath a Steel Sky, it was created using technology developed from LucasArts. After it was released as freeware in 2004, support for playing the game was added to ScummVM.

To start with Beneath a Steel Sky, select Games → Adventure → Beneath a Steel Sky from the K menu. After playing a cartoon that sets up the story (you can skip it by selecting Esc), you take on the role of Robert Foster. After being kidnapped by storm-troopers from the futuristic Union City, Foster sets out to unravel the mystery of his past and discover a way out of the city.

Game play consists of using the mouse to move Foster, finding objects to help him get further along, and interacting with other characters to get clues about how to proceed. Move the pointer to the top of the screen to see what Foster is carrying (wrenches, cables, ID card, and so on); then select an item and drag it to act on buttons, doors, machines, and other items in the scene.

Here are a few tips on getting started:

- Move your mouse pointer slowly around the screen to search for items. Some items you can't see until the pointer is over them.
- Use the left mouse button to choose where to go. Use the right mouse button to select items.
- Ask a lot of questions. Sometimes you can't proceed until someone has given you information.

TABLE 2-1 Keyboard Commands for NetHack Games

KEY	DESCRIPTION	KEY	DESCRIPTION
?	Displays the Help menu.	^R	Redraws the screen.
/	Tells what a symbol represents. Choose a location or give a symbol argument.	s	Searches for secret doors and traps around you.
&	Tells what a command does.	S	Saves the game.
<	Goes up a staircase (if you are standing on it).	t	Throws an object or shoots a projectile.
>	Goes down a staircase (if you are standing on it).	T	Takes off armor.
.	Rests, does nothing for one turn.	^T	Teleports, if you are able.
_	Travels via a shortest-path algorithm to a point on the map	v	Displays the version number.
a	Applies (use) a tool (pick-axe, key, lamp, and so on).	V	Displays a longer identification of the version, including the history of the game.
A	Removes all armor.	w	Wields a weapon. w - means wield nothing, use bare hands.
^A	Redoes the previous command.	W	Wears armor.
c	Closes a door.	x	Swaps wielded and secondary weapons.
C	Calls (names) an individual monster.	X	Switches the game to explore (discovery) mode.
d	Drops something. d7a: Drops seven items of object a.	^X	Shows your attributes.
D	Drops multiple items.	z	Zaps a wand.
^D	Kicks (for doors, usually).	Z	Casts a spell.
e	Eats food.	^Z	Suspends the game.

continues

TABLE 2-1 Continued

KEY	DESCRIPTION	KEY	DESCRIPTION
E	Engraves a message on the floor. E- - writes in the dust with your fingers.	:	Looks at what is here.
f	Fires ammunition from a quiver.	;	Looks at what is somewhere else.
F	Followed by direction, fights a monster (even if you don't sense it).	,	Picks up some things.
i	Displays your inventory.	@	Toggles the pickup option.
I	Displays selected parts of your inventory, as in I* (lists all gems in inventory), Iu (lists all unpaid items), Ix (lists all used-up items that are on your shopping bill), and I$ (counts money).	^	Asks for the type of a trap you found earlier.
o	Opens a door.	)	Tells what weapon you are wielding.
O	Reviews current options and possibly changes them.	[	Tells what armor you are wearing.
p	Pays your shopping bill.	=	Tells what rings you are wearing.
P	Puts on an accessory (ring, amulet, and so on).	"	Tells what amulet you are wearing.
^P	Repeats last message (subsequent ^P commands repeat earlier messages).	(	Tells what tools you are using.
q	Drinks (quaffs) a potion.	*	Tells what equipment you are using; combines the preceding five.
Q	Selects ammunition for a quiver.	$	Counts your gold pieces.
r	Reads a scroll or spellbook.	+	Lists the spells you know; also rearranges them, if desired.
R	Removes an accessory (ring, amulet, and so on).		

Figure 2-5 shows a screen shot from Beneath a Steel Sky, where Robert Foster needs to get into the store room to find the putty he needs to short-circuit the control panel:

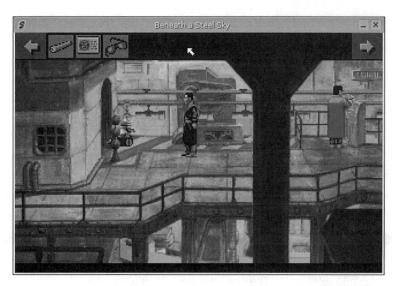

FIGURE 2-5 Help Robert Foster escape from Union City and find the secrets of his past.

It can be very time-consuming to figure out how to progress with this game. To help you get started, here are the first few steps you can try: Locate the metal bar and take it (right-click). Pry open the fire escape door. After the officer checks the door, go down the stairs to the room to your right.

Find something in the trash to use as Joey's (your robot's) body and drop the circuit board on it. Try to start the transport robot. When it doesn't start, go in the room to the right and ask Hobbins questions until he tells you what's wrong with the transport robot. Go back to the room to the left and ask Joey to fix the transport robot. When the transport begins bringing barrels to the lift, jump down the hole when the lift is down.

Next, try the lock on the door out of the furnace room. When you can't open it, have Joey open the door. When Officer Reich comes in and gets shot by Linc, go over and take his ID card and sunglasses. Exit the furnace room and try to figure out how to get an elevator to take you down. You're on your way.

If you find the game difficult after a while (which you probably will), you can find lots of walkthroughs of the game on the Internet. An example of a walkthrough is located at http://home.alo.com/gametown/beneath.html. Otherwise, just search for the terms *walkthrough* and *Beneath a Steel Sky*.

Running Card Game, Board Game, and Strategy Game Clones

Nearly every board game or card game you can imagine in the real world has a version available that you can play in Linux. Likewise, many popular computer and arcade games have been cloned to run as open-source applications. Some games that are diverting to play if you need a bit of brain downtime include the following:

- **Card games**—Select Games → Card Games from the K menu and select a card game to try. You'll find several solitaire games, Cribbage, Go Fish, XScat, and a clone of Mille Borne.
- **Board games**—Select Games → Board Games from the K menu to select from dozens of board games. You'll find traditional board games such as chess, backgammon, Go, and mahjongg, as well as clones of commercial games, such as Monopoly.
- **Strategy games**—Select Games → Strategy from the K menu to choose from a variety of original and cloned strategy games. Select Freeciv to try the free clone of the popular Civilization games. Choose Freecraft to try a clone of the WarCraft II real-time strategy game.

You can include plenty of games in these categories on a live Linux CD. KDE and GNOME desktop environments themselves offer packages that include a well-rounded set of game packages.

For information on issues that go into producing your own gaming CD, refer to Chapter 11. Besides choosing the types of games you want to include, you need to carefully consider licensing issues and requirements for video hardware (especially for games requiring 3D hardware acceleration).

RUNNING A MULTIMEDIA LIVE CD (MOVIX AND DYNEBOLIC)

Playing and displaying multimedia content are among the most fun activities to do with a computer. Desktop-oriented live CDs, such as Knoppix, typically offer several choices for playing audio, digital images, and some form of video. People have also developed a variety of specialized live Linux CDs for both presenting and creating multimedia content. Here are some examples:

- **Specialized media players**—There are live Linux CDs made primarily for playing video. Because there is little overhead with just being a media player (no bulky desktop required), these tiny multimedia live CD systems often play audio CDs and digital images as well. Low resource demands also mean you can run them on minimal PCs (a Pentium II with 64MB of RAM often works fine).

Examples of popular live CD, such as MoviX (http://movix.sourceforge.net), GeeXboX (www.GeeXboX.org), Womp (http://womp.sourceforge.net), and Limp (http://limp-vkk-ver1.sourceforge.net), offer small footprints to run in RAM, so you can pop out the CD and use your CD or DVD drive to play content. Often you can also access your multimedia content from a local hard disk, an NFS shared directory, or a Windows shared folder (SMB).

Media player live CDs are prime candidates for hooking up with your personal audio, video, or digital image content. In fact, an offshoot of the MoviX project called eMoviX is made especially for you to combine your own video files with a scaled-down Linux system and mplayer media player to boot up and start playing your video files.

- **Multimedia production**—The Dynebolic live Linux CD (www.dynebolic.org) is a treasure chest of free and open-source multimedia production applications. Not only does it include applications for creating and editing sound, video, and digital images, but it also include tools for playing and streaming that content. To make this live CD truly useful for producing multimedia content, Dynebolic also offers procedures for saving multimedia content to a type of persistent desktop (called a nest) on a medium such as a USB flash drive. Dynebolic can also be installed and run from hard disk.

Finding fun and useful tools for playing and producing multimedia content is easy, but finding open-source software that works with some popular multimedia formats can be a big problem. In particular, certain video and audio codecs (for compressing and decompressing audio and video streams) are encumbered by software patents and other issues. (Chapter 12, "Customizing a Multimedia Live Linux CD," covers these issues in detail.)

The good news, however, is that if you are producing, editing, and playing your own audio, video, or digital images, free software alternatives exist for every type of medium you might want to produce. For example, you could produce a video clip, convert it to Theora (video) and Ogg Vorbis (audio) with ffmpeg2theora, edit the file with Cinelerra, and play the results in Totem (or several other video players).

In terms of multimedia live Linux CDs, the DVD that comes with this book contains the Dynebolic live Linux CD and the MoviX multimedia player live CD. Also included on the DVD is a custom version of eMoviX that can be booted to directly play a video produced for this book.

Playing Video, Music, and Images with MoviX

The MoviX project, created by Roberto De Leo, consists of several small Linux-based live CDs that are used to play a range of multimedia content. By offering a minimal operating system that includes only the software needed to access and play multimedia content, MoviX projects can run on low-end computers with minimal amounts of memory.

The MoviX2 multimedia player is the most versatile of the MoviX projects. The main focus of MoviX2 is a simple X Window system display and the mplayer multimedia player. Because of its size, MoviX2 can fit on a mini-CD, 64MB USB pen drive, or other small bootable medium. When it's running, you can play video, music, or digital images from CD, DVD, hard disk, or various network interfaces.

A key element of any multimedia live CD is its capability to properly detect and configure your video card configuration. MoviX2 offers several boot options that let you take best advantage of your video hardware. For example, MoviX2 includes proprietary NVIDIA drivers that you can select (at the boot prompt) to use instead of the open-source NVIDIA drivers. Likewise, you can set your monitor frequency manually (also at the boot prompt), if that is not being properly detected.

The following procedure steps you through some of the features of MoviX2:

1. Burn the MoviX2 ISO image to CD, as described in Appendix A.
2. Insert the MoviX2 live CD into your computer and reboot.
3. When you see the MoviX2 boot screen, you can either simply press Enter or type any of the following boot labels, depending on your situation:

   - `MoviX2`—This is the default label.
   - `NVidia`—If you have an NVIDIA video card, you can try this label to use the driver made available by NVIDIA. (Otherwise, the open-source nv driver will be used.)
   - *Frame Buffer*—If your video hardware cannot be detected properly, you might be able to identify it as a frame buffer device so you can use MoviX2. You can instead use a label for a generic frame buffer (`vesaFB`) or use a frame buffer at a particular resolution (`vesaFB640`, `vesaFB800`, `vesaFB1024`, `vesaFB1280`, or `vesaFB1400`, for 640×480, 800×600, 1024×768, 1280×1024, or 1400×1050 resolutions, respectively).
   - `vesa`—This label starts MoviX2 with a generic vesa driver (nonaccelerated).
   - `aa`—Use the aa label to display video in ASCII.

   If you have further trouble getting MoviX2 to run properly, press F5 or F6 at the boot prompt to see other X display boot parameters and system boot parameters, respectively.

   The kernel then boots and begin copying MoviX2 into RAM. When it's finished, you will see the MoviX2 screen, ready to begin playing your multimedia content.

4. Eject the CD. Now you can use the drive to insert a CD or DVD containing the content you want to play.

5. Right-click the desktop to see a modified Mplayer menu. Then select Switch to MoviX. The MoviX main page appears, as shown in Figure 2-6.

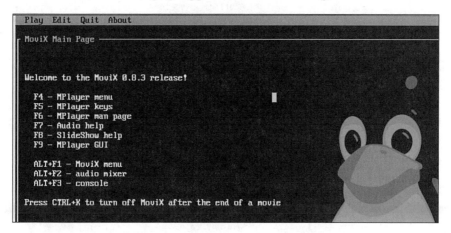

FIGURE 2-6 Play video, audio, or slide shows from the MoviX main page.

Here are some of the things you can do from the MoviX main page:

- **Play video**—Press F9 to start the Mplayer media player graphical user interface. Right-click the desktop and select Open → Play File. You can then browse your computer to find any supported video to play. You can check your CD or DVD (/cdrom0), your hard-disk partitions (mounted on /discs), and any remote-mounted file systems (mounted on /mnt).

- **Play music**—Insert a music CD into the drive. Select Play → Audio CD → Play to play music from an audio CD. MoviX2 displays the artist, album, and track name (song title) on the screen (provided that it can access a CDDB database over the network) as each track plays from the CD. The player has simple controls. Use the up and down arrow keys to move between tracks. Press 9 to reduce volume and 0 to increase volume. Press Esc to exit.

 NOTE

MoviX2 cannot play commercial movie DVDs as it is delivered. If you can obtain the libdvdcss library and add it to the /usr/lib directory on the Movix2 CD, you can use MoviX2 to play commercial DVDs. See Chapter 12 for a deeper discussion on why the library to decode commercial DVD movies is not always included with Linux distributions.

- **Play digital images**—To display a slide show of a directory of digital images, select Play → SlideShow, then select the location of the images (CD drive or disk partition). Use Page Up or Page Down to go to previous or next images, respectively. Zoom in and out with + or - keys. For images larger than the screen, use arrow keys to scroll. To get help, press H. Press P to pause the slideshow and Esc to exit.

If you want to adjust your audio, press Alt+F2 to display the alsamixer audio mixer. To access a shell, press Alt+F3.

Most sound cards that the ALSA project supports work with MoviX2. If your card doesn't work, you can try loading the OSS sound module (enter the OSS=y boot option). For ISA sound cards, you might need the DETECT=all boot option for it to work properly. See the ALSA project (www.alsa-project.org) for further suggestions.

Creating Multimedia Content with Dynebolic

The Dynebolic live CD was created as an open-source tool kit for working with multimedia content. It was designed to be something that a digital artist can carry around and use on just about any standard PC that can be rebooted.

Instead of offering a full-blown KDE or Gnome desktop, Dynebolic boots up to a lightweight window manager (Windowmaker) and focuses on providing tools for getting data from a variety of sources, then for displaying and manipulating that data.

Touring Dynebolic

The following is a quick tour of the Dynebolic live CD on the DVD that comes with this book. To get the official ISO image of Dynebolic, follow the download link from the Dynebolic home page (www.dynebolic.org).

1. Burn the Dynebolic image to CD, as described in Appendix A.
2. Insert the Dynebolic image into your CD drive and reboot.
3. Either check boot options (press F2 or F3 to see boot options) or just press Enter. Dynebolic should boot to a desktop similar to the one shown in Figure 2-7:
4. Check out the Dynebolic desktop. You should note a few features about the desktop:
   - **Storage devices**—The panel in the upper-right corner of the screen represents storage devices. Use the house icon at the top of the panel to open the home directory (/home) in a file manager (the XFE, X File Explorer). You can use XFE to explore your file system.

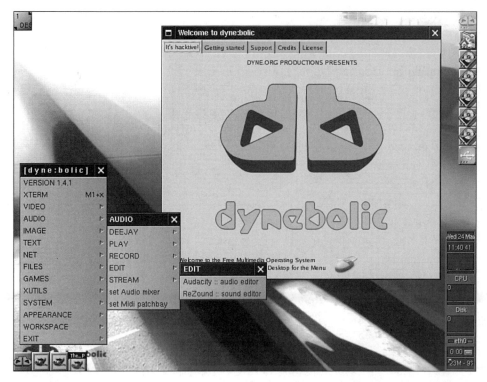

FIGURE 2-7 Create and manage multimedia content from the Dynebolic desktop.

For ease of use, an icon represents each hard-disk partition on the computer. Those partitions are automatically mounted with read-write permission on the /vol directory, so all you have to do is open the icon for the partition you want to access files and directories from there.

If you have a USB flash memory drive inserted into a USB port, you can select the USB icon on the bottom of the upper-right panel. The first USB device should be mounted on /rem/usb and opened by the XFE file manager, for you to access.

- **System monitor**—The GNU Krell Monitor is anchored to the lower-right corner of the screen. By default, it is set to display date/time, CPU usage, disk activity, network (Ethernet) activity, and memory usage. Select any of those items to see additional details or configuration information.

- **Dynebolic menu**—Right-click the desktop to see the menu of available applications. Choose from a selection of video, audio, and image-editing and playing applications. The Files menu offers ways of accessing local folders (XFE), remote folders (XFSamba and LinNeighborhood), encrypted storage (Gringotts), and CD burning (gCombust). Some examples of applications to try are described later.

5. Do basic configuration. Select the Getting Started tab if you need to configure certain features. For example, you can change the language, reconfigure
your Ethernet connection (Network), set up a dial-up connection (Modem),
configure printing (Printer), or change video settings (Screen). You can also
set up a Nest feature from the Getting Started screen (described later).

6. Set up Nest. If you are ready to start using Dynebolic and you want to be
able to keep the data you work on, you should consider setting up a type
of persistent desktop that Dynebolic refers to as a Nest. The Nest feature
lets you store the files you store with Dynebolic on a hard-disk partition or
USB drive.

To create a Nest, select the Getting Started tab on the Welcome to Dyne:bolic
window. Then select Nest. Choose either the Nest on Hard Disk or Nest on
USB Key option (if you have a USB key inserted). Choose the amount of storage space you want to consume for your Nest on the disk partition or USB
drive, and select OK.

A file called `dynebol.nst` is created on the USB drive or hard-disk partition
you selected. Reboot Dynebolic. During the boot process, Dynebolic should
find the `dynebol.nst` file you saved and ask if you want to use it as your
Nest. Either type **Y** or wait for it to time out; Dynebolic boots with your nest
now available to be able to save files permanently in your `/home`, `/etc`, `/var`,
and `/tmp` directories as you use Dynebolic.

Trying Multimedia Applications in Dynebolic

The collection of open-source multimedia tools available in Dynebolic will keep
you busy for quite a while. The following list covers some of the things you can do
with Dynebolic and the applications you can use to do those things:

- **Play video**—Mplayer and Xine are among the most popular open-source
multimedia players. Both can play video from a variety of popular formats,
such as MPEG (1, 2, and 4), DivX, Windows Media Video, motion JPEG,
Sorenson SVQ1/SVQ3, and others. Supported audio formats include MP3,
Ogg Vorbis, DivX audio, Real Media, and others. In Dynebolic, Mplayer is
not compiled to use graphical controls (`gmplayer`), so you need to launch it
from the command line. To see features that Xine and Mplayer support, refer
to their Web pages (http://xinehq.de/index.php/features and http://mplay-
erhq.hu/info.html, respectively).

- **Record and edit video**—Dynebolic includes the Kino digital video
recorder and editor and the Avidemux video cutter for working with video. It
also includes powerful command-line recording tools, including `mencoder`,
`ffmpeg`, and `nuvrec`.

- **Play audio**—Xmms is a popular graphical audio player. From the command line, you can play compressed music in Ogg Vorbis format using ogg123. The mpg123 command can play MP3 music files.

- **Edit audio**—The ReZound audio editor (http://rezound.sourceforge.net) is an open-source tool for doing fast and efficient sound editing. It currently can work with files in WAVE, AIFF, raw audio, Ogg Vorbis, MPEG (3, 2, 1), FLAC, and MIDI sample dump standard. Audacity (http://audacity.source-forge.net) is another graphical audio editor that you can use to edit sound and music, add effects, and save the output in a variety of formats. Figure 2-8 shows the Audacity window.

- **Edit images**—GIMP is a popular tool for editing digital images. If you want to edit vector graphics, you can try InkScape. Use Blender to create 3D models. To browse your digital images, use GQview. You can select all of these tools from the IMAGE menu on the main Dynebolic menu.

Dynebolic has dozens more multimedia applications available. For information on other software tools included with Dynebolic, refer to the project's Web site (www.dynebolic.org/index.php?show=features).

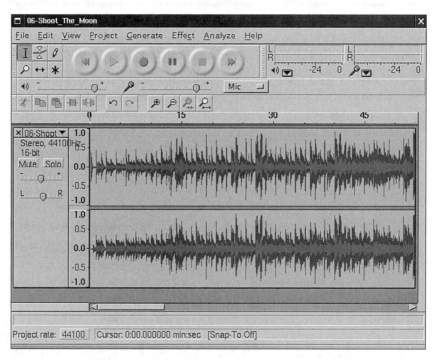

FIGURE 2-8 Edit audio files with Audacity.

Running a Security Live CD (BackTrack)

BackTrack (www.remote-exploit.org/index.php/BackTrack) is a suite of network security tools on a Linux live CD. It is based on the SLAX live CD, a slackware derivative, and combines features from two security-oriented live Linux distributions: Whax and Auditor.

The BackTrack CD contains more than 600MB of tools for fixing file systems, tracking down exploits, monitoring networks, and doing many, many other repair and maintenance tasks. The CD also includes archives of information on known exploits from Metasploit (www.metasploit.com) and SecurityFocus (www.securityfocus.com), with tools (such as an archive browser) available to access that data. (See Chapter 9, "Customizing a Security Live Linux CD," for further descriptions of BackTrack.)

Using BackTrack

The approach to BackTrack's design reflects the kind of features you might expect from a live CD that is brought in to check or repair a broken system or network. Here are some examples:

- **Boot messages**—Normally when you boot a live CD, messages stream by so quickly that you can miss something important. BackTrack offers a debug mode (type `slax debug` at the boot prompt) to open a shell at several points during the boot process. If something is wrong, you can correct it from the shell. If everything is okay, you press Ctrl+D to continue to boot.

  When control is handed to the init process, services are started up. If certain features fail, BackTrack tells you what to turn off from the boot prompt. For example, if BackTrack fails when starting PCMCIA services, the message on the screen tells you to type `slax nopcmcia` the next time you boot. The same applies if Hotplug fails (`slax nohotplug`).

- **Boots to a text prompt**—BackTrack boots to a text prompt, assuming that you might not have an available (or working) graphics card. However, six virtual terminals are available (Ctrl+Alt+F1, Ctrl+Alt+F2, and so on).

- **Mounting file systems**—BackTrack assumes that you want total access to your system when you are booting from a security live CD. Every partition that can be mounted from a storage medium is detected and mounted with read-write permission turned on. For example, partitions from the first hard disk (`/dev/hda1`, `/dev/hda2`, and so on) are mounted on the `/mnt` directory (`/mnt/hda1`, `/mnt/hda2`, and so on.). Likewise, USB flash drive partitions (which are viewed as SCSI devices) are mounted on `/mnt/sda1`, `/mnt/sda2`, and so on.

Each partition is mounted to allow devices to be accessed and files to be executed from that partition. You can check /etc/fstab to see which partitions were detected, as well as where and how they were mounted.

- **Desktop**—After logging in as the root user, run the **startx** command to start the GUI (a KDE desktop, by default). If you are in a low-resource environment, you can run a more efficient window manager instead of the full-blown KDE desktop.

- **Available tools**—Tools needed to bring up, configure, check, and repair computers are easily available on the BackTrack desktop. The bulk of the security tools are organized in more than a dozen categories under the Back-Track menu on the KDE menu (select the K menu button). Supporting services from the KDE menu let you set up and use a network connection (Internet menu), configure the desktop (Settings menu), search the computer (Find Files/Folders selection), and do screen captures.

Besides having a lot of available tools, BackTrack (and any security CD) needs to support lots of different kinds of hardware and file system types. BackTrack includes support for NTFS partitions and tools for configuring different wireless networking cards, for example.

Trying Security Applications

Despite the fact that the BackTrack live Linux CD includes hundreds of security tools, you can find many of the best tools from the well-organized BackTrack menu. Because many of these tools are command-line utilities (no GUI), some of the menu selections simply launch a shell displaying the help text for the selected command. The following text contains a sampling of some of the security tools you can run from BackTrack:

- **Scanners**—BackTrack contains tools for scanning your network ports (to see where someone might break in) and for scanning your system for general vulnerability.

  The Nessus (www.nessus.org) vulnerability scanner relies on an updated security database to check for the latest exploits. Besides checking the security of your computer from the outside (such as open ports and misconfigured network services), Nessus checks vulnerable applications (such as Web browsers and mail clients) to find flaws and missing patches.

  Nmap (www.insecure.org/nmap) can check the ports on your network interfaces to find potential vulnerabilities. A graphical front end to Nmap is available from the K menu by selecting BackTrack → Scanners → Port Scanners → NmapFE.

  From NmapFE, you can type the IP address of the target computer you want to scan, select a scan type (such as a SYN Stealth Scan or Connect Scan), and click the Scan button. NmapFE displays a list of ports that respond to the scan (implying that a service is available on that port), as well an indication of the number of ports that appear to be closed. It also indicates the type of operating system running on that computer.

- **Sniffers**—A network sniffer, such as Ethereal, can monitor an Ethernet port on your computer to watch all traffic received on that port. Open Ethereal (select BackTrack → Sniffers → Ethereal), select Capture → Interfaces, and then click the Capture button for the local interface you want to scan. After a few minutes, select Stop to see a list of packets received on the interface.

  The output from Ethereal shows you the packets sent and received over that interface. You should see such things as DNS queries, BROWSE packets from Windows shares, available printer announcements, and (if you are Web browsing) lots of HTTP GETs. You can sort the data in various ways (by time, source, destination, protocol, and so on) or select Filter to filter by protocol type, IP address, or other attributes.

- **Forensic tools**—Select BackTrack → Forensic Tools to choose from a variety of applications for analyzing systems after a suspected attack. A typical way to do forensics on a hard-disk partition is to back it up to an image file (select Acquiring Tools and then use a tool such as AIR or the dd command to create an image file).

  The Autopsy Forensic Browser (www.sleuthkit.org/autopsy) provides a graphical interface for investigating problems on UNIX and Linux systems using a set of Sleuth Kit tools. To start Autopsy in a browser, from Forensic Tools, select Analysis → Autopsy. You can use Autopsy to run a variety of tests on that image, such as File Analysis or Keyword Search, as shown in Figure 2-9.

If you find in the course of using BackTrack that you need more information about problems you encounter, open the Firefox Web browser from the BackTrack panel. In the Bookmarks toolbar you can find links to locations that provide information on security problems. These include links to Milw0rm.com (to look up exploits by platform, port, or other identifier), Metasploit.com (for penetration testing information), Securityfocus.com (for a wide range of security information), and Packet Storm (http://packetstormsecurity.org, for security tools, exploits, and advisories).

GETTING A LIVE CD WORKING JUST RIGHT

Despite all its wonderful autodetection and configuration, a live CD still might not be working exactly right when you just boot it. For a live CD that fails right from the start, you don't have the advantage of all the fancy configuration tools that come with the distribution. Your greatest friends, in that case, are boot options. If you don't get to the boot screen at all, however, you need to check the BIOS.

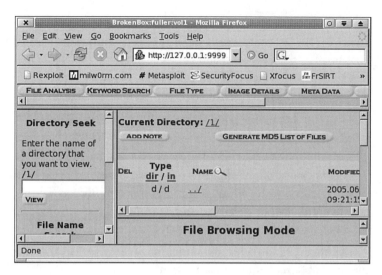

FIGURE 2-9   Run forensics on file-system images using Autopsy.

Before you get to boot options, if when you try to boot a live CD, DVD, or USB drive, your computer ignores it completely and boots straight to hard disk, you might need to change the system BIOS. As the system is first booting, go to the BIOS screen (by pressing a function key, the Del key, or another key as instructed on the screen). From the BIOS, look for an option that lets you change the boot order so that your CD, DVD, or USB drive comes before your hard disk. Save the changes and continue to boot.

If you see the live CD or DVD splash screen or boot prompt, you can proceed. From the boot line prompt for any live Linux CD, you can pass options to the kernel that tell it how to handle certain types of hardware, or possibly to ignore certain hardware as you boot up.

The first thing to warn you about is that you have to be quick. From a boot screen, you typically have only a few seconds to pause the boot process before it continues on to boot the default system. From an Isolinux boot screen, typing any letter keeps the boot process from proceeding. From a GRUB boot screen, use the arrow keys to move to the CD image you want to boot, and press the letter **e** to be able to add options to the selected kernel line.

Different live CDs might have different boot options. You enter boot options by entering the label (such as `knoppix` or `linux`), followed by one or more options. For example, to run Knoppix using US English language and the fluxbox desktop, you type the following at the boot prompt:

```
boot: knoppix lang=en desktop=fluxbox
```

Although knoppix is the default label to use as the boot prompt, Knoppix has other labels available. The expert label lets you interactively configure hardware during boot-up. The debug label results in more messages when Knoppix boots. The failsafe label boots with almost no hardware detection. Several other frame buffer labels set the video display to different resolutions: fb800×600, fb1024×768, and fb1280×1024.

Table 2-2 contains a list of boot options that are available with Knoppix. Most of these options are listed in the knoppix-cheatcodes.txt file on any Knoppix CD. Many of them also appear when you press F2 and F3 and the Knoppix boot prompt.

Other boot options that are not listed here can be used to provide special features for running Knoppix. They include options for having a persistent desktop, saving configuration settings, and running Knoppix from RAM or hard disk. Chapter 3 covers the options you can enter to create and use a persistent desktop.

The feature for running a Knoppix live CD entirely from RAM requires a simple boot options called toram. If you have at least 1GB of RAM available, you can run your Knoppix live CD from RAM by typing the following at the boot prompt:

```
boot: knoppix toram
```

Booting Knoppix with the toram option can take longer to boot because the entire image must be loaded into RAM. However, performance of the live CD should then be much improved over running from the CD or DVD. Also, you can then pop out the CD or DVD and use the drive for other purposes.

SUMMARY

Because live Linux CDs are made to run from read-only media, running a live Linux CD has some differences from running Linux from a hard disk. Developers of live Linux CDs have gotten around problems such as slower performance by allowing the system to run from RAM. They have gotten around the read-only issue by allowing you to save data to memory. Also, by implementing features such as persistent desktops and nests, the data you save doesn't just disappear when you reboot.

This chapter featured several different types of live CD. Knoppix is featured as the most popular desktop live CD. Games Knoppix contains a large number of games. BackTrack contains a slew of security-related applications. Exploring how these and other live CDs work should give you ideas about building your own live Linux CDs.

TABLE 2-2 Knoppix Boot Options

GENERAL BOOT OPTIONS	DESCRIPTION
lang=*id*	Indicates the language/keyboard to use for the live CD. Replace id with ch, cn, de, da, es, fr, it, nl, pl, ru, sk, tr, tw, or us.
gmt	Uses time based on Greenwich mean time (GMT) instead of local time.
tz=*id*	Uses a specific time zone with Knoppix. Replace *id* with the name of the time zone you want to use.
desktop= *id*	Replace *id* with the name of the desktop environment or window manager you want to use for your desktop. Although not all of these are on the Knoppix CD, valid values include fluxbox, gnome, icewm, kde, lg3d, larswm, openbox, twm, wmaker, xfce, and xfce4.
screen= *id*	Enter a specific screen resolution. Replace *id* with 640x480, 800x600, 1280x1024, or another resolution.
DISPLAY OPTIONS	DESCRIPTION
xvrefresh= *id*	Enter a vertical refresh rate. Replace *id* with 60, 72, 80, or some other refresh rate in hertz (based on your monitor specifications).
xhrefresh= *id*	Enter a horizontal refresh rate. Replace *id* with 80, 93, or some other refresh rate in hertz (based on your monitor specifications).
xserver= *id*	Enter either XFree86 or *XF86_SVGA* to identify the X server project to use.
xmodule= *id*	Identify a specific X driver to use for your video card. Replace *id* with ati, fbdev, i810, mga, nv, radeon, savage, s3, or svga.
1 2 3 4 5	Adding a number at the end of the boot options tells Knoppix to boot up to a specific run level. Type 1 for single user mode, 2 for multiuser no-network mode, 3 for multiuser plus network but no GUI, or 5 for multiuser plus GUI. Run level 4 is reserved for someone to set up custom run level scripts.

continues

TABLE 2-2 Continued

Hardware Options	Description
noapic	Avoids problems with the Intel 440GX chipset BIOS.
noagp	Doesn't detect the graphics card in any AGP slot.
noapm	Doesn't enable advanced power-management support.
noaudio	Doesn't enable audio.
noddc	Doesn't use display data channel detection to configure the monitor.
nodhcp	Doesn't try starting your network connection using the DHCP protocol.
nofstab	Ignores the /etc/fstab file when trying to find file systems to mount.
nofirewire	Disables firewire detection.
nopcmcia	Disables PCMCIA detection.
noscsi	Disables SCSI detection.
noswap	Doesn't try to detect a swap partition.
noudev	Disables UDEV device detection.
nousb	Doesn't try to detect USB version 1 ports.
nousb2	Doesn't try to detect USB version 2 ports.
pnpbios=off	Turns off PNP BIOS initialization.
acpi=off	Turns off ACPI BIOS initialization.
acpi=force	Requires ACPI BIOS initialization.

## CHAPTER 3

Customizing a Live CD

If you find that you love your live Linux CD, you'll probably want to use it more than once. The problem is that as soon as you reboot the live CD, you lose all your custom settings, data, and added applications. The solution is to find a way to save the data you have changed or added during a live CD session so that it is available the next time you reboot that live CD.

Remastering (modifying and remaking an existing CD) and starting from scratch (essentially doing a fresh Linux install that results in a new ISO image) are two ways to get exactly what you want on your live CD. However, those approaches require some time and a fair amount of Linux expertise (see Chapters 6, "Building a Custom Knoppix Live CD," through 8, "Building a Basic Gentoo Live CD"). Also, if you are working with a read-only medium, you can't add software to it as you go along.

Different live CDs offer different approaches to letting you save your custom settings, data files, and applications so they can be used the next time you reboot the live CD. Using those features requires little or no special expertise. And by having your data returned to the same places in the file system (such as /home or /etc), your settings can be automatically used to keep your desktop's look and feel or incorporate the system settings you need (network addresses, printers, exported file systems, and so on).

This chapter begins by covering some great ways of customizing your live CD systems. Some of these features are ones you can do on most any Linux system (such as change the desktop look and feel); others offer features that work well on a live CD (such as setting up the live CD to run in kiosk mode).

Next, the chapter tells you how to set up your live CD so that your data can be saved and reused from a USB flash memory drive, hard-disk partition, floppy disk, or other writeable medium. This feature is sometimes referred to as a persistent desktop. The chapter also tells how to put the operating system itself on a rewriteable USB flash drive so that the operating system and data don't have to be carried around separately.

Knoppix is used primarily here to provide examples of how to customize your live CD and configure it to save those customizations across reboots. Because many other live Linux distributions are based on Knoppix, most of the procedures described here work on those live CDs as well. After that, the chapter includes information on how other live CDs use different means of saving your data across reboots.

Customizing a Live CD

This section gives you ideas on how to customize your live CD. These techniques for changing the look, feel, and content of a live CD (without the pain of remastering) let you really make a live CD your own. Knoppix provides two primary ways of saving your custom settings: persistent desktop and backup archive. Before you start configuring the settings you want to save, you should be aware of how these two approaches differ:

- **Persistent desktop**—With this approach, you set up a writeable file-system image that is stored on a writeable USB flash memory drive or a hard disk. You should set this up before making customizations because you need to reboot for this feature to take effect. After that, all custom settings are stored in that file-system image as they are made.

- **Backup archive**—With this approach, when you have your settings and files the way you want them, you can back them up to a compressed archive (in bzip2 and tar formats) that is stored on any writeable medium (hard disk, USB flash drive, or zip drive) you choose. With this approach, you can save only files in your home directory and settings in the /etc directory. However, you can save this archive after you make your settings because it backs them up to a single file.

Refer to the "Keeping Your Customized Files and Settings" section later in this chapter to learn ways of saving your customizations. That section describes both the persistent desktop and backup archive approaches.

For several reasons, this section focuses on KDE as the desktop environment to demonstrate customization techniques. One reason for using KDE is that it is the default desktop environment for Knoppix. Another is that it is loaded with bells and whistles that GNOME (which is a simpler, business-oriented desktop) and other window managers just don't have.

If you want a custom server-oriented live Linux CD, the section "Making Server Customizations" describes how you can add data and custom settings to a live CD. Without having to remaster, you can have a live CD that lets you offer a variety of services and data from your live CD.

Making Desktop Customizations

KDE has a wealth of features for customizing the look and feel of your desktop environment. You can store the settings you change in your home directory. Live CDs such as Knoppix and Damn Small Linux enable you to back up those desktop settings with just a few simple mouse clicks.

The examples in this section use the KDE desktop (3.5.2) included with Knoppix 5, which comes on the DVD with this book. Start by booting up the DVD and typing the following at the boot prompt:

```
boot: knoppix
```

When Knoppix boots up, open the KDE Control Center. To do that from the K menu, select Control Center. Figure 3-1 shows an example of the KDE Control Center, with the Appearance & Themes section selected.

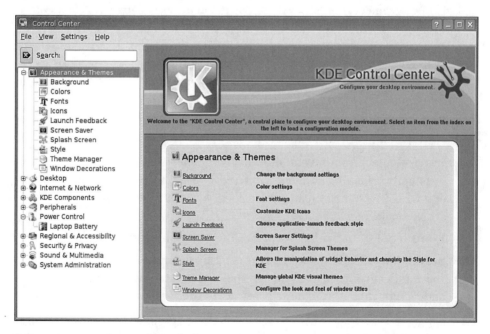

FIGURE 3-1 Change KDE desktop settings through the Control Center.

Creating a Custom Theme

If you are using a live CD as a personal desktop, you might want to select backgrounds, themes, colors, fonts, and other graphical elements to reflect your taste. If you want to create a live CD to represent a business or product, you might want those elements to enhance your presentation.

KDE lets you create entire desktop themes or just select individual elements to change on an existing theme. The following list provides a quick reminder of many theme-related features of the KDE desktop that you can change by selecting Appearance & Themes from the KDE Control Center:

- **Theme Manager**—Start by selecting a theme that is close to one that you want, or select Create New Theme to create your own. The new theme goes into a file in the .kde/share/apps/kthememanager/themes directory in your home directory. For example, I created a theme directory named LinuxToys. Next, you can start modifying the elements of your theme (as described next).

- **Background**—Add an image you want to use for your background (to the /home/knoppix/.kde/share/wallpapers directory). Select Get New Wallpapers to find images from the Internet to use. To rotate the backgrounds in a slide show from the wallpapers directory (or another directory you choose), select Slide Show and choose Setup to adjust how often the background changes.

- **Colors**—Select from a variety of color schemes to change the colors used in window borders, buttons, links, menus, and other desktop components. You can create and save your own color scheme, if you like. To have the scheme available, place it in the .kde/share/apps/kdisplay/color-schemes directory (or just save one by selecting Save Scheme after you select colors you like from the Widget Color box).

- **Styles**—Select a style for how the buttons, tabs, and various widgets are displayed on the KDE desktop.

- **Icons**—Select from several different complete sets of icons to use on the desktop by selecting a theme. Try Kids for a fun icon theme; Industrial or KDE-Classic for a clean, professional look; or Slick Icons for a more artistic look.

- **Fonts**—Select individual fonts for different parts of the desktop.

- **Screen Saver**—The screen saver is off by default in Knoppix. However, if you want to enable it, you can set when the screen saver comes on (after how many minutes) and whether a password is required. After that, select from more than 100 screen savers to use for your KDE desktop.

You can customize the screen saver to include your own content in several ways. For example, under Banners & Pictures, you can choose Flag and then Setup to have any text and bitmapped image you enter wave like a flag. Select Slide Show to have a folder of images rotated as your screen saver, using different effects.

Figure 3-2 shows a custom KDE desktop to be used on a live CD that goes with the LinuxToys.net Web site.

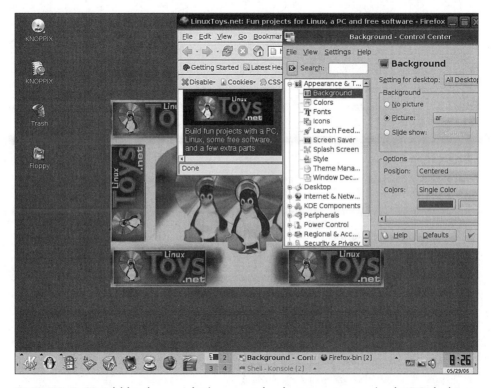

FIGURE 3-2 Add backgrounds, icons, and colors to a customized KDE desktop on your live CD.

To give you some ideas of how you might customize your own KDE desktop theme, for this example, I made a background that includes logos from my personal Web site, LinuxToys.net. I chose Kids icons, to go with the fun theme, and red and black colors from the icon to use behind the background image, for window title bars, and for link colors. With the logo displayed, I just selected the eyedropper to choose colors from the logo to use in different locations.

As a screen saver, I created a directory of images that represent inexpensive projects to build with Linux. I used a Slide Show screen saver to rotate those images every minute. With KDE, you could also set up the background to show a slide show, if you like.

If you can't make the theme you want, you can download tons of whole themes or individual elements from the KDE-look.org site (www.kde-look.org). These items are free for you to download. Although you are encouraged to register to participate in the site, registration isn't required for downloading themes and elements. If you have questions about developing themes, refer to the Themes Dev KDE Wiki (http://wiki.kde.org/tiki-index.php?page_ref_id=18).

Making Custom Menus

Live Linux CDs that offer tool chests of particular types of applications typically add custom menus to the K menu for selecting those applications. To simply change the appearance of the K menu, you use the Control Panel. To add and remove menus and items from a K menu, you use the menu editor.

To begin changing the appearance of the K menu, select Desktop → Panels from the Control Center. Here are some of the features you can then change on the K menu:

- **Menu item format**—A name and short description (in parentheses) appear for each menu item by default. Instead, you can choose to show the name only, description only, or description followed by name.

- **Optional menus**—You can add optional menus under the Actions section of the K menu. Only Bookmarks and Quick Browser are added by default. You can also add menu items to be able to quickly access printers (Print System), configuration settings (Settings), file and Web searches (Find), and network resources (Network Folders).

- **QuickStart menu items**—At the top of the K menu, applications that were started most often appear under the Most Used Applications heading. Instead, you can choose to have the most recently used applications appear on the K menu. You can also change the number of applications shown under that heading from the default five applications.

To make more substantial changes to the arrangement of items on your K menu, select the Edit K Menu button from the Panels module on the Control Center. From the KDE Menu Editor, you can add, remove, and rearrange items that appear on the K menu. You can add new items, new submenus, and separator lines. You can also cut and paste to rearrange items and change information associated with each item (such as name, description, icon, and commands run).

Here's a quick procedure for adding a new submenu to the K menu from the Panels module, along with several items (applications, links, and so on):

1. From the Control Center, select Desktop → Panels, and then select the Menus tab.

2. Click the Edit K Menu button. The KDE Menu Editor appears.

3. Click the New Submenu button. A New Submenu pop-up window appears.

4. Add a name for the new submenu and select OK. A blank form appears.

5. Fill in the name, description, and comments for submenu. You can also select the icon to browse for an icon to represent your submenu.

6. With your new submenu item highlighted, select New Item to add an application to your submenu. A New Item pop-up window appears.

7. Select a name for the new item and click OK. A blank form appears.

8. Fill in a description, comment, and command for the item. You can click the folder icon to browse the file system to find your application. If you need to, you can have the command run in a terminal window (which you need to do for non-GUI commands). You can also select to have the application run as a different user.

9. Repeat the previous three steps for each application you want to appear under your new submenu.

10. When your submenus and items are all entered, click Save to save your changes.

11. Once you get everything working the way you want it to, be sure to save your persistent desktop to hard disk or USB flash memory (as described later in this chapter) so you will have all your settings available the next time you reboot your live CD.

Using the procedure I just described, I created a custom submenu called Lin-uxToys.net. I added my own icon to that submenu. Then I added several items to that submenu, including an item that opens the LinuxToys.net site in a Web browser and several applications. Figure 3-3 shows an example of the KDE Menu Editor for creating those entries (right) and the actual resulting KDE menu that includes the new submenu and applications (left and above).

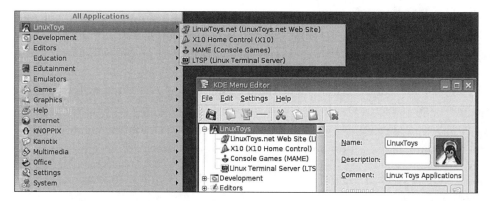

FIGURE 3-3 Add custom applications by creating a submenu on the KDE menu.

Autostarting Applications

When KDE first starts up, it launches applications that are included in the /home/knoppix/.kde/Autostart directory. By default, the only file in that directory is the showindex.desktop file. Its contents cause the Konqueror window to open, displaying the Knoppix Info page. Here's what the contents of showindex.desktop look like:

```
[Desktop Entry]
Name=KNOPPIX
# Exec=kfmclient openProfile webbrowsing /cdrom/index.html
Exec=konqueror -geometry 850x600x85x70 file:/cdrom/index.html
Type=Application
Icon=html
Terminal=0
```

By removing that file, you can prevent the initial Knoppix Info page from starting. To open your own Web page, replace file:/cdrom/index.html with a file you choose. Or replace the whole address with a Web site (http://www.example.com).

The .desktop file is the same format used to launch applications from the KDE desktop. If you want to see more examples of .desktop files, refer to the /usr/share/applications directory on the Knoppix live CD.

Changing Other Features

Because both the persistent desktop and the custom archive features let you retain any changed files in the system, you can change system-wide settings in the /etc directory and have them used the next time you reboot Knoppix. This can result in a highly customized CD that knows about your computer peripherals, network, users, or other special information about your environment.

For example, files in the /etc/sysconfig directory contain settings used when Knoppix boots up. The desktop file indicates which desktop environment/window manager to use. To change your desktop from KDE to fluxbox, change the first line of /etc/sysconfig/desktop to read DESKTOP="fluxbox".

The /etc/sysconfig/knoppix file contains a consolidation of settings relating to your display, keyboard, language, and other features. The xserver file identifies your X server (Xorg or XFree86) and X module (such as vesa). The sound file identifies your sound driver.

Any system-wide configuration you do to set up printers, network connections, Windows file sharing (samba), Linux file sharing (NFS), or other features that end up in the /etc directory can be saved with the persistent desktop.

Locking Down KDE

If you want to restrict what someone using your live CD can access from the KDE desktop, you can use the Kiosk Admin Tool (kiosktool command) to customize your live CD. Using the Kiosk Admin Tool, you can lock down nearly every aspect of the KDE desktop, effectively mandating what a user of that desktop can access and change.

 NOTE

The Kiosk Admin Tool is not included on the Knoppix 5 CD included on the DVD that comes with this book. To try out this feature as described here, you can use the Knoppix 5 DVD that you can get in several different ways from the Knoppix.net Web site (www.knoppix.net/get.php).

In the physical world, a kiosk can be a stand-alone booth that incorporates a self-service terminal for getting information. By locking down the desktop interface (such as KDE) for a general-purpose operating system (such as Knoppix), a computer can become like a kiosk to securely provide a contained set of features (such as a presentation or information service).

Some KDE desktops, including the one with Knoppix, come with the Kiosk Admin Tool installed. Using the Kiosk Admin Tool, you can create a profile containing the components you want the user to see (background, desktop icons, menus, and so on) and rules restricting the user's ability to change those items or access items outside the desktop (shells, context menus, and so on). Then you assign that profile to one or more users. In this example, the profile is owned by the root user and assigned to the knoppix user.

NOTE

Some of the settings you select in the Kiosk Admin Tool will be overridden by settings in the /etc/skel directory and by features launched by Knoppix-specific scripts.

The following procedure takes you through some features of the Kiosk Admin Tool and suggests some results you might be looking for:

1. Assign a password to the root user. Open a shell and type the following:

```
$ sudo passwd root
Enter new UNIX password: ********
Retype new UNIX password: ********
```

2. Select System → Kiosk Admin Tool (to launch the kiosktool command). The Kiosk Admin Tool window opens on the desktop.

3. From the Add New Profile screen, assign a name, short description, profile owner (the root user), and directory for this profile. Then select Add. You are prompted for the root password.

4. Type the root password and click OK.

5. Back at the main menu, with the new profile highlighted, select Setup Profile. The window displays icons representing the components you can lock down for the profile.

6. Select the component you want to change. A list of items for that component is displayed. Select the check box next to an item to restrict access to the component by the user. Figure 3-4 shows an example of the Kiosk Admin Tool window.

Here are examples of some components you might want to change:

- **General**—Items under this heading prevent users from getting access to features outside of the restricted application you are running. For example, you can prevent access to the shell, the window manager context menu (Alt+F3), the run command box (Alt+F2), the capability to start another X session, the logout option, and the lock screen option.

  If multiple people are using the same login from the desktop, you might want to disable input line history so a user can't see what other users have done before. Also, you can keep all tasks that require root access from being included on menus available to the user assigned to this profile.

FIGURE 3-4 Configure and lock down KDE components with the Kiosk Admin Tool.

- **Desktop icons**—You can choose a predefined set of icons to appear on the desktop for this profile (click Setup Desktop Icons). Drag and drop menu items from the K menu to copy them to the desktop. After that, you can disable context menus and lock down your desktop settings and desktop icons.

- **Desktop background**—Select and lock down a particular background.

- **KDE menu**—Set up the K menu as you would like; then prevent the user from changing that menu. Select File → Save to save your changes.

- **Theming**—Change colors, fonts, widget style, and window decorations.

- **Panel**—Change and lock down panel items and attributes.

- **Network proxy**—If needed, configure the profile to cause the user to connect to the Internet via a proxy server. By default, the user would connect to the network directly.

- **Konqueror**—Disable the user's capability to display the context menu or use the Open With or Open in New Tab actions on the Konqueror file manager window. You can also prevent Konqueror from browsing for files outside of the user's home directory. This is a good feature if you want the user to view only a restricted set of information that you set up in that user's home directory.

- **Menu actions**—Disable the capability to use menu items that are available to many applications. For example, you can disable File → Save to prevent someone from saving any displayed information.

- **Desktop sharing**—Desktop sharing is off by default. You can enable it and add invitations if you want others on the network to be able to access your desktop. Then you can lock down those settings.

- **File associations**—You can change which applications are run by default when different types of content (audio file, image, video file, and so on) are encountered.

7. When you are finished setting up the profile, select Finished to return to the main menu.

8. With the profile highlighted, select Assign Profiles.

9. From the Assign Profiles screen, assign the profile to either an individual user or a group. By assigning the profile to the knoppix user, you ensure that the settings for the policy will be in use the next time you restart the live CD (provided that you save the settings using the persistent desktop feature).

10. When you are finished, select File → Quit.

Because you have created a root password in this procedure, you can lock down other aspects of the knoppix user. For example, you should comment out the line in the sudoers file that gives knoppix complete access to the running Knoppix systems. After you comment it out, it should read as follows:

```
# knoppix ALL=NOPASSWD: ALL
```

To have the settings you just made be used the next time you reboot, you can create a persistent Knoppix disk image. Later, when you restart the live CD using the persistent desktop, as described later in this chapter, you need to indicate that you want to overwrite stored system configuration files for the Kiosk Admin Tool features to take effect.

Using a Live CD as a Kiosk

Knoppix 5 actually offers a feature that lets you boot up your desktop directly to kiosk mode. By adding a kiosk option to the boot prompt, you can tell Knoppix to start up the Firefox Web browser in kiosk mode and display a selected Web page (which you can indicate using a url option from the boot prompt).

Setting up Knoppix to boot to a kiosk desktop is a great way to set up a dedicated Web browser or a presentation with HTML content. You can either use this feature in tandem with the Kiosk Admin Tool described in the previous section or combine the kiosk desktop with a window manager other than what you get with the KDE desktop. This procedure describes how to set up Knoppix to run as a kiosk Web browser:

1. If you want to change the window manager used for the kiosk, set up a persistent desktop as described in the "Setting Up a Persistent Desktop" section.

2. Set the window manager you want to use. Because you will identify kiosk as the desktop, if you don't want to use KDE as the underlying desktop environment; you need to make an additional setting. For example, as described earlier in this chapter, to use fluxbox as the window manager, you can change the first line of /etc/sysconfig/desktop to read DESKTOP="fluxbox".

3. Open the Firefox Web browser (from an icon on the desktop) and change any setting you want. For example, you can change the default colors, fonts, or menu bars that are displayed.

4. Save your settings. This happens automatically with a persistent desktop, but you must do it explicitly (as described in the next section) if you want to back up the settings to an archive. (If you want to have the data files in your home directory saved, you have to indicate explicitly that you want to save them.)

5. Reboot your computer, leaving the Knoppix medium in the drive and the medium holding your saved settings (such as a USB flash drive) still connected to the computer.

6. At the Knoppix boot prompt, indicate that you want to start Knoppix in kiosk mode and to scan for the persistent desktop. That command line might look like this, for example:

   boot: **knoppix desktop=kiosk url=http://knoppix.net home=scan**

   After the knoppix tag, the desktop option is set to kiosk. The url option indicates the address of the HTML page you want to display when the Web browser comes up in kiosk mode. Use the home=scan option if you need to reinstate your settings.

When your desktop boots up, a single application (your Firefox Web browser) should appear on the desktop. No other applications, panels, or icons should appear on the desktop. You should be able to begin browsing from that window. However, this feature alone doesn't lock down your desktop (for example, you can still press

Ctrl+Alt+F2 to get a virtual terminal). So you need to use other features to lock down your desktop, as described earlier.

Making Server Customizations

Most Live CDs include some features that allow them to operate as servers as well as desktop systems. Because the server software is the same software you might get on professional-quality servers, the complexity and security you can achieve running servers from a live CD, such as Knoppix, is limited only by the time and expertise you put into them.

Knoppix makes configuration of certain servers easy to get started. Using the Knoppix Firewall Tool, you can open access to selected services (ports) to provide such things as domain name system service (named), secure shell (sshd), TELNET, FTP, and mail access (POP3 and IMAP). From the Knoppix menu, you launch servers for such features as a Windows file-sharing server (Samba) or a, SSH remote-login server.

This chapter isn't intended to describe how to configure and lock down professional 24×7 servers, but it does show you how, with a few quick steps, you can get a live CD server (from Knoppix) up and running quickly in a pinch. Then, of course, using persistent desktop features, you can keep the settings and data so you can have it all on the next reboot.

Most network services in Linux are configured by opening a port in your firewall to access the service and then starting a daemon process to listen on the network for requests for that service. Knoppix includes a simple tool for configuring an iptables firewall. With access open to the necessary ports, you can configure and start up services that you are interested in offering. The following sections describe the firewall tool and several servers.

Adding a Simple Firewall

From the Knoppix menu (the penguin icon on the desktop), you can select the Knoppix Firewall tool to configure a simple iptables firewall. If you have configured a persistent desktop, you can preserve your firewall settings and have the firewall enabled each time you reboot your live CD.

Start this procedure with your live Knoppix CD booted and a persistent desktop enabled (see the next section for information on setting up a persistent desktop). Then do the following to set up your firewall:

1. From the Knoppix menu, select Services → Knoppix Firewall. The Knoppix Firewall Tool window appears. Figure 3-5 shows an example of the Knoppix Firewall Tool window, displaying information in expert mode.

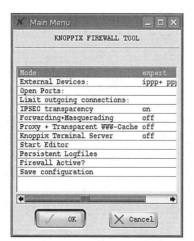

FIGURE 3-5
Open ports in your firewall to allow access to Web, login, and other services.

2. Select Mode and click OK. By default, Easy is selected (allowing only outgoing connections from your machine).

3. Select Expert and click OK.

4. Select External Devices and click OK. Select the network interface that faces your network (that is, where you want to offer your services). Typically, this is eth0 or eth1 for a wired Ethernet card. However, it might be ppp for a dial-up or ippp for an ISDN connection.

5. Select Open Ports and click OK. Select the names that represent the services you want to make available to the network. For the server examples that follow, you need to open ports to allow access to a Web server (www and/or https) and secure login shell (ssh).

6. Select Firewall Active. Then select Start Firewall now and click OK.

7. Select Save Configuration and click OK. Click OK again when you are warned that you need a persistent desktop (because you should have already set one up before you started this procedure).

8. Select Cancel to close the Knoppix Firewall Tool.

9. To start the firewall immediately, open a shell and type the following:
```
# sudo /etc/init.d/firewall start
```

10. To set up the firewall to start each time you reboot your live CD, type the following:
```
# sudo ln -s /etc/init.d/firewall /etc/rc5.d/S15firewall
# sudo ln -s /etc/init.d/firewall /etc/rc0.d/K15firewall
# sudo ln -s /etc/init.d/firewall /etc/rc1.d/K15firewall
# sudo ln -s /etc/init.d/firewall /etc/rc6.d/K15firewall
```

The command just shown adds the firewall script to the `/etc/rc5.d` directory in a way that it will be run when the system boots up to the default run level (5). The other lines cause the firewall to shut down in run levels 0 (off), 1 (single user), and 6 (reboot). The firewall is now in place to proceed to setting up your services.

The settings you just entered in the previous procedure result in settings being stored in the `/etc/sysconfig/firewall` file. If you are handy with iptables and you need to add any special rules that are not available from the Knoppix Firewall Tool, you can add iptables rules to the `/etc/sysconfig/firewall.iptables` file.

Adding a Remote Login Server (sshd)

To access your live CD from another computer on the network, you can configure a secure shell daemon (`sshd`) to run. Knoppix offers a quick method of setting up and starting the sshd daemon from the Knoppix menu:

1. From the Knoppix menu, select Services → Start SSH server. After setting up encryption keys for your `sshd` server, you are asked to enter a password for the knoppix user.

2. Enter and reenter a password for the knoppix user. Assuming that you opened the `ssh` port in your firewall, you should now be able to log in to this live CD over the network when you know the IP address.

3. To determine the live CD's IP address, type the following:
   ```
   # /sbin/ifconfig | grep "inet addr"
   inet addr:10.0.0.205 Bcast:10.0.0.255 Mask:255.255.255.0
   inet addr:127.0.0.1 Mask:255.255.255.0
   ```

4. Assuming that the IP address of the live CD is 10.0.0.205 (yours will probably be different), from another Linux system on your LAN, you could type the following to log in to your live CD server:
   ```
   # ssh knoppix@10.0.0.205
   ```

When prompted, type **yes** to verify the authenticity of the host. Then enter the knoppix password you set for the live CD system previously. You can now start using the live CD from the computer on your network you just logged in from.

Adding a Simple Web Server

If you want to set up a quick Web server without a lot of fuss, you can configure the `thttpd` Web server quite efficiently. For example, if you want to put up a temporary Web server to offer content to a classroom of students on the same LAN or to put up a temporary server when your real server fails, running `thttpd` with a live CD might be a good solution.

The following procedure tells how to set up a thttps Web server from your Knoppix live CD in a way that requires very little configuration change. It assumes that you have already configured your firewall to allow https (port 443) and/or www (port 80) access to your server. To begin, boot up Knoppix in a way that incorporates a persistent desktop, as described in the next section:

1. To start the `thttpd` Web server immediately, type the following command:

   ```
   # sudo /etc/init.d/thttpd start
   ```

2. To start the `thttpd` Web server so it starts up every time you reboot Knoppix, type the following:

   ```
   # sudo ln -s /etc/init.d/thttpd /etc/rc5.d/S20thttpd
   # sudo ln -s /etc/init.d/thttpd /etc/rc0.d/K20thttpd
   # sudo ln -s /etc/init.d/thttpd /etc/rc1.d/K20thttpd
   # sudo ln -s /etc/init.d/thttpd /etc/rc6.d/K20thttpd
   ```

   The command just shown creates a link from the `thttpd` start-up script to the `/etc/rc5.d` directory in such a way that the `thttpd` server will run when Knoppix boots to the default run level (5). The other links stop the `thttpd` service when you move to a lower run level, including shutdown (0), single user (1), and reboot (6).

3. Assuming that your network interface is already up and running, determine the address of your network interface as follows:

   ```
   # /sbin/ifconfig | grep "inet addr"
   inet addr:10.0.0.205 Bcast:10.0.0.255 Mask:255.255.255.0
   inet addr:127.0.0.1 Mask:255.255.255.0
   ```

   In this example, the IP address of the eth0 network interface is 10.0.0.205 (the loopback interface is 127.0.0.1, but this is not the number we are looking for here).

4. From a Web browser on your network, check that the Web server is working by displaying the `index.html` page. Do this by typing the following in the Web browser's location box:

   ```
   http://10.0.0.205/index.html
   ```

   Strictly speaking, `index.html` doesn't have to be typed in for this to work. You should see the sample "Welcome to Your New Home in Cyberspace" page. If you do, this shows that the server is working and available on your network.

5. Next, replace the `index.html` file in the `/var/www` directory with your own `index.html` file, along with any other HTML content that is accessible from your Web server. Because the root user owns the directory, you need to use the `sudo` command to write to it from the shell as the knoppix user.

For example, to copy an `index.html` file from your USB flash memory drive, you might type the following:

```
# sudo cp /mnt/sda1/index.html /var/www/
```

6. Because you set up this server using the Knoppix persistent desktop feature, to have your content served up when you reboot, you simply have to identify the location of your persistent desktop at the boot prompt. (Using your persistent desktop image is described in the "Booting with Customized Files and Settings" section.)

The procedure you just completed uses all the default settings for the `thttpd` daemon. To change the default settings, edit the `/etc/thttpd/thttpd.conf` file. For example, if you would rather add your HTML content to another location, change the value of `dir=/var/www` in the `thttpd.conf` file to reflect the directory you want to use. You can also change the default port number (currently, 80), the user running the `thttpd` daemon (www-data), the log file used (`/var/log/thttpd.log`), and the location of any CGI scripts you want to use (`/var/www/cgi-bin`, by default).

The `thttpd` server daemon also has many command-line options available (type **man thttpd**). One special feature the `thttpd` server daemon has is the capability to do URL traffic-based throttling. Throttle settings can be made in the `/etc/thttpd/throttle.conf` file.

NOTE

For some reason, the `/var/run/thttpd.pid` file was not being consistently removed when I restarted Knoppix. When that happened, the `thttpd` service refused to start because it believed the service was already up. If this happens to you, type the following before rebooting:

```
# sudo rm /var/run/thttpd.pid
```

If you want to add other servers to your computer, I recommend checking the `/etc/init.d` directory for other available services. Most network services represented by start-up scripts in that directory can be easily started and linked to different run directories (to be set to start more permanently) in the same ways that were done in this procedure. Look for configuration file for those services in the `/etc` directory.

KEEPING YOUR CUSTOMIZED FILES AND SETTINGS

The first live CDs had problems related to writing and saving data you create during your live CD session. The problem was that most of the running live CD's file system was being used from the read-only CD. Only a few directories, such as /home (where users keep personal files) or /etc (where the system keeps configuration files), were even writeable. And those writeable areas were stored in memory so they disappeared when you rebooted.

The first solutions were to add features that let you back up your /home and /etc files to an archive file that could then be written to a floppy disk (or other medium). Those files could later be returned to their original locations when you rebooted the CD. This worked for storing configuration files and personal data, but it didn't work in particular when it came to installing new software (which needed to write to places such as /usr or /sbin).

To deal with this problem, Knoppix, Morphix, Slax, and other live CDs began using the UnionFS stackable unification file system. The beauty of UnionFS is that it can combine several file systems (some read-only and some read/write) so that they appear as one file system. Any added, changed, or deleted files and directories are noted in the read/write file systems, so the modifications can be overlaid on the read-only areas from the live CD. (See Chapter 5, "Looking Inside Live CD Components," for further discussions of UnionFS.)

The following sections describe two approaches available in Knoppix to save information created during a Knoppix live CD session:

- **Persistent desktop**—You create a writeable file system image file. That writeable file system is overlaid onto root file system so that files saved or changed anywhere on the file system are automatically saved on the writeable image.

- **Configuration archive**—This essentially backs up system-configuration files (mostly from /etc) and personal files (from /home) to a single archive file that can be restored later. Changes are not saved as they are made, so you need to select to back up the files again, to keep any configuration changes you make subsequently.

Setting Up a Persistent Desktop

When you select to set up a persistent desktop, Knoppix detects your computer's writeable media (such as a USB flash memory drive, zip drive, or hard-disk partition) and lets you choose one of those media to hold your persistent desktop files.

You select how much disk space you want to have available, and Knoppix creates an image file (knoppix.img file) of that size that is formatted as an ext2 file system.

The image file created for your persistent desktop holds the changes you make throughout the live CD's entire file system. The next time you reboot your live CD, you tell Knoppix where to find that image (or have Knoppix scan for it), and its contents are merged back together with the live CD contents.

The following procedure steps you through the process of creating and reusing a persistent desktop in Knoppix. After that are descriptions of how other live CDs handle similar features.

1. Insert the USB memory device, zip disk, or other writeable drive. Alternatively, you can use a hard drive on your computer to store the Knoppix image (of course, it won't be portable then).

2. Boot Knoppix; then press Enter to boot to the Knoppix desktop.

3. From the KNOPPIX menu in the panel (represented by a penguin icon), select Configure → Create a Persistent KNOPPIX Disk Image. You are asked whether you want to create a persistent home directory.

4. Select Yes. You will see a list of devices representing the storage partitions available on your computer, along with the partition type and the space available on each. Figure 3-6 shows an example of the window listing available storage partitions.

FIGURE 3-6
Select the disk partition for storing your persistent desktop.

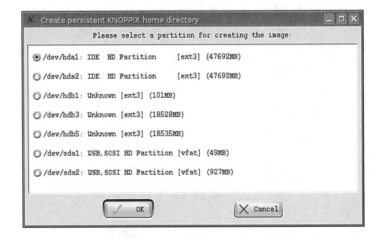

Notice in Figure 3-6 that the first IDE hard drive has two writeable partitions (hda1 and hda2). A second IDE hard drive has three (hdb1, hdb3, and hdb5). The USB memory stick has two VFAT partitions (sda1 and sda2). If you have a SCSI hard drive, it might be listed as /dev/sda instead.

5. Select the partition you want to contain your persistent desktop (check that there is enough available space on the device to hold your persistent desktop) and click OK. You are asked if you want to encrypt your persistent desktop using AES 256 encryption (requiring a password of at least 20 characters).

NOTE

The Advanced Encryption Standard (AES) is an encryption algorithm the U.S. government approved in 2001 for securing nonclassified data. In 2003, AES was approved for protecting U.S. classified information. AES256, which you can use to protect your persistent desktop in Knoppix, is the version of AES that uses 256-bit keys.

6. Select Yes if you want to use AES256 (requiring you to enter a long password and then re-enter that password each time you reboot the live CD to access your persistent desktop) or No if you don't want to use a password. You are asked how large you want to make your persistent desktop.

7. Type a number (in megabytes) to indicate the size of your persistent desktop and select OK. This results in a file of the size you indicate (called knoppix.img) being placed on the disk partition or USB drive. That image file will be used to hold all data you store on the file system as you use Knoppix. It takes a few moments to create the image file. If you selected to use an encrypted password, you are prompted to enter that password.

8. Type at least a 20-character password, verify it, and select OK to protect your saved persistent desktop. A message appears letting you know that the image was successfully created.

At this point, the knoppix.img file exists but is not yet in use. For that to happen, you need to reboot. Before you do, however, two tips relate to your persistent desktop:

- **Leaving images around**—If you don't password-protect your persistent desktop image, it is essentially unprotected. Knoppix creates the image with the knoppix user as the owner and permissions open (rwxrwxrwx). If you leave your USB memory stick lying around or forget to remove knoppix.img from the hard disk of the person's computer you are working on, other people will have access to your personal settings and data.

- **Multiple images**—Some people like to create different persistent desktop images for different uses. For example, you might have an image that you use for your general portable desktop. You might also have one that includes files for a presentation you are giving or to use as a portable file server or Web server.

Now, if you are ready to use your persistent desktop, you can reboot your computer. Refer to the "Booting with Customized Files and Setting" section for information on boot options to take advantage of your saved knoppix.img file.

Keeping Just Configuration Files

Instead of saving your entire Knoppix file system to a read/write image, you can just back up your configuration files to an archive file. When you reboot Knoppix later, you can reuse that archive file. This feature is useful as an efficient way to not have to reenter your desktop settings, printer configuration, video card settings, or other configuration files stored in your home directory or in /etc.

When you save your configuration settings, they are stored in a compressed tar file on a device that you choose (such as a hard disk or USB memory stick). The following procedure describes how to back up your Knoppix configuration:

1. From the Knoppix desktop, select the Knoppix menu on the panel.

2. Select Configure → Save Knoppix Configuration. (This launches the save-config command, which you can run from the command line instead, if you prefer.) You are asked to choose which types of configuration files you want to back up.

3. Select to back up any of the following types of configuration files and click OK:

   - **Personal configuration**—Select this to have configuration files in your home directory saved. These are files and directories that begin with a dot (.), such as .kde directory. This option won't save any data files (documents, music, spreadsheets) you create in your home directory, nor will it save cache files from browsing the Web.

   - **All files on the desktop**—Select this to save any files you created on the desktop (represented by icons).

   - **Network settings**—Select this to back up any network settings that are not stored in your home directory. Use this feature to store settings used to configure your Ethernet connections (LAN) or dial-up (modem), ISDN, or DSL (ADSL) connections. You might not need to select this to save dial-up settings that are stored in your home directory (such as those KPPP created).

- **Graphics subsystem settings**—Select this to save settings related to your video card and monitor that your X display server (XF86Config) uses.

- **Other system configuration**—Select this to save other system-configuration files in the /etc directory. These might include files for storing printer, scanner, sound, or password settings.

You are asked where you want to store your configuration settings.

4. Choose the location where you want to store your configuration settings and click OK. If you selected to save to floppy disk, you are asked to insert a floppy disk.

5. Insert a floppy disk and select OK. The archive is created. When it is finished, a pop-up tells you that the configuration is complete.

At this point, you should have custom settings saved on your floppy disk or other medium. The knoppix.sh file is the script that is executed to restore the files from the compressed archive (configs.tbz file). Here are some suggestions on how you might want to modify those two files:

- knoppix.sh—Instead of just using the knoppix.sh file that is created during this procedure, you can modify that script or create one of your own. Having your own knoppix.sh file is another way you can customize your live CD without remastering the KNOPPIX/KNOPPIX file that contains the read-only Knoppix file system from the CD. That script can copy or change the files contained in your live CD's file system as you like.

- configs.tbz—All the files from /etc and from your home directory that you selected to store are combined into a single archive file (a tar file) that is then compressed using the bzip2 utility. So you can manipulate the contents of that file as you would any tar archive. Because the knoppix.sh script expects the file in configs.tbz to contain full paths, you need to add and remove files from that archive using full path names.

To change the contents of your configs.tbz file, you can start by copying the file to a temporary directory, unzipping it, and then adding and removing files as you please. Here is an example of how to do that. It starts by assuming that your configs.tbz file is on /mnt/sda1 and that you have enough space in your /tmp directory to edit this file. You can do this:

```
$ cp /mnt/sda1/configs.tbz /tmp
$ cd /tmp
$ bunzip2 configs.tbz
```

Now, with the archive unzipped to the file configs.tar, here are a few commands for adding and removing files from your archive. The –list option to tar lists the contents of the tar archive. The –delete option is used here to remove the file /etc/X11/XF86Config from the archive. The -r option is used to add the file /home/knoppix/index.html to the archive (with -P indicating to keep the leading /). After that, the archive is zipped up again and returned to its original location.

```
$ tar –list –file=configs.tar |less
$ tar –delete –remove-files –file configs.tar /etc/X11/XF86Config
$ tar -r –file=configs.tar -P /home/knoppix/index.html
$ bzip2 configs.tar ; sudo cp configs.tar.bz2 /mnt/sda1/configs.tbz
```

At this point, the modified configs.tgz file is ready to be reused the next time you reboot Knoppix.

Whether or not you change knoppix.sh or configs.tbz, to restore your setting the next time you reboot, you simply have to add an option to the boot line when you start your live CD. Available options are described in the next section.

BOOTING WITH CUSTOMIZED FILES AND SETTINGS

After you have saved custom settings for Knoppix in either a persistent desktop image or a custom setting archive, you can reapply the information in those files by noting their location when you boot Knoppix. Here are some examples of boot options you can enter to reuse your custom data:

- **Scan for persistent desktop**—To have Knoppix scan your writeable storage partitions (hard disks, memory sticks, and so on) for the existence of a stored persistent desktop image (knoppix.img), you can use the following command:

  boot: **knoppix home=scan**

- **Select partition for persistent desktop**—As an alternative, you can identify the specific disk partition on which the knoppix.img file exists. For example, the first partition for a USB flash memory drive often is identified by /dev/sda1. So to specifically request that the knoppix.img file from the first partition from this device be used, you would enter the following:

  boot: **knoppix home=/dev/sda1**

When the persistent desktop image (knoppix.img) is found, you are prompted to indicate the information you want to use from that image. Your options include these:

- **home**—Select this setting if you want to restore the /home/knoppix directory from your persistent desktop image.

- **system**—Select this setting to have the entire file system be writeable so your persistent desktop will store files that are changed or added throughout the file system.

- **overwrite**—Select this setting (it's off by default) if you want saved settings on your persistent desktop to be overwritten by those from the live CD.

- **init**—Select this to start up initialization scripts associated with system services. These scripts primarily start daemon processes to listen for requests for services, such as login, mail, and printing services. The init process start only those services that were configured to start during the current run level. By default, that is very few services. (See the "Making Server Customizations" section for more information on starting up services.)

  Select OK after selecting the options you want. Knoppix boots, with your persistent desktop image being used as you just indicated.

- **Scan to restore configuration files**—If instead of restoring the persistent desktop image you want to restore the configuration archive file you previously saved (knoppix.sh and configs.tbz), you can use the myconf boot options in the same way. For example, to scan for your configuration archive, you could type the following at the boot prompt:
  boot: `knoppix myconf=scan`

- **Select to restore configuration files**—Likewise, to have Knoppix look on a specific partition (in this case, the first partition on a USB flash drive), you would type the following:
  boot: `knoppix myconf=/dev/sda1`

  In both of the cases just shown, Knoppix looks for a knoppix.sh script. That script uncompresses and untars the files back to their original locations on the booted Knoppix live CD.

SAVING AND USING CUSTOM SETTINGS ON OTHER LIVE CDs

The way in which Knoppix lets you save your files and settings is not the only way it can be done. Other live CDs offer innovative ways of keeping your important data across reboots. The following sections describe how you can use several different live CDs to save your data.

Saving Data in Damn Small Linux

Although Damn Small Linux (DSL) was originally derived from Knoppix, DSL developers have added innovations of their own related to saving data across reboots. In fact, DSL includes simplified procedures for saving and modifying a backup archive of your files and writing the entire operating system to a pen drive. You'll even find a procedure for installing specially packaged applications so they can be restored each time you reboot DSL.

Backing Up Data Files

DSL doesn't offer the feature of creating a file-system image and merging it with the file system from your CD (as does Knoppix). However, it does let you easily create an archive that can be restored later. Also, because it backs up your files based on a file list, you can edit that file list to add or delete files as you please.

Start by opening the DSL Control Panel by selecting the DSLpanel icon from the desktop. Next select Backup/Restore, select the device where you want to store your backup files, and select Backup. For the first partition on a pen drive, you would probably enter sda1; the first partition on an IDE hard drive would be hda1. The result is a file in the root of that partition called backup.tar.gz. Figure 3-7 shows an example of the DSL Control Panel, with the Backup/Restore tool ready to save the backup file.

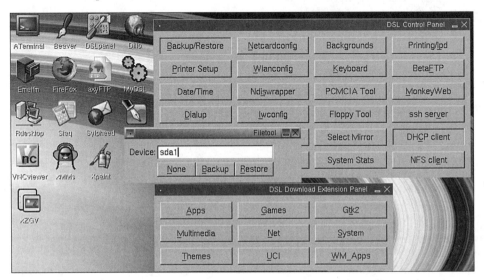

FIGURE 3-7 Backup files and settings using the DSL Backup/Restore tool.

To see what files and directories will be backed up using this procedure, open the file /home/dsl/.filetool.lst in any text editor. You can add and delete files as you like from this file.

Adding DSL Applications

Because directories such as /bin and /usr/bin are not writeable in DSL, DSL uses another approach to add applications to your running DSL system. Using the DSL Download Extension Panel (select MyDSL from the desktop), you can download and install applications that are especially tailored to run on DSL. These applications can be stored (using the Backup tool) and later restored when you reboot DSL. See the bottom of Figure 3-7 to see the DSL Download Extension panel.

After you select a package you want to download, you need to enter a location to store that application. For example, if you have an accessible pen drive for saving your settings, you can save the applications to /mnt/sda1. (You can mount any drive by selecting the drive name from the mounting tool in the lower-right corner of the screen.)

Restoring Files and Applications

As with Knoppix, you can have DSL restore your backup archive from the boot prompt. One difference, however, is that DSL restores your backup archive automatically if it finds it on one of your storage media (even if you don't ask for it). This can cause some confusion if you forgot you left an archive on a hard disk or USB flash memory drive. DSL also has boot options for restoring your DSL applications.

As I noted, you don't have to add any boot options if you have a backup archive on any available storage medium. DSL simply finds it and uses it. However, if you have multiple backup.tar.gz files available (on different media), you can explicitly identify a particular drive to indicate the one you want. For example, to restore the backup file from the first partition on your USB drive (sda1), you could type the following at the DSL boot prompt:

```
boot: dsl restore=sda1
```

To restore your saved applications, you can use the mydsl option. For example, if your applications are on the first partition of your USB drive (sda1), you could type the following at the boot prompt:

```
boot: dsl mydsl=sda1
```

Of course, you can add multiple boot options with DSL, as you can with any live CD. For example, to restore your backup archive and applications from sda1 and have DSL run entirely from memory, you can type the following from the boot prompt:

```
boot: dsl restore=sda1 mydsl=sda1 toram
```

Saving Data in Dynebolic

Dynebolic (www.dynebolic.org) refers to its feature for saving your personal data as a Nest. Using its nest feature, you can create a disk image of any size you choose on an available hard disk or USB flash memory drive. When you reboot Dynebolic later, the Nest is automatically detected and used.

By selecting Nest on the Welcome to Dynebolic window, you can choose HARDDISK or USB KEY to hold your nest. After selecting one of those two, you are presented with a window that lets you select from a list of available devices of that type on your computer, lets you choose the size of your nest (in megabytes), and lets you choose to encrypt it (using 256-bit AES encryption). Figure 3-8 shows the windows just described.

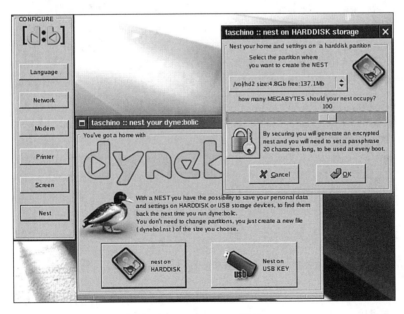

FIGURE 3-8 Dynebolic lets you create a Nest to save your settings.

To enable your Nest, you need to reboot Dynebolic. When it comes up, it looks for the nest file, named `dynebol.nst`. It is actually a writeable ext2 file system image mounted in loopback. All files saved to /etc, /home, /tmp, and /var while Dynebolic is running are written to this image.

Saving Data in Puppy Linux

Although Puppy Linux (www.puppylinux.com) is not included on the DVD that comes with this book, some of the techniques it uses to save your custom settings and files are worth noting. Puppy Linux has gained a lot of popularity among first-time Linux users because it is very lightweight and because so many features just work, without the user having to ask for them.

To begin saving data in Puppy Linux on most computers, you don't have to do anything. If it can find a writeable storage medium when it boots up, Puppy Linux automatically mounts the partition with read/write permission to create an image file (256MB) on that medium. When Puppy Linux is rebooted, the image is automatically restored, making the saved files available again to be used.

NOTE

Because Puppy Linux creates and uses a file system image on an available disk partition without telling you, it is important to first know that it is there. Then it is important to remove that image if you are using Puppy Linux on someone else's computer. Later versions of Puppy Linux might handle this issue differently.

Another interesting feature available for Puppy Linux is the multisession live DVD feature. Making use of a special version of Puppy Linux and burning it to a DVD using the growisofs command, the session can remain open to allow further files to be written to the DVD. You can read about how this feature works on the Puppy Multi-Session Live CD page (www.puppylinux.com/multi-puppy.htm).

ADDING DAMN SMALL LINUX TO A USB FLASH DRIVE

With your live CD image installed on a USB flash drive (also called a pen drive, thumb drive, and several other names), you can save your own software with your live Linux system. Because these drives are rewriteable, you can keep (and add to) the operating system, applications, and data (documents, music, images, and even video) on the same medium.

Most modern PCs come with USB ports from which you can boot, given a working BIOS. The trick is to get a live Linux set up on a USB flash drive so it is ready to boot from one of those ports. This section describes how to create a bootable Linux live USB flash drive using Damn Small Linux (DSL). Configuring DSL in this way requires no special knowledge of Linux.

The procedure for adding DSL so it can boot from a USB flash drive (which is referred to as a "Pendrive") can be done with just a few easy clicks from the DSL desktop. All you need to get started are as follows:

- **A USB flash drive**—Because DSL is only about 50MB total size, the minimum size USB drive you need is 64MB. However, if you plan to add any data, at least 128MB is recommended. I use a 1GB drive, which allows me to keep music, documents, and some extra applications on the drive.

- **Damn Small Linux**—You can use the version of DSL that is included on the DVD that comes with this book. You can burn the DSL ISO image from that DVD and boot it to start this procedure (or simply boot DSL directly from the DVD).

With DSL booted and your USB flash drive handy, run the procedure that follows to install DSL on a USB flash drive:

1. Determine the device name of your USB flash drive. This is very important because this procedure erases the contents of that drive. Type **fdisk -l** to see the available storage devices (hard disks, USB flash drives, Zip drives, and so on). USB flash drives appear as SCSI devices. So, if you have no other SCSI hard drives or other devices on your computer, your USB flash drive will probably be available from /dev/sda.

2. From the DSL desktop, select Apps → Tools → Install to USB Pendrive.

3. Select either For USB-ZIP Pendrive or For USB-HDD Pendrive. Which type of selection you use should depend on where you expect the USB drive to be run:

   - **Any machine**—Some older PCs only include BIOSs that can boot from USB drives that use the older USB-ZIP specification. To boot in this way, the partition that is booted on the USB drive must be smaller than is allowed for USB-HDD specification. As a result, if you select USB-ZIP, DSL creates a small boot partition and assigns the rest of the space on the USB flash drive to a second partition.

     The USB-ZIP procedure creates a boot loader using Syslinux instead of Isolinux. The Syslinux bootloader basically emulates a floppy boot, while Isolinux emulates an El Torito live CD boot. Because most PCs can boot a floppy disk image, installing DSL as a USB-ZIP install results in a USB flash drive that can boot on both older and newer PCs.

- **Newer PCs**—Most newer PCs will let you select the USB-HDD boot type. When you select USB-HDD Pendrive install from DSL, only one partition is created on the USB flash drive. Older PCs might not be able to boot this type of device.

   The USB Pendrive Installation screen appears, displaying information about the installation you are about to perform.

4. If you are ready to proceed with installation, type **y** and press Enter. You are asked whether you want to display your USB storage device information log.

5. Type **Y** to view information about your USB storage device. (When I ran this, the device from my USB drive, sda, appeared in green.) You are asked if this is an installation or upgrade.

6. Type **i** to begin an installation. You are asked for the target device name.

7. Type the device name representing the USB device and press Enter (sda is the most common if you have not other SCSI devices). You are asked where you want to get the DSL image.

8. Type **L** to get the DSL image from the live CD. Alternatively, you could choose F (for file) or W (for Web) to get the image from a local file or from a location on the Web. You are asked whether you want to add any boot time options.

9. Add any options you like. For example, you might want to have services start ups, such as printing (lpd), FTP service (ftp), or NFS (nfs).

10. Choose a language (such as cs, da, de, es, fr, nl, it, pl, ru, sk), if you are selecting a language/keyboard other than Linux. Press Enter to just accept English. You receive your final warning that everything on the device you entered will be destroyed.

11. If you are *sure* that you have that right device name and that it is okay to erase it, type **y** and press Enter. The USB flash drive will be repartitioned (into either one or two partitiond). Then, in the case of USB-ZIP, boot files will be placed on the first partition (/dev/sda1) and all other files will go on the second partition (/dev/sda2). When the install is complete, you are asked to press Enter.

12. Press Enter. Your USB flash drive should now be configured.

   The USB flash drive should now be ready to boot on an available PC. Insert the USB flash drive into a USB port on an available PC and reboot. If DSL doesn't boot (the PC bypasses the USB flash drive and starts your normal boot from hard disk or CD), reboot again and run Setup before you see the boot prompt to change BIOS settings. From the selection that lets you set the boot order, be sure that the USB drive (USB-HDD or USB-ZIP) appears in the boot order before any other drive (CD or hard disk) that might boot.

If you want to add data or applications to your DSL USB flash drive, the larger amount of space from the flash drive is available from these directories: /home, /opt, /tmp, and /var. I recommend you use one of those locations to add content to your USB flash drive.

Summary

By their nature, live Linux CDs usually are run from a read-only CD or DVD, so making and saving custom settings and data that you create during live CD sessions has always been an issue. By including popular desktop environments (such as KDE) and many configurable features (printers, network interfaces, and servers, for example), you have no shortage of ways to customize a running live CD system.

Live CD developers have come up with innovative ways to keep the settings and files you create during a live CD session. The first solutions focused on backing up changed files to a compressed archive file. When the CD was rebooted, those files could then be restored to where they were needed. A more recent solution is to create a persistent desktop that relies on a writeable disk image stored on a local hard disk or USB flash memory drive.

With persistent desktop images, changes are immediately applied to the writeable medium. When you reboot, the files are still available from their same locations, without having to back them up. Combining a writeable file system image with a UnionFS file system means that the persistent desktop doesn't have to be restricted to the /home and /etc directories. Files throughout the entire file system can be can be changed and then merged with files from file systems mounted from read-only live CDs and DVDs.

Examples of customizing and saving customizations associated with a live CD in this chapter were done using Knoppix. However, because many other live CDs are based on Knoppix, these techniques work with other CDs as well. Later, the chapter also described techniques for customizing settings, files, and even applications for live CDs such as Damn Small Linux, Dynebolic, and Puppy Linux.

Part II

Creating a Custom Bootable Linux

## CHAPTER 4

Understanding How Live Linux CDs Work

From the moment you turn on your computer to the time when the operating system and services are up and running from your live CD, a lot of activities take place. As someone who wants to create and use live CDs, you can mold nearly every aspect of that process.

By learning how live Linux CDs work, you enter some of the magical areas of how BIOSes and boot loaders operate before Linux even starts up. Seemingly no less magic, however, are special live CD scripts (such as linuxrc) that enable the features needed to set up the environment in which the live CD will run.

Following along with the process of how a live CD boots up takes you on the road to creating your own live CD. To get beyond point-and-click customizing described to this point in the book, however, you must bring some knowledge of Linux with you. In other words, the book covers special live CD file systems (such as Squashfs and UnionFS) but expects you to already know how to mount, list, and get around file systems in Linux.

NOTE

Although I won't discourage you from trying the projects described in this book, if you are not familiar with Linux, you should at least get hold of a good reference book on the subject. In particular, you should become familiar with the shell and common shell commands.

UNDERSTANDING THE BOOT PROCESS

In this chapter, I take you through the entire process of booting a live CD. Because the boot process can go in different directions, I step you through the boot process of a particular live Linux CD. Along the way, I note how the process might branch off into different directions. The thrust of the descriptions, however, cover the following:

- **PC with x86 architecture**—As with most of the discussions in this book, PCs are used in the examples.

- **Knoppix**—Because of its popularity, Knoppix is the live CD used in this example.

- **CD-ROM (El Torito)**—The ISO 9660 Knoppix image boots from CD-ROM because when the Knoppix ISO image was created, components described in the El Torito specification were added (such as a boot image and boot catalog). El Torito is an extension of the ISO 9660 standard that places boot information on a well-known place on the CD so that a computer Basic Input Output/System (BIOS) that supports El Torito can find it and boot from it.

In general, the following sections fill out the boot process of our live CD example:

- **Boot medium**—The boot process begins with PC x86-compatible hardware and the medium you add to that hardware. Although we are bypassing the normal "boot from a hard disk" process, the discussion of boot media isn't limited to CD-ROMs. It also includes booting from other non–hard disk media: floppy disks, USB flash memory drives, Zip drives, and network cards (PXE boot).

- **BIOS**—BIOS settings initially determine what gets booted when a computer starts up. You can set the order in which bootable devices (floppy drive, hard disk, CD-ROM, and so on) are checked for information that would allow the computer to boot from those devices.

- **Boot loader**—When the BIOS determines which medium to boot from, the computer looks for a boot record on that medium. That boot record points to a boot loader (such as Isolinux, GRUB, or LILO) that can be configured to let the user choose among various boot labels. Each boot label represents a different combination of operating system and boot options to launch.

- **Kernels and initial RAM disk**—When the selected boot label is started for a Linux system, an initial RAM disk is identified and mounted, and the root file system and a kernel are started that draws from that initial RAM disk.

- **First script run (linuxrc)**—After starting the kernel and before starting up system services associated with the system run level, Knoppix (and other live CDs) start up a script that prepares the operating system to run. In Knoppix, that script is called linuxrc and is located in the root directory of the live CD.

- **Init process (SystemV init)**—By the time the live CD hands off control to the init process, most setup that is specific to a live CD has already been accomplished. Services that the init process start up provide system services (such as the system log facility) and network services (such as Web, FTP, or remote login services).

- **Desktop**—If the live CD includes a desktop system, that desktop can be set to launch automatically when the live CD boots up. Getting the desktop working typically requires the live CD to properly detect the available video hardware (or guess at some good default settings) and configure the X display server (using an X.org or XFree86 X server).

Figure 4-1 illustrates the boot process for a Knoppix live CD. Aside from some of the particular scripts that Knoppix uses during the boot process, the boot process is similar on most live Linux CDs.

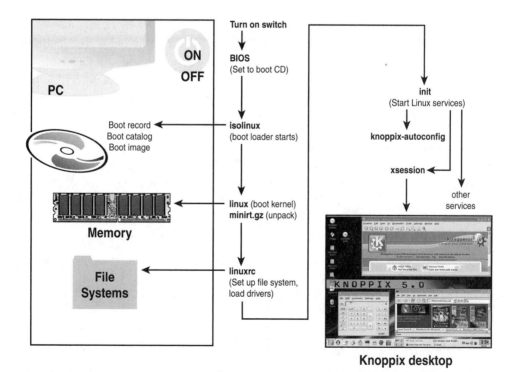

Knoppix desktop

FIGURE 4-1 Nearly every aspect of a live CD boot process can be customized (from boot-up to desktop display).

FROM BIOS TO BOOT LOADER

When you first turn on (or reboot) a PC, the computer's BIOS is run to direct the start-up process. The BIOS must determine where to look for the boot information that will either boot the operating system or present a boot screen (so the user can select the operating system to boot). The BIOS has these primary duties related to running live CDs:

- **Enable drives**—Depending on the BIOS, you might have to specifically enable the particular hardware drive you want to boot from. For example, with some BIOSes, you might need to enable USB BIOS support to even be able to select USB flash drives or USB hard disks as bootable devices.

- **Set the boot order**—The boot order set in the BIOS determines which device is searched first for bootable media. On systems most often booted from hard disk, floppy and CD drives still typically precede hard disks in the boot order. In these cases, bootable CDs and floppies are expected to be in those drives only during the boot process to start them instead of starting the installed operating system.

  If an inserted live CD is bypassed during the boot process, you should check the boot order to make sure that it appears in the boot list before the medium (probably the hard disk) that actually booted. Also, other media that you might want to boot from (such as a USB device or Zip drive) likely will not be in the default boot order list; you must change the boot order to boot from those devices.

In most cases, a PC's BIOS is set so that simply inserting a live Linux CD into a computer's CD drive and rebooting cause the boot information on the CD to be found and booted. However, with some computers (especially older ones), the boot order doesn't include the CD drive before the hard disk. A more likely problem with older computers, however, is that a computer's BIOS doesn't include less popular boot devices (such as a USB drive or Zip drive) in its boot priority order.

In other cases, BIOS is supposed to be capable of booting from a particular drive, but some bug in the BIOS prevents that from happening. In those cases, you might try to track down an updated BIOS for your computer.

Checking and Changing the BIOS

To check and possibly change your computer's BIOS, turn on the computer and watch the screen as the computer checks the available memory. Look for the message that tells you which key to press to go into Setup (such as the F2 function key or the Delete key) and press that key. At this point, you should enter a BIOS setup utility.

The BIOS setup utility should tell you some things about your computer that will help you boot a live CD. It also should give you the opportunity to change some of those settings. Here are some items to look for:

- **Boot order**—This is the most likely feature you will need to change in your BIOS to use your live CD. Because many BIOS setup utilities are different, you need to look for and select a heading that reads something like Boot. Under the Boot heading, you should see a listing of boot devices, shown in priority order. Some PCs will let you simply select floppy, CD, and hard drives; others enable you to boot from a variety of devices. Figure 4-2 shows an example of a boot priority order for the BIOS on an IBM Thinkpad.

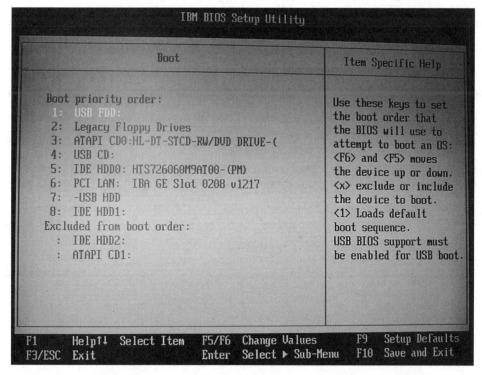

FIGURE 4-2 Some BIOS setups let you choose from a variety of boot devices.

Follow the instructions to make sure that the device you want to boot from appears in the boot order before another device (in particular, your first hard disk) is booted. Notice in this example that the first USB floppy disk drive (FDD) is checked for boot media. Then regular (legacy) floppy drives are checked, followed by a regular ATAPI CD drive and a USB CD driver.

As noted on this screen, you might need to enable support for USB devices before you can boot from a USB floppy, CD, or flash drive. You should also note that entries for booting from USB flash drives typically do not appear before hard disks in the boot order, by default.

- **Total memory**—By checking the amount of available RAM, you can see whether enough memory is available to meet the minimal required memory to run the live CD you are choosing. This also tells you whether you can use the toram boot option (with live CDs such Knoppix and Damn Small Linux) to load the entire live CD image to RAM and run it from there.

- **BIOS version**—Usually on the first setup page, you will see information about the version of BIOS being used. If you are unable to select the device you want to boot, or if you believe that your live CD won't boot because of a bug in the BIOS, you can see whether an update for your BIOS is available.

Start looking for BIOS updates at the Web site for the manufacturer of your motherboard. Although most BIOSes are based on those that come from only a handful of BIOS vendors (Phoenix Technologies, Award Software International, and so on), because the manufacturers often adapt the BIOS they get from one of those companies, the original BIOS vendor typically won't have the updated BIOSes available.

NOTE

Updating your BIOS is dangerous. If you try to update (flash) your BIOS and you are using the wrong BIOS, or if an error occurs, you can render your motherboard useless. Therefore, if you decide to update your BIOS (as described in the following paragraphs), you do so at your own risk.

BIOS updates for older computers are usually offered as files that create floppy-disk images that you can download directly from the motherboard manufacturer's Web site. Often you can just click on one of these files from a Windows desktop to automatically write a boot floppy containing the update to a floppy disk inserted in your computer.

As motherboard manufacturers adapted to the fact that not everyone has a floppy drive anymore (and that not everyone uses Windows), BIOS updates have become available in different formats. For example, Intel now offers BIOS updates in the following formats:

- **Recovery BIOS update**—If a BIOS update is interrupted, an available `.BIO` file can be used to restore the BIOS to a usable state. A recovery BIOS update can be used to recover the motherboard from this situation.

- **Express BIOS update**—On a Windows system, this type of BIOS update can simply be downloaded and launched from a Windows desktop to update the BIOS. You can do this if you have a dual-boot Windows and Linux system.

- **IFlash BIOS update**—A self-extracting `.exe` file can be launched from a Windows system to create an image that is written to floppy disk and then booted to update the BIOS (regardless of which operating system is being used). This can be useful if you have a Windows system for creating the boot floppy that can then be rebooted on your Linux machine.

- **ISO image BIOS update**—This BIOS update comes in the form of an ISO 9660 image that can be burned to CD and rebooted on any computer for which the BIOS is intended. For Linux, simply download the ISO, burn it to a blank CD (using `cdrecord` or another CD-writing utility), and then reboot the CD on the computer on which you want to update the BIOS. This is usually the best choice for computers running Linux systems, when it is available.

If your computer is running Linux and the only way you can get the BIOS update you need is in the form of a floppy image, you can convert that floppy image to a bootable ISO image and burn it to CD. The "Motherboard BIOS Flash Boot CD from Linux Mini HOWTO" describes how to make a boot CD that incorporates an updated BIOS so you can flash that BIOS to your motherboard. You can find that mini HOWTO at www.nenie.org/misc/flashbootcd.html.

Before you update your BIOS, view your current BIOS settings (press F2 or another key as required when you turn on the computer). You should write down all settings that you have changed because you might lose those settings during the update process. With some BIOSes, you have the choice of saving custom defaults. If that is the case, when the BIOS is updated and the settings are cleared back to the defaults, you will have the opportunity to restore those custom settings.

Starting from BIOS

For the first PCs, the BIOS was set to try to boot first from the floppy drive and then (if no floppy was inserted) from hard disk. BIOS enhancements that made it possible to boot from CD-ROM were added later in a specification referred to as the "El Torito" Bootable CD-ROM Format Specification.

When the computer is turned on, BIOS is the first code that is run. This is what the BIOS does:

- **Runs POST**—The Power-On Self Test (POST) is a routine that initializes and tests the hardware components attached to your PC. If something goes wrong, an error code is written to IO port 080h (that can be displayed with special hardware). An error message is also typically displayed on the screen.

- **Beeps**—To indicate that the speakers are working, BIOS often sends a beep to the speakers after POST completes.

- **Checks boot order**—The default boot order for your PC might attempt to boot from the floppy drive, then the CD drive, and finally the hard disk. A newer BIOS might also offer the option to boot from many different devices (USB drives, Zip drives, and so on) but typically requires you to change the order yourself by going into setup mode.

- **Boots the indicated device**—By going through each boot device in order, BIOS looks for boot information on each device and attempts to boot the operating system or boot loader indicated by that device.

Because our interest here is live CDs, let's assume going forward that a CD is inserted into the CD drive and that it is the first bootable medium encountered. A BIOS that implements the El Torito specification looks at the CD to determine whether it has boot information available. If the CD contains no boot record volume, the BIOS bypasses the CD, moving on to the next bootable device. However, if the CD contains one of the following types of boot information, the BIOS attempts to boot from that CD:

- **Single boot image**—If a single boot image is encountered, the BIOS accesses the boot record volume to determine the location of the boot catalog. The boot record volume, in turn, checks the boot catalog on the CD and starts the initial/default entry. That entry points to the boot disk image on the CD that starts the operating system.

- **Multiple boot images**—As with the single boot image, here the BIOS checks the boot record volume to find the boot catalog. However, if the boot catalog contains multiple boot entries, a boot loader can be used to enable the user to select the boot image to start up. Boot entries can point to one of multiple available boot images to start up. Those images can exist on the CD or on other devices (such as a hard disk).

  To access different boot images on the CD, the BIOS can use INT 13 calls. If the BIOS has problems booting from a multiboot live CD, often there will be errors related to INT 13 calls.

The format of Linux live CDs is compatible with the ISO 9660 standard. The El Torito spec is incorporated into the ISO 9660 CD standard to make the CD bootable. When the BIOS tries to boot an El Torito CD, information about how to boot that CD is sought in the following order:

- **Boot record**—The BIOS looks for a boot record volume descriptor that resides in sector 11 in the last session on the CD. This boot record points to the boot catalog.

- **Boot catalog**—A boot catalog contains a list of boot entries. Each entry in the boot catalog points to a boot image, if that boot entry is selected.

- **Boot image**—The boot image represents the operating system that is launched for the selected entry. Instead of being a complete operating system or a boot loader, the boot image can represent a specialized boot floppy image.

You can see where each of these items came from when someone first created the live Linux CD ISO image using the `mkisofs` command. This is an example of an `mkisofs` command line to create a bootable live Linux CD ISO image:

```
# mkisofs -R -b isolinux/isolinux.bin -c isolinux/boot.cat \
   -no-emul-boot -boot-load-size 8 -boot-info-table . > ../livecd.iso
```

In this example, a boot record is created that points to the boot catalog file (`boot.cat`, located in the `isolinux` directory on the CD). The `boot.cat` file was created automatically by the `mkisofs` command and points to the `isolinux.bin` file (located in the `isolinux` directory on the live CD). The `isolinux.bin` file is the boot image that represents the second stage of the boot process. When launched, `isolinux.bin` starts the Isolinux boot loader. The `isolinux.bin` file enables the user to select bootable images listed in the `isolinux.cfg` file.

NOTE

Different boot loaders come with their own stage2 boot images. For example, for the GRUB boot loader, instead of `isolinux.bin`, you can use the stage2_eltorito boot image included with the GRUB package.

The El Torito boot image can be booted in different modes. As someone running a live CD, you don't need to know the mode in which this image is running. However, as someone building a live CD, you need to tell the `mkisofs` command which mode this boot image was built to run in. The `-no-emul-boot` option to `mkisofs` shown earlier indicates that this live CD boots in El Torito no emulation mode. You can boot an El Torito CD in the following emulation modes:

- **Floppy mode**—By default, El Torito live CDs are assumed to include a floppy boot image as the boot image (indicated by the -b option). For this to take place, the floppy image included on the CD must be exactly 1200, 1440, or 2880K in size. A drawback of using floppy mode is that the boot loader can reference only items on that image (which restricts the size of the boot images and other files you want to include). The advantage of using floppy mode is that you can simply copy a working boot floppy and use that on your CD to boot from.

- **Hard disk mode**—Adding the -hard-disk-boot option to mkisofs removes the size restrictions related to floppy emulation for someone creating a live CD. However, hard-disk emulation tends to work less reliably with different BIOSes.

- **No emulation**—This is the mode most commonly used to create live Linux CDs (by using the -no-emul-boot option to mkisofs, as described earlier). In this mode, boot problems are most typically caused by older BIOSes that don't fully support El Torito. In these cases, creating a live CD in floppy mode or by using Syslinux (http://syslinux.zytor.com) instead of Isolinux can overcome the problem.

When the El Torito boot image starts up, the boot loader takes over the process of booting the computer.

Proceeding to the Boot Loader

When the boot loader has taken over the boot process, you typically get some choices about how the boot process will proceed. Here are the things you will see once the boot loader takes over:

- **Boot prompt**—Whether you are in text mode or graphics mode, the Isolinux boot loader displays a boot prompt (boot:) when the boot loader takes over. A timeout period (often about 5 seconds) usually passes, during which you can type any labels defined for the boot loader. If you don't type anything, the boot loader times out and boots the default boot label.

  Pressing any key usually stops the boot process from proceeding while you try to figure out what to type at the prompt. Often message files (described later) are available by pressing functions keys (F1, F2, and so on) that indicate both available labels and options to those labels.

  If your live CD uses the GRUB boot loader instead of Isolinux, you might have a menu interface available instead of seeing a boot prompt. In that case, use the arrow keys to select the label you want to boot from a menu.

- **Splash screen**—The initial boot screen and any message screen available during the boot process can also include an image, sometimes referred to as a splash screen. For Isolinux, images must be in a special LSS 16-color format (described in Chapter 5, "Looking Inside Live CD Components"). GRUB allows someone creating a live CD to use an image in gzipped XPM format.

- **Message screens**—Live CDs that use the Isolinux boot loader usually include additional message screens you can display by pressing different function keys. The live CD developer identifies the files representing these screens in the `isolinux.cfg` file by assigning each file to a function key from F1 through F10. Function keys from F1 through F9 are each represented by those tags, and the F0 tag represents the F10 function key.

By simply pressing Enter or waiting for the live CD to time out, someone using a live CD has it boot the way that the live CD creator most commonly intended the live CD to be used. The default boot image (in our case, typically a Linux kernel at this point) is started with a file system that is provided from an initial RAM disk (typically, a compressed file-system image).

Along with the kernel and the initial RAM disk, a useful set of options is typically appended to the kernel command line. For an Isolinux boot loader, that information is defined in the `isolinux.cfg` file when the live CD is created.

Different labels are made available from the live CD for a variety of reasons. For example, typically special labels exist for booting with different types of hardware (especially for different video modes). The live CD developer might also have included several different floppy boot images on the CD.

You can tailor Isolinux or GRUB boot loaders to have the live CD behave the way you want it to. You can present a simple boot prompt, menus, or images. Then you can allow the user to choose exactly what to boot (by selecting a boot label and/or adding options), or bypass the user altogether and proceed straight to booting the operating system. These choices and others are covered in descriptions of the Isolinux and GRUB boot loaders in Chapter 5.

The next section describes how the live CD boots the Live Linux system after continuing forward from the boot loader. The description focuses on booting Knoppix as your selected live CD.

BOOTING THE LIVE LINUX SYSTEM

After the boot loader has presented its boot screen, the user chooses how to go forward and boot the live CD, based on the label and options selected. Depending on the live CD you are booting, the processing going forward can vary from one live CD to another. In this section, descriptions follow what happens when you boot a Knoppix live CD.

Linux Kernel and Initial RAM Disk

From a Knoppix CD, simply pressing Enter or typing knoppix uses the following information configured in the isolinux.cfg file:

```
LABEL knoppix
KERNEL linux
APPEND ramdisk_size=100000 init=/etc/init lang=us apm=power-off vga=791
    initrd=minirt.gz nomce quiet BOOT_IMAGE=knoppix
```

Based on this label, the boot loader identifies the kernel named linux as the one to boot and the minirt.gz file as the initial RAM disk (both of which are stored in the isolinux directory). Other information shown on the APPEND line is passed as options to the linux kernel to be used later in various ways. Options that the user might have added to the knoppix label at the boot prompt (for example, knoppix nodma to turn off DMA support on local disk drives) are added to the end of the appended options.

One of the first things the linux boot image (containing the Linux kernel) does when it starts up is unzip (using the gunzip utility) and mount the initial RAM disk (minirt.gz). minirt.gz is the root file system that the linux boot image uses; it contains the minimum amount of software needed to set up the full Knoppix system. Most of the files that the ultimate Knoppix system needs are contained in the KNOPPIX compressed image file in the KNOPPIX/ directory on the CD.

With the linux boot image running the Knoppix kernel and the minimum file system mounted (minirt.gz), the linuxrc script in the root directory can kick in. The linuxrc script relies on a couple of nonstandard directories it uses during setup that are contained on the minirt root-mounted file system: /modules and /static:

- **/modules**—The /modules directory contains the loadable modules and related commands (insmod and rmmod) for working with those modules. For example, in /modules, the cloop modules are needed to uncompress files from the KNOPPIX image on the fly. The unionfs module is there to create merged UnionFS file systems (so the end user can save files to a directory that are otherwise read-only). A scsi directory is also located in the /modules directory, in case the CD drive is a SCSI device in need of a module to access it.

- **/static**—The /static directory contains the ash shell required for the shell environment that is needed at this point.

Both /modules and /static will be deleted later in the Knoppix boot process. In the mean time, however, those directories contain important components needed to set up the Knoppix environment. To see what's in these directories, as well as other components, you can start by unzipping the initial RAM disk file and mounting it in loopback. With a running Knoppix system, here's how to check out the contents of the initial RAM disk file:

1. Unzip and mount the minirt.gz initial RAM disk:

```
$ cd /cdrom/boot/isolinux
$ gunzip -dc minirt.gz > /tmp/minirt.ext2
$ sudo mkdir /tmp/mini
$ sudo mount -o loop -t ext2 /tmp/minirt.ext2 /mnt/mini
```

2. List the contents of the initial ram disk:

```
$ ls -CF /mnt/mini
KNOPPIX/   boot@   dev/   lib@    media/   modules/   proc/
static/    tmp/    bin@   cdrom/  etc/     linuxrc*   mnt/
opt@       sbin@   sys/   usr/
```

You can see from this output which items are directories (/), which are links to other directories (@), and which are executable files (*). This is the actual file system that Knoppix adapts into the file system that it will ultimately use when Knoppix is finished booting. So, when directories such as /static and /modules are done being used, they are removed.

NOTE

When you try to remaster Knoppix later, as described in Chapter 6, "Building a Custom Knoppix Live CD," you might decide that you want to make your own initial RAM disk to include (or exclude) drivers or add commands to run. With that file unzipped and mounted as described already, you can make any changes you like. When you are done, just unmount the file (umount /mnt/mini) and zip up the file again (gzip /tmp/minirt).

After the initial ram disk is mounted, it's time to start setting up the file system and additional drivers to run the live CD. Knoppix, Fedora, and live CDs built with other technology use a linuxrc file to set up the live CD environment. How those components are directed to set up the Knoppix environment mostly comes from a script that is located in the root of the initial RAM disk: the linuxrc file.

> **NOTE**
>
> Instead of using the file system from the initial RAM disk going forward, as Knoppix does, Fedora live CDs built using kadischi set up the permanent file system structure separately from the initial RAM disk. When the new environment is set up, the pivot_root command is run to change the running kernel to use the new file-system structure.

The linuxrc Script

A linuxrc script in the root directory of the initial RAM disk file (minirt.gz in Knoppix) directs much of the initial setup of the live CD environment. Most of what this script does is mount the file systems that the live CD will use when the boot process is completed. However, in Knoppix, the linuxrc script also makes sure that modules are loaded to handle any special hardware requirements (such as SCSI devices) that the live CD might encounter.

The work that linuxrc does at this point is accomplished with the limited number of commands and modules available at this point. Most of the work is done using commands that are built into the Linux kernel, the ash shell, and commands for adding and removing modules (insmod, rmmod, and modprobe). These are some of the things the linuxrc script does:

- **Sets colors**—As Knoppix boots, you will notice that different types of messages are displayed in different colors. These color changes make it a bit easier to see what is going on as Knoppix boots up. In the linuxrc script, the following variables are set to the color names they represent, to output different types of messages: RED (failure or error messages), GREEN (success messages), YELLOW (descriptions), BLUE (system messages), MAGENTA (found devices or drivers), CYAN (questions), and WHITE (hint).

  You might also notice that Knoppix uses these colors in some fun ways. The "Welcome to KNOPPIX" message displays each of the letters in KNOPPIX as a separate color.

- **Mounts system file systems**—The /proc and /sys file systems are mounted within the linuxrc script. The /proc file system provides an interface to data structures used by the kernel. The /sys file system contains data registered by built-in drivers that can be accessed from processes in user space.

- **Checks options**—The linuxrc script checks options that the user or the isolinux.cfg file might have set. These values cause environment variables to be set that are used later in the linuxrc script. Many of the values consumed here turn off features (noscsi, nousb, or nofirewire, for example) or set modes of operation (such as debug or expert modes).

- **Sets the location of KNOPPIX**—The KNOPPIX_DIR variable sets the directory containing the Knoppix image file (the KNOPPIX directory, by default). The KNOPPIX_NAME variable sets the name of the Knoppix archive (KNOPPIX, by default). This image file contains a compressed archive of most of the file system (file, directories, applications, settings) used to run Knoppix. As a result, the Knoppix image is located at /KNOPPIX/KNOPPIX from the root of the CD's file system.

 NOTE

If you ever set up a live DVD to contain multiple versions (or derivatives) of Knoppix, changing the value of KNOPPIX_DIR in the linuxrc file for the initial RAM disk of each version can allow multiple Knoppix distributions to coexist (and be bootable) from the same disk. For example, one distribution could use /KNOPPIX/a as the location of the KNOPPIX file-system image. Another might use /KNOPPIX/b, and so on. If you name the initial RAM disks differently (minirta.gz, minirtb.gz, and so on), different labels can point to different versions.

- **Runs in different modes**—If debug was set as a boot option, linuxrc sets a special shell to start up in debug mode. If expert mode was set as a boot option, the person running the live CD is asked whether they want to install additional modules from a floppy disk.

- **Probes and configures devices**—The linuxrc script checks for PCI devices (cat /proc/pci) and searches that output for SCSI devices that might require modules to work. It also checks and tries to install modules for any IDE raid devices, USB devices, and Firewire devices.

- **Finds KNOPPIX**—With all available CD and hard-drive storage devices (IDE, SCSI, etc.) now properly detected and configured, the linuxrc script tries to find the KNOPPIX archive that will be used to make most of the KNOPPIX file system available (including the applications and settings).

- **Mounts KNOPPIX**—When found, the KNOPPIX image is mounted. If multiple KNOPPIX images are found, they are mounted as KNOPPIX2, KNOPPIX3, and so on. Each image is mounted as a cloop device, so as files and directories are requested from one of those file systems, they can be uncompressed on the fly.

If the person running Knoppix requested to have the KNOPPIX image written to and run from hard disk (tohd) or RAM (toram), linuxrc makes sure enough space is available to write KNOPPIX there. The linuxrc script also checks whether the user asked for KNOPPIX to be booted from hard disk or from an ISO.

- **Mounts RAM disk**—After checking for a reasonable size to create a RAM disk, linuxrc creates a RAM disk (/ramdisk). Writeable directories are created on /ramdisk that can be used (via symbolic links) elsewhere in the file system. These locations include /home and /tmp.

- **Creates the UnionFS file system**—To make all the read-only directories from the live CD available as read-write directories, the linuxrc scripts merges them with writeable directories on /ramdisk using UnionFS. To see which directories are linked from the UnionFS file system (/UNIONFS), type **ls -l /** | **less** with Knoppix booted. Chapter 5 describes how UnionFS is used to enable you to write to merged read-only directories (from the CD) and read-write directories (from the RAM disk).

- **Sets up the** /etc **directory**—Certain files and directories in the /etc directory cannot be links but must be real files. To make sure that this is true, the linuxrc script removes files in the /etc directory that include ftpusers, passwd, shadow, gshadow, group, ppp, isdn, ssh, ioctl.save, inittab, network, sudoers, init, localtime, dhcpc, and pnm2ppa.conf. It then copies real versions of these files from the CD.

- **Performs final cleanup**—To clean up the /etc/mtab file, the linuxrc script grabs information from /proc/mounts. It then removes the /linuxrc file and exits.

With the linuxrc script finished, control of the boot process is passed to the Linux kernel. The kernel then passes control to the init process.

Starting init (and the inittab File)

The init process takes over the boot process to direct the startup of systems services and to set system parameters. The init process is referred to as the parent of all processes. In fact, the process ID number of init is 1 because it is the first process to start on the running system and it sets all other processes in motion.

The init process keys off the contents of the /etc/inittab file. The services that init runs are based on the run level passed to init and on the services that are set up to start at that run level. For Knoppix, the default is to boot to a desktop run level (run level 5) and to run at least one start-up script that is specific to Knoppix.

To understand what happens after init starts up, follow the settings in the /etc/inittab file. Unless overridden, Knoppix starts at run level 5, based on this entry in the /etc/inittab file:

```
id:5:initdefault:
```

Entries identified as sysinit processes are executed when init first starts up. The following entry in /etc/inittab causes the rcS script to run all init scripts that begin with the letter S and are located in the /etc/init.d/rcS.d directory to be executed:

```
si::sysinit:/etc/init.d/rcS
```

By default, the only script that is set to start at system initialization (from the /etc/rcS.d directory) is the knoppix-autoconfig script. The link S00knoppix-autoconfig points to the /etc/init.d/knoppix-autoconfig script. This is where a lot of Knoppix configuration occurs. (The knoppix-autoconfig script is described a bit later.)

The next set of lines in the /etc/inittab file indicate what is launched next, based on the current run level. (For the run level to be something other than 5, you must have changed the value of the initdefault line or passed a run level number as a boot option.) Here are the lines:

```
# What to do in single-user mode.
~~:S:respawn:/bin/bash -login >/dev/tty1 2>&1 </dev/tty1

# /etc/init.d executes the S and K scripts upon change
# of runlevel.
#
# Runlevel 0 is halt.
# Runlevel 1 is single-user.
# Runlevels 2-5 are multi-user.
# Runlevel 6 is reboot.

10:0:wait:/etc/init.d/knoppix-halt
11:1:wait:/etc/init.d/rc 1
12:2:wait:/etc/init.d/rc 2
13:3:wait:/etc/init.d/rc 3
14:4:wait:/etc/init.d/rc 4
15:5:wait:/etc/init.d/rc 5
16:6:wait:/etc/init.d/knoppix-reboot
```

Valid run states that you can boot into include single-user modes (S or 1) and multiuser modes (2, 3, 4, or 5). In single-user mode (S), Knoppix opens a root shell and starts no other services. In single-user mode (1), Knoppix runs the /etc/init.d/rc script with 1 as an option. This causes all scripts beginning with S in the /etc/rc1.d directory to be started. Likewise, the other run states you might boot to (2, 3, 4, or 5) each run scripts starting with *S* from their run level directories (/etc/rc2.d, /etc/rc3.d, and so on).

In Knoppix, because it is primarily a desktop system, services that might be run on a server system from those directories (such as Web server, FTP server, MySQL server, and so on) are not enabled (that is, added to those directories) by default.

NOTE

Many of the scripts representing services are available in Knoppix in the /etc/init.d directory. So if you were creating your own custom Knoppix, you could link any of those scripts to a file in any runlevel directory to get it to run at that runlevel. For example, while you were customizing Knoppix, you could type the following:

```
# ln -s /etc/init.d/apache2 /etc/rc5.d/S85apache2
```

This command creates a link from the apache2 script (for starting the Apache Web server) to a file (S85apache2) in the /etc/rc5.d directory. The next time the computer enters runlevel 5 (the default desktop runlevel), the Apache Web service will start up.

The other scripts that are run when you change run levels begin with the letter *K*. For example, if you changed from run level 5 to run level 3, the K10xsession script would be run to shut down your X server (the desktop interface) and drop you to a shell. The desktop is turned off at every run level except run level 5, so this is one of the first services shut off when you shut down the computer (run level 0) or reboot (run level 6).

As you might guess from the previous sentence, you should never set your run level to 0 or 6. With the run level set to 0, your system would simply shut down when init kicked in. With it set to 6, it would continuously reboot. Most Linux systems are set to 5 (to boot to a desktop) or 3 (to boot to a predefined set of services, but no desktop). There are historical meanings to run states 2 and 4 from old UNIX systems, which no longer have much meaning.

The next set of lines in the /etc/inittab file that apply to starting up Knoppix have to do with starting up virtual terminals:

```
# 4 virtual consoles with immortal shells
1:12345:respawn:/bin/bash -login >/dev/tty1 2>&1 </dev/tty1
2:2345:respawn:/bin/bash -login >/dev/tty2 2>&1 </dev/tty2
3:2345:respawn:/bin/bash -login >/dev/tty3 2>&1 </dev/tty3
4:2345:respawn:/bin/bash -login >/dev/tty4 2>&1 </dev/tty4
```

These lines show that one bash shell is started as a login shell that is connected to a specific tty device (/dev/tty1) for run levels 1 through 5. For run levels 2, 3, 4, and 5, three additional run levels are created (tty2 through tty4). You can get to those different virtual terminals by pressing Ctrl+Alt+F1, Ctrl+Alt+F2, and so on. Virtual terminals are a useful way to get to a shell if your desktop interface becomes scrambled.

The last line in the /etc/inittab file that relates to starting up your system has to do with starting up your X desktop. When Knoppix goes into run level 5 (the default), the following lines are the last ones that are executed:

```
# Run X Window session from CDROM in runlevel 5
w5:5:wait:/bin/sleep 2
x5:5:wait:/etc/init.d/xsession start
```

After pausing for 2 seconds (sleep 2), the xsession script is run with the start option. The xsession script starts your X desktop interface based on settings that were determined during start-up (stored in the xserver and knoppix files in the /etc/sysconfig directory). It also tries to load modules that could be useful for running your video card (such as loading AGPGART and DRM modules).

At this point, your Knoppix desktop interface should have started up and you should be ready to start using Knoppix.

UNDERSTANDING THE RUNNING LIVE LINUX SYSTEM

With the Linux system up and running, you can gain further understanding of how your live Linux system was started. For Knoppix, as mentioned earlier, the knoppix-autoconfig script sets many Knoppix values when the live CD is first booted. You also can try commands on the running system to see how various values are set.

Understanding knoppix-autoconfig

When the init process takes over during a Knoppix boot-up, the knoppix-autoconfig script is run from a link in the system-initialization directory: /etc/rcS.d/S00knoppix-autoconfig. By looking at this file, you can see how a lot of runtime features are set in Knoppix. When you go to customize your own live CD, this is a script you might consider modifying.

Here are some highlights of the processing that occurs in the knoppix-autoconfig script:

- **PATH**—The PATH (where the shell finds the commands you run) is set to include /bin, /sbin, /usr/bin, /usr/sbin, and /usr/X11R6/bin. This is significant because, even for nonroot users (for example, the default knoppix user), the /sbin and /usr/sbin directories, typically used only by root, are included in the PATH. This is probably because Knoppix expects the regular knoppix user to run system-administration commands using the sudo command.

- **Colors**—Colors are defined in this script so they can be used to indicate different types of information, as they are in the linuxrc script. As Knoppix boots up and after you see INIT starting, output from the processing in this script can appear in RED (failure or error message), GREEN (success message), YELLOW (description), BLUE (system message), MAGENTA (found devices or drivers), CYAN (questions), or WHITE (hint). If you were to add your own features to this script, you could incorporate these colors as well.

- **Boot options**—This script rereads the boot options, in case any of those options are needed during the processing of this script. Because those options are stored in /proc/cmdline, the script can simply run the cat command on that file to get the boot options.

- **Config files check**—The script checks whether you want to restore configuration files that you previously saved from Knoppix. It does this by checking the boot options for strings beginning with *myconf*, *custom*, *config*, or *floppyconf*.

- **Language**—The language and keyboard used are based on the lang= value set as a boot option. For example, U.S. English is us and German is de. Based on this value, the values country, language, keytable, xkeyboard, kdekeyboard, character set, and timezone are also set. The language is enabled immediately, so error messages can be translated as well.

- **Desktop**—The desktop boot option is read so that Knoppix knows which type of desktop interface to start. The default is kde (K Desktop Environment). This information is checked again in the xsession script.

- **Hostname**—The hostname is set to Knoppix.

- **Clock**—Based on boot options, the clock can be set to GMT or UTC. Normally, local time is used. Also, the hardware clock (hwclock command) is set based on the time zone.

- **Live CD or installed Knoppix**—Because Knoppix can be installed and run from hard disk, some different processing needs to be done depending on which medium Knoppix is running from. If Knoppix is running from hard disk, this script does such things as performs file system checks on hard-disk partitions, remounts the root directory (/) as read/write, and regenerates module dependencies on hard disk.

- **Configuration files**—A handful of configuration files are recreated in the knoppix-autoconfig script. This is important to note because if you tried to save any of these files, the previous versions are erased and the new files will be populated with information gathered during the boot process. Configuration files that are recreated include several that are stored in the /etc/sysconfig directory, such as: i18n, keyboard, desktop, and knoppix. The /etc/environment file (used by OpenOffice.org applications and others) is also re-created.

> **NOTE**
>
> To determine whether Knoppix is being run from a live CD or from hard disk, the knoppix-autoconfig script checks for the existence of the /KNOPPIX/bin/ash command. If it isn't there, the install is assumed to be a hard disk install. If you remaster Knoppix at some point, you should be sure to either not remove that command or change the test for it in this script.

- **CD/DVD integrity tests**—If the testcd or testdvd options were given as boot options, the integrity of the CD or DVD is checked against md5sum data stored on the CD (see /cdrom/KNOPPIX/md5sums). Every file on the CD or DVD is checked to make sure that it is not corrupted. (Note that the files on the compressed images are not checked individually, but the KNOPPIX image itself is checked.)

- **Enables hardware features**—Unless turned off by boot options (noapm, nopcmcia, and so on), several hardware features are enabled. Those features include Advanced Power Management (apm), PCMCIA cardbus slots (pcmcia), USB ports (usb and usb2), Firewire ports (firewire), and Udev dynamic device manager (udev). A variety of devices are also created to work with the udev facility.

- **Additional hardware features**—The /etc/modules and /etc/modules.conf files are checked and their contents loaded, to enable additional hardware features.

- **Hardware information**— Information that is gathered about system hardware in the /etc/sysconfig/knoppix file relating to your mouse, sound card, and keyboard are checked. Information about how those items are set is displayed. In particular, if any Braille devices have been enabled, that information is noted and the Braille display manager is started.

- **Interactive setup**—If you entered expert as a boot option, you are given the choice at several points in the boot process to change settings. The first chance comes at this point, when you are given the option to reconfigure console keyboard settings (using the kbdconfig command). You then have the option to reconfigure your mouse. When X configuration is done, you will later have the option to reconfigure your graphics subsystem,

- **X configuration**—The latest versions of Knoppix use the X.org X server. To create the X configuration file (`/etc/X11/xorg.conf`) that the Xorg server process uses, the `knoppix-autoconfig` script runs the `/sbin/mkxorgconfig` script.

  The `mkxorgconfig` script reads boot options, such as those that set particular vertical and horizontal refresh rates (`xvrefresh` and `xhrefresh`), vertical and horizontal sync rates (`vsync` and `hsync`), and screen resolution (`screen`), to configure the X server. Likewise, any special mouse and keyboard options are noted and incorporated into the `xorg.conf` file.

  After the new `xorg.conf.new` file is created, it is copied to its permanent location (`/etc/X11/xorg.conf`). Then information about the selected X server and setting is displayed on the screen.

- **Run level**—At this point, the `run level` command is run to determine the current run level. By default, this will be run level 5 (desktop). If another run level was entered at the boot prompt (S, 1, 2, 3, or 4), that run level will be used instead.

- **File systems configured**—Hard-disk partitions, CD drives, and other storage devices are added to the `/etc/fstab` file so they can be easily mounted and unmounted as requested. The `knoppix-autoconfig` script runs the `/usr/sbin/rebuildfstab` script to add partitions to the `/etc/fstab` file.

- **File systems mounted and swap on**—Those file systems that need to be mounted, and have not already been mounted, are mounted at this point. Likewise, `swapon` is run to enable any available swap partitions to be used. If you are running in expert mode, you have the option to create a swap file on any available DOS partition.

- **Network startup**—The `/proc/net/dev` file is checked for any available Ethernet devices (typically `eth0`). If one is found, the `ifconfig` command is run to start the interface and `pump` is run to find an available DHCP or Bootp server on the network. If a server is found, you will have an automatic connection to the network (probably the Internet).

- **Background image**—The background image for the Knoppix desktop is located at this point. The default image is located at `/cdrom/KNOPPIX/background.jpg`.

- **Use backed-up config files**—If you have saved a Knoppix configuration (to floppy, hard disk, or other writeable medium, one of the last actions performed in the `knoppix-autoconfig` file is to restore those setting (provided that you want them restored).

When `knoppix-autoconfig` processing is completed, the `init` process continues on (as described in the previous description of the `inittab` file).

Watching the Live CD Boot Progress

If you watched the live CD boot process on the screen, you could see it pass from one stage to another. Here's an example of output from the DVD version of the Knoppix live CD as it goes through various stages of the boot process. The following messages are output after pressing Enter from the boot prompt.

```
Loading Linux..................
Reading minirt.gz.................                              boot
                                                              loader

Uncompressing Linux... Ok, booting the kernel.
Welcome to the KNOPPIX live Linux-on-DVD!

Scanning for USB/Firewire devices... Done.
Accessing KNOPPIX DVD at /dev/hdb...
 Found primary KNOPPIX compressed image at /cdrom/KNOPPIX/KNOPPIX.
 Found additional KNOPPIX compressed image at /cdrom/KNOPPIX/KNOPPIX2.   linuxrc
Total memory found: 253384 kB                                           script
Creating /ramdisk (dynamic size=192996k) on shared memory...Done.
Creating unionfs and symlinks on ramdisk...
>> Read-only DVD system successfully merged with read-write /ramdisk.
Done.
Starting init process
INIT: version 2.86 booting
Running Linux Kernel 2.6.15.
Processor 0 is Pentium III (Coppermine) 648MHz, 256 KB Cache
apmd[1077]: apmd 3.2.1 interfacing with apm driver 1.16ac and APM BIOS
APM Bios found, power management functions enabled.
USB found, managed by udev
Firewire found, managed by udev
Starting udev hot-plug hardware detection...Started.
Autoconfiguring devices... /                 Done.
Mouse is ImPS/2 Logitech Wheel Mouse at /dev/input/mice
Soundcard: Ensoniq ES1371 [AudioPCI-97] driver=snd-ens1371            init
                                                                     process
AGP bridge detected.
 Video is Intel Corporation 82810E DC-133 CGC [Chipset Graphics
   Controller], using Xorg(i810) Server
 Monitor is Generic Monitor, H:28.0-96.0kHz, V:50.0-75.0Hz
 Using Modes "1024x768" "800x600" "640x480"
Scanning for Harddisk partitions and creating /etc/fstab...Done.
Using swap partition /dev/hda5.
Network device eth0 detected, DHCP broadcasting for IP. (Backgrounding)
INIT: Entering runlevel: 5
Executing /etc/init.d/xsession start:
```

The messages just shown appear on the console terminal. The first few lines (shaded text) are output from the boot loader as the kernel is started and the initial RAM disk is uncompressed. The next section (appearing in bold) shows the output of the linuxrc script as the file systems are set up and merged. The init process takes over in the final section (second set of shaded text). As its last activity, it starts up the X server using the xsession script.

Checking the Running Live CD

Because a fair amount of reconfiguration goes on as the live CD boots up, sometimes the only way to be sure how features were set up is to check around a bit. The following are some commands you can run to see how Knoppix was configured:

```
$ cat /proc/cmdline
ramdisk_size=1000000 init=/etc/init lang=us apm=power-off vga=791
    initrd=minirt.gz nomce quiet BOOT_IMAGE=knoppix BOOT_IMAGE=linux
```

By displaying the contents of /proc/cmdline, you can see the boot options that were used when the live CD first booted. Knoppix uses this on many occasions when it runs its start-up scripts to determine user preferences. Here you can see the maximum amount of RAM that can be assigned to the ramdisk (1,000,000 bytes). /etc/init is the location of the init file, the language is U.S. English (us), and the power-off feature is assigned to the APM system. The vga=791 option sets the display to use 1024×768 resolution and 16-bit color. The boot image, which is originally set to knoppix, ultimately boots the image containing the Linux kernel named kernel.

If you can't understand more boot options, you can check several different places. On the Knoppix CD, check out the knoppix-cheatcodes.txt file. For kernel boot parameters, refer to the bootparam man page (type **man bootparam**).

Just as a quick reminder, these components interpret the options passed to the kernel during the Knoppix boot process:

- linux **kernel**—From the isolinux directory on the CD
- linuxrc **boot script**—Contained in the root directory of minirt.gz
- knoppix-autoconfig—Run as part of the init process
- xsession—Used to start the X desktop
- knoppix-halt **and** knoppix-reboot—Run when you stop or restart Knoppix, respectively

Other services located in the /etc/init.d directory check your boot options. For example, the /etc/init.d/hdparm service checks whether nohdparm is set (it skips the setup of disk parameters if it is).

Viewing mounted file systems also yields interesting results from your live CD. This is the output from the mount command on a Knoppix system:

```
/dev/root on / type ext2 (rw)
/ramdisk on /ramdisk type tmpfs (rw,size=192996k)
/UNIONFS on /UNIONFS type unionfs (rw,dirs=/ramdisk=rw:/KNOPPIX=ro)
/dev/hdb on /cdrom type iso9660 (ro)
/dev/cloop on /KNOPPIX type iso9660 (ro)
/proc on /proc type proc (rw)
/proc/bus/usb on /proc/bus/usb type usbfs (rw,devmode=0666)
/dev/pts on /dev/pts type devpts (rw)
```

The /ramdisk partition stores files that are created during the live CD session. The KNOPPIX image is mounted /KNOPPIX using the cloop driver (so that files from the /cdrom/KNOPPIX/KNOPPIX compressed image can be decompressed as needed. Because the most recent version of Knoppix uses a UnionFS file system, the read/write /ramdisk is jointed with the read-only /KNOPPIX file systems to have all directories (even those from the read-only CD medium) act as read/write media.

You can use a few other useful commands for determining the state of your Knoppix or other live CD system. Type the following to see whether your Ethernet network connection is active:

ifconfig eth0

Type the following to see the previous run level, followed by the current run level:

runlevel
N 5

Type the following to see what modules have been loaded for your system:

lsmod | less

Type the following to see a list of your PCI hardware:

lspci -v

Type the following to see the version of Knoppix you are using:

cat knoppix-version

For more details on how the boot process generally works in Linux, you can refer to several different man pages, including boot, inittab, run level, and init.

SUMMARY

Although the BIOS, which runs when the computer is first turned on, is typically supplied by the manufacturer of the motherboard, nearly every other aspect of the boot process involves open-source software. For that reason, someone creating a live Linux CD can control nearly every aspect of the live CD boot process when control is handed off from the BIOS.

The control a user can exert over the BIOS is typically done from the BIOS setup screen. Most important, the user might need to make sure that the device containing the live CD (CD, DVD, USB flash drive, or other medium) is enabled. The next step is to be sure that the device falls in the boot order so that another device (such as the computer's hard disk) doesn't boot first.

The BIOS passes control of the boot process to the boot loader next. For Linux Live CDs, that typically means the Isolinux boot loader. With Isolinux, the user can type a boot label and options to control the boot process going forward. GRUB is another type of boot loader that is sometimes used with live Linux CDs (however, it is more often used to boot from hard disk).

After the selected label is booted, the Linux kernel takes over with the help of some drivers and commands made available from an initial RAM disk. The kernel and initial RAM disk represent the most basic components needed to mount the permanent file system structure, load the needed drivers, and begin the initialization of the system services.

For Knoppix, the next step is to run the `linuxrc` script. The `linuxrc` script, which is contained on the initial RAM disk, is responsible for mounting the file systems and loading the drivers needed to proceed to the next stage of the boot process.

System services are started next by way of the `init` process. The `init` process relies on the contents of the `/etc/inittab` file and run level directories for the current run level. For Knoppix, the default run level is 5. This means that the live CD is intended to boot up to a graphical desktop system.

Many of the features described in this chapter are common to many Linux systems. Some features are more specifically used on live CDs. The next chapter describes features such as file systems that are particularly useful to live CDs (squashfs and UnionFS) and boot loaders used to boot live CDs (Isolinux and, to a lesser extent, GRUB).

## CHAPTER 5

Looking Inside Live CD Components

Although many of the components you find in live CD systems are the same ones you find in installed Linux systems, some components are of particular interest to live CDs. Live Linux CDs are different than installed systems in these areas:

- **Boot loaders**—Isolinux (part of the Syslinux project) is the boot loader most often used with live CDs because it implements the El Torito standard, which most BIOSes understand, for booting from CD-ROM. Other boot loaders, such as GRUB or LILO, can be used as well but tend to be less popular for use with live Linux CDs.

- **File systems**—Issues related to file system types relate to the facts that live CDs are typically a read-only medium and that they have much more space limitations than a typical hard disk. The UnionFS file system type is an interesting file system type because it can be used to merge read-only and read/write file systems to enable you to save files in what would otherwise be a read-only environment on a live CD. Live Linux CDs such as Knoppix use UnionFS in tandem with file systems compressed for use with the cloop driver, allowing more than double the amount of software to be included on the live CD.

  The Squashfs file system has become a popular file system type because it compresses software in a way that it can be uncompressed on the fly. Live Fedora CDs created using Kadischi can incorporate file systems compressed with Squashfs.

After the live Linux CD boots up, the live CD often runs a script that does a lot of the magic needed to make it operational. Knoppix runs a `linuxrc` script, which mounts file systems, loads modules, and copies files that are needed. After that, the live CD typically passes control to the `init` process to start up the system processes. From that point forward, how services start and the ways that you use the system are very similar to the ways you would use a Linux system installed on your hard disk. The differences tend to relate to the Linux distribution on which the live CD is based.

Before you begin the process of remastering or putting together a live CD from scratch, it helps to understand some of the differences among the different Linux distributions used to create the live CD you are building:

- **Software packaging**—Although you can install software from tarballs (even building the software you want from source code, if you want), using software that is prepackaged for the Linux distribution on which your live Linux CD is based can save you some trouble. Packaging formats described in this book include RPM (for building Fedora CDs), Deb (for Debian, Knoppix, and other live CDs), and emerge (for Gentoo live CDs).

  Some live Linux CDs also have their own methods of installing software that are prepackaged for their own particular live CD. Damn Small Linux has a MyDSL feature that lets you install tarballs of software live and across reboots. SLAX lets you add software packaged as compressed modules to activate software on-the-fly.

- **Installers**—Instead of remastering an existing live CD, certain tools available with some Linux distributions enable you to use the installer that comes with the distribution to create a live CD. One example of this is the Kadischi project, which uses the anaconda installer that comes with Fedora and Red Hat Enterprise Linux to run through a fresh software installation that results in a live CD ISO image. Another example is the Gentoo Catalyst installer, which can likewise be used to create a live CD from scratch.

Use the topics covered in this chapter as background for the procedures for remastering or creating from scratch the different types of live CDs covered in the chapters that follow. The first section covers how to use boot loaders in live CDs.

USING BOOT LOADERS IN LIVE CDS

When the computer's BIOS is directed to boot from a live CD, the boot loader takes over. Most live Linux CDs use Isolinux as their boot loader. However, if you choose to use GRUB as your boot loader, you can choose different boot labels from a menu instead of typing in the label you want. The following sections describe how to use Isolinux and GRUB boot loaders with a live CD.

Using the Isolinux Boot Loader

Isolinux provides a lot of control over the boot process by allowing the user to enter different boot labels and options to control what image is booted and which features of that image are on or off. Isolinux is one of several projects in the Syslinux suite (http://syslinux.zytor.com) of boot loaders. The different Syslinux boot loaders differ based on the type of medium each is made to boot. The Syslinux boot loaders include the following:

- **Isolinux**—Used to boot ISO 9660 standard CD-ROMs. The Isolinux boot loader is the one most often used to boot live CDs and DVDs (or images made for those media).

- **Syslinux**—Used to boot MS-DOS and Windows FAT file systems. Often used to create a bootable floppy disk.

- **Pxelinux**—Used for booting a computer from a network server. Often Pxelinux boots a program (such as Nilo, http://nilo.sourceforge.net) that has been loaded as a PXE-compliant boot PROM on a network card.

- **Extlinux**—Used to boot from an ext2 or ext3 file system.

This book focuses on Isolinux because it is used for booting live CDs or similar removable media. What you need to know about Isolinux differs based on whether you are using a live Linux CD or creating your own live Linux CD:

- **Using an Isolinux live CD**—As someone booting a live Linux CD, you might just press Enter and forget about Isolinux completely. However, to boot the live CD in different ways, you can try different boot labels (defined using Isolinux features) and options. Often pressing a function key from the boot screen (F1, F2, F3, and so on) shows different boot labels and options.

  To see for yourself what boot labels and options can be chosen, you can refer to the isolinux.cfg file on the live CD (it's probably in the /boot/isolinux or /isolinux directories in the root of the live CD). Chapter 2, "Playing with Live Linux CDs," and Chapter 3, "Customizing a Live CD," describe some boot options used by different live CDs.

- **Building an Isolinux live CD**—If you are creating or remastering a live CD, you can set up Isolinux features to enable users to boot up your live CD in different ways. For example, you might set up labels to boot the live CD in different video modes or to start at different run levels. You might also add special labels to do such things as check your RAM (`memtest` command) or boot to a Linux installer instead of a live CD.

If you are building a live CD, Isolinux also enables you to control what the users see from the boot screen. Using Isolinux, you can incorporate an image that you choose on the splash screen. You can also create message screens on which you can place information that is useful to the person booting the live CD (such as boot options and licensing information).

The following describes different ways of configuring the Isolinux boot loader to direct the boot process of your live CD.

Understanding Isolinux

Isolinux is made to be compatible with the El Torito Bootable CD-ROM Format Specification (search for the `specscdrom.pdf` file at www.phoenix.com). That specification defines what a CD-ROM must include to be bootable and what a computer's BIOS needs to boot such a CD. Because the El Torito spec has been widely accepted since it was created in 1994, most PCs made in the past decade are capable of booting El Torito–compatible CDs and DVDs.

El Torito extends the ISO 9660 standard (which describes the format of data CD-ROMs) by identifying the location of a *boot record* volume descriptor that points to a *boot catalog*. The boot catalog contains information on available images that can be selected and booted.

Isolinux operates in the El Torito mode referred to as *no emulation* mode. This means that the computer executes the image without performing floppy emulation (which limits how much space you can access on the CD-ROM) or hard-disk emulation (which doesn't work on all BIOSes). Using "no emulation" mode lets you access the whole CD or DVD from the Isolinux boot loader. For example, accessing more than 8GB of compressed data on a DVD-9 is no problem.

Setting Up the isolinux Directory

Isolinux is designed to have the files it needs stored in a single directory on the live CD. Files in that directory can include kernels, initial RAM disks, message files, a splash screen, and related files. A boot catalog in the `isolinux` directory is inserted into the CD header to identify the available images. A configuration file also identifies available kernels and options.

To see some real-world implementations of Isolinux, you can look in the `/isolinux` or `/boot/isolinux` directories of a Linux live CD, such as Knoppix.

The Isolinux boot process keys off the isolinux.cfg file. Besides setting some options about the boot loader (such as how long to wait before timing out), this file contains one or more labels. Each label identifies the kernel file to run and options that are appended to that kernel.

Options identified in the isolinux.cfg file can include the location of the initial RAM disk, along with many options related to hardware issues. For example, Knoppix includes multiple labels that boot the same kernel, but in different video modes (including fb1280x1024, fb1024x768, and fb800x600 for using Frame Buffer mode at various video resolutions).

The following is part of the isolinux.cfg file that comes with Knoppix:

```
DEFAULT linux
APPEND ramdisk_size=100000 init=/etc/init lang=us apm=power-off
       vga=791 initrd=minirt.gz nomce quiet BOOT_IMAGE=knoppix
TIMEOUT 300
PROMPT 1
DISPLAY boot.msg
F1 boot.msg
F2 f2
F3 f3
LABEL knoppix
KERNEL linux
APPEND ramdisk_size=100000 init=/etc/init lang=us apm=power-off
       vga=791 initrd=minirt.gz nomce quiet BOOT_IMAGE=knoppix
LABEL expert
KERNEL linux
APPEND ramdisk_size=100000 init=/etc/init lang=us apm=power-off
       vga=791 initrd=minirt.gz nomce BOOT_IMAGE=expert
LABEL memtest
KERNEL memtest
APPEND initrd=
LABEL knoppix-txt
KERNEL linux
APPEND ramdisk_size=100000 init=/etc/init lang=us apm=power-off
     vga=normal initrd=minirt.gz nomce quiet BOOT_IMAGE=knoppix
LABEL debug
KERNEL linux
APPEND ramdisk_size=100000 init=/etc/init lang=us apm=power-off
     vga=normal initrd=minirt.gz debug BOOT_IMAGE=debug
LABEL fb1280x1024
KERNEL linux
APPEND ramdisk_size=100000 init=/etc/init lang=us apm=power-off
     vga=794 xmodule=fbdev initrd=minirt.gz nomce quiet
     BOOT_IMAGE=knoppix
```

The `isolinux.cfg` file is a plain-text file in either Linux (UNIX) or DOS formats. It contains a set of keywords and values to provide default settings and user options. Using the portions of the `isolinux.cfg` file that comes with Knoppix as an example, here are some ways that this file can control the boot process of a live CD.

- **Default boot command**—The DEFAULT line sets the default command line to run if the user simply presses Enter at the boot prompt (the Linux kernel with no options is run by default).

- **Boot timeout**—The TIMEOUT value of 300 causes the live CD to wait 30 seconds before automatically booting the default boot command. The value of TIMEOUT represents [1/10] of a second. A user can prevent the timeout from occurring by pressing any key from the keyboard after the boot prompt appears.

  The value TOTALTIMEOUT can be set instead to boot the default command after a set number of [1/10] seconds, regardless of whether the user pressed a key. Both TIMEOUT and TOTALTIMEOUT can be set to allow the user a short period of time to stop the default boot process (maybe 30 seconds), but ultimately just boot after a few minutes (maybe 5 minutes) if the user hasn't entered a command by that point.

- **Boot prompt**—Setting PROMPT 1 causes the boot: prompt to always be displayed from the Isolinux boot screen. By setting PROMPT to 0 instead, the prompt is displayed only when the user presses the Alt or Shift keys (or if the Caps Lock or Scroll Lock key is on).

  By setting the NOESCAPE flag to 1, you can disable the escapes just described. For example, if you set PROMPT 0 and then set NOESCAPE 1, the user has no way of entering anything to the boot prompt. As a result, the default boot command runs every time. This approach is good if you know the exact hardware environment you are using and don't want any user intervention in the boot process.

- **Initial boot screen**—The DISPLAY value points to the file whose contents are displayed as the initial boot screen. Often, as is the case with Knoppix and many others, the file reads in an image file that is displayed at the top of the boot screen. The upcoming section "Creating Boot Screens" describes the format you can use with this file.

- **Additional boot screens**—You can have ten boot screens in addition to the initial boot screen. Using the keywords F1, F2, F3, F4, F5, F6, F7, F8, and F9, you can assign a particular file to each function key of the same name. You can assign F0 to the F10 function key.

Usually, as is done with Knoppix, F1 is assigned to the same boot screen file (boot.msg) as is assigned to the DISPLAY keyword. In that way, the user can return to the original boot screen (by pressing F1) after visiting the other boot screens. The boot: prompt remains at the bottom of all boot screens, so the user can type in the desired label and options from any of those screens.

In the case of Knoppix, the content of the boot.msg file appears on the initial boot screen and when the F1 function key is pressed. The f2 and f3 files are assigned to the F1 and F2 function keys, respectively. For information on how these files are formatted, refer to the "Creating Boot Screens" section.

- **Boot labels**—The LABEL keyword identifies the string of characters that users type at the boot prompt if they don't want to use the default boot command. Often labels represent the name of the live CD (such as knoppix for Knoppix or ds1 for Damn Small Linux). Other boot labels, however, indicate special-purpose commands or settings that come with the live CD.

Typically at least two keywords follow each LABEL keyword. The KERNEL keyword identifies the image file containing the Linux kernel to boot for that label. For example, the file linux contains a bootable Linux kernel with Knoppix.

The other keyword typically used is APPEND. Any options added to the APPEND keyword are appended to the command indicated by KERNEL for the LABEL. Options that users type with the label at the boot prompt are added to the end of the APPEND options.

Some of the options added to an APPEND line direct how the kernel boots, while other options are passed along and consumed at different points in the boot process. For example, the initrd=minirt.gz option tells the boot kernel to use the minirt.gz file as the initial RAM disk. The BOOT_IMAGE option tells the linuxrc script (which is run after the kernel boots) what mode to start in.

NOTE

You might notice that an APPEND line near the beginning of the isolinux.cfg file is not associated with a LABEL. Options attached to this APPEND keyword are set as global defaults. Those options are appended to the KERNEL for any LABEL that doesn't have its own APPEND line. To avoid using the global APPEND options for a particular KERNEL line, you must add an APPEND - line after that KERNEL line.

Boot labels shown in the previous Knoppix example include knoppix, expert, memtest, knoppix-txt, debug, and fb1280x1024. These labels, described in the upcoming section "Creating Different Boot Labels," can be used to boot Knoppix in text mode (knoppix-txt), debug mode (debug), or with special video settings (fb1280x1024). A label also can be used to run a different command altogether (such as the memtest label, which runs the memtest command for checking your system RAM).

- **Capability to run from a serial port**—In most cases these days, you would expect a computer running a live CD to have a monitor available that supports VGA. However, Isolinux can also boot on a computer that uses a dumb character terminal that connects to a serial port as its console instead of a graphics display.

  To have your live CD work on a computer with the console connected to the computer's serial port, you must add a SERIAL line as the first entry in your isolinux.cfg file. For example, to use a dumb terminal (with a null modem cable, no flow control or RS-232 status signals) connected to the COM1 port (/dev/ttyS0 in Linux) of the computer running your live CD, add the following to the beginning of your isolinux.cfg file:
  SERIAL 0

  By default, parameters for the serial port are hard-coded to 8 bits, 1 stop bit, and no parity. The connection defaults to a 9600bps baud rate and no flow control. However, if you want to change baud rate and flow control, you can add them as options to the SERIAL line. To get the flow-control features you want, you need to combine the bits associated with those features. Table 5-1 shows the hex values for flow-control features.

  The Isolinux project recommends several flow-control values you might want to use, other than the default (0) of no flow control. For null modem cable detection, use 0x303. Use 0x023 for DTR/DSR flow control or 0x083 for DTR/DCD flow control. For RTS/CTS flow control, you can use 0x013 or 0x813 (with the latter adding modem input).

  For example, you might want to change the baud rate to 14400bps and the flow control to 0xab3. The 0xab3 would include all values needed for RS-232 compliance (marked with asterisks in Table 5-1). For this example, the SERIAL line (as the first line in you isolinux.cfg file) would appear as follows:
  SERIAL 0 14400 0xab3

When you set out to create the isolinux.cfg file and related boot files for your own live CD, you should keep some issues in mind:

TABLE 5.1 Hex Values for Flow Control Options on Serial Terminals

FLOW-CONTROL FEATURE	VALUE NEEDED	HEX FOR RS-232?
Assert DTR	0x001	*
Assert RTS	0x002	*
Wait for CTS assertion	0x010	*
Wait for DSR assertion	0x020	*
Wait for RI assertion	0x040	
Wait for DCD assertion	0x080	*
Ignore input unless CTS asserted	0x100	
Ignore input unless DSR asserted	0x200	*
Ignore input unless RI asserted	0x400	
Ignore input unless DCD asserted	0x800	*

- **Comments**—To add comments to the `isolinux.cfg` file, simply add a pound sign (#) to the beginning of a line you want to be a comment.

- **File and label names**—It is safest when creating filenames in the `isolinux` directory and label names in the `isolinux.cfg` file to use DOS file-naming restrictions. Although Isolinux can mangle DOS filenames, if you use more than eight characters with a three-character extension, you run some risk of having nonunique names.

- **Restricting options**—Using the ALLOWOPTIONS 0 keyword and value, you can prevent users from entering any options to the kernel they boot from the boot prompt. This can be useful for locking down the behavior of a live CD for a kiosk or similar use.

- **Error conditions**—If error conditions occur when you boot the live CD kernel image, you can set up Isolinux to respond in some way. If you require the user to respond to the boot prompt, you can set the ONTIMEOUT keyword to a kernel and options to run if the timeout value is reached (pressing Enter still triggers the default). In case the requested kernel isn't found, the value of ONERROR can be set to a different command and options to run.

The following sections describe ways in which you can modify the isolinux.cfg file and associated kernels, boot screens, and other items to steer the boot process of your own live CD.

Creating Boot Screens

To present information related to your live CD before it even boots up, Isolinux lets you create an initial boot screen and up to ten other boot screens, accessible to the user by pressing function keys. Although the environment for presenting the boot screens is fairly rudimentary at that point, the boot screens can display the following:

- **Text**—Add text describing your live CD, boot options, licensing, and other important information.
- **Colors**—Display your text and background in any of 16 different colors.
- **Images**—Import image files (created in a special format) that can include up to 16 colors and be up to 640×480 pixels.

Any of the boot screen files you create can contain plain text in DOS or UNIX (Linux) format. If no formatting is entered, text is displayed as white characters on a black background. However, by adding certain control codes, you can change colors, include graphics, or clear the screen.

Entering control codes into a plain-text file can be a bit tricky. If you are editing a text file with the vi or vim command, you can enter a control code by pressing the Ctrl key along with the V key. After that, you can enter the control code you want. For example, to add a Ctrl+X (so you can add an image to a boot screen), you would type Ctrl+V, Ctrl+X while you are in input mode. The result should look like the following:

^X

The following examples describe how you can add different features to your Isolinux boot screens:

- **Changing colors**—To change to any of 16 different colors (4bpp) on your boot screen, you can use Ctrl+O (that's the letter O) to indicate the foreground and background colors to use. Each color is represented by a single hexadecimal digit (0 to 9 and a to f). Table 5-2 lists the available colors.

  For example, to assign a dark red background and white lettering (while editing a boot screen file in the vi editor), you could type Ctrl+V, Ctrl+O, 4, f. The resulting characters in the file would appear as follows:

  ^04f

TABLE 5-2 Add Background and Foreground Text Colors to an Isolinux
Boot Screen

Hexadecimal Digit	Color	Hexadecimal Digit	Color
0	Black	8	Dark gray
1	Dark blue	9	Bright blue
2	Dark green	a	Bright green
3	Dark cyan	b	Bright cyan
4	Dark red	c	Bright red
5	Dark purple	d	Bright purple
6	Brown	e	Yellow
7	Light gray	f	White

Notice that the darker colors are assigned to numbers 0 through 7. Lighter
colors are assigned to 8 and 9, and a through f. To cause the foreground
color to flash, pick a dark color for the foreground and a light color for the
background.

■ **Adding an image**—Assuming that the boot screen where your live CD
will eventually run has a VGA display available, you can add an image to
any of the boot screens. Display mode for the image is 640×480 and 16
colors. Also, the image must be in a simple Run Length Encoding (RLE)
format, referred to as Syslinux SLL16 format. The `syslinux` package includes
the `ppmtolss16` command, which lets you convert an image file from PPM
to SLL16.

Although the available display is 640×480 pixels, when you create your
image, you will not want it to consume the entire 480 pixels so that there is
room for other information. That information typically tells you how to boot
the live CD or find other boot options.

For example, in the `isolinux.cfg` file for Damn Small Linux (DSL), the file
`boot.msg` is identified as the initial boot screen (`DISPLAY` keyword). The following is the content of the `boot.msg` file:

```
^017^L^Xlogo.16
DSL is based on Knoppix Debian GNU Linux Technology.
Press <enter> to begin, F2 and F3 for boot options.
```

The information in boot.msg starts by setting the screen colors (^O). It sets the background color to dark blue (1) and the foreground color to light gray (7). It then identifies the image file (^X) as the file logo.16. That file is a 640×400–pixel in SLL16 format that is available with the other files in the isolinux directory.

The rest of the text in the boot.msg file appears after the image. Then the boot prompt (boot:) automatically is appended at the bottom of the page. Figure 5-1 shows the initial DSL boot screen, created from the contents of the boot.msg file.

FIGURE 5-1 DSL uses Isolinux to include a graphic on its initial boot screen.

To add an image to a boot screen (also called a splash screen) from your own live CD, you need to create an image that will fit on the 640×480 display. You must save that image to include only 16 colors and be in PPM format. Then you can use the ppmtolss16 command to convert the image to the proper format.

Keep in mind that the image will need to look good at 640-pixel width and 16 colors. (You will notice a loss of quality as you go through this process on an image with many more colors.) Also, if you are trying to keep file sizes low, the less busy the image is, the more efficiently the ppmtolss16 command will be capable of compressing it.

To run the following procedure, you need to be on a system that includes the GIMP and has the `syslinux` package installed (so you have the `ppmtolss16` command available). Knoppix works fine for this case. Here's an example of how to create an image for your boot screen using the GIMP image-manipulation program:

1. Acquire an image you want to use for your boot screen. You can start with any image format that the GIMP can read.

2. Open the image in GIMP (look on the Graphics menu for most Linux desktop systems to launch the GIMP).

3. Scale the image to fit inside the 640×480 boundary (as noted earlier, 640×400 or similar enables you to include extra text) by selecting Image → Scale Image. Try resizing the width to 640; the height adjusts automatically (provided that the two numbers are locked together).

4. Convert the image to use only 16 colors by selecting Image → Mode → Indexed. Under the Colormap section of the Indexed Color Conversion screen that pops up, select Generate Optimum Palette and choose 16 for Maximum Number of Colors.

5. Save the image as a PPM file by selecting File → Save As. When prompted to name the file, name it with a `.ppm` extension and choose Select File Type (By Extension) to have the image saved as a PPM file. For example, you might save the file as `mylogo.ppm`. To avoid naming problems, be sure to keep the filename to eight characters or less, with an extension of up to three characters.

6. Open a shell and change to the directory containing the image you just created. Next, use the `ppmtolss16` command to convert the image to the RLE format. The command itself (`/usr/bin/ppmtolss16`) is a Perl script. You can open that script in a text editor to read about the file format and the processing the script does. Here's an example of using the command to convert the image file just created (`mylogo.ppm`) to an image file you can use with Isolinux on your boot screen (`mylogo.rle`):

```
# ppmtolss16 < mylogo.ppm > mylogo.rle
244480 pixels, 27018 bytes, (77.90% compression)
```

7. Copy the file you just created (`mylogo.rle`) to the `isolinux` directory where you are building or remastering your live CD.

8. Edit the boot screen file that is being used for your initial boot screen (or any other boot screen associated with a function key) so it includes your

image file. For example, if you are simply remastering DSL or Knoppix, edit the `boot.msg` file and change `logo.16` to `mylogo.rle`.

■ **Returning to text mode**—To have a screen that contains only text, you can start by telling Isolinux to switch to text mode. A text-only screen is useful for such things as showing boot options or displaying licensing information. With text-only screens, you can still change foreground and background colors as you like. To go to text mode, use Ctrl+Y.

The following line changes the screen to text mode (^Y), sets the background to dark blue and the foreground to light gray (^017), and then clears the screen and home the cursor (^L).

```
^Y^017^L
```

After that, you can begin entering text as you like. Keep your text lines under 80 characters so they don't wrap on most displays.

Creating Different Boot Labels

Adding different boot labels to your `isolinux.cfg` file is one technique for helping those who use your live CD get it running properly. Although the default label that usually launches your live CD is the mode that you expect to be used (for example, to a KDE desktop or to a shell), you can use alternate labels for some of the following cases:

■ **Check memory**—Instead of running a Linux kernel, a particular label might run a different command altogether. For example, some live CDs use the `memtest` label to run the `memtest` command. This is a good way to determine how much RAM is available and how much of it is working properly. With the `memtest` command in the `isolinux` directory, the following label is used in Knoppix to start that command:

```
LABEL memtest
KERNEL memtest
APPEND initrd=
```

In this case, the `memtest` command runs when the `memtest` label is typed at the boot prompt. No initial RAM disk is needed, so the `APPEND` line is basically blank.

■ **Run in selected video modes**—Because an inability to get the X display server working properly can be a great challenge in some cases, often a live CD offers specific labels so the CD can run in particular video modes. Video for many laptops works in framebuffer mode. You can set different framebuffer specifications using the `vga` option. For example, `vga=769` sets a very basic framebuffer console (640×480 with 256 colors). Table 5-3 shows a list of available video modes.

TABLE 5-3 Indicate Video Depth, Colors, and Resolution with the vga= Option

DEPTH	COLORS	640×480	800×600	1024×768	1280×1024	1600×1200
8-bit	256	769	771	773	775	796
15-bit	32,768	784	787	790	793	797
16-bit	65,536	785	788	791	794	798
24-bit	16,800,000	786	789	792	795	799

In Knoppix, separate labels exist for different framebuffer modes. For example, the following label (fb1024x768) starts Knoppix with vga=791. This sets the screen resolution to 1024×768 and colors to 16-bit color (65,000 colors). This is a listing of that label:

```
LABEL fb1024x768
KERNEL linux
APPEND ramdisk_size=100000 init=/etc/init lang=us apm=power-off vga=791
       xmodule=fbdev initrd=minirt.gz nomce quiet BOOT_IMAGE=knoppix
```

The xmodule value is set to fbdev and vga is set to 791. In Knoppix, other fb labels (fb800x600, fb1280x1024, and so on) are set to different vga values. To have the user prompted for a mode, you can set vga=ask instead.

You can set other xmodule values as well, depending on which drivers your kernel supports. In Knoppix, open-source drivers exist for ATI (ati), Radeon (radeon), Savage (savage or s3), NVIDIA (nv), and Intel i810 (i810) chipsets.

If you are remastering a live CD, another option is to add video drivers from NVIDIA or ATI. Because these drivers are not open source, they are not available with most Linux distributions. However, you can add those drivers to your live CD for private use because they are distributed freely from NVIDIA and ATI.

A few other issues relate to LABEL lines. If a user types the LABEL name at the boot prompt, followed by one or more options, those options are appended to the end of the options listed on the APPEND line. If a LABEL has no APPEND line, the APPEND keyword at the beginning of isolinux.cfg is used to provide global options. To not use the global options, you can add an APPEND line followed by a dash (APPEND -).

- **Labels for failsafe and debug**—If your live CD won't boot, it's nice to provide the live CD user with labels that include failsafe and debug options. A failsafe label might be used to start a Linux kernel with many features disabled that might be causing the boot to fail (options such as nodma, noscsi, nousb, nofirewire, and so on) that then drops you to a shell instead of a desktop.

  Using a debug label, where the debug option is added to the APPEND line, you can see many more messages relating to the live CD startup, so you can figure out what is causing any problems that occur during the boot process.

Other Files in the isolinux Directory

Depending on how you set up your live CD boot configuration, the files you have in your isolinux directory (or boot/isolinux directory) will vary. By way of a quick checklist, you need to have these files in your isolinux directory before you can build your live CD:

- **Boot image (El Torito)**—Copy the isolinux.bin file to the isolinux (or boot/isolinux) directory where you are creating your live CD. On a Fedora system, the file is located in /usr/lib/syslinux. This file contains the El Torito boot image that the mkisofs command uses when you are making the live CD ISO image. When the ISO image is created, a pointer is placed in the image header to point to isolinux.bin. The isolinux.bin image must be 1200K, 1400K, or 2800K in size.

  You can create your own isolinux.bin file as you would create a boot floppy. In fact, you can simply copy the contents of a boot floppy to your isolinux directory and use it. For example, you could place a boot floppy into the floppy drive and type the following:

  ```
  # dd if=/dev/fd0 of=isolinux.bin bs=10k count=144
  ```

  You don't need to name the file isolinux.bin. However, any name you use you must identify with the -b option when you run the mkisofs command.

- **Boot catalog**—El Torito requires a boot catalog file (usually boot.cat). The mkisofs command creates this file automatically, so you don't have to worry about creating this file. However, you must identify its name and location using the -c option when you run the mkisofs command.

- **Isolinux configuration file**—The isolinux.cfg file must be created and stored in the isolinux directory, as described earlier in this chapter.

- **Boot screen files**—Files containing the initial boot screen and any boot screens you make accessible using function keys F1 through F10 need to be added to the isolinux directory. Knoppix uses boot.msg to contain information for the initial boot screen (and also when pressing the F1 function key).

It uses files named f2 and f3 to create boot screens available by pressing the F2 and F3 function keys, respectively. You can name these files anything you like (although a limit of 8 characters with a 3-character extension used with DOS file names is recommended). To enable them, however, you need to identify them in the isolinux.cfg file.

- **Graphics file**—If you incorporate a graphical image (of the special format described earlier in this chapter), you need to place it in the isolinux directory. Knoppix calls this file logo.16, but other bootable CDs call this image splash.lss.

- **Kernel**—The isolinux directory must contain a kernel (often named kernel) that is identified on the KERNEL lines in the isolinux.cfg file.

- **Initial RAM disk**—An initial RAM disk file must be placed in the isolinux directory. In Knoppix, this file is named minirt.gz and is identified using the initrd option (initrd=minirtgz) on the APPEND line for each LABEL that requires it.

  An initial RAM disk is mounted as the root file system for the kernel that's started by the boot loader. It contains commands and modules that the initial kernel might need at this early stage of the boot process. When the real root file system is available to be mounted, the initial RAM disk file system is unmounted.

- **Other executables**—You can include multiple kernels or other executables to launch as identified on the KERNEL line for each LABEL. The memtest command is an executable that is often included with live CDs.

When all the files you need are in the isolinux directory, that directory can be joined up with the file system to be used with the live CD. Then you build ISO images from those files using the mkisofs command (as described in Appendix B, "Building, Testing, and Burning ISOs").

Using the GRUB Boot Loader for a Live CD

The Grand Unified Bootloader (GRUB) is the most popular boot loader used to boot Linux systems that are installed to hard disk. Its popularity stems from the fact that it can boot a wide range of computer operating systems, plus it understands different file systems and kernel executables (so GRUB can boot using the name of the kernel, instead of needing to know where the kernel is physically located on the disk).

GRUB's flexibility also extends to its user interface. Command-line and menu interfaces are available with GRUB. As a developer, you can change the look of the boot screens by adding your own images. As a user, you can edit boot labels before launching the selected operating system.

Configuring GRUB centers on the grub.conf file. Like the isolinux.cfg file used with Isolinux, grub.conf can set a variety of options, followed by specific labels that represent the operating systems GRUB can boot. The grub.conf file is a plain-text file that you can edit with any text editor.

From a live CD point of view, GRUB comes with an El Torito–compatible stage2 boot file. That boot file is placed with other GRUB-related files in the /boot directory. The location of this boot file (called stage2_eltorito) is identified on the mkisofs command line when you go to produce the ISO image for your live CD.

To illustrate how GRUB can be used as the boot loader for a live CD, the following steps describe how to remaster a Knoppix live CD to use GRUB. The steps were done on a Fedora system that had the grub package installed and the contents of a Knoppix CD copied to the /knoppix/master directory. If you are using a different Linux system, you need to get the grub package for your system or download it from the GNU GRUB site (www.gnu.org/software/grub).

1. From the root of the directory where you are remastering Knoppix (it should contain several autorun files, as well as boot/ and KNOPPIX/ directories), make a grub directory. For example, if your remaster directory is /knoppix/master, you would type the following:

```
# cd /knoppix/master
# mkdir -p boot/grub
```

2. Copy the stage2_eltorito file to the grub directory as follows:

```
# cp /usr/share/grub/i386-redhat/stage2_eltorito boot/grub
```

3. Copy the files you want from the isolinux directory. I chose to use the kernel file (linux), the initial RAM disk (minirt.gz), and the memtest command (memtest):

```
# cd /knoppix/master/boot/isolinux
# cp linux minirt.gz memtest ../grub
```

4. Next, you can create your own splash screen to use as the background for the GRUB menu when you first boot the live CD. For the background, you can use an XPM image that is 640×480, has a 14-color palette, and is compressed with gzip. You can use GIMP to convert your image to this size or use the convert command. This example converts a JPEG image to one that can be used on a GRUB splash screen:

```
# convert -colors 14 -resize 640x480 mypic.jpg mysplash.xpm
# gzip mysplash.xpm
# cp mysplash.xpm /knoppix/master/boot/grub
```

5. Create a grub.conf file in the boot/grub directory, using any text editor. I got many of the options used here from the isolinux.cfg file that comes with Knoppix:

```
default=0
timeout=10
splashimage=(cd)/boot/grub/mysplash.xpm.gz
title KNOPPIX 5
  root (cd)
  kernel /boot/grub/linux ramdisk_size=100000
    init=/etc/init lang=us apm=power-off vga=791
    nomce quiet BOOT_IMAGE=knoppix
  initrd /boot/grub/minirt.gz
title KNOPPIX 5 expert
  root (cd)
  kernel /boot/grub/linux ramdisk_size=100000
    init=/etc/init lang=us apm=power-off vga=791
    nomce BOOT_IMAGE=knoppix
  initrd /boot/grub/minirt.gz
title KNOPPIX 5 knoppix-txt
  kernel /boot/grub/linux ramdisk_size=100000
    init=/etc/init lang=us apm=power-off vga=normal
    quiet nomce BOOT_IMAGE=knoppix
  initrd /boot/grub/minirt.gz
title MEMTEST
  root (cd)
  kernel /boot/grub/memtest
```

The default line indicates which entry to boot by default (after the timeout expires). With default=0 set, the first title (KNOPPIX 5) is booted by default. The timeout is set to 10 seconds (pressing any key from the splash screen prevents the timeout). The splashimage value indicates that the image file that will appear behind the GRUB menu (created earlier in this procedure) is located at /boot/grub/mysplash.xpm.gz on the CD.

A title label indicates each boot entry. For this example, I simply re-created a few of the entries from the isolinux.cfg file for Knoppix. I put the APPEND boot options from that file on the line with each kernel (the options should all be on the kernel line, although they are shown as indented here). So the kernel is linux and the initial RAM disk is minirt.gz. I also added an entry to run the memtest command.

This example shows just a few of the neat features in GRUB. You can find more options by typing **info grub** on a Linux system where GRUB is installed.

6. Assuming that you have remastered Knoppix (or other live CD) the way you like, you can now create the ISO image of your live CD. This is an example of a mkisofs command you can use, using the example we created to this point:

```
# cd /knoppix/master
# mkisofs -R -b boot/grub/stage2_eltorito \
    -no-emul-boot -boot-load-size 4 \
    -boot-info-table . -o ../knoppix.iso
```

In this example, mkisofs creates a boot image (knoppix.iso in the /knoppix directory) from the current directory (notice the dot on the last line). The -b option indicates the location of the El Torito boot image added earlier. The ISO image (knoppix.iso) is created in no emulation mode (-no-emul-boot) and -boot-load-size is 4 (meaning that four 512-byte sectors are used). The -boot-info-table option inserts a 56-byte boot information table into the boot file (indicated by the -b option). (See Appendix B for more information on the mkisofs command.)

You should now be able to test your knoppix.iso by burning it to a CD and booting it or by using an emulator (such as qemu). Figure 5-2 shows an example of the GRUB boot screen I created using the previous procedure.

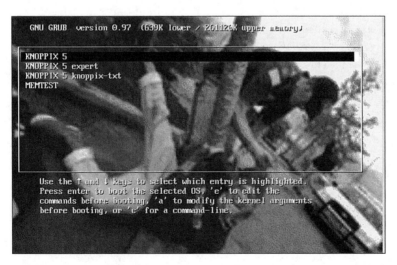

FIGURE 5-2 Add your own image to the GRUB boot screen and boot from a menu.

In this example, you can see the background image (a war protestor in Washington state) behind the GRUB menu. You can use arrow keys to move among the five menu items, and then press Enter to boot the selected item. By pressing the E key on an item, you display and edit that item (to either add or remove boot options). Press Esc to return to previous screens. Then press B to boot the selected entry.

The menu interface shown previously appears by default with GRUB. However, you can choose instead to have a command-line interface (a grub shell) or a hidden menu interface (where you see a graphic and must press a key before the timeout to see the menu). Add hiddenmenu on a line by itself to hide the menu interface.

To go to a grub shell from the menu, press the C key. To see available commands from the grub shell, type help. To return to the menu, type **reboot**.

UNDERSTANDING FILE SYSTEMS FOR LIVE CDS

A live Linux CD can include and access any type of file system that Linux supports (ext2, ext3, reiserfs, VFAT, and so on). However, two facts about operating systems that run from read-only, limited-space environments (as live CD-ROMs do) make it useful to include special kinds of file systems:

- **Read-only**—A CD-ROM itself cannot (in most cases) be written to again after the image has been burned on it. Because the file system used by the live CD is stored on the CD itself, you can't just save and modify files from that file system as you would on file systems stored on a hard disk.

  Ways to get around the problem of running from a read-only medium include loading the entire file system into RAM (which might not be reasonable with a 700MB live CD) and having only selected directories available from RAM (such as home and temporary directories). The second solution, however, might not allow you to install software that needs to reside in multiple directories.

  The special file system type that can be used to deal with the read-only problem is called UnionFS. Using UnionFS, read-only and read/write file-system branches can be combined to appear as one file system to the end user. As a result, the previously read-only file system looks like a read/write file system to the user. When the user tries to change or add files to the file system, those changes are actually stored on the read/write branch.

- **Limited space**—Compressed file systems can be used to allow more data to be saved on live CDs. Knoppix has used the create_compressed_fs command to create a compressed cloop-compatible version of its file-system image. When Knoppix is running, the cloop module decompresses files as needed on-the-fly. This allows nearly 2GB of compressed data to be on a 700MB CD.

Another way of doing file system compression on live CDs is with the Squashfs file system. Using Squashfs, directories, files, and even inodes are compressed (including files up to 4GB). It can provide greater compression than some other compressed file-system types by supporting block sizes of up to 64K. Kadischi enables you to create Squashfs file systems when you produce live CDs of Fedora or Red Hat Enterprise Linux.

The following sections describe some details on UnionFS, Squashfs, and the cloop driver.

Using the UnionFS File System

UnionFS (www.unionfs.org) is referred to as a stackable unification file system. When it is implemented on a live CD, it allows a combination of read-only and read/write branches to be joined to form a single file-system view to an end user. This enables end users to write to directories containing data from read-only live CDs in a way that the entire file system appears to be writeable.

With UnionFS, changed and added data is actually written to a writeable file-system branch, which can be stored on a separate medium from the read-only medium. With the new data stored separately, it can be used during the current session and even can be backed up so it can be restored the next time the live CD is booted.

More than two dozen live CD projects (most notably, Knoppix and its derivatives) incorporate UnionFS file systems. Earlier versions of these projects tended to have areas that could be written to (such as /home and /tmp directories) that were separate from directories taken from the live CD. Now, with UnionFS enabled at the root of the file system, files can be changed and added anywhere (given proper Linux file permissions). This greatly simplifies the capability to mix content from the live CD with new content, such as software installed from standard packages.

NOTE

As a quick aside, UnionFS has other uses beyond live CDs. For example, UnionFS can be used to merge multiple archives of music, images, or video so they can be accessed from a single point in the file system. Likewise, home directories from different disk partitions or networked file systems can be merged to form a single home directory structure.

To use UnionFS on a Linux live CD or other Linux system, UnionFS support must be added (it is not part of the basic Linux kernel). You can get the latest

UnionFS software (it's actively being developed) from a UnionFS mirror site (for example, ftp://unionfs-mirror.linux-live.org/unionfs).

To see how UnionFS is used in Knoppix, boot up Knoppix and type the following:

```
# mount |grep -i union
/UNIONFS on /UNIONFS type unionfs (rw,dirs=/ramdisk=rw:
    /KNOPPIX=ro:/KNOPPIX2=ro.delete=whiteout)
```

In this example, the /UNIONFS mount point consists of a union of three branches. The /KNOPPIX and /KNOPPIX2 branches are read-only. The /ramdisk branch is a writeable tmpfs file system, stored in RAM. With UnionFS file systems, the leftmost writeable branch holds changes to any files in that file system. In this case, because there is only one writeable branch (/ramdisk), all changes are stored on /ramdisk.

To use the files and directories from the combined /UNIONFS file system, Knoppix sets up symbolic links from directories in /UNIONFS to their rightful places in the file system. To get a sense of how this is done, you can list the directories in the root of the file system:

```
# ls -ld /* | less
drwxr-xr-x  23 root root  4096 Feb 23 07:44 /KNOPPIX
dr-xr-xr-x   5 root root  2048 Feb 26 07:57 /KNOPPIX2
drwxrwxrwt  31 root root   140 Jun 20 06:35 /UNIONFS
lrwxrwxrwx   1 root root    12 Jun 20 02:34 /bin -> /UNIONFS/bin
lrwxrwxrwx   1 root root    13 Jun 20 02:34 /boot -> /UNIONFS/boot
dr-xr-xr-x   1 root root  2048 Feb 21 23:33 /cdrom
drwxr-xr-x  15 root root 13740 Jun 20 06:35 /dev
lrwxrwxrwx   1 root root    12 Jun 20 02:35 /dvb -> /UNIONFS/dvb
lrwxrwxrwx   1 root root    12 Jun 20 02:34 /etc -> /UNIONFS/etc
lrwxrwxrwx   1 root root    15 Jun 20 02:35 /floppy -> /UNIONFS/floppy
lrwxrwxrwx   1 root root    13 Jun 20 02:34 /home -> /ramdisk/home
lrwxrwxrwx   1 root root    15 Jun 20 02:35 /initrd -> /UNIONFS/initrd
lrwxrwxrwx   1 root root    12 Jun 20 02:34 /lib -> /UNIONFS/lib
drwxr-xr-x  10 root root  1024 Jun 20 06:35 /media
drwxr-xr-x   2 root root  1024 Jun 20 06:35 /mnt
lrwxrwxrwx   1 root root    13 Jun 20 02:35 /none -> /UNIONFS/none
lrwxrwxrwx   1 root root    12 Jun 20 02:35 /opt -> /UNIONFS/opt
dr-xr-xr-x  75 root root     0 Jun 20 02:34 /proc
drwxrwxrwt   7 root root   160 Jun 20 06:57 /ramdisk
lrwxrwxrwx   1 root root    13 Jun 20 02:35 /root -> /UNIONFS/root
lrwxrwxrwx   1 root root    13 Jun 20 02:34 /sbin -> /UNIONFS/sbin
drwxr-xr-x  10 root root     0 Jun 20 02:34 /sys
lrwxrwxrwx   1 root root    12 Jun 20 02:34 /tmp -> /ramdisk/tmp
lrwxrwxrwx   1 root root    12 Jun 20 02:35 /usr -> /UNIONFS/usr
lrwxrwxrwx   1 root root    12 Jun 20 02:34 /var -> /UNIONFS/var
```

Looking at this listing (which I edited somewhat to save space), you can see that most directories in root (/) are linked to /UNIONFS directories. This enables you to combine the read-only files from the live CD with any changes you make to, for example, install software or change configuration files in /etc. Notice that /tmp and /home exist only on /ramdisk because they don't need to be joined with files from the live CD. Also notice that directories associated with system functions (such as /dev, /proc, and /sys) are not associated with a UnionFS file system.

When files are deleted, UnionFS can be set to either delete the files physically or mask out the real file using what is called whiteout mode. Whiteout is used in this case. Whiteout files are indicated by .wh files in the writeable branch. For example, type **ls -a /ramdisk/etc** to see files that have been deleted or replaced in the /etc directory.

If you want to further control UnionFS file systems, you can try the unionctl command. For example, to list the branches of an existing UnionFS file system, you could use the –list option as follows:

```
# unionctl /UNIONFS –list
    /ramdisk (rw-)
    /KNOPPIX (r-)
    /KNOPPIX2 (r-)
```

You can see from this example that /UNIONFS is a union of the /ramdisk, /KNOP-PIX, and /KNOPPIX2 directories. Permission on a branch can be read/write (rw-), read-only (r-), or read-only for an NFS file system (r-n). You can also use unionctl to add (–add), remove (–remove) or change the read/write mode (–mode) of a branch.

Using the Cloop Driver

Cloop is a technology used by some live CDs, such as Knoppix, to compress a supported Linux file system so that it can be uncompressed on-the-fly later when the live CD is used. To compress the file system, the create_compressed_fs command is used. To uncompress data as it is requested, the cloop driver (which needs to be added to the Linux kernel) is used.

Using cloop technology, you can more than double the amount of software and data you can get on a live CD. For example, the KNOPPIX file-system image that consumes less than 700MB on a Knoppix CD holds more than 1.7GB of data. The 1.8GB KNOPPIX image on a Knoppix DVD holds about 4.5GB of data. As you can see, using cloop compression, you can have about 2.5 times the amount of software available on your live CD than you would if it were not compressed.

If you have remastered Knoppix (as described in Chapter 6, "Building a Custom Knoppix Live CD"), you have probably already used the create_compressed_fs command. With your remastered Knoppix file system completed and gathered into an ISO image, you run this command to compress that image so that the cloop driver can access it later. As shown in Chapter 6, you often can just pipe the output of the mkisofs command to the create_compressed_fs command to create the compressed image named KNOPPIX.

When the live CD goes to use the compressed image when the live CD boots, the compressed image is mounted using a cloop device. For example, in Knoppix, the /KNOPPIX/KNOPPIX file on the CD is mounted on /KNOPPIX of the running live CD, using the /dev/cloop0 device. As files are requested from that image, they are uncompressed individually. Because accessing the CD drive tends to be more of a bottleneck than the processing required to uncompress the files, using the cloop driver adds little or no overhead to the process.

Because the cloop driver is maintained by Klaus Knopper as part of the Knoppix project, you can get the source code for cloop the same place you can find Knoppix source code (at www.knopper.net/knoppix/sources).

Using the Squashfs File System

The Squashfs file system type (http://squashfs.sourceforge.net) is a read-only file system, primarily designed for archival backups. Because Squashfs was designed for low-overhead environments, it can work well on embedded systems or, as is our interest, live CDs.

Because Squashfs was created for Linux systems, it supports many Linux features that might not be found in other compressed file system types. It stores complete user ID and group ID (32-bit) information and creation time. Large files (2^{64} bytes) and file systems (2^{64} bytes) are supported. Likewise, directory and inode data can be efficiently compressed. Some people claim that they can get about to 50% compression using Squashfs.

Squashfs support is available when you create live Fedora Linux CDs (using Kadischi). Developers on the Kadischi project have discussed adding extended attributes (xattr) to Squashfs so that Fedora live CDs will ultimately be capable of supporting security features from SELinux.

CHOOSING AN APPROACH TO CREATING YOUR OWN LIVE CD

When you create live CDs based on Linux systems, you have access to literally thousands of open-source software applications and utilities. In most cases, you are free to use and distribute the software from these projects as you like, as long as you adhere to the terms of the GPL or similar license. Most of those terms have to do with not restricting other people's access to that code.

When you are ready to begin building your own live CD, you can start from scratch or you can start with an existing Linux distribution. Starting with an existing distribution offers many advantages:

- **Prepackaged software**—One feature that sets different Linux distributions apart is the way that software is packaged for each distribution. Although you can usually get software directly from the software project that made it, most of the popular software projects already have been compiled, packaged, and tested for the major Linux distributions.

  The three distributions illustrated in this book (Knoppix/Debian, Fedora, and Gentoo) each use a specific packaging format. Because Knoppix is based on Debian GNU/Linux, you can add precompiled .deb software packages that match your particular distribution's release. Fedora can include packages in RPM format that are maintained in Fedora Core or Fedora Extras, or from third-party sources. Gentoo maintains packages using the Portage packaging system.

- **Software tools and repositories**—To maintain consistency among the software you install on a particular distribution, Linux distributions set up software repositories that contains thousands of packages. Each distribution also includes tools for installing and managing software.

  For Debian, the dpkg system was created to manage software that was packaged into .deb format. Later, APT utilities came along to point installation requests at software repositories on the Internet. Gentoo uses the emerge command, along with other Portage tools, to let you grab, compile, and install any of about 10,000 packages from Internet repositories

  Fedora and other Red Hat–sponsored Linux systems package software in RPM format (.rpm). To build live CDs, you can use the same anaconda installer used to install Fedora to hard disk, but have the result be a live CD ISO image instead. Typically, you copy the RPM packages to hard disk to create the live CD. However, anaconda and other software tools in Fedora have moved toward supporting online repositories that are constructed for use with the yum utility. So, in other words, you can build a live CD entirely from software repositories outside of the local system.

Before we launch into a description of the software tools just mentioned (and how to use them when you are creating your own live CDs), I want to mention a few other approaches to gathering the software you want and building live CDs that are not covered in this book. You might want to look into these approaches to building live CDs if the procedures in this book don't suit you:

- **Linux From Scratch (www.linuxfromscratch.org)**—If you really want to make decisions about every aspect of the live CD you create, Linux From Scratch provides a way to do just that. As the name implies, Linux From Scratch (LFS) helps you pull together the software you want and compile it and configure it into a useful, installed system. You can then package up that system into a live CD.

  You can get instructions for creating an LFS live CD from the Linux From Scratch site (www.linuxfromscratch.org/livecd/documentation.html). The basic procedure involves installing an LFS system (complete descriptions are available), adding packages, and modifying boot scripts and systems settings to your needs.

  When the basic LFS system is in place, you create an initial script (one is supplied to start with) that you use to set up the CD environment. Then, as with other live CDs, you configure that boot loader and package the LFS file system into an ISO image.

  LFS relies on Squashfs to create a compressed, read-only file system. Instead of using `initrd` as the initial RAM disk, LFS uses `initramfs` to provide the basic file-system environment when the live CD first boots and before the final file system is mounted. Instead of a `linuxrc` file, LFS uses an `init` file (created in C language) to set up the environment.

- **Linux Live Scripts (www.linux-live.org)**—Linux Live Scripts provide a means of creating a live Linux CD from any installed Linux system. The Slax project (www.slax.org) used these scripts to create several different Slax live CDs based on the slackware distribution.

  To build a live CD using the Linux Live scripts, you need an installed Linux system with a kernel that includes support for UnionFS and Squashfs file systems. Download the archive containing the latest scripts from the linux-live.org site, unpack the archive, and run the `./runme.sh` script to get going.

The approaches to creating your own live Linux CD that the coming chapters illustrate were chosen because they let you leverage a lot of work that has been done for other Linux distributions. Unless you are purely in it for the learning process of how Linux works, you can start creating your live CD with Linux distributions that have thousands of software packages ready, well-tested installers, and proven components for compressing, booting, and running live CD software.

The following sections provide brief introductions to the different software-packaging systems you will encounter when create live CDs based on Knoppix (Debian), Fedora, and Gentoo.

Using dpkg and apt-get Software Tools for Knoppix

If you create a live CD by remastering Knoppix (as described in Chapter 6), you set up an environment in which you can add and remove software packages to suit your needs. Because Knoppix is based on Debian GNU/Linux, it can use the same tools to get software packages from Debian software repositories and install them with utilities such as dpkg and apt-get.

The dpkg command is the basic software-packaging tool and is most appropriate for installing individual packages. The more commonly used tool is apt-get, which not only can install software packages, but also can grab selected packages from online repositories. It can even grab and install additional packages that the packages you request depend on having there.

You can run these example commands from a chrooted environment as you remaster Knoppix (see Chapter 6 for details):

- **Updating packages**—Because you might lack some of the latest security fixes, the first thing you want to do is update the packages on the live CD you are creating. Assuming that you have an Internet connection from the system on which you are remastering Knoppix, type the following command from your chrooted environment to update your packages:
  # **apt-get update**

- **Remove packages**—Because the Knoppix CD is already near capacity of what can fit on a CD-ROM, you might want to remove some packages before adding your own. To do that, you can also use the following apt-get command (replacing *package* with the name of the package you want to remove):
  # **apt-get remove** *package*

- **Add packages**—To add a new software package to your live CD, you can use the following apt-get line (replacing *package* with the package name you want to add):
  # **apt-get add** *package*

Plenty of options are available for querying, listing, adding, and removing Deb software packages using the apt-get and dpkg commands. Refer to the man pages for those commands for further information.

Using yum and rpm to Manage Fedora Software

The best way to choose which software packages go into your Fedora live CD is to use the kadischi command to run the anaconda installer to ultimately produce the live CD ISO image. It is possible to set up a chroot environment to install packages

using either the rpm command (to install a single package from the local hard disk)
or the yum command (to install selected packages and their dependent packages
from an online repository. However, this is not the recommended approach for
Fedora live CDs.

Despite that fact, you can still use the rpm and yum commands to get information
about software installed on your live CD and packages available from repositories.
The following are a few examples of commands to get information on RPM packages
installed on a Fedora live CD.

- **List package contents**—The first command lists the contents of the
  coreutils package:

```
# rpm -ql coreutils | less
/bin/basename
/bin/cat
/bin/chgrp
/bin/chmod
...
```

- **List package description**—The following command lists a description of
  the coreutils package:

```
# rpm -qi coreutils
Name       : coreutils             Relocations: (non relocatable)
Version    : 5.93                  Vendor: Red Hat, Inc.
...
Description:
These are the GNU core utilities. This package is the combination of
the old GNU fileutils, sh-utils, and textutils packages.
```

- **List installed package names**—The following command lets you list all
  installed packages on your system. I piped the output to grep to be able to
  list only those packages that have xorg in the name:

```
# rpm -qa |grep xorg
xorg-x11-xkbdata-1.0.1-7
xorg-x11-xdm-1.0.1-1.2
xorg-x11-fonts-Type1-7.0-3
...
```

- **Get software information with yum**—In the previous examples, the rpm
  command queries the local RPM database. If you want to query Fedora software repositories for packages that are not yet installed on your computer,
  you can use the yum command. This is an example of using yum to get a
  description of the pan software package, which is in the Fedora Extras software repository:

```
# yum info pan
...
Available Packages
```

```
Name     : pan
Arch     : i386
Version: 0.14.2.91
...
Summary  : A GNOME/GTK+ news reader for X
Description:
 Pan is a newsreader which attempts to be pleasant to new and
advanced users alike.
...
```

You can use many other options with the rpm and yum commands that you can find on their respective man pages. Of course, along with those options shown, there are options for adding and removing software packages using those two commands.

Using emerge to Manage Software in Gentoo

The Portage software system is complex and powerful, but the emerge command that you can use to add, remove, and list software from Portage to work with Gentoo (for a live CD or otherwise) can often be used in very simple forms. The emerge command can also update the Portage tree, which contains the latest list of Gentoo packages.

- **Get latest Portage tree**—The emerge command shown next is used to make sure that you get the latest Portage tree installed on your system (this command could take a while to run):

  # emerge –sync

- **Search packages**—The following command line searches the list of available packages and finds any that contain the string ogg123:

  # emerge –search ogg123

- **Add packages**—To add a software package to Gentoo, you simply use the emerge command with the package name you want to install. For example, the following command installs the xmms package:

  # emerge xmms

Many other options are available with the emerge command. Refer to the emerge man page for further information on ways of using emerge to manage software in Gentoo.

Building Live CDs Using Linux Installers

Remastering an existing live CD is one way to build the live CD you want. Another way is to use an installer and related tools to essentially create a software installation to make your live CD. Two projects illustrated in this book offer tools for running a modified installation to produce a live CD ISO image:

- **Fedora Kadischi Project (with anaconda)**—Using the kadischi command from the Fedora project of the same name, you can start a process that launches the Fedora installer (called anaconda) to create the live CD ISO image. With kadischi, you can install all the packages you want to include in your live CD to a directory on your hard disk, and then start up kadischi to run through a modified anaconda installation procedure.

  To save you some trouble as you perfect your live CD, you can create a kickstart file. Information you put in your kickstart file can save you the trouble of clicking through installation screens. You can simply modify the script and run it again (after you have made your corrections).

- **Gentoo Catalyst Project**—Catalyst is the installer used with Gentoo. Using Catalyst, along with a spec file, you can tailor a live CD "install" so that it controls the build process to the smallest detail. The result can be a highly tuned, highly configured Linux system.

Whether you choose to create your live Linux CD by remastering or by using a modified installer, understanding how packaging, file systems, and boot loaders work on your live CD will help you make a quality live CD.

SUMMARY

Although a live Linux CD is, in many ways, like any installed Linux system, some components are of special interest when you are building a live CD. With an installed Linux system, you typically set up everything when the software is first installed so it is tuned to work with your specific hardware. Because a live CD is typically expected to boot up and be configured quickly on different computer hardware, setting up a boot loader with options to overcome potential problems can be helpful.

Isolinux is the boot loader most often used with live Linux CDs. With Isolinux, you can configure the look of the boot screens, timeout values, and multiple labels to boot from. Each label can contain different options to help overcome problems with video settings or failed X display configuration. As an alternative to Isolinux, this chapter describes how to configure GRUB as your live CD's boot loader. GRUB can be used to select different boot labels from a menu interface.

Because of limited space on live CDs and the need to write to what the CD saves as read-only files and directories, the types of file systems used with live CDs are very important. To be able to compress file system data, some live CDs compress their file systems into single archives that can be decompressed on-the-fly using the cloop driver. Other live CDs use the Squashfs file system to provide a read-only file system to use.

To be capable of writing to files and directories from the CD, some live CDs use the UnionFS file system. Using UnionFS, a file system can join read-only and read/write branches to give the user the appearance of a completely writeable file system. This also provides a means of saving changes to files and directories so that they can persist across reboots.

When you set out to remaster an existing installer or create one using a Linux installer, the Linux distribution you choose to base your live CD on is very important. This chapter described the different tools, software repositories, and software packaging formats available with Knoppix (Debian), Fedora, and Gentoo.

## CHAPTER 6

Building a Custom Knoppix Live CD

Not only is Knoppix the most popular live CD to use, but it is also the live CD distribution that has seen the greatest interest in customizing and remastering. Unlike a Fedora live CD, in which you use scripts from the Kadischi project to essentially build a live CD from a Fedora install, the common way to remaster Knoppix is by copying, changing, and rebuilding files from a live Knoppix CD itself.

The remastering process is different than the customization steps described in Chapter 3, "Customizing a Live CD." Whereas customization can pull desktop settings or even applications into an existing Knoppix system, remastering lets you change what is in the Knoppix CD itself. The result is a live CD that can do everything you want it to do, from start to finish.

Much of the procedure shown in this chapter is derived from the Knoppix Remastering Howto (www.knoppix.net/wiki/Knoppix_Remastering_Howto), as well as others available on the Web. Refer to that document for further information on Knoppix remastering as it becomes available. The forum for Customizing and Remastering Knoppix is located at www.knoppix.net/forum/viewforum.php?f=2.

Because the commands you will use to remaster Knoppix are on the Knoppix CD itself, you can learn about other options for those commands using the man command while Knoppix is running. In particular, you might want to check out man pages for mkisofs (for creating ISO images) and create_compressed_fs (for compressing the KNOPPIX image).

When you know how to create a basic custom Knoppix CD, information at the end of this chapter describes different ways of doing specialized customization. These include tips for using some custom scripts to make the setup process easier.

UNDERSTANDING KNOPPIX REMASTERING

Remastering Knoppix begins from a computer with a lot of disk space, a bunch of memory (RAM and swap), and a running Knoppix live CD. The basic steps for creating your own remastered live CD include these:

- **Choosing a Knoppix distribution**—This procedure uses the Knoppix live CD, but you can choose to start from an already customized Knoppix derivative that includes content that might be closer to what you want.

- **Setting up the build machine**—Prepare the computer to have enough disk space and memory to complete the procedure.

- **Copying Knoppix software to hard disk**—This involves copying both the Knoppix file system structure from the CD for you to modify (source directory) and the files needed to boot the CD (master directory).

- **Modifying the Knoppix software**—You can add and delete software, set up features, and configure the user desktop environment. You do this in a chroot shell.

- **Compressing the Knoppix software**—After you have made your modifications, you compress the Knoppix software into a single image (named KNOPPIX) that is copied to the master directory.

- **Modifying boot files**—If you choose, you can change the splash screen that appears when the CD boots or modify isolinux boot files.

- **Creating the CD image**—Combine the boot files and KNOPPIX image into a single CD image that you can burn to CD, DVD, or other medium to boot up your final customized Knoppix.

Figure 6-1 shows the general flow of what happens when your remaster Knoppix to make your own custom live CD. It begins by booting a Knoppix CD on a PC that has enough available memory and disk space to handle the process and ends when you burn your custom ISO image to a blank CD. In between, you modify the contents of the Knoppix system you copy to disk so it includes the software and settings you want.

If you are ready to start creating your own customized, remastered Knoppix CD, you can begin by choosing the Knoppix distribution you want to use as the basis for your custom Knoppix CD.

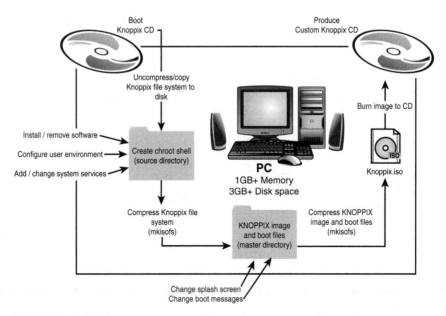

FIGURE 6-1 Uncompress, modify, and recompress Knoppix to create a custom CD.

CHOOSING A KNOPPIX DISTRIBUTION TO CUSTOMIZE

Because a variety of customized Knoppix distributions already are available, to save yourself some work, you can begin with a Knoppix distribution that most closely matches the live CD you eventually want to create. These different Knoppix live CD or DVD distributions (among others) are available:

- **Knoppix**—The standard Knoppix CD distribution contains a well-rounded set of desktop and server applications. The ISO image is just less than 700MB.

- **Education**—Knoppix customizations made for educational purposes include Freeduc (www.ofset.org/freeduc-ecole) and Knoppix for Kids (www.osef.org). Check www.knoppix.net/wiki/Education_Live_CD for a list of other educational Knoppix customizations.

- **Games**—The Linux Live Game Project (www.llgp.org) and Knoppix Games (http://games-knoppix.unix-ag.uni-kl.de) are among the Knoppix-based gaming distributions available. (The Linux Live Game Project live CD is described in Chapter 11, "Customizing a Gaming Live Linux CD.")

NOTE

Using the standard Knoppix distribution offers the best opportunity to use the latest Knoppix technology. Also, there is more risk of getting broken or even malicious software if you just grab some random distribution off the Internet. For those reasons, the procedure in this chapter uses the standard Knoppix distribution for illustration.

- **Server**—Lamppix (http://lampix.tinowagner.com) is primarily a Web server live CD. LiveOIO (www.txoutcome.org) is a CD to demo Zope Web server and the OIO on Zope medical application.
- **Small**—The Damn Small Linux (www.damnsmalllinux.org) and Feather Linux (http://featherlinux.berlios.de) live CDs are good to start with if you want a mini live Linux CD that starts at about 50MB. (Damn Small Linux offers some of its own customization tools.) An example of a remastered Damn Small Linux distribution is described in Chapter 10, "Customizing a Presentation Live Linux CD."
- **Security/recovery**—Because rescue, recovery, and security applications are natural tools for live CDs, several Knoppix-based distributions focus on such tools. Popular security live CDs include the Auditor security collection (www.remote-exploit.org) and Knoppix STD (www.knoppix-std.org). You can find a list of security live CDs at www.knoppix.net/wiki/Security_Live_CD.

For a long list of Knoppix customizations, refer to the Knoppix Customizations page: www.knoppix.net/wiki/Knoppix_Customizations. To find out how to get the standard Knoppix distribution used in examples in this chapter, refer to www.knoppix.net/get.php.

SETTING UP THE BUILD MACHINE

If you have a computer with a Linux system installed on your hard disk, you might already have the configuration you need to remaster your own custom Knoppix live CD. To effectively remaster Knoppix, you need good chunks of RAM, swap, and hard disk space. The space you need varies, depending on whether you are creating a CD or a DVD. You also need a connection to the Internet:

- **Memory (RAM and swap)**—At least 1GB of memory (RAM plus swap) is recommended to create a CD iso image, while 5GB of memory is recommended to create a single-layer DVD. For example, if you have 512MB of RAM, you need at least 512MB swap for a CD and 4.5GB of swap for a DVD.

- **Hard-disk space**—For hard-disk space, you need between 3GB (CD) and 15GB (DVD) of space on a Linux file system. Linux file systems such as ext3 or xfs should work fine.

- **Internet connection**—Knoppix automatically configures most wired Ethernet cards and connects to the network (assuming that a DHCP server is available). If needed, Knoppix can also be configured manually for many wireless network cards or for a static Ethernet network connection.

The procedure that follows here assumes that you have a Linux system installed on your hard disk (with the memory and disk space available as just described). To carry out the customization, however, the procedure assumes that you are booting Knoppix and carrying out the instructions from there. Knoppix should detect your swap area automatically, so you need only be sure that the hard disk space you will use is on a Linux file system that Knoppix can support.

Remastering Knoppix

With your computer prepared as described previously, you can start the process of remastering Knoppix. This procedure was done using a standard Knoppix 5.0.1 CD (about 696MB). The procedure is split into the following major parts: preparing for remastering, working in the chroot environment, modifying boot files, creating the final CD image, and testing and burning the CD image.

Preparing for Remastering

To begin the process of remastering Knoppix to create a custom Knoppix live CD, you need to work from the computer you just prepared by booting Knoppix. While Knoppix is running, you will copy the files you need from the Knoppix CD to your hard disk. Here's how:

1. **Boot Knoppix**—Insert the DVD that comes with this book (or other Knoppix CD) into your computer's DVD drive and reboot. At the boot prompt, type **knoppix** and press Enter. Wait several minutes for Knoppix to boot up to the desktop.

2. **Open a shell as root**—From Knoppix, select the terminal icon (Konsole) from the desktop panel. When the Konsole window opens, type **su -** to become the root user. (Run this entire procedure as root.)

3. **Check Internet access**—To check that you have Internet access, you can use the ping command. For example, type the following command (then use Ctrl+C to end it):

```
# ping www.knoppix.net
PING www.knoppix.net (xxx.xx.xx.xxx): 56 data bytes
64 bytes from xxx.xx.xx.xxx: icmp_seq=0 ttl=235 time=64.3 ms
```

If you don't have Internet access, you might need to configure it manually. Utilities for configuring network connections in Knoppix are available from the K menu by selecting KNOPPIX → Network Internet and then selecting from the available connection types.

4. **Access hard-disk partition**—Determine which partition on your computer's hard disk is the one to use for this procedure (minimum of 3GB to 5GB of disk space) and open it with read-write permissions. Open the icon on the desktop that you believe is the partition you want. Then close the window displaying the partition, unmount the partition, and remount it with read-write permission.

   For example, after closing the window, if the partition you want to use is /dev/hda1 (mounted on /media/hda1), type the following into the terminal window:

```
# umount /media/hda1
# mount -o rw /media/hda1
```

   Your hard-disk partition should now be accessible. (Knoppix recently also added a feature to remount a partition with read-write permission from the desktop. Right-click on the partition's icon and select Change Read/Write Mode.)

5. **Make a work directory**—For example, if the partition you are using is mounted on /media/hda1, you can create a knoppix directory as follows:

```
# mkdir /media/hda1/knoppix
```

6. **Check available memory**—To check whether you have enough memory and hard-disk space, you can use the free and df commands, respectively. Here are some examples:

```
# df -h /media/hda1
Filesystem          Size   Used Avail  Use%  Mounted on
/UNIONFS/dev/hda1   46G    876M  43G    2%   /media/hda1
# free -m
```

```
           total       used      free    shared  buffers  cached
Mem:        724         232       492         0        0     109
-/+ buffers/cache:      113       611
Swap:       996           5       990
```

You can see in this example that the partition mounted on /media/hda1 has 43GB of available disk space. You can also see that there is 724MB of RAM and 996MB of swap space. There is more than 1.5GB of RAM and swap free together. If you don't have enough memory available, you can create an additional swap file. Here's an example of creating a swap file on the partition we just mounted:

```
# dd if=/dev/zero of=/media/hda1/knoppix/myswap bs=1M count=1000
1000+0 records in
1000+0 records out
# mkswap /media/hda1/knoppix/myswap
Setting up swapspace version 1, size = 1048571 kB
no label, UUID=595a3efe-9cd8-4fb3-9892-37e05e2ee651
# chmod 0600 /media/hda1/knoppix/myswap
# swapon /media/hda1/knoppix/myswap
```

The commands just shown create a 1000MB empty file named myswap, closes the permissions to all but root, identifies that file as a swap area, and enables it as a swap file.

7. **Create master and source directories**—You need to create two separate directories to work in. The master/KNOPPIX directory contains the files needed to start up the CD, while the source/KNOPPIX directory contains the files that will make up the KNOPPIX file system on the CD (compressed into a single image file named KNOPPIX).

Type the following to create those two working directories:

```
# mkdir -p /media/hda1/knoppix/master/KNOPPIX
# mkdir -p /media/hda1/knoppix/source/KNOPPIX
```

8. **Copy Knoppix files**—The /KNOPPIX directory on running a KNOPPIX live CD or DVD system contains the Knoppix file system structure you want to customize. To copy those files and directories to your work directory, type the following:

```
# cp -Rp /KNOPPIX/* /media/hda1/knoppix/source/KNOPPIX
```

When I ran this command, it took about 13 minutes to complete and resulted in 2.1GB of data in the source/KNOPPIX directory.

NOTE

If you are remastering an official Knoppix DVD, you will notice that there is a KNOPPIX and a KNOPPIX2 image. Allowing multiple KNOPPIX images (KNOP-PIX2, KNOPPIX3, and so on) to exist lets you maintain KNOPPIX images that are a reasonable size to work with. When Knoppix boots up, all KNOPPIX images are merged using the UnionFS file system. For the purposes of this procedure, only the single KNOPPIX image that comes on the Knoppix CD is described.

9. **Copy boot files**—The boot directory on the Knoppix CD contains the files needed to boot the live CD. You also need to copy the modules directory. To copy those files to your master directory so you can use and modify them, type the following:

```
# cp -ar /cdrom/boot /media/hda1/knoppix/master/boot
# cp -ar /cdrom/KNOPPIX/modules /media/hda1/knoppix/master/KNOPPIX
```

10. **Copy start-up pages**—To copy the first HTML page that appears when Knoppix boots (or if you open the Knoppix CD in Windows) to your master directory, type the following:

```
# cp /cdrom/index.html /media/hda1/knoppix/master
# cp /cdrom/autorun.* /media/hda1/knoppix/master
# cp /cdrom/cdrom.ico /media/hda1/knoppix/master
```

11. **Copy files from CD**—You want to copy all the other files needed when the CD starts up (FAQs and home pages in different languages, license information, and some images) to your master directory. The following command line (suggested by the Knoppix Customization Howto) copies all files from the CD that are less than about 10MB (to exclude copying the 690MB KNOPPIX file):

```
# cd /cdrom/KNOPPIX && find . -size -10000k -type f -exec \
  cp -p –parents '{}' /media/hda1/knoppix/master/KNOPPIX/ \;
```

NOTE

The two command lines shown here can actually be typed as a single command line. The backslash (\) at the end of the first line enables you to press Enter and still have the second line be part of the first.

Now you should have all files needed to boot your live CD in the master/KNOP-PIX directory. The entire KNOPPIX file system you are using should be in the source/KNOPPIX directory. Your next step is to change your root directory (chroot) to the source/KNOPPIX directory and modify that directory structure to contain the applications, files, and directories you want to include on your live CD.

Working in the chroot Environment

By changing your root directory to the source/KNOPPIX directory, you change the contents of your custom Knoppix CD image by working within that directory structure. Within that environment, you can add and remove software packages, set up a desktop, and configure system settings.

When you run the chroot command, as shown next, you begin working from a copy of the same Knoppix system you just booted from CD. Therefore, you have to do a few steps to make that environment capable of accessing the Internet and downloading software packages. Remember that everything you do to the file system while you are in this environment ends up on the CD you produce.

Here's what you do:

12. **Add network access**—To use the chrooted environment to access the Internet, you need a working resolv.conf file. If you were able to get an Internet connection from the live CD (via DHCP), you can copy the resolv.conf file that was created when you booted Knoppix:

```
# cd /media/hda1/knoppix/source/KNOPPIX/etc/dhcpc
# cp /etc/dhcpc/resolv.conf .
cp: overwrite './resolv.conf'? y
```

13. **Run chroot**—To assign the source/KNOPPIX directory as your root directory, type the chroot command and mount the /proc file system as follows:

```
# chroot /media/hda1/knoppix/source/KNOPPIX
# mount -t proc /proc proc
warning: can't open /etc/fstab: No such file or directory
```

 NOTE

If the partition you chroot to was mounted with the nodev option, a /dev/null error message might appear ("/dev/null: Permission Denied"). You can get around this problem by adding the dev option to the entry in /etc/fstab and then unmounting and remounting the partition. For example, the new fstab entry for /dev/hda1 might then appear as follows:

```
/dev/hda1/media/hda1 ext3 noauto,users,exec,dev 0 0
```

Ignore the /etc/fstab warning (/proc should mount despite that). At this point, your shell looks at the /media/hda1/knoppix/source/KNOPPIX directory as your root directory until you exit that shell. Make sure you use this shell for the steps that follow.

14. **Add network access**—Because you added the resolv.conf file earlier to your chroot environment, you should now have Internet access from the chrooted shell. To check, try the ping command:

```
# ping www.knoppix.net
```

If you are only adding new software packages you get from the Internet, you can proceed to the next step. However, if you want to add data files, applications, or other software from your LAN, consider configuring the following network connection types:

- **Samba**—By starting the Samba server from the Knoppix desktop (KNOPPIX → Services → Start Samba Server), you can mount SMB shares from Windows clients to copy files from those shares to your chroot environment. If you do this, you might need to make changes to your /etc/samba/smb.conf file in the chrooted environment (such as the workgroup name) for this to work on your LAN.

  With Samba running on your desktop, you can mount an SMB share from your LAN by creating a mount point and using the mount command. Consider this example:

```
# mkdir /tmp/share
# mount -t smbfs //host1/home /tmp/share
```

  Assuming that a share named home is available from a computer named host1 on your LAN, the share will be mounted on the /tmp/share directory in your chrooted environment. You can then copy files across to your chroot environment from that mounted share. (Remember to unmount the share and remove the mount point before building the CD image.)

- **NFS**—Likewise, you can start the NFS server (a popular service for sharing files among Linux and UNIX systems) to use that service to share files with other Linux systems. Here is what you would type from your chroot shell to mount a shared NFS directory (/home/chris) from a host at IP address 10.0.0.1:

```
# mkdir /tmp/nfs
# mount -t nfs 10.0.0.1:/home/chris /tmp/nfs
```

Updating, Adding, and Removing Software

Now you are entering the meat of customizing your CD. With your chroot build environment in place, you can begin modifying the software content of your custom CD. This entails updating the software that's there, removing what you don't want, and adding what you do. (Refer to the sidebar "Getting the Most from apt" for some tips on using apt to customize your Knoppix CD.)

15. **Updating software**—Knoppix is configured to enable you to get new or updated software packages from Debian software repositories over the Internet. With your Internet connection working, you can update all software in your chroot environment by typing the following:

    ```
    # apt-get update
    ```

16. **Removing software**—Because Knoppix is already near the maximum size to fit on a CD, if you want your remastered Knoppix to fit on a CD, you need to remove some packages. To see which packages are installed on your Knoppix chroot environment, type the following (press the spacebar to page through the output and Q to exit):

    ```
    # dpkg-query -W –showformat='${Installed-Size} ${Package}\n' | sort -nr|less
    353204   openoffice-de-en
    63132    sun-j2se1.4-jre-binary
    57852    kde-i18n-es
    52252    linux-image-2.6.17
    48158    wine
    ```

    The command just shown displays a list of packages, sorted by their file size. Note the names of the packages you might want to remove. If you are not sure what a package contains, you can list its description or the files it contains. For example, to see what openoffice-de-en contains, type the following:

    ```
    # dpkg-query -s openoffice-de-en
    Package: openoffice-de-en
    Status: install ok installed
    Priority: optional
    Section: unknown
    Installed-Size: 2353204
    Maintainer: Klaus Knopper <knoppix@knopper.net>
    Architecture: i386
    Version: 2:2.0.2-1
    Replaces: openoffice-de-en
    Depends: libnspr4
    Description: The OpenOffice suite, see
        http://www.openoffice.org/
     This release uses a quick&dirty hack to support english
     as well as german layout and templates in KNOPPIX.
    ```

For example, if you don't need an office suite for your live CD (or can live with a lightweight word processor), you can remove that package using the apt-get command. The following command removes (remove) the openoffice-de-en package and all its dependencies (–purge):

```
# apt-get remove –purge openoffice-de-en
Reading Package Lists... Done
Building Dependency Tree... Done
The following packages will be REMOVED:
  openoffice-de-en*
0 upgraded, 0 newly installed, 1 to remove and 871 not upgraded.
Need to get 0B of archives.
After unpacking 362MB disk space will be freed.
Do you want to continue? [Y/n] Y
```

Press Y to remove the package. In this example, you can see that removing the package enables you to save 362MB of disk space (before compression) that you can use for other software. Use the same command to remove any other packages you don't want on your live CD.

17. **Adding software**—With the packages removed that you no longer need, you can now add other packages you want on your CD. You can choose from any of the thousands of packages available from Debian software repositories.

NOTE

Chapter 9, "Customizing a Security Live Linux CD," through Chapter 14, "Customizing a Cluster Live Linux CD," describe software packages that are appropriate for different types of live CDs. Refer to those chapters if you want to look into additional software packages to add to a remastered Knoppix live CD.

Because Openoffice.org was removed from the previous step, the following example adds a stand-alone word processor in its place:

```
# apt-get install abiword
```

You can repeat this command for every package you want installed on your live CD.

18. **Cleaning up software**—When you have finished deleting and adding the software you want, you should do some cleanup to ensure that extraneous files and packages created in the process are not left on your CD. Here are a few things to do:

To see whether all your deleting and adding of packages left behind any unneeded packages, you can run the deborphan command:

```
# deborphan | less
```

You can remove any orphaned packages using the `apt-get remove` command, shown earlier. Or, as the *Knoppix Remastering Howto* suggests, you can simply pipe the list to `apt-get remove` and delete them all as once, as follows:

```
# deborphan | xargs apt-get -y remove
```

A removed package can sometimes leave behind configuration files. To find out whether this happened, you can list those packages that you chose to remove (R) but left behind a configuration file (C). The following command lists those packages:

```
# dpkg -l | grep ^rc
```

You can then remove the files left behind by typing the following:

```
# dpkg -l | grep ^rc | awk '{print $2}' | xargs dpkg -P
```

Because `apt-get` saves all software packages you downloaded and installed in cache, you should clean out those files before proceeding. Here's how:

```
# apt-get clean
```

Testing Applications

Although applications that rely on particular hardware configurations are best tested after you build your custom Knoppix CD, most command and graphical utilities that you install can easily be tested from your `chroot` environment. These are a couple of ways to go about launching an X application from your `chroot` environment:

- **Local X desktop**—You can launch an application on your local desktop from your chrooted environment by setting the `DISPLAY` variable and simply running the application. For example, to run the `xmms` application from your `chroot` environment to the local desktop, type the following:

```
# export DISPLAY=localhost:0
# xmms &
```

- **Nested X desktop**—If you want to try out a different window manager, you can run Xnest from your chroot environment. Xnest is an X server that can run as a client window on your X desktop. After running Xnest, you can launch a window manager that you choose and then run any application you like in that Xnest window.

  For example, from your `chroot` shell, you could type the following:

```
# export DISPLAY=localhost:0
# Xnest -ac :1 &
# export DISPLAY=localhost:1
# icewm &
# xclock &
```

GETTING THE MOST FROM APT

To help you install and work with applications for your custom Knoppix CD, you can do several things with the apt facility. Here are some ideas:

- Get the apt-spy application (apt-get install apt-spy) and use it to check for the best mirror sites to use from your area. The apt-spy command will modify your sources.list file (so you should probably make an extra copy of that file as a backup). Here's an example of an apt-spy command line that finds four Debian stable mirrors that offer good response times to North America and updates the /etc/apt/sources.list file with the new servers:

  # **apt-spy -d stable -a north-america -e 4**

- Don't upgrade packages (apt-get upgrade). Upgrades are more likely to break software than simply doing an update.

- Consider changing the default packages installed by apt-get for Knoppix from testing to stable. You can do this by changing the word testing to stable in the /etc/apt/apt.conf file.

- Watch the messages produced by apt-get to get information that you might need, such as empty directories left behind after uninstalling a package.

- Instead of using apt-get, you could try the aptitude utility. Besides being able to work with packages in the same way that apt-get does, aptitude also provide information about disk space you are using or saving.

Figure 6-2 shows an example of the steps just run. Inside the Xnest server window, you can see icewm window manager, the xclock application, and two other applications I ran from menus within that window (Firefox browser and xboard chess application). The Terminal window in the lower-left corner of the screen is where Xnest, the icewm window manager, and xclock were launched.

Configuring the Desktop and User Environment

You can customize nearly every aspect of the desktop and user environment that goes into your custom Knoppix desktop. Knoppix relies both on common Linux files and directories for determining user setting (such as /etc/skel directory) and on Knoppix-specific configuration files (such as those in /usr/share/knoppix/profile).

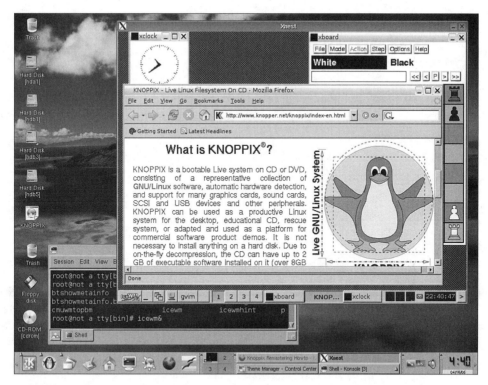

FIGURE 6-2 Check a window manager from a chroot shell in a nested X window (Xnest).

In Knoppix, the process of starting up the desktop is directed by files in the /etc/X11/Xsession.d directory on the CD (in your chroot environment). The following items describe each of the scripts in that directory for Knoppix 5 and what each script does:

- **20x11-common_process-args**—Settings in this determine what is run for different arguments passed during desktop startup. With no arguments, X boots up with the default behavior (a KDE desktop). With the failsafe argument, only a terminal window is opened so you can begin running commands from the shell.

- **30x11-common_xresources**—This is where system-wide X resources are merged into the X server.

- **45xsession**—A lot of the good stuff goes on in this file. Most of the activities of setting the look, feel, and behavior of your Knoppix desktop take place here. In fact, it actually puts together a lot of the user configuration files

(files beginning with a dot that end up in the /home/knoppix directory) on the fly. (More on this file a bit later.)

- 50x11-common_determine-startup—In the case where no X session start-up program was set, the settings in this file cause a user-defined or system default session manager, window manager, and terminal emulator to start up.

- 75dbus_dbus-launch—This script activates the session bus when the X session is started.

- 90x11-common_ssh-agent—This file contains settings that turn on the ssh-agent to authenticate clients that run on the X desktop.

- 99x11-common_start—The single exec line in this file launches the desktop set by $STARTUP.

As I mentioned earlier, much of the activity for setting the user environment and desktop happens in the 45xsession file. This file is commented well, so an experienced Linux user can get a sense of what is happening when a Knoppix desktop starts up by just reading that file. The following describes the default activities that occur when a Knoppix desktop boots up (by default) and how you can change those items that are set:

- **Global variables**—Variables that are active for all desktop types are set (home directory, username, host name, default cursor, language, keyboard, and so on).

- **Start KDE**—With the default KDE desktop set, the startkde settings are run.

- **Play audio**—The playsound script runs to play the /usr/share/sound/ startup.ogg file ("Initiating start-up sequence"). You can substitute any .ogg audio file you like for startup.ogg to have that play instead.

- **Copy desktop files** (/etc/skel)—If no persistent desktop is available (from a previously saved session), all files contained in the Desktop and .kde directories are copied from /etc/skel to the knoppix home directory. By default, you get Floppy and Trash icons in the Desktop directory (and, therefore, on your desktop). Other icons representing disk partitions and CD-ROM drives are added as those devices are available. The .kde directory is where most of your KDE desktop settings come from. Copy your personal set of KDE configuration files to the /etc/skel/.kde directory to have those settings used when you boot up your custom Knoppix.

- **Copy knoppix files** (/usr/share/knoppix/profile)—Several dot files for such things as Mozilla, Netscape, and encrypted keys are copied from this directory to the knoppix home directory. You can modify these files or add your own.

- **Knoppix start page**—An HTML page (/cdrom/index.html) containing links to Knoppix information is displayed when the desktop starts up. You can replace this file with your own HTML page, if you choose.

- **Desktop background**—The desktop background (wallpaper) is set to knoppix.jpg (located in /usr/local/lib on the CD). Change that to a different file to have the new file used as the background instead.

- **Desktop themes**—If custom themes are available from /cdrom/KNOPPIX/ksplash, those themes are copied into the Knoppix home directory under .kde/share/apps. You can add to that directory themes that you want to make available to the user.

- **Change desktop icons**—Icons are placed on the desktop with the mkdesktophdicons script (in /usr/bin/). Edit that script to change which icons go on the desktop.

- **Initialize KDE**—The kdeinit script starts to bring up the KDE environment. This includes dcopserver, clauncher, kded, kxkb, kaccess, kmserver, kwin, kdesktop, and other processes used in the KDE environment.

If instead of using the default KDE environment you pass a different desktop name at the boot prompt using knoppix desktop=*window_manager* (such as twm, icewm, or fluxbox), search for any of those window manager names in the 45xsession file to see how startup is handled for it. For example, starttwm indicates the TWM window manager and starticewm is for the Ice window manager. The script also supports desktops that aren't installed.

NOTE

When Knoppix is running, if you want to restart the desktop with a different window manager, you can press Ctrl+Alt+Backspace to end the current session. Then change the value of DESKTOP in the /etc/sysconfig/desktop file and type **startx** to start the new desktop.

Available window managers include icewm, twm, larswm, and fluxbox. The script also supports gnome, windowmaker, xfce, ratpoison, lg3d, openbox, xfcd4, kiosk, tdp, and nx, but they're not available unless you install them yourself.

Configuration files or data files you add to the user environment don't have to be limited to those that support desktop features. Any files or configuration settings that you want to apply to the user directory can simply be added to the /etc/skel directory.

Although you can also add any data files you want the knoppix user to have by placing them in the /etc/skel directory, for a large amount of data, you should use a different location in the file system, such as a directory under /var.

Changing or Adding System Start-Up Services

Knoppix lets you use the standard System V init scripts facility for starting system services. Using this facility, you can add any system services you like (Web server, mail server, login server, and so on) so that the service starts when Knoppix boots up.

Regardless of which run level (also called system state) the system boots up to, the first init script run is the knoppix-autoconfig script (located in /etc/rcS.d/S00knoppix-autoconfig). This script defines many basic settings (language, keyboard, and so on) and loads modules so Knoppix can interact with hardware ports and storage devices (USB, firewire, udev, and others).

By default, Knoppix starts up in init state 5. That state is the one most commonly used to start an X desktop system that is connected to a network. When the computer boots up to init state 5, any service start-up scripts in the /etc/rc5.d directory beginning with the letter S are started (run with the start option), while start-up scripts beginning with K are stopped (run with the stop option).

Many applications that include start-up scripts place those scripts in the /etc/init.d directory. For example, if you want to have any of the services in /etc/init.d start up when you boot your custom Knoppix, you need only link the script for that service script to a file in /etc/rc5.d that begins with a letter S. Here is an example:

```
# cd /etc/rc5.d
# ln -s ../init.d/ssh S55ssh
```

In the example just shown, the ssh service start-up script is linked to a file named S55ssh in the /etc/rc5.d directory. The convention of that filename is the letter S (for "start"), followed by a number (indicating the order the script will be run), and ending with the script name. (You can use any number you like, although the convention is to use numbers above 40 for services that require the network to be running and all local file systems to be mounted.) In this case, the sshd daemon starts automatically when you boot Knoppix, so remote users can log into the computer using ssh.

Although Knoppix supports this facility, it makes little use of the SysV init facility itself. However, if you want to see the start-up features that Knoppix runs itself (and possibly change those features), I suggest checking the following files:

- /etc/inittab—This file defines the initial run level, as well as some features that are started at different run levels. For example, the last line in this file launches xsession for run level 5 to start your X desktop session.

- /etc/init.d/knoppix-autoconfig—This script is executed when the system boots to single-user mode or higher (in other words, every time Knoppix starts up). It contains many of the basic settings needed to run Knoppix (keyboard, language, boot options, file system mounting, and so on). This script is run from a link to /etc/rcS.d/S00knoppix-autoconfig. See Chapter 4, "Understanding How Live Linux CDs Work," for a longer description of this file.

Cleaning Up the chroot Environment

Before you leave the chroot environment, you need to make sure that everything is cleaned up. Anything you leave behind in the file-system structure will go on your live CD. The first thing you need to do is unmount the /proc directory you mounted, as follows:

```
# umount /proc
```

Next remove any temporary files or configuration files that you changed during the course of creating your custom Knoppix. Here are a few places to check:

- **/root directory**—Type ls -lat /root and remove any files that were created unintentionally in the process of working as the root user.

- **/var/log directory**—Check for any log files left behind from applications you tried out (such as the X server).

- **apt files**—Remove files from the /var/lib/apt/lists directory that were put there when you installed applications using apt-get. From that directory, you can type rm *debian* *knoppix* to remove extraneous package files left behind.

One way to make sure that no files created during the customization process are left behind is to search the entire source directory structure for any files created from the time you started the customization process. Here is a find command line that list all files created in the past two days:

```
# cd /media/hda1/knoppix/source
# find . -type f -mtime 1 -exec ls -ld '{}' \; | less
```

You can page through the list that appears to see the new files that were created. Remember that this list also includes software you have installed and want to keep; think carefully about the contents of this list before you begin deleting files.

When you feel that your Knoppix customization is complete, you can get out of the chroot environment by simply exiting the chroot shell:

```
# exit
```

Next you can begin putting together the KNOPPIX image that will go on the CD.

Making the Compressed File-System Image

With everything set up in the file system that will go on your Knoppix live CD, the next step is to gather that file system into a single compressed image. That image (named KNOPPIX) will go into the final CD ISO, where parts of that image can be uncompressed later (by the cloop driver), as they are needed.

When making the compressed file system image, you need the amount of memory (RAM plus swap) described near the beginning of the chapter. Refer to that section again on how to check the amount of available you need before proceeding.

NOTE

Although in this example we are using a single KNOPPIX image, you can have multiple KNOPPIX images in the /KNOPPIX directory (KNOPPIX, KNOPPIX2, KNOPPIX3, and so on). They will all be picked up and merged into a single root file system (/) when Knoppix boots up.

Allowing multiple KNOPPIX images not only makes each of those images a more manageable size, but it also reduces the total amount of memory you need, instead of producing a single, massive KNOPPIX image. The official Knoppix DVD includes KNOPPIX and KNOPPIX2 images that are merged.

The mkisofs command is the tool used to make a set of selected files into a single ISO 9660 file-system image. Because this file system needs to include Linux/UNIX file system features that are not part of the official ISO 9660 standard, several options were added to the command line to support those needed features. The image we create here is not itself bootable (no -b or -c options to add El Torito boot information). It will, however, be included on the bootable image.

In this example, after the ISO 9660 image is created, it is piped to the create_compressed_fs command to reduce the size of that image. Here's an example of that command line:

```
# mkisofs -R -U -V "My Knoppix File System"      \
      -publisher "John W. Jones"                 \
      -hide-rr-moved -cache-inodes -no-bak -pad \
      /media/hda1/knoppix/source/KNOPPIX         \
      | nice -5 /usr/bin/create_compressed_fs - 65536 > \
      /media/hda1/knoppix/master/KNOPPIX/KNOPPIX
```

The -R option adds SUSP and RR records that must have file-system attributes that a Linux or UNIX system expects (longer filenames, symbolic links, permission bits, and so on). The -U option allows filenames that might include characters that violate the ISO 9660 standard (such as leading dots, multiple dots, mixed-case files, and so on). The hide-rr-moved option hides the RR_Moved directory on the image (if it exists) by renaming it to .rr_moved.

Using the -cache-inodes option saves space on the CD by causing files that are hard-linked (multiple names for a single file) to physically appear only once on the CD. The -no-bak option excludes backup files (ending in .bak or including # or ~ characters) from the CD. The -pad option causes the end of the image to be padded by 300K (150 sectors).

Note the location of the source directory and make sure it matches where you put your source/KNOPPIX directory. Likewise, note the location where the image file (KNOPPIX) will end up (in this case, /media/hda1/knoppix/master/ KNOPPIX/KNOPPIX).

The output of mkisofs is piped to the create_compressed_fs command. (That command is run with the nice command, which attempts to increase the processor priority to -5). The create_compressed_fs command will run for a while to convert the image file to a compressed file-system image that the cloop driver can mount and access. The block size (65536) is set to a multiple of 512 bytes.

When this command line was run on a 1.7GB source directory structure, the resulting KNOPPIX image was 627MB (about a 39% compression ratio). With the KNOPPIX file inserted into your master/KNOPPIX directory, you can now take a look at all the files that will appear on your CD. Most of these files are associated with how the CD will boot up. You can customize those boot files as well.

Modifying Boot Files

Up to this point, you have been modifying files and software that are used after you boot Knoppix. This section describes how to modify components that are used before Knoppix boots up. Files in the isolinux directory can be modified to direct the boot process as you like. Ultimately, isolinux starts a bootable kernel image with an associated initial RAM disk.

Changing Isolinux Files

You might consider changing these files located in the /boot/isolinux directory of the Knoppix CD:

- isolinux.cfg—Describes how the CD responds to input from the boot prompt. Labels listed in this file define which kernel and options are run when those labels are typed at the boot prompt. Function key definitions determine which message files are displayed. Also, you can enter several different options to define such things as how long the system should wait at the boot prompt (without input) before the system boots (TIMEOUT) or what text to display before the boot prompt (DISPLAY).
- boot.msg—Defines the text that appears before the boot prompt.
- logo.16—Contains the splash screen image in syslinux SLL16 image format that appears on the initial boot screen.
- f2—Contains text that appears when the user presses the F2 function key from the boot prompt. This text describes boot options available with Knoppix.
- f3—Contains text that appears when the user presses the F3 function key from the boot prompt. This text describes cheat codes available with Knoppix.

If you like, you can add more message files to go with function key definitions (f4, f5, f6, and so on). For example, you might want to create message files that describe the contents of the CD or licensing information.

Because the isolinux files are basically the same from one type of live CD to another, Chapter 5, "Looking Inside Live CD Components," has general descriptions of Isolinux files. Refer to that chapter for information on creating your own splash screens and modifying configuration and message files.

Besides the isolinux files, you might consider changing informational text and HTML files that are available from the CD when it first boots up. These files include the index.html file that appears in the root directory on the CD. That file points to introductory files in the KNOPPIX directory that are in a variety of languages (French, Italian, Spanish, Japanese, and others). You might also look at the FAQ files in that same directory (also available in different languages) to see whether you want to change or replace them.

Understanding Kernel Image and Initial RAM Disk

Ultimately, most the stuff in the `isolinux` directory is just there to help you get to the right kernel image to boot. For Knoppix, that kernel boot image (in the `boot/isolinux` directory) is named `linux`. During the initial boot process the `linux` kernel image also relies on modules and commands contained on the initial RAM disk. For Knoppix, that initial RAM disk is a compressed (gzip) file system image named `minirt.gz`.

The `linux` Linux kernel image has gone beyond the 1.4MB boundary needed to run on older floppy disks because of the size of the 2.6 kernel. The `linux` file is now 1.7MB. If you want to create your own custom Knoppix kernel, refer to the *Knoppix Custom Kernel Howto* (www.knoppix.net/wiki/Knoppix_Custom_Kernel_Howto).

If you want to add or remove modules or other components to the initial RAM disk, you can unzip it, make the changes you like, and then zip it back up again. That process is described in detail in Chapter 5.

Creating the Final CD Image

If you have rechecked your `master/KNOPPIX` directory to make sure it has everything you want (and that it doesn't have things that you don't), you're ready to create the final CD/DVD image. That process includes running a command line to generate md5sums to verify the files in the CD image and running another `mkisofs` command to produce the final ISO image that contains your custom Knoppix live CD.

The `KNOPPIX` directory contains a `md5sums` file that includes the MD5 checksums for each of the files on the live CD. Because you will have changed some of these files, you need to run `md5sum` commands on the files and direct the output to the `md5sums` file.

Change to the master directory. Then run the following `find` command to create `md5sums` for each of the files on your custom Knoppix:

```
# cd /media/hda1/knoppix/master
# find -type f -not -name md5sums -not -name boot.cat \
  -not -name isolinux.bin -exec md5sum '{}' \; > KNOPPIX/md5sums
```

The command line just shown gathers all files in the master directory and its subdirectories (excluding the `md5sums`, `boot.cat`, and `isolinux.bin` files), runs the `md5sum` command on them, and copies the resulting `md5sum` for each file to the md5sums file. The content of this file shows each md5sum followed by the file it represents. For example:

```
65311f3570a8f9f2bfdb164dc93a3729  ./KNOPPIX/background.jpg
b820d6bfaa53dcf1b170a581661136d9  ./KNOPPIX/avm-license.txt
7383e6da11f2801dbf09980dff20746d  ./KNOPPIX/background.jpg
7aa99ddd714a6f0e565555e7eb2a4953  ./KNOPPIX/images/knoppix-24-1.jpg
b72b38f6b70f1cda7d0a73b995f97a11  ./KNOPPIX/images/knoppix-header.png
a19ea9bd8e2701163d22f98cc3da804c  ./KNOPPIX/index.html
b346de5c68adc774927725a50740cfdc  ./KNOPPIX/index_dk.html
           .
           .
           .
```

After the CD is produced, you can check the integrity of each file by running the command md5sum *filename*. The results should match the left side next to the filename you just checked; this is a good way to check the integrity of any file that might be in question.

The final step in producing your custom Knoppix live CD image is to run another mkisofs command. This time, however, you need to add options to that command line that make it possible to boot the contents of the CD image. Here's an example:

```
# cd /media/hda1/knoppix/master
# mkisofs -pad -l -r -J -v -V "MyKnop" -no-emul-boot -boot-load-size 4 \
    -boot-info-table -b boot/isolinux/isolinux.bin  \
    -c boot/isolinux/boot.cat -hide-rr-moved         \
    -o /media/hda1/knoppix/knoppix.iso /media/hda1/knoppix/master
```

The mkisofs command line shown converts the directory structure you just created for your custom live CD (assuming that you placed it in /media/hda1/knoppix/master) into a single file (-o /media/hda1/knoppix/knoppix.iso). That file is an ISO 9660 CD-ROM file system that allows long filenames (-l), SUSP extensions and permissions that are useful for a Linux or UNIX system (-r), and Joliet directory records (-J).

You should add your own volume name (-V) instead of the "MyKnop" as was done here. Several options make the CD bootable:

- Indicating the location of the El Torito boot image (-b boot/isolinux/isolinux.bin)

- Specifying that the El Torito image load and execute without performing disk emulation (-no-emul-boot)

- Indicating the location of the boot catalog file (-c boot/isolinux/boot.cat)

The -hide-rr-moved option moves the RR_MOVED directory (if one exists) to a directory named .rr_moved at the top of the file-system tree (effectively hiding it from view). The -boot-load-size option is set to 4, indicating that four sectors (of 512 bytes) are used to load in no-emulation mode.

When the mkisofs command finishes, the resulting boot image named knoppix.iso is stored in your /media/hda1/knoppix directory. That image is ready to be tested and burned to CD or DVD.

Testing and Burning the CD Image

The procedure for testing and burning an ISO image to CD or DVD is the same for any live CD. You can test the live CD before burning it to disk using an emulation package such as qemu. Then you can burn the image using a variety of tools available in Linux or Windows. See Appendix B, "Building, Testing, and Burning ISOs," for details on testing and burning live CD images.

The following quick examples illustrate how you can test and burn the knoppix.iso ISO image you just created. From a Knoppix desktop or other Linux system that has the qemu package installed, you can use a command such as the following to try out your live CD image on your desktop:

```
# cd /media/hda1/knoppix/
# qemu -cdrom knoppix.iso -k en-us -m 512
```

The image should boot up in a window on your desktop. Unless you have a ton of RAM on your computer, you probably won't have the 512MB of RAM available (as suggested earlier with -m 512), and your custom Knoppix will probably run slowly on your desktop. However, this is a good way to make sure that the image is basically working before you start burning up your CDs.

The following simple cdrecord command (with a blank CD or DVD medium in a writeable drive) can probably be used to burn your CD image to CD or DVD:

```
# cdrecord -v -data knoppix.iso
```

TRYING OTHER KNOPPIX REMASTERING TECHNIQUES

Now that you have gone through the basic procedure for remastering your own custom Knoppix CD, you might want to try some different approaches to remastering or modifying some different components. Descriptions in this section cover some automated scripts to help you remaster Knoppix.

Using Other Remastering Howtos

Because remastering consists of taking apart an existing Knoppix CD, fiddling with it, and putting it back together, a lot of Knoppix enthusiasts have gone about doing that in their own ways. If you have gone through this procedure and want to review some other approaches to the task, here are a few other Knoppix remastering howtos you can try out:

- **Knoppix Mini-Howto (Daniel Stirnimann)**—This mini-howto (located at www.stirnimann.com/mystuff/doc/knoppix.txt) offers some nice ideas for using X to work on your remastering within the `chrooted` environment.
- **HOWTO: Remaster KNOPPIX (James Pryor)**—This howto (located at www.virtualacuity.com/james/knoppix-howto) offers some useful details on getting a proxy network connection going in the `chroot` environment and working in a `chroot` environment.

Many of the Knoppix remastering howtos that you can find on the Web have also been posted to the Knoppix customizing and remastering forum.

Checking Out Custom Remastering Scripts

The remastering procedure just described is a rather manual endeavor. To avoid retyping the same set of commands when you do a Knoppix remastering, Knoppix enthusiasts have created a variety of scripts for carrying out parts of the process.

One popular script is the `knoppix-remaster` script created by Fabian Franz, which lets you click through most of the process of starting and finishing the Knoppix remastering process. You can get a `deb` package or a tarball for the remaster package at http://debian.tu-bs.de/knoppix/remaster.

When the package is installed, you can launch the `knoppix-remaster` script from a desktop icon or from the shell. For example, with the tarball downloaded to the current directory and enough memory and hard disk space available on your computer (see how much you need earlier in the chapter), here's how to use the `knoppix-remaster` script:

NOTE

This script has not been updated for some time now. Although the following procedure eventually resulted in a working ISO image, the script failed sporadically in some terminal windows.

1. Unzip/untar the remaster package:

   ```
   # tar xvfz remaster_*.tar.gz
   # cd remaster-*
   ```

2. Launch knoppix-remaster:

   ```
   # ./knoppix-remaster &
   ```

   A pop-window asks if you want to create a new remaster.

3. Select Yes and select OK. You are asked to select the directory to use for remastering.

4. Select a directory and click OK. The script begins copying files to your remastering directory (this takes a while). When the copying is done, you are presented with a list of activities, as shown in Figure 6-3.

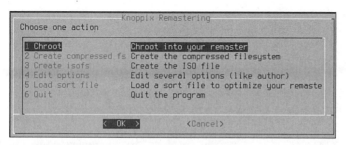

FIGURE 6-3
After Knoppix files are copied to disk, choose a remastering task.

5. Choose Chroot into Your Remaster and select OK. When the shell prompt appears, you are ready to begin working in your chroot environment.

6. Follow the instructions from earlier in this chapter for working in the chroot environment.

7. When you have done everything you want to do with your remaster, type **exit** (to return to the menu).

8. Select Edit Several Options. From the screen that appears, you can change the name of the file system, the author of the CD, and a home page. Then click Quit when you are done.

9. Select to compress the file system. The script gets any available updates and compresses the file system to a single ISO image.

10. Choose the Create isofs option. The script compresses the file system to a single ISO image. (This takes a while.)

11. When you are done, select Quit to exit the script.

You can now test and use the ISO image as described earlier in this chapter.

SUMMARY

The process of remastering a custom Knoppix CD is largely a manual process, but many people have managed to do it successfully. The general steps to remastering Knoppix involve unpacking the Knoppix files directly from a running Knoppix system, changing the unpacked files to make the system suit your needs, and then repacking it all into an ISO file that can be burned to disk.

By modifying the Knoppix file system that was copied to your hard disk in a chrooted environment, you can install and remove packages, change settings, and test out your changes as though you were working directly from the live CD itself. After you recompress the file system and add it back into a full, bootable ISO image, you can test that image using emulators such as qemu or by burning the image to CD and trying it out.

## CHAPTER 7

Building a Basic Fedora Live CD

To start building your own bootable live Linux CD system, you should set up the tools you need to build your live Linux and the software packages you plan to put into it. Because this chapter steps you through creating Live Linux CDs based on Fedora Core using a project called Kadischi, I describe how to do the following:

- Obtain and set up the Fedora Core distribution and Kadischi tools needed to create the live Fedora CD
- Run the commands to create your first Fedora live CD
- Learn about the many opportunities to customize your Fedora live CD

When you understand the basics for building a Fedora live CD with Kadischi, you can go on to use many of the techniques in the third part of this book to create specialized live Linux CDs and DVDs.

Unlike Knoppix, which is itself a bootable Linux distribution, Kadischi is really a set of tools you can use to produce your own live Linux distribution based on the Red Hat–sponsored Fedora Core Linux project. Using the Red Hat anaconda installer, Kadischi essentially creates a live Fedora Core CD or DVD (in the form of an ISO image).

UNDERSTANDING HOW TO BUILD A FEDORA LIVE CD

The process of building a Fedora-based live CD using Kadischi is very similar to doing a typical permanent install of Fedora to your hard disk. The process consists of the following:

- Launching an install of Fedora Core (typically from a repository of Fedora Core software located on your hard disk)
- Installing the Fedora system as you selected (language, keyboard, network settings, packages, and so on) to a temporary directory on your hard disk
- Gathering the installed software from the temporary directory and molding it into a form that can be used in a live CD environment
- Creating a bootable ISO image of that software

Essentially, you need the following items to get started:

- **Fedora Core installed**—This procedure describes how to create a live Linux CD from an installed Fedora Core system. This procedure was tested and run on an installed Fedora Core 6.
- **Kadischi Tools installed**—You need to install the Kadischi software included on the DVD that comes with this book. The software is packaged as a binary RPM that was tested to run on Fedora Core 6.
- **Fedora Core repository**—The actual live Linux CD you create will be made from a selection of packages from Fedora Core. You can get those packages in several ways, but I describe how to install them on a directory on your hard disk and use them from there.
- **Fedora Core kickstart file**—You have the option of using a kickstart file to indicate the software packages and other installation options used to create your Fedora Core live Linux CD. Using a kickstart file, you can easily repeat the process of creating your live Fedora ISO without having to manually step through the Fedora Core install process each time.

Kadischi works by installing a Fedora system to a directory structure on your hard drive and then executing scripts that will let the system run from a CD, DVD, or other read-only medium. Kadischi compresses the Fedora system tree that was created and joins that image with a newly created initial RAM disk (initrd) to form the ISO image that is the bootable Fedora system.

The live CDs you can produce using Kadischi tools and Fedora Core software repositories won't have the bells and whistles you get with Knoppix, but the approach Kadischi takes to producing live CDs has some wonderful advantages.

In fact, in some ways, Kadischi can produce live CDs that are more secure and easier to fix and rebuild than Knoppix live CDs. Here's how:

- **Read-only file system**—By default, Kadischi uses Squashfs as the file system that holds most of the files on a Fedora live CD. The drawback is that those files and directories used directly from the live CD cannot be changed, deleted, or added to once the CD is running. By keeping those files and directories read-only, however, fewer opportunities exist to hack into areas that might be vulnerable. Although making most of the file system readable in Knoppix with UnionFS is user-friendly, it is inherently less secure.

- **Kickstart**—By using a kickstart file, you can define all the options you want to build your live CD. Instead of having to maintain a chroot environment (as is done with remastering Knoppix), you can simply rerun Kadischi using the same kickstart file. Small changes or updated packages in the software repository can be immediately picked up and incorporated into a new ISO image.

- **Easy firewall and service setup**—During the process of producing a live CD with Kadischi, you have the opportunity to turn on and configure a secure firewall. Likewise, you can add users (with passwords) and even turn on or off services that are needed on the live CD (such as remote shell, FTP service, or Web service).

Kadischi was created by Darko Ilic as part of the Google Summer of Code project in 2005 (http://code.google.com/soc-results.html). Discussions of the development process on the Fedora Live CD mailing list (www.redhat.com/archives/fedora-livecd-list/index.html) can give you some insights into the design decisions. Information about Kadischi is maintained on the Fedora Project Wiki (www.fedoraproject.org/wiki/kadischi).

The technology on which Kadischi is based includes software from the Stateless-linux project (http://fedora.redhat.com/projects/stateless)—in particular, the readonly-root package. Some ideas used for creating Kadischi were also taken from the Linux4All project (www.linux4all.de), which created the Basilisk Fedora–based live CD.

Like many other Linux live CD projects, Isolinux (http://syslinux.zytor.com/iso.php) is the boot loader used by default to manage the live CD's boot process for Fedora. The mkisofs command, used to produce the resulting ISO image, is part of the cdrecord project (http://cdrecord.berlios.de/old/private/cdrecord.html).

Going forward, a fair amount of development is going on with Kadischi. As more Kadischi features are added to the basic Anaconda installer, building live CDs based on Fedora will become a more mainstream activity that is built into

Fedora Core itself. As for new features that are currently being worked on, a graphical front end for Kadischi is in the works. Tools also are being developed for adding user-friendly live CD features, such as the capability to keep a persistent /home directory.

Now that the Kadischi tools are becoming stable, you can expect more Fedora-based live CDs to begin appearing. A good place to start looking for Fedora live CDs is from the Fedora Unity project (www.fedoraunity.org). The first live CDs that organization produced were based on Fedora Core 5 and Fedora Core 6, Test 2.

SETTING UP TO BUILD A FEDORA CD

The Kadischi tools used to build your live Linux using Fedora Core are made to run on a Linux system. Because there are dependencies on particular packages from Fedora Core, this procedure assumes that you have a Fedora Core system installed on your hard disk. You can find specific hardware and disk-space requirements for installing Fedora Core in the Fedora Core Release Notes (http://fedora.redhat.com/docs/release-notes/).

Although no additional hardware requirements specify using Kadischi (other than that you need a DVD drive to use the DVD with this book and a CD/DVD burner to ultimately burn your ISO images), you need more than the minimal amount of disk space. I recommend that at least the following additional disk space should be available after Fedora Core is installed:

- **Software repository space**—Allow for at least an additional 3GB of disk space for the Fedora Core binary RPM packages you will use to build your live Linux CD. (You can install from Fedora Core CDs or over a network, if you prefer.)
- **Build directory space**—Allow at least 1.5 times the ultimate size of your ISO image in free disk space for the directory where you will build the ISO image. To build a CD ISO image, you should have at least 2GB of free disk space. For a standard, single-side DVD, have at least 8GB of disk space available in the build directory. (The default location of the build directory is a subdirectory of /tmp that is automatically named by Kadischi.)

INSTALLING FEDORA CORE

I installed Fedora Core 6 on my hard disk as the operating system on which I built the live Linux with Kadischi. The default install should work well for this procedure. However, whatever set of Fedora packages you choose, you should be sure to have at least the following packages installed:

- anaconda—Contains parts of the Fedora Core installation software used to install and reconfigure Fedora software.

- busybox-anaconda—Contains the busybox binary, which implements a simple shell and a large number of basic commands run from a shell.

- syslinux—Contains bootloader software used on live CDs to start a Fedora install process or boot the live CD.

- mkisofs—Contains the mkisofs command for creating ISO images from any set of selected files (including the bootable CD's file systems you create).

- squashfs-tools—Contains tools for working with Squashfs file systems. Squashfs file systems are made for read-only environments where high compression is desired.

- zisofs-tools—Contains the mkzftree command for compressing an ISO 9660 file system using ZF compression records.

- e2fsprogs—Contains tools for creating and working with ext file systems.

- createrepo—Contains the createrepo command, which you will need if you want to add software packages to your Fedora repository.

- yum-utils—Contains utilities for downloading software packages in a way that you can use them in your Fedora repository.

- gnome-python2-gtkhtml2—Contains components to allow Kadischi to run in graphical mode. (When you install this package, it also installs gnome-python2-extras and gnome-python2-libegg if those dependent packages are not already installed.)

- perl—Contains components needed to handle Perl scripts on the Fedora system.

After you have installed Fedora Core, if you are missing any of the packages just listed, provided that you have an Internet connection, you can install those packages using the yum command. Add any of the missing packages to the yum command line, for example:

```
# yum install anaconda busybox-anaconda
```

With Fedora Core installed, you are ready to begin setting up Kadischi.

INSTALLING KADISCHI TOOLS

There is no official software package (in RPM format) for the Kadischi project as of this writing. Because the tools are under active development, the official way to get Kadischi is to download the latest software from the Fedora CVS system and install it as described on the Fedora Project's Kadischi page (http://fedoraproject.org/wiki/Kadischi).

For the purposes of this procedure, however, I have created an RPM containing the Kadischi tools that you can install on your Fedora Core 6 system. Although the software in this RPM works as of this writing with Fedora Core 6, if you want the latest software (or if updates to Fedora 6 break the Kadischi RPM provided with this book), refer to the Fedora Project's Kadischi page to get the latest software.

From a running Fedora Core 6 system, you can install the Kadischi RPM using the DVD included with this book. For example, with the DVD inserted, type the following from a terminal window:

```
# rpm -Uhv /media/LiveCDs/RPMS/kadischi*rpm
```

The Kadischi software you use to create your live Linux distros is installed in the following locations:

- **/etc/kadischi**—Contains configuration build files used to create your live Linux CDs.

- **/usr/share/kadischi**—Contains scripts and examples used to configure your live Linux CD.

- **/usr/sbin**—Contains the kadischi command, which is used to build the ISO image containing your live Linux distribution.

- **/usr/libexec/kadischi**—Contains some commands used in the process of building the live CD. These include eject-live-cd, find-live-cd, and scanswap.

In addition, kadischi and kadischi.conf man pages are in the /usr/share/man directories. The next section describes how to set up the Fedora Core software repository you will draw from to create your live Linux CDs.

SETTING UP THE FEDORA CORE REPOSITORY

Through the Fedora Core anaconda installer, Kadischi can grab the Fedora Core packages it needs to create your live CD from a software repository on your local hard disk, removable medium (CD or DVD), or network location (via NFS, HTTP, or FTP protocols). For the purpose of this procedure, I describe how to copy the Fedora Core distribution to your hard disk and use it from there to create your live CD.

 NOTE

You can download the complete Fedora Core 6 installation DVD from a Fedora mirror site (see http://fedora.redhat.com/download/mirrors. html). The Fedora Core DVD is also packaged with several books on Fedora, such as the *Fedora 6 and Red Hat Enterprise Linux Bible,* by Christopher Negus (Wiley Publishing).

Setting Up the Fedora Core Repository on Hard Disk

By copying the Fedora Core distribution to your hard disk, you get better performance for your builds and can modify the packages included in the repository. This procedure assumes that you are working from the computer with Fedora Core 6 installed on your hard disk with the required software packages (anaconda, busybox-anaconda, syslinux, and so on) installed on that system (as described earlier in this chapter).

If you have recently installed Fedora Core 6, you may have the Fedora Core 6 installation DVD handy that you need for this procedure.

1. Insert the Fedora Core 6 installation DVD into the DVD drive. (If you don't have the Fedora Core 6 DVD, refer to previous note for information on how to obtain one.) The DVD should mount automatically.

2. Create a directory to contain the entire Fedora Core distribution. For example:
   ```
   # mkdir $HOME/FC6
   ```

3. Next, copy the entire contents of the Fedora directory on the DVD that comes with this book. Those contents consist of the base system and all binary RPMs delivered with Fedora Core. For example, if the mount point of your DVD is /media/cdrecorder, you could type the following:
   ```
   # cp -a /media/cdrecorder/Fedora/ $HOME/FC6/
   # cp -a /media/cdrecorder/repodata $HOME/FC6/
   ```

The contents consist of about 3GB of data, so the copy should take a few minutes. Remember the location of your repository directory (in this case, $HOME/FC6). That is the location that you need to identify later when you build your live Linux with Kadischi.

TIP

Software Repositories

If you want to use a different version of Fedora Core than you have available, or if you don't have enough disk space to store Fedora Core locally, you use a public software repository. Here's an example of a public Fedora repository address; the process will take a lot longer but should work just as well:

```
http://download.fedora.redhat.com/pub/fedora/linux/core/6/i386/os
```

Creating a Custom Software Repository

With the Fedora Core software repository in place, when you go to generate your live CD, packages are picked up from that repository based on package groups and individual packages that are selected. The comps.xml file contains definitions of available packages and package groups.

When you copied the repodata directory to your hard disk in the previous section, the comps.xml file was copied there as well (for example, $HOME/FC6/repodata/comps.xml). The screens used to select software categories, packages, and groups that you see from the anaconda installer come from this file. The tags used to indicate categories, groups, and packages are <category>, <group>, and <packagelist>, respectively.

Figure 7-1 shows an example of screens that anaconda presents during Fedora installation (or a live CD build) that reflect the available categories, groups, and packages. Those entries shown come directly from the comps.xml file.

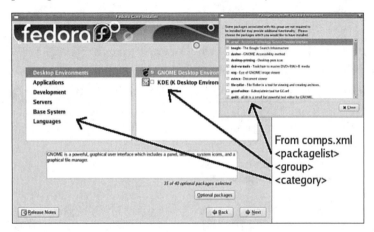

FIGURE 7-1 Select packages to include on your live CD from those listed in comps.xml.

You might wonder why you should care about comps.xml. Well, if you want to add packages to a Fedora live CD that are not in Fedora Core, those packages need to be included in the comps.xml file you are using. Then you can choose to add those packages when you build your live CD (either from an anaconda screen or from a kickstart file).

Starting with the Fedora Core software repository you added to your hard disk in the previous section, here is how you might go about placing other packages into your repository so they can be added later to your live CD.

1. **Enable yum repositories**—You can get the packages you want and add them to your repository using the yum facility. With Fedora Core installed, yum is already enabled to get additional packages from Fedora Core and

Fedora Extras. However, if you want to get packages from the rpm.livna.org repository, you can do so by typing the following command as root user:

```
# rpm -ivh http://rpm.livna.org/livna-release-6.rpm
```

NOTE

A new feature in anaconda for Fedora Core 6 allows you to merge comps.xml files from different repositories. So, for example, you could build a live CD using both Fedora Core and Fedora Extras packages without having to add everything to a single comps.xml file. You could even add packages from third-party repositories, such as http://rpm.livna.org.

Chapter 11, "Customizing a Gaming Live Linux CD," describes how to use this new feature to create a gaming live CD from Fedora Core and Fedora Extras. Use this section as a means of understanding how the underlying comps.xml structure works.

2. **Download packages**—To download a package you want (and all packages that package depends on), you can use the yumdownloader command (provided that you have installed the yum-utils packages as noted earlier). Because the livna repository is enabled, here's how to get the mplayer media player plus all packages mplayer depends on:

```
# cd $HOME/FC6/Fedora/RPMS
# yumdownloader --resolve mplayer
```

The mplayer package, along with all packages mplayer depends on, are downloaded to the current directory. You can continue to download other packages you want to add to your repository.

3. **Configure** comps.xml—Edit the comps.xml file to create software groups to install to your live CD. You can then add those groups to existing categories or create your own category. With the repository at $HOME/FC6, open comps.xml in any text editor (for example, vi $HOME/FC6/Fedora/base/comps.xml). Here are some changes I made:

```
<group>
  <id>myextras</id>
  <name>MyExtras</name>
  <description>Packages from Fedora Extras.</description>
  <default>true</default>
  <uservisible>true</uservisible>
  <packagelist>
    <packagereq type="default">bittorrent</packagereq>
```

```
              <packagereq type="default">bittorrent-gui</packagereq>
              <packagereq type="default">ncftp</packagereq>
            </packagelist>
          </group>

          <group>
            <id>multimedia</id>
            <name>Multimedia</name>
            <description>Packages from Livna.</description>
            <default>true</default>
            <uservisible>true</uservisible>
            <packagelist>
              <packagereq type="default">mplayer</packagereq>
            </packagelist>
          </group>

          <category>
            <id>extras</id>
            <name>Extras</name>
            <description>Packages from Fedora Extras.</description>
            <display_order>01</display_order>
            <grouplist>
              <groupid>multimedia</groupid>
              <groupid>myextras</groupid>
            </grouplist>
          </category>
```

I created two groups: MyExtras and Multimedia. In MyExtras, I added packages from Fedora Extras (just `bittorrent`, `bittorent-gui`, and `ncftp` to start with). In Multimedia, I added just `mplayer`. Then I added the group ID for each group to a new category I called Extras. By setting the display order of that category to 01, I ensured that it would appear at the front of the category list on the anaconda screen.

4. **Run `createrepo`**—Next I ran the `createrepo` command to update the repository information with the stuff I just added to the `comps.xml` file. Here's how:

```
# cd $HOME/FC6
# createrepo -g Fedora/base/comps.xml $HOME/FC6
```

Files in the `repodata` directory will be updated with the new package, group and category information just added. Later, when you run Kadischi to generate a live CD, the new category, groups, and packages can be displayed. Figure 7-2 displays the package-installation screen for anaconda that appears when the `comps.xml` changes shown earlier are included.

With all the packages you want added to your repository and the `comps.xml` file updated to include those packages, you are ready to start configuring Kadischi.

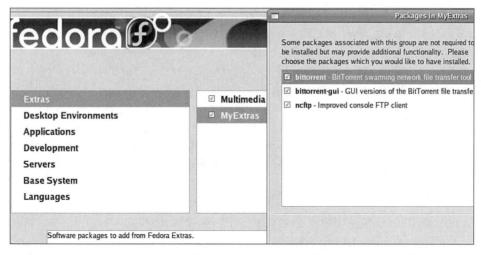

FIGURE 7-2 Create custom software categories and groups on your live CD.

TRYING A TEST BUILD

With the repository in place, you can run the kadischi command to try your first test build of an ISO image. As I noted earlier, you basically go through the same process you would to install Fedora Core to a hard disk. However, instead of the result of the installation being a Fedora Core system installed on partitions of your hard disk, the result is a single ISO image containing an entire bootable Fedora Core system.

To start the process of creating you own live Fedora CD, run the kadischi command as follows:

```
# kadischi $HOME/FC6 $HOME/FC6-live.iso
```

At this point, you should see the Kadischi Fedora LiveCD Creator Tool. Type in the following information, based on how you set up your repository and where you want your final ISO image to be placed:

- **Enter a Repository**—Type the full path to the directory where you added your repository. For example, I created my Fedora software repository in the directory /home/chris/FC6/.

- **Enter a filename and its location**—This is where you want the ISO image to go. In my case, I entered /home/chris/FC6-live.iso.

You can add the -f option to the command line to overwrite the location of the previous ISO file when the new one is created. Add the --text option to the command line if you want to do the live CD creation process in text mode. If Kadischi is unable to run in graphical mode on your desktop, it will automatically step back to text mode. Select OK to continue.

The next steps are part of a standard Fedora Core installation process. You can find detailed descriptions of this process in many books on Fedora Core (such as *Red Hat Fedora and Enterprise Linux Bible,* ISBN 0-47-008278-X, by Christopher Negus). The following is a checklist covering the install process.

1. **Welcome screen**—Click Next (or OK) to continue.
2. **Language selection**—Select your primary language.
3. **Keyboard configuration**—Select the language/layout for your keyboard.
4. **Network configuration**—Configure the Ethernet setup.
5. **Time zone selection**—Select the time zone in which the system will run.
6. **Set root password**—Select a password for the root user.
7. **Installation type**—Select one or more sets of software to get the basic groups of software you want on your live CD (Office and Productivity, Software Development, and Web Server). Choose Customize Now to make more specific selections.

   A new feature on the Installation Type screen is the Additional Repository feature. Select Fedora Extras to allow software packages from the Fedora Extras repository to be included on your live CD. Select to add additional software repositories to type the location of additional software repositories (such as those from rpm.livna.org or atrpms.org). (See descriptions in Chapter 11 on building a Fedora Gaming live CD to learn about incorporating packages from other repositorites.)

8. **Package group selection**—Select the packages you want included in the system. (Be sure to select Base System → Base and add the Squashfs optional package.)
9. **Beginning of installation**—When package dependencies have been worked out, click Next to start the install.

   When you select your packages, keep in mind that a bootable CD can hold about 700MB of compressed data; for a standard, single-layer DVD, you can use an ISO image of about 4.4GB. Because the file system is being compressed before being made into the ISO image, you will be able to fit more on your CD or DVD than the anaconda installer will indicate.

From the terminal window where you launched the install, you can see the install and ISO build process as it progresses. Depending on the size of the ISO you are building and your processing power, compressing the tree can take a while.

At the same time, you will see the Fedora Core installation screens, which look the same as they would for a regular install of Fedora Core. However, a few screens that aren't appropriate to building a live CD are not included in the process (such as disk partitioning). Figure 7-3 shows an example of the install process started from the kadischi command (in the terminal window) and Fedora install screen.

FIGURE 7-3 Installing packages to build the Fedora Core live CD.

When the software packages are installed to the build directory on your hard disk, the Fedora Core installation screen alerts you that the installation is complete.

10. **Completed installation**—Click Reboot to complete the installation.

Look back at the original terminal window (or other shell) where you started the kadischi command. From this terminal window, you are asked to enable or disable your firewall.

11. **Firewall configuration**—You can enable or disable your firewall. You can also customize settings on it.

12. **Services selection**—Press arrow keys to go to a service you want to enable. Press the spacebar to have that service enabled (*) or disabled. Enabling first boot allows the person booting the live CD to add a user and set up some other features (but prevents the CD from booting right to a login prompt). You can learn about many of the services by simply typing man *service*, where *service* is replaced by the name of the service you are interested in.

13. **Nonroot user creation**—You can add a nonroot user (any name you choose) to the live CD by typing **yes**. (Typing **no** skips adding a new user.) If you add a new user, you need to select a username, a shell (such as /bin/bash), and a password (twice).

    Kadischi now creates the initial RAM disk (initrd) image and compresses the file system tree. It takes a while to compress the file system; be patient. After that is done, watch as messages on the screen report as the ISO image is created and the build directory is cleaned up.

14. **Burn CD image?**—After Kadischi finishes creating the ISO image, you are asked if you want to burn the image to CD or DVD. Provided that you have a CD/DVD burner on your computer, you can type **yes** to have the image burned to CD or DVD. When prompted, type the name of the device to which you want to burn the image (such as /dev/cdrom). Whether you typed **yes** or no, the ISO image is now complete and ready for you to use and share as you like.

The kadischi command shown is about the most basic one you can use. Here are other options that might interest you that work with kadischi:

- **Fedora install type**—Using Kadischi, you can add an option to indicate the mode of the Fedora installation portion (anaconda) of creating the live CD. Add the --graphical option (default) or the --text option to run the Fedora installer in GUI or text modes, respectively. Use -C to run the installer in command line mode (with no user interaction). To use command mode, you must provide a complete kickstart file (--kickstart option).

- **Install from kickstart**—Using kadischi, you can enter the --kickstart option to indicate that information be fed to the install process using a kickstart file. For example, to indicate that a kickstart file is called ks.cfg in

your home directory, you could add the following kickstart option:
--kickstart=$HOME/ks.cfg.

 NOTE

See the section "Building from a Kickstart File," later in this chapter, for information on using kickstart files to provide some or all of the information needed during a Fedora install.

- **ISO image overwrite**—By adding -f to the kadischi command line, you can have kadischi overwrite the ISO image indicated on the command line (if one already exists).

BURN THE IMAGE TO CD OR DVD

When you have created the ISO image, you can test the image using qemu or burn that image to a CD, DVD, or other bootable medium (such as a USB flash drive). For Fedora, the qemu package is included with Fedora Extras. So, with an Internet connection, you should be able to install the qemu package by simply typing the following as root user:

```
# yum install qemu
```

If you used the same locations as shown in the procedure, the ISO image will be named FC6-live.iso in your home directory. Here is an example of a qemu command line for testing that Fedora live CD iso:

```
# qemu -cdrom ~/FC6-live.iso -boot d -m 768
```

In this example, qemu boots the FC6-live.iso image so that it appears in a window on the desktop. The -cdrom option tells qemu that the file is a CD-ROM image. The -boot d option indicates that the image is booted as an El Torito CD. The -m option, in this example, tells qemu to use 768MB of RAM as virtual RAM to boot the live CD (you should use as much as you have available).

The qemu command and the process of burning ISO images to one of those media are discussed in further detail in Appendix B, "Building, Testing, and Burning ISOs."

CUSTOMIZING A FEDORA LIVE CD

Although customizing a Fedora Live CD or DVD can be as simple as just selecting the features you would put in a normal Fedora Core installation (selecting software packages, keyboard, language, network configuration, and so on), you can customize your live Fedora CD with Kadischi in many other ways.

To help understand where your opportunities are for customizing a live Fedora CD, here is a list of activities that occur when the kadischi command runs:

- **kadischi command options and configuration files**—Options on the kadischi command line indicate the location of the Fedora software repository and the filename of the resulting ISO image (the actual bootable image you will burn to CD). Most of the other options you might add let you indicate how anaconda will run. (See the kadischi options described at the end of the "Trying a Test Build" section, earlier in this chapter.)

  The kadischi command sets the location of the build directory to a subdirectory of /tmp. You can override that location by adding the --tempdir variable to the command line (for example, --tempdir=/home/chris/build). You can also change the location where Kadischi scripts and files are stored (/usr/share/kadischi by default) by changing the value of INSTALLDIR in the /etc/kadischi/kadischi.conf file.

- **Fedora (anaconda) installer**—The anaconda installer used to install the Fedora distribution to the build directory that is created for your live CD is a new version of the standard Fedora anaconda installer that has been updated to be able to build live CDs. To use anaconda to build live CDs, kadischi runs anaconda with the --livecd option.

  Based on the options given to the kadischi command, anaconda can be run in different modes: GUI, text-based, or command (based entirely on selections from a kickstart file you provide). The screens you see are the standard Fedora Core installation screens. You can also bypass those screens by feeding the required information via a kickstart file.

- **Kadischi post-install scripts**—When Fedora is installed to the build directory, a set of post-install scripts are run from the /usr/share/kadischi/post_install_scripts directory. Those scripts modify the standard Fedora install so it can run from a live CD.

- **Initial RAM disk**—The /usr/share/kadischi/livecd-mkinitrd.sh script creates the initial RAM disk (initrd.img) used as the file system when the kernel initially boots the live CD.

- **Compressed files**—Any files and directories that need to remain writeable are copied to a single directory and compressed to the kadischi.tar.gz file (using the movefiles.py script). Then the entire file system is compressed into a single file, and files such as the kernel and initrd.img file (that are not compressed) are added to the compressed archive.

- **Build directory cleaned**—The directory (named /tmp/kadischi.xxx) that was created during this process in the build directory is removed. The xxx is replaced by a set of random numbers and letters, so each live CD build directory has a name that is unique.

The following sections describe how to modify your Kadischi configuration to change how your live CD is created. Step through those sections to find where configuration files are located and ideas on ways you can change them.

Besides describing existing Kadischi configuration files and scripts, I cover how to create your own kickstart file to bypass some or all of the Fedora (anaconda) installation process. You need to use a kickstart in most cases when you are fine-tuning a live CD, and you don't want to have to step through (and remember) all the options you want to set along the way.

Changing Scripts and Configuration Files

The /usr/share/kadischi directory contains scripts and other content in Kadischi that you might want to modify to adapt to your own custom Fedora live CD. Two configuration files for Kadischi (kadischi.conf and buildstamp files) are located in the /etc/kadischi directory.

Before you start changing the contents of your kadischi directory, however, I recommend that you make a copy of that entire directory, in case you have a problem and want to go back to any of the original files. For example:

```
# cp -a /usr/share/kadischi /usr/share/kadischi-original
```

The scripts you can modify in the kadischi directory are python (.py), perl (.pl), or shell (.sh) scripts:

- livecd-mkinitrd.sh—This script creates the initial RAM disk (initrd.img) that is used on the live CD.

- install-boot.sh—This script creates the files needed to initially boot the live CD. It copies the initial RAM disk (initrd.img) and kernel, and creates configuration files in the isolinux directory. You can modify this script to change message files, boot options, and other features that relate directly to when the live CD boots up (as described later in this chapter).

- kadischi.py—This is the python script that runs (along with the contents of the build.conf file) when you launch the kadischi command (/usr/bin/kadischi). If you like, you can set variables in this script to add options (such as arguments to anaconda) or override settings (such as the locations of your build directory or ISO image).

Another opportunity for customizing how Kadischi creates your live Fedora CD is with scripts in the /usr/share/kadischi/post_install_scripts directory. After the Fedora software is installed temporarily in the build directory, kadischi runs the post-install scripts. Names of scripts in the post_install_scripts directory begin with numbers to indicate the order in which they are executed. Scripts include these:

- 01prelink.sh—This script does a chroot to run prelink on the build directory.
- 02install.sh—This script installs system start-up scripts to the live CD that uncompress files and mount file systems needed to start the live CD.
- 03fstab.py—This script modifies the /etc/fstab for the live CD to include file systems that need to be mounted. You might want to add features to detect and mount hard disk or other storage media partitions to this script.
- 04userconfig.pl—This script runs the authconfig and lokkit commands to turn on requested security features used for the live CD. By default, those commands enable shadow passwords and disable the firewall and SELinux features. This script also runs the ntsysv command to let the live CD's user select which installed services are turned on or not turned on.
- 05fsclean.py—This script removes or cleans out directories and files (such as temporary and log files) that aren't needed on the live CD.
- 06sysconfig.py—This scripts creates special links and directories needed for live CD functions. It also configures firstboot (to let the user do initial configuration when the CD boots) and kudzu (to do hardware detection each time the CD boots). (Changing RUN_FIRSTBOOT from YES to NO is one way of disabling the firstboot process.)
- 07accounts.sh—This script lets you add a nonroot user to your live CD. This is a way to get a username and password of your choice added to the live CD needing to run firstboot and have users enter their own user name before the CD fully boots up.

You can modify existing scripts or add your own scripts to this directory to change how the live CD is set up to run. For example, you could change the type of password protection done by changing the 04auth.sh script.

Changing Boot Parameters and Splash Screens

As with most Linux live CDs, the initial boot process of a Fedora live CD is directed by the Isolinux bootloader. By adding or modifying files in the /boot/isolinux directory, you can add options, message files, and splash screens to change the look and behavior of your live CD. (See Chapter 5, "Looking Inside Live CD Components," for more information about how isolinux works.)

Probably the best way to modify the isolinux files for your live CD is through the /usr/share/kadischi/install-boot.sh file. Besides copying files needed to initially boot the CD to the /boot/isolinux directory, it creates the /boot/isolinux/isolinux.cfg file, which defines the initial boot screens and activities.

WARNING

Be sure to have a backup copy of the install-boot.sh file before proceeding. If there is a mistake in this file, it could prevent your live CD from booting at all.

The following procedure steps you through modifying the install-boot.sh script to add or change text appearing on your boot screens, add an image to your initial boot screen, and change kernel parameters:

1. Create a directory to hold the extra files. For example, I created a directory named myfiles in my home directory (/home/chris):

   $ mkdir $HOME/myfiles

2. For this example, I create two boot message files (plain text) in the (/home/chris/myfiles) directory. The first boot screen (boot.msg) will include an image (splash screen) and a few words; the second screen (about.msg) will include a description of the live CD being created. Here is the boot.msg file I created:

```
^L
^Xsplash.lss
 -  Press <ENTER> or type linux to boot directly to Fedora Core Live
 -  Type test <ENTER> to test your hardware.
 -  Press F2 to read about this live CD

^00f[F1-Main Menu] [F2-About this CD]^007
```

The following is an example of a file named about.msg that I created:
```
^000
^L
```

```
^009My Own Fedora Live Security CD^007

Software for testing and securing your systems and networks are
contained on this live CD. The CD image itself was created using
Kadischi along with Fedora Core/Fedora Extras software packages.

Press <Enter> to boot the CD
Type test<Enter> to boot the CD with additional debug information.
```

```
^00f[F1-Main Menu] [F2-About this CD]^007
```
You can create multiple .msg files and assign them to appear in function keys from F1 (usually used for the first boot screen) to F10. For this example, boot.msg will be assigned to F1 and about.msg will be assigned to F2. (To indicate a message file for the F10 function key, you need to use the F0 label.)

3. Using any image you like, create a splash screen and convert it to an lss file. For this example, I used Tux the penguin (www.isc.tamu.edu/~lewing/linux) and created a file called splash.lss. Figure 7-4 shows an example of what the resulting initial boot screen looks like.

4. Next, you need to identify the two boot screens and splash screen in the isolinux.cfg file and then have them copied to the /boot/isolinux directory on the CD. To do that, edit the Kadischi file that creates isolinux.cfg: /usr/share/kadischi/install-boot.sh. For example, using a text editor (as root user), I added the lines shown in bold to my install-boot.sh file.

```
#!/bin/bash

sysdir=$1
csysdir=$2
kernel=$3
    .
```

FIGURE 7-4 Create your own splash screen image for when the live CD boots up.

NOTE

See Chapter 5 for information on creating splash screens and .msg files (including how to enter control codes to change colors) that can be used during the isolinux boot process.

```
        .
        .
        .
cp $sysdir/boot/isolinux/initrd.img $csysdir/boot/isolinux/initrd.img
cp $sysdir/boot/vmlinuz-$kernel $csysdir/boot/isolinux/vmlinuz
cp /usr/lib/syslinux/isolinux.bin $csysdir/boot/isolinux/
cp /home/chris/mydata/boot.msg $csysdir/boot/isolinux/
cp /home/chris/mydata/about.msg $csysdir/boot/isolinux/
cp /home/chris/mydata/splash.lss $csysdir/boot/isolinux/
cp /home/chris/mydata/memtest $csysdir/boot/isolinux/
        .
        .
        .
cat > $csysdir/boot/isolinux/isolinux.cfg <<_EOF_
default linux
prompt 1
display boot.msg
timeout 600
F1 boot.msg
F2 about.msg
F3 general.msg
F4 license.msg
```

```
label linux
  kernel vmlinuz
  append initrd=initrd.img quiet $kernel_params 5
label debug
  kernel vmlinuz
  append initrd=initrd.img INITRD_DBG=x $kernel_params
label memtest86
  kernel memtest
  append -
_EOF_
```

In the previous procedure, I added cp lines to copy the boot.msg, about.msg, and splash.lss files to the CD's /boot/isolinux directory. I also added a display line to indicate that the boot.msg file appears on the original boot screen. In addition, I indicated that the boot.msg and about.msg files should be displayed when the F1 or F2 function keys are pressed from the boot screens, respectively. If you like, you can identify msg files for function keys up to F8.

One other argument I added to the end of the append line after the first label is the number 5. This causes the default label (linux) to be booted to initialization state 5. As a result, when my live CD boots, I get a graphical first boot screen and graphical login screen instead of text-based first boot and login screen. You do this only if you have selected to install a graphical interface, such as the GNOME Desktop Environment on your live CD. To force a non-graphical login, use 3 instead of 5.

You can pass other arguments to the kernel that is initially booted by adding other options to the append line following a label. For example, you could turn off certain features (such as nodma, noscsi, or noapm). Chapter 1, "Starting Up with Live Linux CDs," describes boot options, although not every live CD supports all boot options.

Another thing you might want to do is add your own labels. In this example, there are three labels: linux, test, and memtest86. The memtest86 label is used to have a memory test option from the boot prompt, as the regular Fedora Core installation CD does. You can add your own labels to run a single bootable command (such as memtest) or use existing kernels that simply append different options (such as different vga settings). Examples of boot labels you might want to add are described in Chapter 5.

Notice that everything between the isolinux.cfg line and the final EOF is added to the resulting isolinux.cfg file. If you like, you can add another label, change the timeout, or add boot options to the vmlinuz lines. Refer to the isolinux section in Chapter 5 for further information relating to working with the isolinux.cfg file.

Building from a Kickstart File

One of the installation types Fedora Core supports is called a kickstart install. By creating a kickstart file that contains information needed to direct the Fedora Core installation process, you can bypass some (or all) of the anaconda installation screens.

Kickstart files are often used to do unattended Fedora Core installations. If you are installing Fedora Core on multiple computers (especially if they are configured similarly), a kickstart install can make sure you get the exact installation you want each time.

Using a kickstart file to create your Fedora live CD with Kadischi offers several advantages. As you tune up and customize your live CD with Kadischi, you want to make continuous rebuilds with kadischi as automated as possible. Creating a kickstart files saves you from having to click through the install screens over and over. It also makes sure you get the exact packages, languages, network settings, and other Fedora features you want as you continuously rebuild your live CD.

Here are some ways you can create a kickstart file to use to make your live CD:

- **Sample kickstart files**—You can start with a minimal kickstart file that comes with Kadischi. The sample, minimal kickstart file in Kadischi is named `minimal-livecd.cfg` and is located in the `/usr/share/kadischi/ks_examples` directory. Also in that directory is `standard-livecd.cfg` (which can build a more complete desktop system) and `xen-livecd` (which can build a live CD with a Xen-enabled kernels so the live CD can run multiple virtualized operating systems). The other kickstart file in that directory is `standard-livedvd.cfg`, which builds a DVD-sized ISO image that includes most of the Fedora Core distribution.

- **`system-config-kickstart`**—Run the `system-config-kickstart` GUI utility to create a custom kickstart file. The `system-config-kickstart` package (which includes the utility of the same name) is part of Fedora Core, but it isn't installed by default.

- **Kickstart file from installation**—After a normal permanent Fedora Core install to hard disk, anaconda places a kickstart file called `anaconda-ks.cfg` in the `/root` directory. That file contains the settings you used during that installation. So, essentially, you could use that same kickstart file to repeat the same installation (without having to step through the install screens) or create a live CD with the same settings and software packages.

To use a kickstart file to create a live CD with the kadischi command, you need to create the kickstart file and then identify it with the --kickstart option. Here is an example of a kadischi command with the minimal kickstart file I copied to start with:

```
# cd /usr/share/kadischi/ks_examples
# cp minimal-livecd.cfg $HOME/mydata/
# cd
# kadischi ./FC6/ ./FC6-live.iso --kickstart=./mydata/minimal-livecd.cfg
```

The kadischi command shown here will run without your intervention. However, it will cause the Fedora Core installation screen to pop up as packages are being installed. To keep the installation screens from appearing at all (for example, if you are running from a text-only shell environment), add the -C option to the command line (along with the kickstart file), as shown in the following example:

```
# kadischi -C ./FC6/ ./FC6-live.iso --kickstart=./mydata/minimal-livecd.cfg
```

You can try out the minimal kickstart file yourself. With the previous command line shown, a minimum Fedora Core installation is used to create the live CD (about 163MB total size after compression). The minimal-livecd.cfg file contains the following (note that a \ indicates a line that wraps because of our page size and should actually appear on one line):

```
# Kickstart file automatically generated by anaconda.

install
lang en_US.UTF-8
langsupport --default=en_US.UTF-8 en_US.UTF-8 en_US en \
      en_US.UTF-8 en_US en en_US.UTF-8 en_US en
keyboard us
#xconfig --card "RIVA TNT2" --videoram 4096 --hsync 31.5-37.9 \
      --vsync 50-70 --resolution 800x600 --depth 16
#network --device eth0 --onboot no --bootproto dhcp \
      --hostname fedora.livecd
#network --device sit0 --onboot no --bootproto dhcp \
      --hostname fedora.livecd
rootpw --iscrypted $1$XM/k9ZA1$GMYPu/4Mr3PKKqcbneMeL.
firewall --enabled
selinux --disabled
authconfig --enableshadow --enablemd5
timezone Europe/Belgrade
bootloader --location=none
# The following is the partition information you requested
# Note that any partitions you deleted are not expressed
# here so unless you clear all partitions first, this is
# not guaranteed to work
```

```
#clearpart --linux

# We shouldn't expect to be prompted when finished, let's not.
reboot

%packages
# Packages to exclude for minimal package set
- atk
- bind
- bind-libs
- bind-utils
- bluez-libs
- bluez-pin
- bluez-utils
- caching-nameserver
- cairo
- cyrus-sasl-plain
- expat
- freeglut
- GConf2
- htmlview
- irda-utils
- libglade2
- libICE
- libIDL
- libSM
- libX11
- libXau
- libXcursor
- libXdmcp
- libXext
- libXfixes
- libXft
- libXi
- libXinerama
- libXmu
- libXrandr
- libXrender
- libXt
- libXxf86vm
- mesa-libGL
- mesa-libGLU
- NetworkManager
- numactl
- ORBit2
# End package set

%post
```

Before you use the provided kickstart file, you should change at least the rootpw line (to set your own encrypted password) and timezone (to set the time zone in which the live CD is expected to run). Also, uncommenting and using a network line saves you from having to deal with the network configuration screen. Those and other kickstart options you might want to use are also described here:

install
: Indicates that the Fedora installation is a new install instead of an upgrade.

lang
: Indicates the primary language to use during the installation process.

langsupport
: Indicates the language to be installed on the live CD. If more than one language is installed, a --default= option must be set to indicate which language is used by default.

keyboard
: Sets the type of keyboard to be used.

xconfig
: If you are installing GNOME, KDE, or other X desktop software, you can set specifics about your X server configuration. If you don't set xconfig, Fedora tries to probe for your monitor and video card. If your display configuration is not properly detected, you might need to set your X configuration after you boot up using the system-config-display utility.

network
: You can set your network configuration so that your network comes up when you boot your live CD. If a DHCP server is available, you can use a line such as the following to have your network come up automatically:

```
network --bootproto=dhcp –device=eth0
```

rootpw
: Using rootpw with iscrypted expects an encrypted MD5 password to be assigned to the root user. To create an MD5 encrypted password to use on the rootpw line, type the following:

```
# openssl passwd -1
Password: mygnucar
Verifying - Password: mygnucar
$1$oobl1gYQ$PhbOsJQjHyTYYRcxrEwKNO
```

Type the password you want to use (twice) as prompted. The previous example shows the encrypted string resulting from the password mygnucar. (Of course, you want to select your own password and use the string that results.)

In your kickstart file, replace the string after `rootpw`
`--iscrypted` with the string produced by the `openssl` command. The password you entered to get this result is what
you use to log in as root to your live CD.

firewall

Setting `firewall` to `--enable` turns on the iptables firewall
but doesn't allow any incoming connections unless you
specifically enable ports to allow them. You can allow individual incoming services (`--ssh`, `--telnet`, `--smtp`, `--http`,
or `--ftp`) or allow access to specific port numbers
`--port=XXX` (where you replace *XXX* with a port number on
which you want to allow incoming connections). You can
turn off iptables service completely (effectively blocking all
incoming requests) by setting `--disable` for the firewall
option.

selinux

Setting this value to `--disabled` will disable the Security
Enhanced Linux feature.

authconfig

Sets how authentication is done. The `--enablemd5` option
expects you to use MD5 encrypted user passwords. The
`--enableshadow` option causes passwords to be stored in the
/etc/shadow file instead of the /etc/passwd file. Other methods, such as NIS (`--enablenis`), LDAP (`--enableldap`), Kerberos 5 (`--enablekrb5`), Hesiod (`--enablehesiod`), or SMB
server (`--enablesmbauth`), can be used instead.

timezone

Sets the default time zone used for the live CD. Use the
`system-config-date` utility to see a list of available time
zones.

bootloader

Because Kadischi uses isolinux to boot from the live CD, you
don't need a GRUB or LILO bootloader on your live CD. The
bootloader is therefore set to the value of `--location=none`.

%packages

After the `%packages` directive, you add any software packages
you would like to add beyond the minimal set of packages.
The minimal package set doesn't include a desktop interface
and includes very few server packages. (Those packages
shown in the minimal example, preceded by a hyphen, are
actually those that are excluded from the normal hard-disk
minimal install.) See the sidebar "Choosing Software Packages for Your Fedora Live CD" for further information on
adding packages either from the Fedora Core distribution or
outside of it.

TIP

Excluding Docs

You can save some space on your live CD by excluding documentation that comes with Fedora packages. An Everything install of Fedora Core results in more than 200MB of documents, man pages, and info files in /usr/share/. To exclude documentation from packages you install to your live CD, %packages should appear as %packages --excludedocs.

%post   You can add scripts you want to run after packages are installed on separate lines following the %post directive. This is a good place to do some initial configuration of your live CD. For example, you could use useradd to add a user. Using the encrypted created earlier for root, here are some commands to add a user after the %post line:

```
%post
/usr/sbin/useradd chris
/usr/sbin/usermod -p '$1$oob11gYQ$PhbOsJQjHyTYYRcxrEwKNO' chris
/usr/bin/chfn -f "Chris Jones" chris
```

In the example just shown, the user named chris is added to the live CD, with a home directory /home/chris created by default. The usermod command then enters the password for chris. Finally, the chfn -f command sets the user's full name to Chris Jones.

To find more information about these and other options you can set in your kickstart file, refer to the kickstart-docs.txt file in the /usr/share/doc/ anaconda* directory. To get that file, you must have the anaconda RPM package installed.

Adding Post-Install Scripts

You can change any of the post-install scripts (which are located in the following directory: /usr/share/kadischi/post_install_scripts) to modify the contents of the live CD you are creating after Fedora Core is installed to the build directory and before the file system is compressed and made into an ISO image. Likewise, you can add your own scripts to the post_install_scripts directory.

The post-install scripts are run with the location of the build directory (containing the newly installed Fedora Core live CD system) as an argument. Script names begin with a number, to indicate the order in which each script is run.

CHOOSING SOFTWARE PACKAGES FOR YOUR FEDORA LIVE CD

To select packages to install on your Fedora live CD, you can indicate either groups of packages or individual packages after the %packages line. You can also indicate that selected packages not be installed from a group that has been selected.

In most cases, you will probably want to add groups of packages. Indicate a group with an @ sign followed by either the group name (such as X Window System) or ID (such as base-x). For individual packages, just enter the package name without the @ sign. The following is a list of groups names you can consider adding to your live CD (to install all groups, simply use @ Everything instead):

```
%packages
@ Basic X Window System
@ GNOME Desktop Environment
@ KDE (K Desktop Environment)
@ Editors
@ Engineering and Scientific
@ Graphical Internet
@ Text-based Internet
@ Office/Productivity
@ Sound and Video
@ Authoring and Publishing
@ Graphics
@ Games and Entertainment
@ Server Configuration Tools
@ Web Server
@ Mail Server
@ Windows File Server
@ DNS Name Server
@ FTP Server
@ PostgreSQL Database
@ MySQL Database
@ News Server
@ Network Servers
@ Legacy Network Server
@ Development Tools
@ X Software Development
@ GNOME Software Development
@ KDE Software Development
@ Compatibility Arch Development Support
@ Legacy Software Development
@ Java Development
@ Eclipse
@ Language Support
@ Administration Tools
```

```
@ System Tools
@ Printing Support
@ Java
@ Compatibility Arch Support
@ x86 Compatibility Arch Support
```

To see a description of each of these groups, run the system-config-packages utility. Click the Details link for a group to see what packages it contains and to see which are installed by default.

To install an individual package, put the package name on a line of its own. To not install a package that is part of a group's package list, put a hyphen before the name of a package. For example, the following package list installs the Basic X Window System, while adding the cdrecord and rhythmbox packages:

```
%packages --resolvedeps
@ X Window System
cdrecord
rhythmbox
```

SUMMARY

Using Kadischi, you can create custom bootable CDs and DVDs of Fedora Core. Kadischi works by accessing a Fedora Core software repository and installing the software packages you select to a build directory on the local system. Kadischi then modifies the contents of that directory so it can run from a CD. The result is an ISO image that can be burned to a CD or DVD.

You have many opportunities to customize your Fedora live CD with Kadischi. Because the anaconda installer runs as part of the kadischi process, you can choose the packages that are installed, the keyboard and language used, your Ethernet connection, and other basic anaconda features. You can also modify scripts that come with Kadischi to change boot screens or modify the contents of your Fedora live CD file system.

If you choose to use an optional kickstart file, you can automate much of the process normally done by clicking through anaconda install screens. Using the kickstart file, you can also add post-install scripts to run at the end of the live CD build process.

## CHAPTER 8

Building a Basic Gentoo Live CD

Tools for building live CDs are a natural extension of the Gentoo project. Although prebuilt binaries are available for many Gentoo packages, many people are drawn to Gentoo because it is geared toward those who like to select and build installed Linux systems from scratch.

Although it is possible to build your own Gentoo live CD from scratch, the main procedure in this chapter has you start with an existing `stage2` tarball and builds from there. After you have built a live CD with that procedure, the following section describes how to use tools from the Catalyst project (the Gentoo release building tool) much the same way as you would install Gentoo to hard disk. The difference is that the result is an ISO image instead of an installed system on hard disk.

The procedures contained in this chapter are based on two different approaches to creating a Gentoo live CD:

- **Remastering a Gentoo live CD**—This procedure is, essentially, a remastering of an existing Gentoo live CD. You install Gentoo to hard disk (to create a working environment), copy live CD components (from a `stage2` tarball) to a directory on the hard disk, then add and remove software for that directory structure. That directory structure is then used to create the new ISO image. (http://gentoo-wiki.com/HOWTO_build_a_LiveCD_from_scratch). This is an unofficial process for creating Gentoo live CDs and is only capable of building a live CD for AMD64 or x86 architectures.

- **Building a Gentoo live CD with Catalyst**—Starts by using a `stage` tarball to create a base image. You then install the packages you want to that image and ultimately produce a custom live CD image. This procedure relies on the recently enhanced Catalyst release building tool.

If you choose to use Catalyst to create your Gentoo live CD, refer to the mailing list and other resources associated with the Catalyst project that are described later in this chapter. Because the project is still in early stages of development, it will help to find out the latest versions that people have gotten working before you get started.

ABOUT GENTOO LINUX

Gentoo Linux (www.gentoo.org) is a great Linux system for performance tweakers and cutting-edge users. Its primary claim to fame is its software-distribution system, based on the BSD ports system, called Portage. Key elements of Portage include these:

- The Portage tree (`/usr/portage`), containing more than 10,000 software packages prepared to use in Gentoo.
- The `emerge` command, which lets you select, download, and build on-the-fly any of those software packages. This command also lets you search and update your Portage tree and installed packages.

With Gentoo, not only do you get exactly the packages you want, but you also build them to run specifically for your hardware configuration. Gentoo is set up to take advantage of the latest changes that are constantly being rolled into the Portage tree. A single command updates all your packages (`emerge -u world`) or gets the latest Portage tree (`emerge –sync`).

When you use prebuilt binaries from a Linux project, there are always features built in that you don't need and possibly others not built in that you do. For example, you might not need Kerberos authentication or Oracle database support. By building the packages yourself with `emerge`, using the USE flag, you can request which features are and are not built into the software capable of supporting those features.

If you are trying to set up Gentoo yourself, a challenge is that you need to know a lot of Linux to use it effectively. Even with the recent graphical installer and Gentoo Reference Platform (a set of prebuilt packages), a lot of decisions require you to be Linux-savvy. Also, if something goes wrong, you won't be able to fix it by just clicking a button.

Because Gentoo is in such a constant state of change, it's very possible that something will go wrong in the procedure described in this chapter for building live CDs. So, the other great challenge is to learn how to track down and fix problems. The Gentoo community has a lot of resources you can draw on to help:

- **Documentation (www.gentoo.com/doc)**—Gentoo Linux comes with an active document effort to produce instructions to go with Gentoo software. If you are new to Gentoo, start with the Frequently Asked Questions and Installation Related Resources documents from the main documentation page. It's best to have read these documents before you start asking questions in Gentoo forums.

- **Forums (http://forums.gentoo.org)**—Some Gentoo forums contain literally hundreds of thousands of posts.

- **Mailing lists (www.gentoo.org/main/en/lists.xml)**—More than 50 mailing lists are associated with different Gentoo topics. Mailing lists are available in multiple languages as well.

In general, building a live CD based on Gentoo is more difficult than starting with a Debian-based live CD (such as Knoppix) or a Fedora Linux package set (using Kadischi tools). But if you have a lot of time, bandwidth, disk space, and patience, you have the potential of ending up with a highly tuned Linux live CD.

SETTING UP TO BUILD A GENTOO LIVE CD

To build a Gentoo live CD, you should start with an installed Gentoo Linux system. Because a Gentoo system can be many things to different people, I started the installation with a Gentoo live CD (2006.1) and selected most of the Gentoo Reference Platform (GRP) packages to have a stable platform to begin with. With Gentoo running, I later added packages needed specifically for building live CDs.

The Gentoo project doesn't have system resource guidelines you need to follow to be able to create live CDs. After running through the process, here is what I came up with for my build system:

- **Memory**—A minimum 512MB of RAM and 1GB of swap space seemed to be enough to effectively run the Gentoo system needed to build the live CD. Of course, more will get the job done faster.

- **Hard disk**—I used a 10GB partition for the Gentoo system I used to build the live CD. By selecting the GRP packages and adding those packages needed specifically for building the live CD, I consumed about 3GB of disk space. Creating the build environment to have a copy of the file system structure and produce a 700MB live CD used about another 3GB. That left about 4GB for keeping around extra software and a few versions of the live CD ISOs.

- **Internet**—You need an Internet connection to perform this procedure. Even if you have a Gentoo live CD to start with, you will need to grab software tools (catalyst in particular) and probably will want to grab package updates.

If you have a machine with enough resources to get started, the first thing you need to do is install Gentoo to your hard disk.

INSTALLING GENTOO

The recently added Gentoo graphical installer is available from an official Gentoo live CD. You can begin installing Gentoo to your hard disk by getting the Gentoo live CD and booting it on the machine you want to use as your build machine.

For this procedure, I used the 2006.1 Gentoo live CD (livecd-i686-installer-2006.1.iso), which is included with this book's DVD. You can find Gentoo download locations by selecting Get Gentoo from the Gentoo.org site. I got the live CD I used from http://gentoo.osuosl.org/releases/x86/2006.1/livecd. You can burn the ISO image to CD, as described in Appendix A, "On the DVD," or simply boot Gentoo directly from the DVD.

The quickest way to install is to use the kernel and packages contained on the live CD. This will get you up and running quickly. However, I had some trouble with the kernel that came with the live CD, so I chose to download and recompile the gentoo-sources for the kernel and it seemed to work better for my situation (although it took about an hour longer to run).

NOTE

Refer to the Gentoo Linux Installation Guide (select the appropriate document from www.gentoo.org/doc/en). It will help you understand some of the issues presented to you during the install process.

Running the Installer

Here's the procedure I used to install Gentoo from the official Gentoo live CD for x86 platforms:

1. **Boot the live CD**—Insert the Gentoo live CD into your computer and reboot. Boot Gentoo as required from the boot prompt. When the live CD displays the login prompt, wait for a few seconds and the system will log you in automatically.

2. **Start Installer**—From the desktop, open the Gentoo Linux Installer icon. The Gentoo Linux Installer screen appears.

3. **Read the Welcome screen** and select Networkless, then Forward. The Pre-install Config screen appears. You should not need to change anything here. Select Forward and the Partitioning screen appears.

4. **Partition disk**—Select the hard drive you want to install on (if you have more than one drive) in the Devices box. Then do either of these:

   ■ Click the gray part of the bar representing unallocated space on that disk. Then add the partitions you want.

   ■ Select Recommended Layout to have Gentoo create a recommended layout from your unallocated space for you to install Gentoo. The recommended layout requires at least 4GB of unpartitioned space.

   The Gentoo installer recommends a small boot partition (about 100MB), a swap area (two times the system RAM, up to 2GB), and a root partition (/) that consumes the rest of the free space. You can change these items as you choose. If not enough space exists on your hard disk, you can delete one or more partitions (just make sure that you are not deleting anything that contains information you want to keep). Select Forward when you are done. The Network Mounts screen appears.

5. **Connect NFS share**—Because this is a networkless installation, the options will be grayed out on this screen. Select Forward to continue to the Stage screen.

6. **Choose install type**—Because this is a networkless installation, the defaults for a binary install are chosen and the other options are grayed out. Select Forward; the Portage tree screen appears.

7. **Portage tree**— Choosing a networkless install automatically selects using portage from a snapshot, with the snapshot on the CD itself chosen automatically. Select Forward. The `make.conf` screen appears.

8. **Modify settings**—This screen lets you enable distcc or ccache for subsequent builds, as well as to set your MAKEOPTS. Other options are grayed out because this is a binary installation. Click Forward to continue. The Kernel screen appears.

9. **Choose kernel**— The `livecd-kernel` option is already selected to use as the kernel for the installed Gentoo system. Select Forward to continue to the bootloader screen.

10. **Choose bootloader**— The Grub bootloader is automatically chosen for you. Select to have it installed on the master boot record (MBR) for the hard

disk set to boot on your machine. If you have multiple operating systems installed on your computer, you might choose to not install the master boot record on your first hard disk and manually set it to boot your Gentoo install. Click Forward to continue to the Time Zone screen.

11. **Set time zone**—Select the time zone you reside in from the map or list below the map. Click Forward to continue to the Networking screen.

12. **Set up network**—If you plan to use a DHCP connection for your network interface, select your network interface (such as eth0) from the Interface box, choose DHCP, and then click Save. (Or select Static from the Configuration box and add your address information manually.) This configures the network for your installed system. Click Forward to continue to the Daemons page.

13. **Choose cron and logger**—Select the Cron and System Logger daemons to use (the defaults are fine in most cases). For a networkless install, you can choose vixie-cron as your cron daemon, or none, if you wish not to use cron. Click Forward to go to the Extra Packages screen.

14. **Select packages**—Because the intent now is to get the major components of your Gentoo install working, select the packages from the list shown that you want on your system. Only packages marked GRP are available, because pre-built binaries are available for those packages. You can always add more packages when the initial install is done. Click Forward to go to the Startup Services screen.

15. **Turn on services**—Select to have those services that you want to start up at boot time. Select to turn on only services for those packages that you installed on the previous screen. Select Forward to continue to the Other Settings screen.

16. **Select settings**—Choose settings associated with the display manager, keymaps, and other features that interest you. Select Forward to continue to the Users screen.

17. **Set root password**—Add a root password (twice and click Verify to check it) and select Add User to add a regular user account to your Gentoo system. Click Forward to continue to the Review screen.

18. **Review options (last chance!)**—This is your last chance to back out before making any changes to your computer's hard disk. Review the list of current install options and click Save if you want to save these settings for another install. If everything looks okay, click Install to begin reformatting your hard disk and installing Gentoo. Depending on which options you selected during the installation setup procedure, the process of building and installing Gentoo can take quite a while.

19. **Close installer**—When you see the "Install Complete!" message, you can close the installer window.

20. **Log out and reboot**—Select to log out. Then from the login screen, select System and reboot the computer to have the Gentoo you installed to your hard disk booted. (Be sure to remove the Gentoo CD after it shuts down and before Gentoo comes up again from hard disk.)

Configuring the Installed System

After Gentoo reboots, with your newly installed Gentoo system, you can log in to begin the process of gathering the extra software you need to begin building your Gentoo live CD. The first thing you should do is check your system to make sure the major systems you need (and want) are working properly. Here are a few how-tos to help get you going:

- **GNOME Configuration Howto (www.gentoo.org/en/gnome-config.xml)**—Set up the GNOME desktop environment.

- **Alsa Sound Howto (www.gentoo.org/doc/en/alsa-guide.xml)**—Configure your sound system.

- **X Server Configuration Howto (www.gentoo.org/doc/en/xorg-config.xml)**—Starting and tweaking your X display server.

- **Hardware 3d Acceleration Guide (www.gentoo.org/doc/en/dri-howto.xml)**—Turn on 3D rendering for gaming and video.

Adding More Software

You probably want to add other packages as well, just to create a comfortable working environment. If you know the name of some software you are interested in, you can search the Portage database for the name of that software. For example, to look for the abiword word processor, you could type the following:

```
# emerge search abiword | less
Searching...  ..... ..... ..... ..... .....
[ Results for search key : abiword ]
[ Applications found : 2 ]

*   app-office/abiword
        Latest version available: 2.2.11
        Latest version installed: [ Not Installed ]
        Size of downloaded files: 23,390 kB
        Homepage:    http://www.abisource.com
        Description: Fully featured yet light and fast cross platform
                     word processor
        License:     GPL-2
```

From the output just shown, you can see that abiword is a word processor under the app-office category. Before you install the package, you can see its size, the license that covers it, and a brief description. If you want to install it, you can do that with the following emerge command:

```
# emerge abiword
```

I personally like the vim text editor, so emerge vim is one of the first things I do after installing Gentoo. You should install whatever tools you are used to having on your Linux system.

Creating the Gentoo Live CD Remastering Environment

When you get your installed Gentoo system working as you like, you can install the packages needed to start creating your own Gentoo live CD. All of the steps in this procedure should be done as the root user. The procedure also assumes that you will be working from a subdirectory of the /root directory. You should begin with Gentoo booted with yourself logged in as the root user.

NOTE

Although the procedure below can be done entirely from the shell, you may be more comfortable working from a desktop GUI. If you didn't install a display manager, you may have booted to a plain login prompt. To start a GUI after to login, type startx.

1. **Add packages**—After installing Gentoo as previously described, you need to add the squashf-stools and cdrtools packages. You can add them as follows:
   ```
   # emerge squashfs-tools cdrtools
   ```
2. **Create build directory**—You need to create a directory structure for building your live CD. This example creates the directory livecd/source in the root user's home directory (the build scripts described later expect this location):
   ```
   # mkdir -p /root/livecd/source
   ```
3. **Get stage2 tarball and Portage tree**—From any Gentoo mirror, get a stage2 tarball and a snapshot of the latest Portage tree. Here are examples of

wget commands (each should be typed on one line) that get the stage2-x86-
2006.1.tar.bz2 and portage-latest.tar.bz2.

```
# cd ~
# wget
ftp://ftp.ussg.iu.edu/pub/linux/gentoo/releases/x86/current/stages/
stage2-x86-2006.1.tar.bz2
# wget ftp://ftp.ussg.iu.edu/pub/linux/gentoo/snapshots/
portage-latest.tar.bz2
```

4. **Unpack the tarball and Portage tree**—Change to the livecd/source
directory and unpack the stage2 tarball:

```
# cd ~/livecd/source
# tar jxvpf ~/stage2-x86-2006.0.tar.bz2
# mkdir newroot
# cd ~/livecd/source/usr
# tar jxvf ~/portage-latest.tar.bz2
```

5. **Mount directories and devices**—Because you have probably already
downloaded many useful packages for your installed Gentoo system, you can
take advantage of those packages for your live CD by mounting the
/usr/portage/distfiles directory on the directory structure you're building.
Also, before you chroot to the build directory structure, you need to mount a
few special file systems. The last command in this group copies the
resolv.conf file so you can connect with DNS servers to use the Internet
from your chroot environment.

```
# cd ~/livecd/source
# mkdir usr/portage/distfiles
# mount -o bind /usr/portage/distfiles usr/portage/distfiles
# mkdir -p proc dev
# mount -o bind /proc proc
# mount -o bind /sys sys
# mount -o bind /dev dev
# cp /etc/resolv.conf etc/resolv.conf
```

With the build directory now in place, you are ready to chroot to that directory
and begin installing packages and configuring your live CD.

WORKING IN THE CHROOT ENVIRONMENT

Everything installed beneath the /root/livecd/source directory represents the
files that will make up your Gentoo live CD. Using the chroot command, you can
have that directory be the root directory you work from. That way, any time you
install a package or modify a configuration file, that information will go on your live
CD instead of being implemented on your installed Gentoo system.

1. **Change root directory**—Type the following to change your root directory to that of the build directory and open a login shell using the `bash` shell.

   ```
   # chroot /root/livecd/source /bin/bash -login
   ```

NOTE

If you are working from a Gentoo desktop with several Terminal windows open, you want to be sure to run commands intended for the chroot environment from the Terminal window where you just ran the chroot command. To ensure that I'm using the right Terminal window, I change the Terminal Windows title bar to LiveCD. To change the title for gnome-terminal, select Terminal→Set Title and type the name you want to use.

2. **Set up shell environment**—With `/root/livecd/source` as your root directory, commands that you run act only on the file system below that point in your file system. The following commands cause variables to be set in your shell environment so you can begin working from your `chroot` environment. Also, it's a good idea to set the root password for your `chroot` environment.

   ```
   # env-update
   # source /etc/profile
   ```

3. **Prepare to emerge**—As you prepare to start using emerge to install software that will go into your CD, you should understand a few items and modify a few others for your Portage build environment:

   - `make.globals`—Global settings related to using Portage are contained in the `/etc/make.globals` file. Although you should not change this file, it's a good place to check to see where Portage gets files, where it keeps temporary files, and what settings it uses. To override those settings, use the `make.conf` file.

   - `make.conf`—Settings in the `/etc/make.conf` file direct the specific build environment you use to install the packages used on your live CD. Variables you set here override settings in `make.globals` (except for `USE`, `CONFIG_PROTECT*`, and `ACCEPT_KEYWORDS` variables, which are added to existing variable values). For details on what `make.conf` can contain, type **man make.conf** or see the `/etc/make.conf.example` file.

   This is where some knowledge of the Gentoo Portage system can be very useful. The variables you set in the `make.conf` file have a profound effect on both the time it takes to install software and the size of the CD image you end up with. The following is an example of a `make.conf` file for creating a Gentoo live CD:

```
CFLAGS="-march=i686 -O2 -pipe"
CHOST="i686-pc-linux-gnu"
CXXFLAGS="${CFLAGS}"
MAKEOPTS="-j2"
USE="livecd X -doc -gnome -gtk -gtk2 kde udev -kerberos "
```

The CFLAGS variable lets you set the CPU instruction settings and optimization to be used when building the packages for your live CD. To learn how to
build your live CD for different architectures, refer to the Safe Cflags page
(www.en.gentoo-wiki.com/safe_cflags).

The -O2 optimization setting is considered to be safe in most cases (-Os can
be used if there will be limited memory on machines where the live CD will
run; -O3 can be used to try to improve optimization, but the results can be
unstable). If you have a multiprocessor system, you can add -j3 (or higher)
MAKEOPTS to improve your build performance.

The USE variable lets you globally set features (represented by flags) that
should be built into the packages you add. Likewise, you can request that
certain features not be installed or added. Flags can represent compile-time
options or might indicate whether to include certain libraries.

In the example just shown, the livecd option is needed to build the system to
work on a live CD. In this case, a KDE desktop live CD is being built, so the
kde option is used along with kdexdeltas (which saves download time for
updates by grabbing only binary diffs for KDE packages). Support was
removed for GNOME (-gnome, -gtk, and -gtk2) and Kerberos features
(-kerberos). Also, to save space, additional documentation for each package
is not included (-doc).

You can find out more about USE flags in the USE Flags chapter of the Gentoo
Handbook (www.gentoo.org/doc/en/handbook/handbook-x86.xml?part=
2&chap=2). Flags are also listed in the use.desc and use.local.desc files,
located in the /usr/portage/profiles directory. To find out which flags a particular package supports, run the emerge -pv command. For example, to check
which USE flags are available for Firefox, type this:

```
# emerge -pv mozilla-firefox
```

To see which use flags are on by default, refer to the make.defaults file in
the /usr/portage/profiles/default-linux/x86/directory for your distribution (for example, 2006.1). You can also use the emerge —info command.

4. **Update current packages**—To get the latest versions of the software that
   is currently in your chroot environment, run the following emerge commands.
   Depending on how many packages are needed (and how many of those are
   already available on your system), these steps can take several hours. When
   the two emerge steps are done, change the root password.

NOTE

You can use the `minimal` flag to run a minimal build that disables many nonessential features. If you add the `minimal` USE flag, you need to put in an exemption for the `perl` package. To do that, before changing to the chroot environment, type the following:

```
# echo "dev-lang/perl -minimal" >> ~livecd/source/etc/portage/
package.use
```

Another trick to reducing the size of your build is to edit the `/etc/locales.gen` file to comment out all languages you don't care to have built for your CD.

```
# emerge -e system
# emerge -e world
# passwd root
New UNIX Password: ********
Retype new UNIX password: ********
```

The `system` package class consists of packages needed for your system to run properly. The `world` package class contains system packages plus packages contained in `/var/lib/portage/world`.

If during the `emerge` process the C compiler was upgraded (`gcc` package), you need to instruct your system to use the new C compiler and then run `emerge` again to update your whole system. Upgrading GCC is described in the GCC Upgrade Guide (www.gentoo.org/doc/en/gcc-upgrading.xml).

5. **Change some /etc configuration files**—You should change a few features manually in configuration files. (Note that at this point, nano may be the only text editor available. You might choose to install vim or emacs to use instead, when a text editor is called for.)

First, set your time zone. Replace area/city with information that is appropriate to where you are. For example, to set the time zone to `America/Chicago`, type the following:

```
# ln -sf /usr/share/zoneinfo/America/Chicago /etc/localtime
```

Another suggested configuration file change is to enable the use of `dmraid`. Type the following:

```
# echo "sys-fs/dmraid ~x86" >> /etc/portage/package.keywords
```

Using any text editor, edit the `/etc/fstab` file so that it includes only the following information (be sure to add a blank line at the end of the file):

```
/dev/root    /           squashfs   ro,defaults   0 0
none         /proc       proc       defaults      0 0
none         /dev/shm    tmpfs      defaults      0 0
none         /dev/pts    devpts     defaults      0 0
```

Other changes to configuration files in the /etc directory are described later. You can do many changes by running system-administration utilities, especially after you enable X applications to run from the chroot environment. For example, another way to reset the time zone is by running the time-admin utility and selecting the time zone from a list.

6. **Add required packages**—To make your chroot environment into an image that can be used as a live CD, a few additional packages are needed. The following emerge command adds those packages:

```
# emerge memtest86+ localepurge genkernel sys-fs/fuse
# emerge logger coldplug mingetty slocate
# rc-update add coldplug default
```

rc-update essentially turns on those services listed, using each service's default settings. Most services you can turn on are listed in the /etc/init.d directory.

7. **Add optional packages**—This is where you add the software packages you want on your live CD. For the most part, you need to choose each of the components, beyond the basic system components, that you want on your live CD. You can do that by searching the /usr/portage directories for interesting packages. Exceptions to that rule are the kde and gnome options, which each result in a large set of packages related to those desktop environments being installed.

Chapters 9, "Customizing a Security Live Linux CD," through 14, "Customizing a Cluster Live Linux CD," describe open-source software that might interest you. Most of that software is available for you to install in Gentoo using the emerge command.

8. **Creating the kernel, initrd, and modules**—To create the kernel used on the live CD, get the gentoo-sources package. You can then make the modules and configure the kernel as follows:

```
# emerge gentoo-sources
# cd /usr/src/linux
# make allmodconfig
# genkernel –menuconfig –no-clean all
```

During the genkernel step, you have the option to change which kernel components are and are not included with your kernel, as well as which are included as drivers or loadable modules. Make sure that the following components are compiled in:

- **File systems**—Include SquashFS, CD-ROM/DVD File Systems → ISO 9660 CD-ROM, and `ext2` file system support. To use the live CD as a rescue CD, you will probably also want other file system types, such as Reiserfs, JFS, XFS, and virtual memory file system support.
- **Device drivers**—Include loopback device, RAM disk (default number 16 and default size 192kb), and IDE/ATAPI CD-ROM support. Include Device Drivers → Block Devices → Initial RAM Disk Support. Include Device Drivers → Block Devices → Loopback Device Support.

If all goes well, you should end up, after some compile time, with `initramfs-genkernel-*`, `kernel-genkernel-*`, and `System.map-genkernel-*` files in your `/boot` directory.

With the new kernel and `initrd` created, copy them to an easier name to work with in the boot directory. This makes it a bit easier to set up the boot loader. Here is an example:

```
# cd /boot
# cp initramfs-genkernel-x86-2.6.17-gentoo-r4 initrd
# cp kernel-genkernel-x86-2.6.17-gentoo-r4 vmlinuz
```

9. **Setting up the boot loader**—For this example, `grub` is used as the boot loader for the live CD. First, install the `grub` package as follows:

```
# emerge grub
# rm /boot/grub/menu.1st
```

Next, create a `/boot/grub/grub.conf` file using any text editor. Here is an example of what the `grub.conf` file might contain:

```
default 0
timeout 30
splashimage=(cd)/boot/grub/splash.xpm.gz

title=LiveCD
  root (cd)
  kernel /boot/vmlinuz vga=788 root=/dev/ram0 \
    init=/linuxrc looptype=squashfs loop=/livecd.squashfs \
 cdroot
  initrd /boot/initrd

title=Memtest86+
  root (cd)
  kernel /boot/memtest86plus/memtest.bin
```

Note that the backslashes (\) are there only to indicate that the kernel line (shown as three lines) should actually be only on one line. Be sure to join the three lines together and remove the two backslashes.

As with other live CDs described in this book, you have the opportunity to modify the boot loader to customize how your live CD boots. In the `menu.1st` file, the boot screen displays the image located at /boot/grub/splash.xpm.gz on the CD; it times out after 30 seconds (timeout 30) and boots the first boot label LiveCD (default 0). You can add your own splash screen (a gzipped xpm file) or change any of the other defaults.

The LiveCD label boots the kernel (vmlinuz) and uses the initial RAM disk (initrd) you created in an earlier step. The only other label is to let the live CD user test the system memory (Memtest86+, which runs the memtest.bin utility). See Chapter 5, "Looking Inside Live CD Components," for more information on modifying the GRUB bootloader.

NOTE

If you prefer to use the isolinux bootloader instead of GRUB, you can create an isolinux directory in the target/ directory. Then edit the isolinux/isolinux.cfg file to work with your configuration. In Gentoo, isolinux components are in the syslinux package (emerge syslinux). When you run mkisofs later, be sure to identify the location of the components in the isolinux directory so that isolinux is used as the bootloader.

10. **Cleaning up unneeded files**—Before you finish up in the chroot environment, you can remove files for locales that you don't need on your live CD. Open the /etc/locale.nopurge file in any text editor. Then comment out the NEEDSCONFIGFIRST line and any language at the end of the file that you don't need on your CD. For example, with a live CD for U.S. English only, the last few lines of your locale.nopurge file could appear as follows:

```
# NEEDSCONFIGFIRST
en
# en_GB
# es
# es_ES
# es_ES@euro
# es_ES.UTF-8
```

With locale.nopurge edited, run localepurge to remove files related to those languages you just commented out. Then run makewhatis -u to reindex the whatis database:

```
# localepurge
# makewhatis -u
```

For the rest of the clean-up, you can leave the chroot environment. Start by closing the chroot environment. From the chrooted shell, type the following:

```
# exit
```

Next, you can unmount the items you mounted earlier. To do that, type the following:

```
# cd /root/livecd/source
# umount sys proc dev usr/portage/distfiles
```

Because you have already spent a lot of time creating the files system for your live CD, if you have disk space, consider making a copy of your chrooted file system before you begin cleaning up. Open a terminal window outside of the chroot environment and type the following:

```
# cd /root/livecd
# cp -ar source/ backup
```

With your backup copy in place, begin removing unnecessary files from your live CD. Here are some ways to remove files that you don't want on your live CD:

```
# cd /root/livecd/source/usr/src/linux; make clean
# cd /root/livecd/source
# find .-type f -name ".keep" -print -exec rm {} \;
# rm -rf var/tmp/*
# rm -rf var/run/*
# rm -rf var/lock/*
# rm -rf var/cache/*
# rm -rf var/db/*
# rm -rf tmp/*
# rm -rf etc/mtab
# touch etc/mtab
# rm -rf var/log
# mkdir var/log
# rm root/.bash_history
```

NOTE

Be very careful when you run the following commands to take note of when leading slashes are and are not used. For example, if you mistakenly put a slash (/) before the directory name in rm -rf tmp/* below, you will remove everything from /tmp on your installed Gentoo system and not on the live CD you are building.

Other files you can consider removing include the Portage tree and documentation. For example, here are a few directories you could delete to further save space:

```
# rm -rf usr/portage/*
# rm -rf etc/portage/*
# rm -rf usr/share/doc/*
# rm -rf usr/src/*
```

MAKING THE LIVE CD IMAGE

To make the live CD image from the directory structure you created, you need to first separate the /boot directory from the rest of the file system. Next, you convert the remaining file system to a squashfs file system and use the two elements to create the live CD, using the mkisofs command.

```
# cd /root/livecd
# mkdir -p target/files/source
# cp -a source/boot target/
# cp -p -R -P -d source/ target/files
# cd target/files
```

The next step is to convert the file system into a single squashfs archive. To do that, type the following:

```
# mksquashfs source/ /root/livecd/target/livecd.squashfs
# touch /root/livecd/target/livecd
# cd /root/livecd/target
# rm -rf files/
```

After the previous set of commands, you should now have a /root/livecd/ target directory that contains a /boot directory (that includes the kernel and files needed to boot your computer) and the livecd.squashfs file (that represents a compressed image of your live CD's file system). If you want anything else to go into the root of your live CD (such as a license file or a README file), you can place that in the target directory as well.

The last step in creating the ISO image is to run the mkisofs command. Here is an example:

```
# cd /root/livecd/target
# mkisofs -R -b boot/grub/stage2_eltorito -no-emul-boot \
  -boot-load-size 4 -boot-info-table -hide-rr-moved \
  -c boot.catalog -o /root/livecd.iso /root/livecd/target/
```

The result of the command just shown is a live CD image called livecd.iso in the /root directory. This ISO image is ready to be tested.

TESTING THE LIVE CD IMAGE

You can test your live CD as you would most any live CD. Here are a few reminders:

- **Use qemu**—You can boot your live CD using the qemu package. Install the qemu package and then use the qemu command with the ISO you just built, as shown:
  ```
  # emerge qemu
  # qemu -cdrom /root/livecd.iso -boot d -m 512
  ```

The emerge command installs the qemu software. The qemu command shown boots the livecd.iso image, telling the command that it is a CD-ROM image (-cdrom), that qemu is booting from a CD image (-boot d), and to use 512MB of virtual memory to run the booted image (-m 512).

- **Burn to media**—You can, of course, burn the ISO image to a CD or DVD. Because you will probably redo your CD image a few times, rewriteable media will probably save you money. To do a quick erase and burn, you can use the following commands:

```
# cdrecord -v gracetime=2 dev=/dev/cdrom -tao blank=fast
# cdrecord -v /root/livecd.iso
```

Many other options exist for cdrecord (try man cdrecord). For example, to do a more thorough erase of your CD, use blank=all instead of blank=fast. After the CD is burned, insert it into the CD drive of an available computer and reboot.

If everything on your CD worked perfectly, you are done. If there are problems, assuming that you kept your source directory, you can go back and make corrections. To make corrections to your CD image, return to the step where you mounted the sys, proc, and other directories in your source directory. Then run the chroot command again and continue forward with the procedure from there to make any changes you desire.

CREATING A GENTOO LIVE CD WITH CATALYST

The Gentoo Catalyst project, which is referred to as the Gentoo Linux Release Engineering Metatool, includes features that let Gentoo users extend the "build-your-own" concept to live CDs as well. Catalyst is the official tool for building live CDs in Gentoo. It is provided in this chapter as an alternative method because, for the first-time Gentoo CD builder, it can be a bit trickier to produce live CDs with Catalyst.

 NOTE

Using Catalyst to produce live CDs is not intended for casual users. The information in this section is our attempt to steer more advanced users toward the recommended way of producing Gentoo live CDs.

With Catalyst, you can create your own group of settings and packages in what are referred to as spec files. With those spec files, you execute the commands that are used to make the live CD. You can find more information on Catalyst here:

- **Catalyst project page**—For links to the Catalyst FAQ and Reference Manual, refer to the Catalyst project page (www.gentoo.org/proj/en/releng/catalyst). The documentation on the most recent version of Catalyst was not yet complete at the time of this writing. However, if descriptions of the `catalyst` command are still available, they will better reflect the current state of how `Catalyst` is used than do descriptions of the older `catalyst` command from catalyst 1.1.

- **Catalyst mailing list**—The Catalyst mailing list is probably the best place to ask questions about building Gentoo live CDs. Subscribe to the list by sending an e-mail from your e-mail address to gentoo-catalyst+subscribe@gentoo.org (to receive and post to the list) or gentoo-catalyst+subscribe-digest@gentoo.org (to send a digest of messages every few days).

- **Catalyst documentation**—For information about the `catalyst` command itself, type `man catalyst` or `catalyst -help`. Sample spec files to use for creating live CD stage tarballs are available by installing the `livecd-specs` and `livecd-kconfigs` packages. The former contains spec files for building official Gentoo live CDs, while the later contains files for configuring live CD kernels for different computer architectures. Review spec files in the `/usr/share/doc/catalyst-2.0*/examples/` directory to learn about the setting you can choose to create your live CD.

Building Gentoo live CDs is done in stages. The `livecd-stage1` target is where you gather and compile all the software packages you want to include on your live CD to form an archive for use in `livecd-stage2`. In `livecd-stage2`, you customize the basic `livecd-stage1` archive you built to include such things as custom splash screens, create or remove configuration files, and select which system services to start automatically.

Setting Up the Build Environment

I started with an installed Gentoo system to do this procedure, although you should be able to create a live CD with Catalyst from most any Linux system. To install Gentoo to your hard disk, follow the instructions in the "Installing Gentoo" section earlier in this chapter. When Gentoo is installed, you need to run a few commands to get the software you need to create live CDs with Catalyst.

You can get the Catalyst software you need to create your Gentoo live CD by indicating that you want the new catalyst software and running `emerge`, as follows:

```
# mkdir -p /etc/portage
# echo "dev-util/catalyst ~x86" >> /etc/portage/package.keywords
# emerge catalyst
```

Type this to get the package containing sample spec files:

```
# emerge livecd-specs livecd-kconfigs
```

Although, strictly speaking, you don't need the livecd-specs and livecd-kconfigs packages, they are useful to refer to later. The packages contain the spec files that the Gentoo development team used to create the official Gentoo live CDs, and have recently been updated for the 2006.1 release.

Configuring the catalyst.conf File

With the software you need installed, next you should create and identify the directories for building your Gentoo live CD with Catalyst. For the catalyst command to know where your working directories are located, those locations need to be identified in /etc/catalyst/catalyst.conf. Here are examples of how variables can be set in that file:

```
# /etc/catalyst/catalyst.conf file
distdir="/usr/portage/distfiles"
options="pkgcache kerncache"
sharedir="/usr/lib/catalyst"
storedir="/var/tmp/catalyst"
# envscript="/root/catalyst-env.sh"
```

The following list describes variables you can set in the catalyst.conf file.

- distdir—Use the default distdir in most cases (/usr/portage/distfiles). This directory contains all the files that were fetched when you install packages.

- options—By adding pkgcache and kerncache to the options line, you can set Catalyst to save all built packages and your built kernel, respectively. The seedcache and snapcache do caching for those features. These options are useful because they save time by not having to rebuild components that don't change each time you rebuild your stage files. The autoresume option enables you to save points at which you want to restart a build.

- sharedir—Indicates the location of Catalyst runtime executables. The default /usr/lib/catalyst directory is used in most cases.

- storedir—Indicates the location where stored temporary and cache files are stored. The default is /var/tmp/catalyst.

- envscript—If you need to set any options or environment variables to use when you build live CDs, set the location of a script containing those items with the envscript variable. By default, envscript is commented out.

Understanding the Directory Structure

At this point, it helps to understand the directory structure you are working in to create your live CD. Based on the information just entered into the `catalyst.conf` file, the following is a list of directories and files you should know about for the rest of the procedure:

- `/var/tmp/catalyst`—Contains the `builds` directory (which holds the `stage3` tarball used to build the live CD), `snapshots` directory (which holds the Portage snapshot), and `packages` directory (which holds the packages created by the pkgcache and kerncache that are used to create the live CD).

- `/usr/lib/catalyst`—Contains the scripts catalyst uses to produce the live CD.

- `/usr/portage`—By default, this is the `portage` directory (`portdir`) used to create the live CD. The `distfiles` subdirectory holds source code for package updates that have been applied to the local system.

- `/root/genttoCD/`—This is an arbitrary directory I created to hold the spec files used to create the live CD.

The configuration files you need to work with include the `/etc/catalyst/catalyst.conf` file (defining the location of catalyst components) and spec files for the live CD `livecd-stage1` and `livecd-stage2` archives. To go with those files, you need a portage snapshot and a `stage3` tarball, which you will use to build the `livecd-stage1` archive.

Creating the livecd-stage1 Archive

Building your Gentoo live CD is done in stages. The first stage (`livecd-stage1`) gathers all the software packages you want to include on the live CD and compiles them, based on the USE flags you provide. That `livecd-stage1`archive is then used to create a `livecd-stage2` archive and your live CD image.

Creating the `livecd-stage1` archive starts by configuring a `livecd-stage1` spec file. The spec files are available from the `/usr/share/doc/catalyst-2*/examples` and `/usr/share/livecd-specs-*` directory, under separate directories for each architecture. The examples in this chapter use the i686 (standard PC) architecture. Copy the `livecd-stage1` spec file to a working directory to get started. For example:

```
# mkdir $HOME/gentooCD
# cd $HOME/gentooCD
# cp /usr/share/doc/catalyst-2*/examples/livecd-stage1_template.spec .
```

This file contains a lot of comments to understand how you can modify the file. Here is an example of how you might configure the spec file. You can find more details on variables used in this file, and in Catalyst itself, in the Catalyst Reference Manual (www.gentoo.org/proj/en/releng/catalyst, then select the link to that manual).

```
subarch: i686
version_stamp: 2006.1
target: livecd-stage1
rel_type: default
profile: default-linux/x86/2006.1
snapshot: 20060906
source_subpath: default/stage3-i686-2006.1
livecd/use:
        -*
        alsa
        socks5
        nptl
        nptlonly
        livecd
        dbus
        gnome
        gtk
        -kde
        -qt3
        -qt4
          fbcon
          ncurses
          readline
livecd/packages:
        app-admin/ide-smart
        app-admin/logrotate
        app-admin/passook
        app-admin/pwgen
        app-admin/sudo
        app-admin/syslog-ng
        app-arch/mt-st
        app-arch/unrar
        app-arch/unzip
          app-editors/gedit
          app-editors/nano
        app-misc/livecd-tools

          .
          .
          .
        x11-base/xorg-x11
        x11-drivers/synaptics
        gnome-base/gdm
        gnome-base/gnome-light
```

```
gnome-base/gnome-vfs
gnome-base/gnome-volume-manager
gnome-base/gnome-applets
```

The subarch value sets the computer architecture for the livecd-stage1 tarball. The i686 architecture works well with most computers built in the past few years. If you need the live CD to work with older computers, however, the x86 architecture will work with everything from an i386 to Pentium 4 and Athlon XP processor architectures. So x86 is best to use for a live CD that should work across that range of processors. Subarchitectures for x86 include i386, i486, i586, i686, pentium-mmx, athlon, athlon-xp, athlon-mp, pentium3, and pentium4.

The version_stamp is set to a string of characters to identify the CD. In this example, the version_stamp is set to 2006.1 because the CD is using Gentoo 2006.1 as a base. The target variable indicates what is being built from this spec file (in this case, a livecd-stage1 archive). Use default as the rel_type variable in most cases (you can use a different build profile if you like).

The profile variable defines the location of the Portage profile that catalyst will use. In this case, you will use the 2006.1 file (located in /usr/portage/profiles/default-linux/x86) in the next step. This file contains information about the architecture and build options (same as /etc/make.conf). The snapshot is the name given to the Portage snapshot used to build the livecd-stage1 archive.

The value for snapshot must match a portion of the name of the portage snapshot you will download in a coming step. For example, for the snapshot portage-20060906.tar.bz2, I entered 20060906 (you will probably get one with a later date). The source_subpath indicates the location of the stage3 tarball you will download in a coming step. For example, the value of default/stage3-i686-2006.1 indicates that the stage3 tarball is named stage3-i686-2006.tar.bz2 and is located in the /var/tmp/catalyst/builds/default directory.

Keywords under livecd/use represent USE variables that are used to build the live CD environment. Packages under livecd/packages indicate which packages will be added to the live CD.

NOTE

Don't include the genkernel package to livecd/packages. That would cause livecd-stage1 catalyst to fail.

A couple of the pieces that this spec file points to need to be created or otherwise obtained: a portage snapshot tarball and a stage3 tarball. If you don't want to create your own portage snapshot tarball, there are snapshots available from http://mirrors. tds.net/gentoo/snapshots or you can use the snapshot used by Gentoo's Release Engineering to build the 2006.1 release from http://mirrors.tds.net/gentoo/releases/ snapshots/2006.1. I downloaded one as follows:

```
# mkdir -p /var/tmp/catalyst/snapshots
# cd /var/tmp/catalyst/snapshots
# wget -c http://mirrors.tds.net/gentoo/snapshots/portage-20060906.tar.bz2
```

You might wonder why you need a stage3 tarball when you are creating a livecd-stage1 archive. The reason is that the stage3 tarball is used to create the chroot environment that is used to create the livecd-stage1 archive. With this arrangement, you can select a stage3 tarball that is compatible with the livecd-stage1 archive you create. In this way, the stage3 tarball isolates the livecd-stage1 archive from the local system.

To download the stage3 tarball, you access any official Gentoo mirror and download the tarball to your builds directory. Mirror sites are listed here: www.gentoo.org/main/en/mirrors.xml. Then, for example, to download a stage3 tarball from a gentoo mirror site, you could type the following:

```
# mkdir -p /var/tmp/catalyst/builds/default
# cd /var/tmp/catalyst/builds/default
# wget -c \
http://mirrors.tds.net/gentoo/releases/x86/2006.1/stages/stage3-i686-
2006.1.tar.bz2
```

The wget command line shown should actually be on one line. The point, however, is that you need to get a stage3 tarball from a Gentoo site and place it in the /var/tmp/catalyst/builds/default directory.

With everything in place, the next step is to build the livecd-stage1 archive. Here's what to type:

```
# cd /root/gentooCD
# catalyst -f livecd-stage1_template.spec
```

Depending on how many packages you have selected to use, this could take several hours to complete. You can use the resulting livecd-stage1 archive to build a livecd-stage2 archive and your live CD.

Creating the livecd-stage2 Archive

As with the livecd-stage1 archive, to create the livecd-stage2 archive, you need to create a livecd-stage2 spec file. To begin, you can copy an example livecd-stage2 spec file from the examples directory to a working directory. Here's an example:

```
# cd $HOME/gentooCD
# cp /usr/share/doc/catalyst-2*/examples/livecd-stage2_template.spec .
```

Before you begin editing the `livecd-stage2spec` file, you need to get a kernel-configuration file. I copied one of the kernel-configuration files from the `livecd-kconfigs` package to start from. Then I edited it to contain the kernel drivers and modules I wanted.

```
# mkdir /root/gentooCD/kconfig
# cd /usr/share/livecd-kconfigs-2006.1/x86
# cp livecd-2.6.17.config /root/gentooCD/kconfig/
```

Next I edited the `livecd-stage2` spec file to contain the setting needed to build my live CD. The following is an example of an edited `livecd-stage2_template.spec` file, used to create a `livecd-stage2` archive from the `livecd-stage1` archive created earlier. Although the `livecd-stage2` spec file shown here works, it might not include every feature you want to add to your Gentoo live CD. I recommend that you step through the comments included in the `livecd-stage2_template.spec` file to see other options that you might want to use.

```
subarch: x86
version_stamp: 2006.1
target: livecd-stage2
rel_type: default
profile: default-linux/x86/2006.1
snapshot: 20060906
source_subpath: default/stage1-x86-2006.1
livecd/cdtar: /usr/lib/catalyst/livecd/cdtar/isolinux-3.09-
memtest86+-cdtar.tar.bz2
livecd/fstype: squashfs
livecd/iso: /root/mylivecd-x86-2006.1.iso
livecd/type: generic-livecd
livecd/splash_type: gensplash
livecd/splash_theme: livecd-2006.1
boot/kernel: gentoo
boot/kernel/gentoo/sources: gentoo-sources
boot/kernel/gentoo/config: /root/gentooCD/kcnofig/2.6.12-smp.config
livecd/unmerge:
    acl
    addpatches
    attr
    autoconf
    automake
        .
        .
        .
livecd/empty:
    /etc/bootsplash/gentoo
    /etc/bootsplash/gentoo-highquality
```

```
    /etc/cron.daily
    /etc/cron.hourly
      .
      .
      .
livecd/rm:
    /boot/System*
    /boot/initr*
    /boot/kernel*
    /etc/*-
    /etc/*.old
      .
      .
      .
```

Notice that many of the values identifying architecture and the locations of files and directories are the same as they were in the livecd-stage1 spec file. Interesting new options include the livecd/fstype, which identifies squashfs as the file system type used to hold and compress most of the live CD's file system.

The livecd/iso value identifies where the resulting ISO image is ultimately placed. In this example, the final ISO image will be created automatically and named mylivecd-x86-2006.1.iso. The livecd/type is set to generic-livecd (it's important to get this type right).

You have the opportunity to set the splash screen type you want and the theme associated with that splash screen. As the livecd/splash_type, I chose gensplash. For the livecd/splash_theme, I used livecd-2006.1.

The next entries in the livecd-stage2 spec file determine the kernel that will be built for your live CD. For boot/kernel, I chose gentoo as the kernel and chose boot/kernel/gentoo/sources to be gentoo-sources. Then I indicated the location of the kernel-configuration file (boot/kernel/gentoo/config) to be the location of the configuration file I recently copied and edited (/root/gentooCD/kconfig/livecd-2.6.17.config).

The last entries shown in this sample file have to do with cleaning up the file system when you are done adding everything there is to add. Items listed under livecd/unmerge represent packages that will be unmerged after all kernels are built. With livecd/empty, you can indicate which directories should be emptied of all contents. After livecd/rm is a list of files that should be removed.

In particular, software packages and files that were used to build the live CD or that were left behind during the process of creating the live CD can be removed. I recommend checking the /usr/share/livecd-specs-*/x86 directory to see what software packages, files, and directories get removed from the official Gentoo live CDs.

When you feel satisfied that your `livecd-stage2` spec file is correct, run the `catalyst` command with that spec file as follows:

```
# cd /root/gentooCD
# catalyst -f livecd-stage2_template.spec
```

When the `catalyst` command finishes running, it creates the live CD, based on the contents of the `livecd/iso` entry (`/root/mylivecd-x86-2006.1.iso`, in my example). You can then test (with tools such as `qemu` or `VMWare`) and burn (with tools such as `cdrecord` or `k3b`) that live CD as described in Appendix B, "Building, Testing, and Burning ISOs."

You almost certainly won't get a clean build the first time you try this procedure. If `catalyst` fails as it is building, look for the last error message and try to correct the problem. You might receive suggestions from the error message to change a use flag or a notice that some component is missing. If you are not able to overcome the issue yourself, you can look for help on the gentoo-catalyst mailing list, as mentioned earlier. Read a few posts first and try to ask specific questions. Archives are available at http://archives.gentoo.org/gentoo-catalyst.

SUMMARY

Gentoo is one of the more challenging Linux systems for building a live Linux CD. The procedure in this chapter for producing a Gentoo live CD has you set up a `chroot` environment for your live CD directory structure. Once in that `chroot` environment, you can use `emerge` to add or remove any software packages as you please for your live CD.

To save space for your live CD, the directory structure is compressed by converting it to a `squashfs` file system. Although `isolinux` can be used as the boot loader, this procedure describes how to use GRUB to achieve the same results.

Active development efforts for producing live CDs are mostly associated with the Catalyst project. Using Catalyst and spec files, you can produce highly customized `live CDs`. Development of Catalyst for producing live CDs has been progressing for a few years. However, you should closely follow the Catalyst mailing list and other resources to find out the latest components you should be using to build live Gentoo CDs with Catalyst.

Part III

Making a Specialized Bootable Linux

## CHAPTER 9

Customizing a Security Live Linux CD

Security and system-rescue activities are among the best uses of a live Linux CD. On one read-only medium, you can gather a range of tools to fix a broken operating system, scan file systems for intruders, watch traffic on the network, and do hundreds of other activities to check and protect your computing environment.

Putting together your own security live CD offers a means of having all the tools you need at your fingertips in a way that you can apply to any PC you can reboot. You have fewer worries when you go to fix a broken system because you can start with a clean, freshly booted operating system each time. In this way, less chance exists that the tools you would use to fix a system are themselves broken or infected.

Creating a custom security live CD also can mean adding tools that might not be on other security live CDs. For example, some software is licensed in a way that you can use it for personal use but might not be available for someone to redistribute. Examples of such things are proprietary drivers or utilities that come with a hardware peripheral. So these features that they can't legally put on a widely distributed Linux live CD might legally go on the one you carry around with you to use when it's needed.

This chapter covers some of the features that have been put into live Linux CDs that are used for security and rescue purposes. It also describes additional components you might want to add to your own custom live Linux security CD. For demonstration purposes, the chapter focuses on the BackTrack live CD.

EXPLORING SECURITY LIVE CDS

Many live Linux CDs for security already are available today, so chances are good that you can start your own Live CD based on an existing security-oriented Live CD. Popular security live CDs include some that are based on Knoppix, Slackware, and Gentoo. You can choose where to start based on Linux distribution, as well as on the tools each CD provides.

To begin demonstrating the types of functions you might find on a security Live CD, this chapter starts with the BackTrack network security suite (www.remote-exploit.org). Chapter 2, "Playing with Live Linux CDs," includes an introduction to BackTrack, to help you get started and learn the basics. This chapter looks at Back-Track with an eye toward the following:

- **Understanding how it starts up**—You'll learn how BackTrack boots up and starts services, as well as the state in which users begin using the live CD (such as run levels, graphical and text-based interfaces, and user accounts).

- **Learning which tools it includes**—You'll become familiar with the types of features and tools included in BackTrack to help you put together your own set of custom computer security tools.

NOTE

BackTrack, like other Slax-based live CDs, includes many of the boot files provided from the Linux Live CD/USB Scripts site (www.linux-live.org). Refer to that site to learn more about how the scripts, kernels, and other components from linux-live.org can be used to produce live CDs from an installed Linux system.

Figure 9-1 illustrates the features that BackTrack pulls into its arsenal of security tools. Because BackTrack was created from a combination of tools from two other popular security-centric live Linux distributions (Auditor and Whax), you can get a good sense of the tools you would want to have on your own security live CD.

If you are using BackTrack, open the BackTrack menu (lower-left corner of the screen) to select security tools to try out. In Figure 9-1, the applications displayed include the Autopsy Forensic Browser, the Automated Image and Restore (AIR) tool for creating and restoring disk images, and the AutoScan utility for exploring your network.

FIGURE 9-1 Size up systems, hunt down exploits, and explore networks with BackTrack.

Because security live CDs are not generally meant to be used for gaming or other high-end graphics applications, a lot of disk space can be saved by including a simple window manager (or no window manager at all). Because it is lightweight but carries enough features to launch many useful X applications, the Fluxbox window manager is available on many of the smaller security live CDs (50MB to 180MB). BackTrack includes Fluxbox for users who want to use it; the KDE interface is used with BackTrack by default.

To understand the foundation on which this security tool chest is built, however, the next sections step you through the boot process and basic setup used to support the security tools.

Booting the BackTrack Security Live CD

To begin exploring how BackTrack is configured, look at the boot files it uses. As with most Linux live CDs, BackTrack uses the Isolinux boot loader. The boot loader is configured quite simply and is basically the same configuration you get with other live CDs based on Slax (www.slax.org).

The `isolinux.cfg` file is stored in the root (/) of the live CD, to direct the boot process. Three labels exist: `slax`, `linux`, and `memtest`. The `memtest` label simply runs the `memtest` command to check your RAM. The default `slax` label is the same as the `linux` label, except that the `slax` label sets the default `vga` mode to 1024×768, 16 colors (`vga=0x317`, the hexadecimal equivalent of 791). The following options, that can be used from the boot prompt (using either `linux` or `slax` labels) are described on the message screen by pressing F1:

- `linux debug`—Interrupts the boot process on several occasions to open a shell to check progress.
- `linux copy2ram`—Copies a complete file system to RAM. This can be used only if enough RAM is available.
- `linux floppy`—Enables floppy automounting during startup.
- `linux load=modules`—Loads indicated modules from the `/optional` directory.

You can pass other boot options to BackTrack from the boot prompt, including `nocd`, `nohd`, and `nodma`.

You can set the `probeusb` parameter to find USB devices earlier in the process than it would normally do so. You can also set the specific amount of RAM you want to allow BackTrack to use when it mounts the root (/) directory by setting the `ram-size=` parameter (in bytes). By default, 60 percent of your available RAM is used for the `tmpfs` file system that will eventually hold the live CD's root file system.

Boot Components

These bootloader components are used during the default boot process for BackTrack:

- **Splash screen**—The first screen that appears when BackTrack boots is defined in the `boot/splash.cfg` file. That file reads in the BackTrack splash screen (`boot/splash.lss`) and line of text instructing the user to press Enter. Before booting, the user has the option of pressing F1 (to see several boot options contained in the boot/splash.txt file) and then pressing F2 to return to the original splash screen.
- **RAM disk**—From append options with the `slax` label, a 4MB RAM disk is created (`ramdisk_size=4444`).
- **Kernel**—The kernel is booted from the `boot/vmlinuz` file. The kernel is a 2.6 kernel that includes support for Unionfs and Squashfs file systems.
- **Initial RAM disk**—The initial RAM disk files and directories are provided from the `initrd.gz` file (`initrd=boot/initrd.gz`). This file is unzipped and mounted as the root file system on the RAM disk. After this file is unzipped,

the kernel can direct the linuxrc file (located at the root of this file system) to continue the boot process.

The linuxrc Script

The linuxrc script does a lot of work to set up the file systems for the live CD. Because the linuxrc script is derived from the same script that comes with Slax, the way BackTrack sets up its file systems is similar to that of Slax (and other distributions based on linux-live.org scripts).

Much of the processing of the linuxrc script is done using functions defined in the liblinuxlive script (also in the root of the initrd file). Here are some of the things that the linuxrc script does in BackTrack:

- Mounts the /proc and /sys file systems.
- Checks whether the debug option was given at the boot prompt. If it was, the rest of the script runs in debug mode.
- Runs modprobe to load essential modules. Many of the modules loaded are used to support needed file system types (isofs, squashfs, unionfs, and vfat). If an NTFS file system is present, ntfs support is also added. Support is also added for USB storage devices if the probeusb boot option was given.
- The root file system (/) is ultimately set up as a tmpfs file system. First, individual squashfs file systems, representing /bin, /etc, /root, /usr, /var, and others, are mounted read-only from the /base directory of the CD. Then they are merged with the writeable /UNIONFS directory. (See Chapter 5, "Looking Inside Live CD Components," for descriptions of UnionFS and Squashfs.)

  Later, the entire root file system is converted to a tmpfs file system. The advantage of a tmpfs file system is that it runs from system memory. This enables you to make the files and directories from the read-only medium (CD) writeable. An advantage of tmpfs over other file systems that are stored in memory, such as the ramfs file system, which can write only to RAM, is that tmpfs can store files in both RAM and swap space. A tmpfs file system automatically expands if more space is needed (as long as memory is available).

- An image appears behind text as it scrolls during the boot process. The location of the image is /etc/bootsplash/themes/Linux/config in the file named bootsplash-1024x768.cfg. The actual images used are stored in the /etc/bootsplash/themes/Linux/images directory.

- With the file system completely set up, `linuxrc` changes to the root of the newly formed directory structure (`pivot_root`). Then it runs `/sbin/init` to start the next phase of the boot process.

Customizing the Boot Process

When creating a live Linux security CD, you have many opportunities to customize a BackTrack live CD so it includes the features you want during the boot process:

- **Custom splash screens**—You can add your own images, both to the initial boot screen and as a background as messages scroll by. See Chapter 5 for information on creating images to use on your boot screens.
- **Multiple boot labels**—Just as `memtest` can be run from a boot label, you can add multiple floppy images to be run individually from Isolinux. You can copy any bootable floppy image to the `/boot` directory and add a label to `isolinux.cfg` so it can be launched from the boot prompt. This can be useful if you have utilities on floppy disk that came with hardware you want to configure. You can use the utilities without booting up the entire live CD.
- **Capability to add a file system**—Create a directory structure of files you want to have on the CD and convert that structure to a `squashfs` file system. Add the file system file to the `/base` or `/modules` directory, naming it with a `.mo` suffix.

For more ideas on configuring Isolinux to have your live CD boot as you would like, refer to Chapter 5.

The Initial System State

Security-oriented live CDs might be booting up on a computer that is broken in some way. Because problems might include a dysfunctional video card or a connection to a network from which the computer could be under attack, start-up often takes you to a minimal system state. This section describes the processing that occurs from when the `init` process takes and then continues to the point at which the user is presented with a login prompt.

Default Run Level

Even though BackTrack includes a graphical user interface, you will see a shell interface instead of an X desktop by default. BackTrack does this by starting the system at run level 3 (based on the `initdefault` value set in `/etc/inittab`).

Run level 3 is the most common run level for starting a system that is not using a GUI by default. Instead, it boots to a text-based login prompt and then, after the user logs in, presents that user with a shell interface. This level might or might not start up network interfaces. In the case of BackTrack, the network interfaces are not started automatically. Here are some of the highlights of what occurs after the `init` process sets other processes in motion to start up system services:

- **rc.S script**—The /etc/rc.d/rc.S script is run every time the live CD is started (regardless of the `init` state). This script mounts and checks any file systems listed in /etc/fstab, turns on swap, starts `udev` (to manage removable devices), and configures plug-and-play devices.

- **rc.M script**—The /etc/rc.d/rc.M script runs when the live CD boots up to any multiuser run level (2, 3, 4, or 5). It does some logging (sending `dmesg` output to /var/log/dmesg and running the `syslogd` system log daemon). This script also runs the rc.slax script, which responds to several options that might have been added at the boot prompt. For example, the `noguest` option disables the guest user account and `passwd` causes the script to prompt the user for a new root password. For the `autoexec` option, the script runs the command given (for example, autoexec="date") and then reboots.

- **System V init scripts**—One of the last things the rc.S script does is run the /etc/rc.d/rc.sysvinit script to start any System V `init` scripts that are set to run at the current run level. For example, in run level 3, the script starts any scripts beginning with the letter *S* in /etc/rc.d/rc3.d directory.

- **MySLAX scripts**—The only script currently in the /etc/rc.d/rc3.d directory is the SInstall script. If you added any MySLAX Modulator scripts to this directory (with names that begin with Install_*), they would be executed to install the software it contained. Information on adding MySLAX software is described later in this chapter.

If you had watched as the messages were displayed, the process just described took place between the message beginning with "INIT:" and the login prompt.

Customizing the init Process

Features you add to a security live CD during the `init` process should focus on the kinds of services you want to enable or disable during the live CD session. Here are some customizations you might want to consider:

- **Add boot options**—You can add support for different boot options that are dealt with during the init process. For example, the /etc/rc.d/rc.M script. That script reads the boot options (stored in /proc/cmdline) and turns various services on or off based on those settings.

- **Add system services**—If you want to have a particular service launched at boot time, you can add a script for starting that service to a run level directory. In this case, you could add start-up scripts (beginning with the letter *S*) to the /etc/rc.d/rc3.d directory.

After the boot process completes, the user sees the login prompt and some information on the screen. That information includes the root password and ways to start the GUI and the network.

Logging In

With BackTrack, you are expected to log in as the root user from a text-based login prompt. No other user account is available as a login account.

BackTrack comes with a root password already assigned. That password appears on the screen when you first boot up. Although this might seem like a security concern, remember that there is no network interface at this point, so you can run the passwd command to change the root password before starting up network interfaces and allowing any remote login services to the machine. You could also type passwd as a boot option to be prompted for a root password during the boot process.

Although other active user accounts exist, none is enabled for you to log into. Knoppix boots up to a desktop owned by the knoppix user (who can request root privilege without a password), but you need to add a new user to operate the live CD as a nonroot user (running adduser username steps you through the process).

As noted earlier, the login prompt is text-based and is preceded by instructions (the contents of /etc/issue are listed). Those instructions include the root password and commands for configuring the desktop (xconf), starting the desktop (startx), starting a simpler desktop (gui), and getting an IP address using DHCP (dhcpcd). Figure 9-2 shows the login screen just described.

Ways of configuring the login process include the following:

- Change the text shown before the login prompt by editing the /etc/issue file.
- Set up other user accounts so you don't have to log in as root.
- Configure the user environment. You can modify user environment variables by editing the /etc/profile file.
- Configure the user home directory. The /root directory is populated with configuration files that are set up in advance in the /etc/skel directory. You can add or change configuration files from there.

If the user can successfully log in as a root user, the next areas to look at are those that set up the desktop environment and features for configuring necessary peripherals (network interfaces, printers, sound cards, and so on).

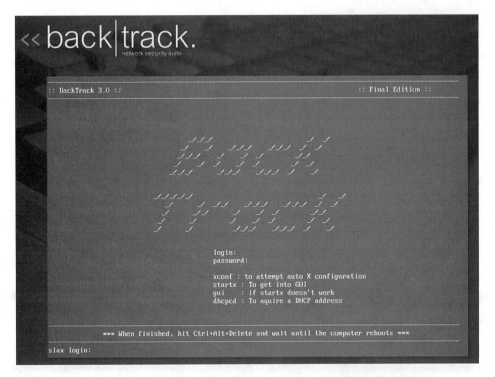

FIGURE 9-2 The text-based login screen includes information from the /etc/issue file.

NOTE

One variable set in /etc/profile that you might look at is the PATH variable. BackTrack added a dot (.) to the PATH. This allows commands to be run from the current directory (an activity that typically needs to be asked for explicitly, by typing something such as ./command). BackTrack needs this feature as part of the way it lets you run commands from the BackTrack menu. It basically opens a terminal window with the shell open to the directory containing the command. It expects you to be able to run the command from there.

Configuring the Desktop

Although many BackTrack features can be used from the shell, BackTrack helps users navigate through the hundreds of commands and utilities by creating a Back-Track menu for the desktop. Some of the design decisions that went into configuring the desktop for BackTrack are worth considering as you go to customize your own security CD.

Desktop Environment or Window Manager

KDE is used by default as the desktop environment for BackTrack. Because Back-Track doesn't have the size limitations that mini security distributions have of fitting on a 50MB bootable business card or 180MB mini disk, there is room for a larger desktop environment, such as KDE. Those mini distributions tend to go for lightweight window managers, such as Fluxbox, to provide a simple GUI.

Other window managers are available with BackTrack, including Fluxbox (fluxbox), Motif (mwm), and Twm (twm). So, with a slow CPU or low amounts of memory, users can switch to another window manager. Of course, you will lose some of the KDE features and tools if you switch to a simple window manager.

In particular, Fluxbox is used with a number of live Linux CDs. For example, Fluxbox is the primary window manager used on other security-oriented live CDs such as INSERT (www.inside-security.de/insert_en.html), PHLAK (www.phlak.org), and Knoppix-STD (www.knoppix-std.org). It is also offered as a Window manager on some mini live CDs, such as Damn Small Linux (www.damnsmalllinux.org).

To change the default desktop environment from KDE to a simpler Fluxbox window manager, edit the /usr/X11R6/lib/X11/xinit/xinitrc file. Then comment out the startkde line at the bottom and add fluxbox on a line by itself. Save the file. Then type startx to start the desktop, using the Fluxbox window manager. Fluxbox has been configured to incorporate the BackTrack menu into the basic Fluxbox menu (right-click the desktop to see it).

Backtrack Menu

The BackTrack submenu on the KDE menu is the most obvious enhancement BackTrack includes. This is where BackTrack gathers hundreds of security tools that are available from the live CD. The tools are divided into 15 categories. Figure 9-3 shows the BackTrack menu displayed from the KDE menu and from the Konqueror window.

Alongside the BackTrack menu in Figure 9-3 is the KDE Menu Editor. By opening the BackTrack menu in the KDE Menu Editor, you can see details about each menu item. For each application, you can see details about how it is run. You can open the KDE Menu Editor to work with the BackTrack menu by right-clicking the K Menu button and selecting Menu Editor.

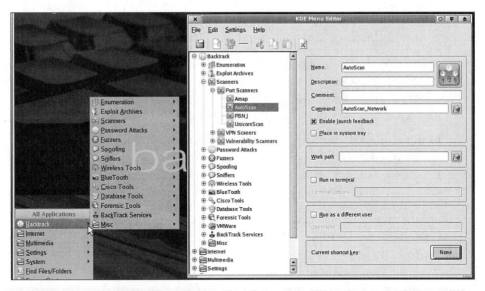

FIGURE 9-3 Security tools on the BackTrack menu are divided into 15 categories.

Because many of the security tools available are commands rather than graphical utilities, BackTrack takes an interesting approach to making those tools available from the desktop. Selecting a menu item that represents a command opens a shell that displays the help message associated with that command. In some cases, the current directory for that shell holds the command and any support files needed by that command. Because the default PATH enables you to run commands from the current directory, you can simply run the command (with the options you want) or refer to the files in that directory for further information.

KDE Settings

Because KDE is the default desktop for BackTrack, you can take advantage of the available tools for configuring the KDE desktop. Most the graphical administrative tools for KDE are available from the Settings and System menus on the KDE menu. To tailor the look and feel of the desktop, refer to Chapter 2. The same features described there for configuring KDE in Knoppix can be used to configure KDE here.

Configuring Network Interfaces

Because network interfaces are off by default with BackTrack, before you can use the tools for scanning network resources and accessing remote computers, you need to turn the interface to your network. Here are two ways to get the interface to a standard wired Ethernet card configured:

- **From the shell**—You can grab an IP address from a DHCP server by typing the dhcpd command. You can have the interface brought up and down by typing `ifconfig eth0 up` (providing that eth0 was assigned to your network interface). To bring the interface down, you could type `ifconfig eth0 down`.

- **From the KDE menu**—Select the KDE menu button → Internet → Set IP address. The network configurator window lets you type in a static IP address, subnet mask, and default gateway. You can also enter the IP addresses of the DNS servers.

For other types of networking interfaces, GUI tools also are available. To configure a dial-up connection, select the KDE menu button → Internet → Internet Dial-Up Tool. To configure wireless LAN connections, select the KDE menu button → Internet → Wireless Manager.

Again, because BackTrack uses KDE, graphical KDE tools also are available for configuring and managing network interfaces and features. Open the KDE Control Center by selecting the KDE menu button → Settings → Control Center. Then select Internet & Network to see Wireless Network (to autodetect or manually configure wireless interfaces) and Network Monitor.

The bottom line is, if you can accept the overhead that comes with using KDE (disk space and memory required), using KDE as your desktop environment on a security live CD offers a lot of the tools you need for basically configuring your system. By offering the Fluxbox, XFCE, blackbox, or other low-end window manager, someone using your security live CD can still switch to those window managers. Although not all KDE tools will be available, they will be capable of running most of the security utilities that come with BackTrack.

 NOTE

In BackTrack, the BackTrack menu has been integrated into the Fluxbox window manager. Although a Fluxbox user will be missing some KDE configuration tools, most of the security tools should be available to run directly from the BackTrack menu that appears when you right-click the Fluxbox desktop.

RUNNING SECURITY TOOLS

With a solid live CD in place, including an appropriate boot loader, user environment, and basic configuration tools, it's time to move on to choosing the software that makes the live CD special. In the case of a security-oriented live Linux CD, that means finding the tools to check systems and networks, evaluate and plug security holes, and deal with problems, such as broken or exploited systems.

Again, BackTrack is used to illustrate the kind of tools you might include on your own security-oriented live Linux CD. Literally hundreds of utilities, resources (such as exploit databases), and services are built into BackTrack that you might find useful for your own Live CD.

Figure 9-4 illustrates the types of features that BackTrack includes.

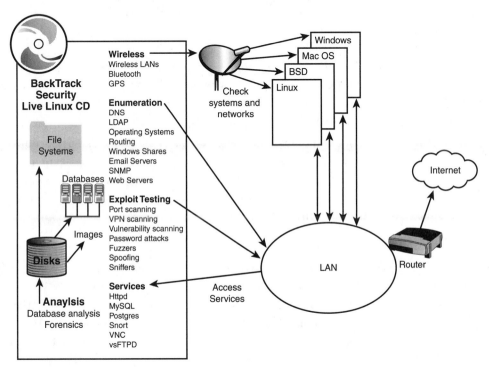

FIGURE 9-4 Features in BackTrack range from remote-exploit to password-cracking tools.

As you can see from Figure 9-4, features added to a security-oriented Linux live CD can go well beyond a password checker and a port scanner. To support the security tools in BackTrack are features such as archives of security information, to check for vulnerabilities to known exploits. Tools also are available for tracking down problems with particular types of devices, such as BlueTooth or wireless LAN cards.

The coming sections take separate looks at the security topics illustrated in Figure 9-4. You can use those sections to learn a bit about how those tools work and to help evaluate the kinds of features you want to have on your own security live CD.

Running Enumeration Tools

Enumeration tools are used to find out what information about a system, network, or service is available to potential intruders. Including enumeration tools on a live CD lets you test the computers on your network so you can shut off access to information that an intruder could use to do you harm.

BackTrack includes dozens of enumeration tools that can be used to find information about your Internet domain, LDAP servers, operating system, routing, and other services. The following enumeration tools come with BackTrack.

Checking Domain Information

To run commands for checking information about an Internet domain from a Domain Name System (DNS) server, select K menu → Enumeration → DNS. About a half-dozen menu items are available to check out DNS information.

Selecting DNS → Walk lets you run the `dnswalk` command (www.visi.com/~barr/dsnwalk) to debug the zone database for your DNS servers. The `dig` command (K menu → Enumeration → DNS → Dig) is a popular utility for looking up a range of DNS information. `dnsenum.pl` (Perl utility) is another useful tool for checking out your domain. With it, you can find DNS servers, try zone transfers, and check for host names from a list you provide.

Checking LDAP Information

Using the `ldapenum` Perl script (http://sourceforge.net/projects/ldapenum), you can get password and system information from LDAP services running on Windows 2000 and 2003 systems. You can get to the script by selecting K menu → Enumeration → LDAP → Ldap Enum. This same tool can be used to try to log into the accounts it finds. The `ldapenum` command can also be used to check for groups and members.

The Luma (http://luma.sourceforge.net) graphical LDAP management tool (K menu → Enumeration → LDAP → Luma) includes eight plug-ins for finding and working with data on LDAP servers. Plug-ins let you search LDAP address books, search selected LDAP servers, manage users, and access other kinds of information from an LDAP server.

Determining Operating Systems

Tools from the Operating System enumeration menu (K menu → BackTrack → Enumeration → Operating System) can help determine the type of operating system being run. Select P0f from that menu to use a passive fingerprinting technique to determine the type of operating system a computer is running, based on TCP/IP packets sent from that computer. The pOf command (http://lcamtuf.coredump.cx/ pOf.shtml) is considered to be passive because it finds information about a system by reading TCP/IP packets on the network to determine the type of operating system and other properties of the host.

Tools such as pOf can get information about a remote system without actually contacting it. The pOf tool can study TCP/IP packets from any system contacting your network. It can also get information from a system based on the remote system accepting or rejecting a connection from the system running pOf.

The nmap command (www.insecure.org/nmap) is another tool that is commonly used to explore a remote system. With nmap, you can scan whole networks or single hosts. By scanning packets, nmap can determine what operating systems hosts are running on a network and what services those hosts are offering. It can also learn what type of firewall each host is running.

The Nmap Front End (nmapfe command) provides a graphical interface to nmap. Figure 9-5 shows the results from scanning a Linux machine on the local network. The system's name is einstein, and TCP ports 21 (ftp), 22 (ssh), rpcbind (111), and X11 (6000) are open. The ftp and ssh services are shown in red, indicating that services are active on those ports.

The sinfp.pl Perl script (www.gomor.org/sinfp) can determine the type of operating system running on a computer, based on the IP address you give the command. For Linux systems, you can also determine information about the version of the current kernel.

The xprobe2 (http://xprobe.sourceforge.net) command can glean a lot of information about a computer's operating system by simply giving the command the system's IP address. It uses several different information-gathering techniques to find out about the selected system. It tries to determine the distance from the remote system, checks open ports on the system, and checks to determine the type of operating system it is running.

Determining Network Routing

Tools for uncovering information about network routing (from the Routing/Network menu) include the Autonomous System Scanner, or ass command (www.phenoelit. de/irpas/docu.html), and the firewalk command (www.packetfactory.net/projects/ firewalk). To trace packets to a destination, you can use the itrace command (http://perfinsp.sourceforge.net/itrace_ppc.html), traceroute command (ftp://ftp. ee.lbl.gov), or tctrace command (www.phenoelit.de/irpas/docu.html). itrace does a traceroute using ICMP echo requests; tctrace uses TCP SYN packets to trace packets to their destination.

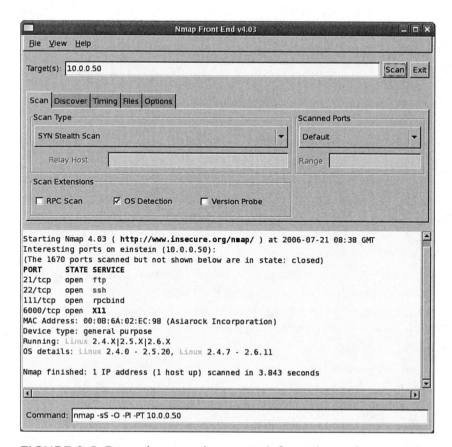

FIGURE 9-5 Determine operating system information and scan ports with nmapfe.

Finding Windows (Samba) Shares

Tools for getting information about shared folders from Windows systems using SMB protocol and from Samba servers enable you to look up a range of information about those shared folders. You can select examples of these tools from the SMB menu (K menu → Enumeration → KDE). Scan a range of IP addresses with the nbtscan command (www.inetcat.org/software/nbtscan.html) to determine which of those machines is capable of sharing files Windows folders and printers.

The nmblookup, net, and smbclient commands are all part of the Samba suite (www.samba.org). To find the IP addresses of computers using NetBIOS over TCP/IP (as Samba typically does), you can use the nmblookup command. The net command can be used to administer Samba servers and is similar to the net command for Windows and DOS. For example, you can view the status of sessions and shares on your computer using the net command.

You can use the smbclient command to create an interactive connection to services on an SMB server. With smbclient, you interact with an SMB server much as you would talk to an FTP server using the ftp command. For example, you can copy files across an smbclient connection.

For a graphical interface to SMB features, you can use the SMB/CIFS Share Browser (smb4k command). Using the SMB/CIFS Share Browser, you can scan your network for SMB servers, look for available shares, and connect to those shares in various ways. You can find out more about SMB4k by visiting its home page (http://smb4k.berlios.de) .

Finding E-Mail Server Information

Two tools for accessing information about an e-mail server are available by selecting Enumeration → SMTP from the BackTrack menu. Select Relay Scanner to run the RelayScanner.pl command to scan selected e-mail servers to see if mail relaying is open. Select SMTP Vrfy against a selected mail server to run the verfy.pl command to try to verify the existence of selected usernames. The command comes with a names.txt file, which includes nearly 9,000 possible usernames to test for. (You would use this tool to confirm that a spammer couldn't verify the existence of any of the usernames from your mail server.)

Finding Simple Network Management Protocol (SNMP) Information

Utilities for checking SNMP resources are available from the SNMP menu (select K menu → BackTrack → Enumeration → SNMP). The Mibble MIB Browser (www.mibble.org) is a GUI tool for parsing Manageable Information Base (MIB) files to interpret their contents. It supports SNMP versions 1, 2c, and 3. You can display the results in tree form and sort them in different ways.

You can use the onesixtyone command (www.phreedom.org/solar/onesixtyone) to scan SNMP enabled devices to glean information about those servers. The command does this by sending many SNMP requests at a time to many different systems. It then logs the responses as they come in. The snmpwalk command (www.net-snmp.org) can retrieve a tree of values under a selected variable from an SNMP MIB object.

Finding Web Server Information

You can glean a lot of information from Web servers, drawing on many different enumeration tools. The WWW menu (select K menu → BackTrack → Enumeration → WWW) includes 11 tools you can use to draw useful information from a Web server.

Using curl (http://curl.haxx.se), you can grab files from a Web server (as well as from FTP, TELNET, and gopher servers). Running curl with multiple Web locations

(URLs), you can download multiple files over the HTTP protocol from a single command line. Using the `dimitry` command, you can gather a whole lot of information at once about a particular Web server (or other type of system). Besides telling you the system's name and IP address, this command searches a variety of information services to find out about the host, including the `whois` database (Inet and Inic), Netcraft, DNS (to find subdomains), and e-mail service.

The `httprint` command (http://net-square.com/httprint) is a tool for fingerprinting Web servers. Instead of relying on what the Web server reports about itself (which might be masked by modified banner strings and plug-ins), `httprint` uses techniques such the Web server's responses to various requests (such as HTTP `DELETE` and `GET` requests) to determine the type of Web server. Select Httprint GUI to use a graphical version of the `httprint` tool.

To find all the URLS on a Web page, select List URLs to run the listurls.py command. Choose Paros Proxy (www.parosproxy.org) to test the security of your Web applications. The Paros graphical utility can intercept and modify HTTP and HTTPS data transferred between the client and server to test for vulnerabilities.

Using Exploit Archives

BackTrack includes several archives of exploits that you can use to test the vulnerability of your systems. It also includes the Metasploit Framework for running exploit modules to test systems for vulnerabilities to selected exploits:

- **SecurityFocus Archive (www.securityfocus.com)**—To access an archive of exploits gathered by Securityfocus.com, select the K menu → Backtrack → SecurityFocus Archive. To update the archive, select Update SecurityFocus from that same menu. This updates and adds exploit information and regenerates the local exploit database. If you have an Internet connection, you can be sure to have the up-to-the-minute information on known exploits.

- **Milw0rm Archive (www.milw0rm.com)**—To access an archive of exploits gathered by Milw0rm.com, select the K menu → Backtrack → Milw0rm Archive. Just as with the SecurityFocus archive, you can update the Milw0rm Archive from the K menu by selecting Update Milw0rm from the Milw0rm menu. This brings up your Milw0rm database to include the latest exploit information from the Milw0rm archives.

- **Metasploit Project (www.metasploit.com)**—The Metasploit Project was set up to help exploit research, as well as assist those who do IDS signature development and penetration testing. In BackTrack, you can access the Metaspolit Web interface from the K menu by selecting Backtrack → Exploit

Archives → Metasploit Framework → Metasploit 2.6 Web-Gui. Other interfaces for using Metasploit are available as well (as described shortly).

By including the Metasploit Framework on the BackTrack live CD, BackTrack enables users to check for vulnerability to known exploits on a variety of systems, including BSD, HPUX, Irix, Linux, OSX, Solaris, Windows 2000, Windows 2003, Windows NT, and Windows XP. You can choose which exploits to run based on application (Apache, Samba, and so on), operating system, or computer architecture (PPC, Sparc, or X86). Figure 9-6 shows the Metasploit Framework Web Console.

The Metasploit Framework Web Console can run as a local service from your Web browser (http://127.0.0.1:55555). By default, you see a list of all available exploits (with updates, BackTrack currently includes 143 exploits and 75 payloads). Figure 9-6 shows the beginning of the list of exploits that appear when Samba was selected. You can see the first three entries in that list, which show the name of the exploit and the operating systems the exploits can be tested against.

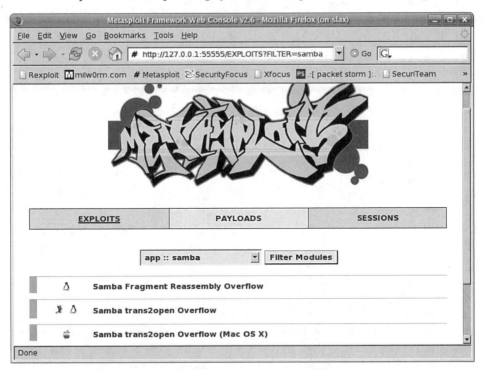

FIGURE 9-6 Metasploit lets you choose exploit modules to test for system vulnerabilities.

The advantage of including Metasploit on a live CD is that you can reboot a computer on a LAN with the live CD and test for exploits on that LAN without connecting that LAN to the Internet. You can select each exploit module to see a description of the vulnerability it attacks. Then links lead you through the process of running each module (selecting options, such as remote systems and port numbers and starting the module).

Besides being a tool for checking exploits, Metasploit is a framework for developing your own security tools. To find out more about how to create and integrate your own tools into Metasploit, a good place to start is the Metasploit documentation page, which includes the project's FAQ: www.metasploit.com/projects/Framework/documentation.html.

Scanning Network Ports

Besides tools such as nmap and nmapfe, described earlier, you can use several tools to find information about open ports for various protocols (such as TCP and UDP) on remote systems. The amap command can scan selected ports on target machines to try to determine what services (if any) are running on the selected ports.

AutoScan (http://autoscan.free.fr) is a graphical tool for exploring and managing your network. When you launch AutoScan, you can select subnetworks to scan in the background. Servers and workstations that are found appear on a list in the left column. You can display available services for each system by selecting that system. You can even start applications to connect to available services (such as ssh, nmap, and nessus). For users who are uncomfortable with Linux shell commands, AutoScan provides an easy-to-use and attractive interface to managing ports and services on your network.

The pbnj command (http://pbnj.sourceforge.net) uses the nmap and amap commands to gather information scanned from ports on selected systems and direct the results to an output file. Using that output file later, you can run the pbnj command again to determine changes to the services in the systems and ports you are scanning.

VPN Scanning Tools

Although virtual private networks (VPNs) were designed to provide secure connections over a public network (usually the Internet) between users and remote systems, VPNs can be exploited. Several tools on the VPN Scanners menu (select K menu → BackTrack → Scanners → VPN Scanners) can be used to test the characteristics of a VPN server for potential vulnerabilities.

By selecting Ike-Scan, you can run the ike-scan command (www.nta-monitor.com/tools/ike-scan) to try to discover the identity of an active VPN server. By watching for transport characteristics during Internet Key Exchange, ikescan can learn about the server being used to set up a connection between a server and remote client. Using that information, an intruder could try attacking any vulnerabilities that might be known about that VPN service.

Select the PSK-Crack entry (psk-crack command) from the menu to use a dictionary file to try to crack a VPN connection during an Internet Key Exchange. By default, the dictionary used is /usr/local/share/ike-scan/psk-crack-dictionary. A brute-force cracking technique is also available with the psk-crack command (–bruteforce option).

Vulnerability Scanning Tools

Network scanners can check for a variety of vulnerabilities. From the Vulnerability Scanners menu (K menu → BackTrack → Scanners → Vulnerability Scanners), you can choose from several different general vulnerability scanners.

The GFI LANguard Network Scanner (www.gfi.com) is a graphical tool for testing a selected system or a range of IP addresses for general information about each computer, specific information about open ports, and alerts related to any of the services that are open on those ports. Figure 9-7 shows an example of the LANguard Network Scanner.

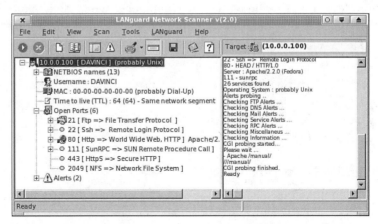

FIGURE 9-7 Scan for a range of vulnerabilities with LANguard Network Scanner.

The example in Figure 9-7 shows the results of scanning a single IP address (10.0.0.100) for a host named DAVINCI. After determining some general information about the systems, such as its NetBIOS names and MAC address, LANguard searches for open ports. When it finds open ports, it tests known vulnerabilities for the active services found on those ports.

In this case, six open ports were found. After the services on those ports were tested, two vulnerabilities were found relating to those ports. You can see the stored information about the scan on the left, with a running output of messages on the right.

SuperScan is another graphical tool for scanning one or more systems over a network. SuperScan is a Windows executable that can be run in Linux using WINE software. Using SuperScan, you can set up a list of ports you want to scan and set timeouts, check ports, and resolve host names.

Nikto (www.cirt.net) is a command-line vulnerability tester that tests for a range of issues that are most useful for evaluating the vulnerability of Web servers. It incorporates testing features using plug-ins. By running the `nikto` command on a name or IP address for a Web server, Nikto first determines general information about the server (such as operating system, Web server type, host name, and port number). Then it goes on to test the server to determine whether a later version of the server software is available and whether the current version unnecessarily exposes too much information about itself when queried.

Password Attack Tools

Trying to steal the passwords for one user (or a whole lot of users) is one of the oldest techniques for breaking into computer systems. Some password-attack tools are designed to be run on live (online) systems, and others are meant to be run offline (for example, when a password file is stolen and the cracker can run the attack at leisure).

Because BackTrack includes so many tools for cracking passwords, I focus on only a few of them. When you open the Password Attacks menu (K menu → BackTrack → Password Attacks), most of the password attacks are divided into offline and online attacks.

Offline Password Attacks

If you have access to a computer's password file (typically /etc/passwd) and shadow file (typically /etc/shadow), you can run commands on those files to try to crack the passwords they contain. As someone trying to protect your own systems, you can use these commands to uncover weak passwords entered by those who use your computers.

Check the Offline Attacks menu (K menu → BackTrack → Password Attacks → Offline Attacks) to see a list of password attack commands available with BackTrack. One example of such a command is `john`. Create a combined password and shadow file. Then run `john` on that file:

```
# unshadow /etc/passwd /etc/shadow > mypasswd
# john mypasswd
Created directory: root/.john
```

```
Loaded 3 password hashes with 3 different salts (FreeBSD MD5 [32/32])
jake      (jake)
toor      (root)
```

In this example, the password for the user jake was discovered to simply be jake. The password for root was found to be toor. If you were able to crack users' passwords on a running system, you should tell those users to change their passwords. Be sure to remove the mypasswd file and .john directory when you are done checking passwords.

Other offline password cracking tools include Rainbow Crack tools BKHive, OPHCrack, Rcrack, Rtdump, Rtsort, SAMDump2, and WebCrack. RainbowCrack uses prebuilt rainbow tables to speed password cracking. (See www.antsight.com/zsl/rainbowcrack site for more information on the RainbowCrack project.)

Online Password Attacks

Online password attacks can be more difficult to carry out. Repeated brute force attacks can easily be detected. A system can be configured to simply prevent someone from repeatedly trying and failing to login to a system.

Hydra (www.thc.segfault.net) is a paralyzed login hacking program. It can be used to try to guess login/password pairs using more than a dozen different service types (telnet, ftp, pop3, imap, and so on). CowPatty is a brute-force password crackdr made for cracking WIFI login/password pairs. Medusa (www.foofus.net) is another parallel password cracking tool, including modules for cracking passwords in CVS, FTP, HTTP, IMAP, MySQL, and other services.

Running Fuzzers

A fuzzer is a program that injects input into an application, hoping that, as a result, the application will crash or cause an exception. By getting programs to crash, the fuzzer hopes to find vulnerabilities in the system that can be exploited by such things as buffer overflows and denial-of-service attacks. You can find fuzzer applications on the Fuzzers menu (select K menu → Backtrack → Fuzzers).

The Bruteforce Exploit Detector (bed command) sends commands to server daemons in an attempt to get those commands to cause the daemons to crash. This can help determine whether the server is susceptible to buffer overflow attacks. The CIRT Fuzzer (fuzz.pl command) lets you identify a host and port to attack. You can include a template.txt file on the fuzz.pl command line.

You can use the clfuzz.py program to help audit binaries that have setuid set. The fuzzer.py program can help find buffer overflow and SQL injection.

BackTrack also comes with the SPIKE Fuzzer Creation Kit. Tools that come with this kit include webfuzz (a combination of small tools for Web application fuzzing) and `msrpcfuzz` (used to send random arguments with the intent of finding bugs that will cause a port to close down).

Doing Spoofing

One way to break into networks or systems is to run programs in which the program pretends to be something it's not, such as a legitimate DNS server or DHCP server, in hopes of fooling an unsuspecting application or user into giving up critical information. BackTrack includes a whole set of spoofing tools (K menu → Backtrack → Spoofing) that you can try out to test for vulnerabilities in your systems.

The `arpspoof` program (part of the `dsniff` package from www.monkey.org/~dugsong/dsniff) tries to trick another computer into believing that it is the gateway machine. It does this by constantly sending the victim machine its own IP address as that of the gateway. When the victim machine eventually caches the `arpspoof` machine's MAC address as that of the gateway, the victim starts sending its IP packets to the `arpspoof` machine instead of the real gateway.

The `dhcpx` program (www.phenoelit.de/irpas) is a DHCP flooder. This technique is also referred to as a DHCP exhaustion attack. The `dnsspoof` command tries to convince other systems on the LAN that it is the DNS server by faking replies to various DNS address queries and pointer queries.

Using the `fragroute` command, you can try to get, change, and rewrite traffic in the LAN that is destined for locations outside the LAN. This type of network traffic is referred to as egress traffic. Although `fragroute` has an effect on only packets that originate on the local machine, the `fragrouter` command can work on other machines as well.

Check the Spoofing menu for other types of spoofing you can do as well. For example, some commands try to redirect ICMP traffic, and others try to gain control by replaying TCP/IP packets.

Network Sniffers

As its name implies, a network sniffer watches a network, trying to "sniff" for information being passed on that network. That information can be used for evil (in the case of someone trying to steal data or connection information) or good (to uncover a potential problem on the network). In some cases, employers use sniffers to make sure employees aren't doing anything against company policy with their computers.

BackTrack includes more than a dozen sniffers that you can use to watch network traffic of various kinds. Check the Sniffers menu to see which ones BackTrack includes (K menu → BackTrack → Sniffers).

You can use the AIM Sniffer (`aimsniffer` command) to log and capture traffic from AOL Instant Messenger sessions. Driftnet (www.ex-parrot.com/~chris/driftnet) is a graphical utility that listens for images in TCP traffic and displays those it finds in the Driftnet window. Figure 9-8 shows the images that appeared on the Driftnet window after selecting Wikipedia.org from a local Web browser.

FIGURE 9-8
Display images encountered in TCP traffic with `driftnet`.

The `dsniff` command (http://monkey.org/~dugong/dsniff) is a password-sniffing command that can listen for passwords on a variety of services. Those services include FTP, TELNET, SMTP, HTTP, POP, X11, AIM, ICQ, and others. With `dsniff` running, it automatically detects the protocols it is sniffing, picks out only relevant password information, and saves that information to an output file in Berkeley DB format.

Ethereal (www.ethereal.com) is a graphical tool for capturing Ethernet traffic on selected interfaces. The Ethereal window contains tools for filtering, sorting, and analyzing network traffic. Ethereal also allows the use of plug-ins, which can be used for many purposes, including outputting the data gathered by Ethereal in various ways.

Iptraf (http://iptraf.seul.org) is an IP network statistics utility you can use to monitor the traffic on your network. The utility is ncurses-based, so it can run in any shell (no need for a GUI). Using the `iptraf` command, you can watch for specific types of traffic or watch only on selected interfaces. Log information is placed in `/var/log/iptraf` unless otherwise specified.

You can use other specialized sniffers in addition to those just mentioned. The SMB Sniffer (`start-smb-sniffer` command) watches for traffic relating to Windows file- and printer-sharing activity. The `mailsnarf` command captures mail traffic based on interfaces you choose and specific patterns you are looking for. The PHoss utility (www.phenoelit.de/phoss) watches network interfaces for clear-text passwords.

To sniff secure shell (SSH) traffic, the sshmitm utility (part of the dsniff package) can be placed between an ssh client and server. By acting as the real ssh server, sshmitm can grab the password information from an unsuspecting client and then complete the transaction for the client with the real server without the client suspecting that anything has gone wrong. The ettercap utility (http://ettercap.sourceforge.net) is a graphical utility that can similarly do man-in-the-middle attacks, but ettercap can grab whole sessions as well as the password information.

As the name implies, URLsnarf (urlsnarf command) can grab Web address information requested on a selected interface (matching any pattern you like). XSpy (xspy command) can track everything typed into an X display and echo that information back to the shell where xspy is running.

To save files that are transferred using the NFS protocol, you can use the filesnarf command. Using the msgsnarf command, you can save messages and chat sessions from many different IRC and messaging protocols. With mailsnarf, you can sniff SMTP and POP traffic to save e-mail messages. All three, mailsnarf, filesnarf, and msgsnarf, are part of the dsniff package.

Wireless Network Tools

You can use tools for working with wireless networks to try to analyze traffic, crack passwords, forge packets, and switch to different driver configurations on your wireless LAN cards. You can see tools available in BackTrack for working with wireless LANs on the Wireless Tools menu (K menu → BackTrack → Wireless Tools).

Kismet (www.kismetwireless.net) is a popular tool for working with wireless LAN interfaces. With Kismet, you can detect intrusions on 802.11 wireless networks (802.11b, 802.11a, and 802.11g). Kismet collects packets passively to detect hidden networks. It detects networks using standard names and can decloak hidden networks over time. Data you log with Kismet is compatible with Ethereal and tcpdump logs.

To test password strength of the nodes on a wireless LAN, you can use tools such as WepAttack (http://wepattack.sourceforge.net), Wep_crack and Wep_decrypt (www.lava.net/~newsham/wlan, as part of the wep_tools package), and Weplab (http://weeplab.sourceforge.net). Each of these tools provides a different set of options for testing the security of the passwords used on your wireless networks.

Some miscellaneous wireless tools are available from the Miscellaneous submenu. The macchanger utility (www.alobbs.com/macchanger) lets you view and change the MAC addresses of network interfaces. If you have a GPS device attached to your system, you can start and stop the GPS tracking daemon by selecting Start GPS Daemon or Stop GPS Daemon, respectively. Several utilities also exist for changing the drivers used on your wireless cards.

For forging packets on wireless networks, a handful of tools are available on the Packet Forging menu. The `aircrack-ng` package (www.aircrack0-ng.org/doku.php) contains a set of tools for auditing the reliability of your wireless network, including `aireplay-ng` (for injecting frames that generate traffic for cracking WEP and WPA-PSK keys). Airsnarf (www.shmoo.com) can be used to set up a rogue wireless access point. WifiTap (`wifitap` command) can be used to capture traffic and inject packets on an 802.11 network (see http://sid.rstack.org/index.php/wifitap_EN).

BlueTooth Device Tools

Tools for monitoring BlueTooth devices (www.bluetooth.org) are available from the BlueTooth menu (K menu → BackTrack → BlueTooth). Blue Snarfer (`bluesnarfer` command) downloads the phonebook of Bluetooth-enabled devices that are not secured against such intrusions. Carwhisperer (`carwhisperer` command) tests the vulnerability of BlueTooth car kits, particularly those that use standard passkeys (see http://trifinite.org/trifinite_stuff_carwhisperer.html).

You can use the HeloMoto utility (`helomoto` command) to exploit the handling of trusted devices by some Motorola phones and other devices. You can learn about HeloMoto attacks from the Trifinite.org site (http://trifinite.org/trifinite_stuff_helomoto.html).

Cisco Router Tools

Look under the Cisco Tools menu (K menu → BackTrack → Cisco Tools) to find tools for checking for vulnerabilities in Cisco Routers. The Cisco Global Exploiter (`cge.pl` perl script) can test for a range of known Cisco equipment vulnerabilities. Using this tool usually just requires a target and the name of an exploit to test for. You can find out about this script from the BlackAngels site (www.blackangels.it).

Cisco Torch is a mass Cisco vulnerability scanner (`cisco-torch.pl` Perl script). With it, you can scan for a variety of services on Cisco devices, including `telnetd`, `sshd`, `snmp`, and `tftp`. You can do fingerprinting scans on Network Time Protocol (NTP) and TFTP servers.

Yersinia (`yersinia` command) is a tool for analyzing network protocols, including the Cisco Discovery Protocol (CDP). You can find out more about Yersinia from its home page (www.yersinia.net). The `cisco-copy-config.pl` and `merge-copy-config.pl` Perl scripts are simple scripts for copying and merging Cisco configuration scripts, respectively, using SNMP.

Database-Analysis Tools

BackTrack divides its tools for analyzing database vulnerabilities into categories of generic database tools, MS-Sql, Mysql, and Oracle. Nearly a dozen tools exist for checking database vulnerabilities.

Absinthe (www.0x90.org/releases/absinthe) is a graphical tool for downloading database schema and content that might be vulnerable to blind SQL injection. It also includes the basics for MS SQL server error-based injection. The tool is used primarily to improve the speed of recovering data.

The SQL-Dict selection runs the `sqldict.exe` Windows binary for launching the SQL Server Dictionary Attacker (http://ntsecurity.nu/toolbox). The window lets you start attacks to test for SQL dictionary vulnerabilities based on target server IP address and target account. You can also load a password file.

For MySQL databases, BackTrack includes Blind SQL Injection (`bsqlbf.pl` script from www.unsec.net), SQL-Miner (`mysql-miner.pl` script), and Setup MySQL (`setup-mysql` Python script). The `setup-mysql` script lets you configure and start a MySQL server on which you can start testing.

Forensic Tools

To check out a system for problems after they occur, BackTrack includes a handful of forensic tools you can run on the system. The Autopsy Forensic Browser (www.sleuthkit.org/autopsy) lets you set up cases to do volume and file-system analysis. As forensics are run, data is stored in an Evidence Locker that is associated with a case.

Using the `pasco` command (www.foundstone.com/resources/proddesc/pasco.htm), you can browse the contents of cache files that Internet Explorer left behind. It takes an `index.dat` file as input and outputs field-delimited data that you can use in a spreadsheet.

Acquiring Tools

To be able to run forensic analysis tools on an infected system, you usually need to copy the file system to an image file to work on it from another location. The standard tool for copying an image file, and possibly converting it in various ways, is the `dd` command (which has been around since the old UNIX days). BackTrack includes several related commands that can also work with those file system images.

The `dcfldd` command is an enhanced version of the `dd` command that is intended specifically for doing forensics. This command can do such things as hashing on-the-fly (to ensure data integrity) and performing flexible disk wipes (using any known pattern you choose). To learn more about dcfldd, refer to its SourceForge page (http://dcfldd.sourceforge.net).

The ddrescue command (www.gnu.org/software/ddrescue/ddrescue.html) is a data-recovery tool that does its best to rescue data in environments where there might be read errors. Because ddrescue runs automatically, it fills in data gaps instead of truncating output or stopping for errors.

A graphical tool for creating file-system image files, already discussed in this chapter, is the Automated Image & Restore (AIR) utility.

Running Services

Because network interfaces and services that run on those interfaces are off by default in BackTrack, the BackTrack Services menu (K menu → BackTrack → BackTrack Services) lets you select to start and stop various system services that can help you with rescue and security activities. You can select the following services from this menu:

- **HTTPD**—Starts and stops an Apache Web server
- **Postgres**—Starts and stops a Postgresql database server
- **SNORT**—Sets up and initializes Snort, and then starts Snort (along with any dependent processes)
- **SSH**—Sets up, starts, and stops an SSH remote-login daemon server
- **TFTPD**—Starts and stops the trivial FTP server
- **VNC Server**—Starts and stops a virtual network computing (VNC) server to allow remote displaying of local desktop displays
- **vsFTPD**—Starts and stops an FTP server

Depending on the types of services you want to be able to test from your live Linux CD, you might want to add other services as well.

Miscellaneous Services

A whole bunch of services that didn't fit into any other category are lumped into the Misc category on the BackTrack menu. Among the tools on that menu are QTParted (a graphical disk-partitioning tool based on the parted command), PDF Viewer (for viewing PDF files with the kpdf viewer), and Screen Capture (to take a screen shot with the ksnapshot command).

ADDING SOFTWARE TO A BACKTRACK LIVE CD

Using the customization and remastering techniques described in Chapters 6, "Building a Custom Knoppix Live CD," through 8, "Building a Basic Gentoo Live CD," for Knoppix, Fedora, and Gentoo live CDs, you can add the components described in this chapter (as well as other components) as you choose. In some cases, software packages will already be available for your chosen live CD type (Deb, RPM, or Emerge packages). In other cases, you can download the software you want from the project Web sites mentioned with many of the components described.

Because BackTrack is based on a slackware (in particular, SLAX live CD) distribution, I next describe how to add SLAX-based packages to a BackTrack live CD. This way, you can download and run any packages (referred to a modules) available from the SLAX software repository.

The technique for adding software modules to a SLAX-based live CD such as BackTrack is much easier than the technique for remastering Knoppix (using a chroot environment) in Chapter 6. You can add SLAX modules to your BackTrack live CD in two ways:

- **Remaster**—Add a SLAX module to the /modules directory on the live CD. You copy the contents of your BackTrack live CD to a directory on your hard disk, adding the SLAX module to the modules directory, and re-creating the ISO image (using mkisofs command); the software in the module you added is installed when you boot that live CD.

- **Live**—You can download any SLAX module and install it live using the uselivemod command while BackTrack is running. The software in that module then is immediately available for use.

To find available software modules that will work with BackTrack and other SLAX-based live CDs, go to the SLAX modules page (www.slax.org/modules.php). There you will find 15 categories of software you can add to your running live CD or to the /modules directory when you remaster. To install a module immediately, find the software you want (either select the category or use the search box to find what you want). Then download the module you choose.

With the module you want to install in the current directory, you can use the uselivemod command to install the module. For example, you could type the following to install the eMovix package:

```
# uselivemod eMovix_0_9_0.mo
```

The software will be immediately available on your live CD to use.

You might need a variety of drivers and firmware to get certain hardware peripherals working properly on your live CD. SLAX comes with a bunch of drivers that might not have been included with the distribution but that might be legal for you to install on your personal live CD:

From the SLAX modules page, select Drivers. These are some examples of drivers you might want to add (depending on your hardware) that are available from the modules page:

- **ATI video drivers**—If your video card uses ATI video chipsets, you can install closed-source, proprietary drivers from the manufacturer that might work better for applications that require hardware acceleration than their open-source counterparts.

- **NVIDIA drivers**—As with ATI video cards, if you have NVIDIA chipsets in your video cards, proprietary drivers from NVIDIA will probably work better for you than open-source drivers for gaming and other software that performs better with hardware acceleration.

- **madwifi**—Several different wireless LAN cards might not work at all in Linux without drivers from the madwifi project.

- **Linux Webcam driver**—The drivers in this package can help the limited number of Webcams that are supported in Linux to work properly.

Besides those packages just mentioned, other drivers are available from this page. They include modem drivers for specific modem types and some firmware packages that are needed to get certain wireless cards working properly.

Summary

With dozens of security- and rescue-oriented live Linux CDs available today, choosing one for yourself can be done based on the tools that are provided and the Linux distribution it is based on. For examples in this chapter, I used the BackTrack network security suite live CD.

Using BackTrack, you can evaluate literally hundreds of security- and rescue-oriented tools to work on Linux systems, networks, and a variety of systems you can reach from a network. BackTrack is based on SLAX (which is based on Slackware) and, therefore, can use many of the resources available to SLAX (such as extra software modules).

The chapter steps you through some of the design decisions in BackTrack and notes where you have opportunities to modify how BackTracks boots up and starts services. Because BackTrack uses KDE as its desktop, you have a wide range of desktop tools to support specialized security utilities that will run from that platform.

## CHAPTER 10

Customizing a Presentation Live Linux CD

If you are creating a live Linux CD for the express purpose of making a presentation, showing your photos, or playing a video, why not have that CD boot directly to applications that play that content? You can create a live CD that offers one or more presentations that you, a friend, or a coworker can select from the boot prompt. By offering your presentation in this way, you can not only go directly to your content, but you also can play that content with the exact players and options you want.

Because I could not find an existing live Linux CD that boots directly to a presentation the way I wanted, I created my own custom live CD. I began with the latest version of Damn Small Linux and remastered using a procedure similar to the Knoppix remastering procedure in Chapter 6, "Building a Custom Knoppix Live CD."

For demonstration purposes in this book, I created a live CD that I call PuppetiX (don't look for it at distrowatch.com), which is designed to promote a puppet workshop and parade. To get a feel for how this type of CD might ultimately work, I have also included content so you can actually see the viewers in action. From the boot screen of this live CD, you can select to launch the following components:

- **Slide Show (GQview)**—A slideshow of images from past puppet parades are displayed in full-screen mode using GQview (`gqview` command).
- **Presentation (Openoffice.org Impress)**—The presentation, displayed as an OpenOffice.org Impress file, describes the puppet workshop and parade. It was designed for live presentations at community groups and schools.

You can add your own presentations or slideshows that can be launched from the boot loader. For this particular project, I chose to use the GRUB boot loader so I could take advantage of the menu interface. I added options to different boot labels to indicate which presentation to launch.

This live CD is used to launch particular content (digital images and an Impress presentation) and applications (GQview and OpenOffice.org Impress), but with some simple remastering, you could remaster this live CD to do the following:

- **Launch any desktop application**—By adding your own label to the boot loader and identifying the command to run based on that label, you can launch any application that you want to run on the desktop. Using the Damn Small Linux MyDSL Extension Tool, you can choose from dozens of applications that are already packaged to run on Damn Small Linux.

- **Play any content you like**—By adding your own content to the live CD, you can be sure that the content will run as you expect. You can even add other types of content, such as music or videos. As long as you can find a player to play it that runs in Linux, you can launch your content directly from the boot prompt using this live CD.

The rest of this chapter describes how PuppetiX works and the ways in which you can use similar techniques in making your own bootable presentations.

TRYING OUT THE PUPPETIX PRESENTATION LIVE CD

The point of the PuppetiX presentation live CD is to select and launch presentations from a boot loader, so the only way to run it is from a separate ISO image. I created two different ISO images of PuppetiX that are on the DVD that comes with this book:

- **puppetix**—The image `puppetix-0.1.iso` contains the software needed to boot right to a full-screen slide show. It also includes the framework for playing OpenOffice Impress presentations, but it doesn't include Impress itself. By not including the OpenOffice.org suite, you can boot on a minimal system and follow along with most of this chapter.

- **puppetix-oo**—The image `puppetix-oo-0.1.iso` is the same as the previous one, except that the entire OpenOffice.org suite has been added. Although this ISO will run the Impress presentation, the ISO itself is much larger (about 160MB) and requires 384MB of RAM to run properly. This ISO also takes longer to load, in part because it uses the MyDSL feature (described later).

To try out PuppetiX, you can copy the ISO you choose to hard disk and then burn it to a blank CD. Here's how to do that from a Linux system:

1. Insert the DVD that comes with this book into the DVD drive on your computer.

2. Copy the `puppetix` ISO you chose from the DVD to your hard drive. For example:

```
# cp /media/livecd/distros/puppetix-1.0.iso /tmp
```

or

```
# cp /media/livecd/distros/puppetix-oo-1.0.iso /tmp
```

3. Remove the DVD and insert a blank CD. Then type the following:

```
# cdrecord -v -eject /tmp/puppetix*.iso
```

When the CD ejects, you can boot it from a spare PC to follow along with the descriptions in this chapter. When you first boot up the CD, you will see a boot screen that looks like Figure 10-1.

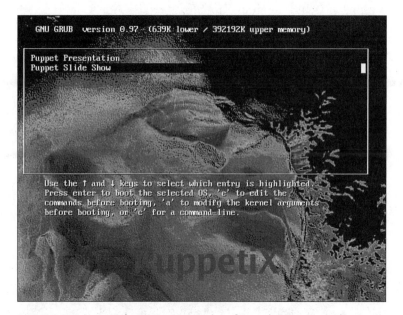

FIGURE 10-1 Select a presentation from the PuppetiX boot screen.

The boot screen contains the head of a large, ugly puppet. Move the cursor (using arrow keys) between the two selections (Puppet Slideshow and Puppet Presentation) to choose which one you want to start. Press e on either selection to see the contents of that boot label. Press e again, this time on the kernel line, to see the boot options being passed to the kernel. Press Esc and b when you are ready to boot.

PuppetiX boots up to a presentation based on the `puppet=` boot option added to the end of kernel lines for the two selections. The Puppet Slide Show label includes a `puppet=slides` boot option, which runs gqview (in full screen, slide show mode) with all the images in the /var/puppets/images directory. The Puppet Presentation label includes the puppet=impress boot option, which ultimately launches an OpenOffice.org Impress presentation that was added to the /var/puppets/presentations directory.

Depending on whether you selected the presentation or slide show, the mylaunch script starts either gqview (for the slide show of digital images) or impress (for the presentation). The data for the two presentations were placed on the live CD itself in subdirectories of /var/local/puppets.

When the presentation is done, you exit to a simple desktop, which has icons for launching the same presentations as were on the boot screen. Although I have added only two selections on this live CD, as I further describe this project, you can see that it would be simple to add as many slide shows, presentations, videos, or other content and players as you like.

Playing GQview Slideshows

Now that you have PuppetiX up and running, you might as well play with it a bit. The GQview image viewer (http://gqview.sourceforge.net) can display digital images of many formats in different ways. Besides simply watching the full-screen slide show play, as happens here by default, GQview can also pan images, zoom in and out, and open them in external applications to manipulate images further.

As the slide show plays, right-click an image. You can select different zooming features or choose to edit the images with Xpaint (or GIMP, electric eyes, or XV, if you added those applications to the live CD). You can also copy, move, rename, or delete the current image.

When you are finished viewing a slide show, press q to quit. In Puppetix, the Fluxbox window manager starts after you exit the viewer. If you want to then restart the slide show, right-click the desktop and select Puppets → Puppet Slideshows → Parade 2006. Exit from full-screen mode to see the GQview file list, as shown in Figure 10-2.

With the file list and menu displayed, you can select more options for working with images. From the Edit menu, select Adjust to rotate, flip, or mirror the image. Select Set as Wallpaper to use the image for the background of your desktop. Choose Select All to be able to work with all the images in the list at once.

Select Options to set the behavior of GQview. For slide shows in particular, you can change the 10-second delay, select to show pictures in order or randomly, or choose Repeat if you want the slide show to loop through the pictures forever.

FIGURE 10-2 Use GQview to play slide shows and work with digital images.

Any settings you choose are stored in the /home/ds1/.gqview directory. If you want to keep those settings to use later, you can copy the .gqview directory to the etc/skel directory where you are remastering the live CD. In that way, you can keep those settings permanently with the live CD.

Playing Impress Presentations

The OpenOffice.org application suite is the premiere set of office-productivity tools available in the free and open-source software world. Besides offering a half-dozen major components for word processing, presentations, math, drawing, spreadsheets, and database access, it can handle file formats from most popular office applications available today.

The OpenOffice.org application suite is not included in DSL by default. Its size, which would nearly triple the size of DSL, would blow out DSL's requirement to fit on a 50MB bootable business card. However, you can add a version of the OpenOffice.org suite to DSL (which, even compressed, comes in at nearly 100MB), as we did for our customized PuppetiX live presentation CD.

If you boot up the puppetix-oo ISO included with this book, the OpenOffice tar/gzip file is added to your running live CD as it comes up. After you decide whether to register with OpenOffice.org, OpenOffice Impress boots up to a full-screen presentation describing the puppet festival shown in the other slide show. Click to move forward or press Backspace to return to a previous slide. Select File → Exit to quit Impress and start the Fluxbox window manager.

You can start the presentation again from the Fluxbox desktop by right-clicking and selecting Puppets → Puppet Presentations → Workshops 2006. The OpenOffice Impress window shows the text and preview windows of the Puppet Workshop presentation, as in Figure 10-3.

FIGURE 10-3 Step through a presentation with OpenOffice.org Impress.

Using Impress, you can edit each slide of the presentation, add more slides, or change a variety of attributes (colors, fonts, layout, and more). You can move around the presentation by selecting from thumbnails of each slide. Besides playing a native OpenOffice.org Impress presentation, Impress can work with PowerPoint presentations and presentations in other formats (such as StarImpress).

Although the OpenOffice.org suite requires a lot of disk space and RAM to run in PuppetiX and other DSL derivatives, if you have those resources, OpenOffice.org lets you handle most every type of office file format that exists today.

The rest of this chapter describes how this live CD was put together. In the process, you learn a bit about using Damn Small Linux to create a minimal live CD that does just what you want it to do.

REMASTERING A PRESENTATION LIVE CD

I began creating PuppetiX by remastering a Damn Small Linux (DSL) live CD. Because Damn Small Linux is based on Knoppix, most of the remastering procedure can be done as described in Chapter 6. In general, here are the steps in remastering Damn Small Linux:

> **NOTE**
>
> In the Knoppix remastering described in Chapter 6, most of the reason for changing to a chroot environment is to run apt-get and related tools to add and remove software for the live CD you build. If you choose to use the MyDSL feature, you might not need to run chroot at all. You can simply copy MyDSL archives of applications, as described here.

1. **Boot DSL**—Boot up Damn Small Linux (an ISO is included on the DVD that comes with this book). The computer you boot up doesn't need quite the resources you would need to remaster Knoppix. However, at least 500MB of disk space and 256MB of RAM probably is a good idea.

2. **Set up directory structure**—As with Knoppix, DSL provides desktop features for easily mounting hard-disk partitions. Because DSL uses /mnt and not /media to mount hard-disk partitions, the directory names used in the procedure should be different for DSL. For example, I set up my directory structure for remastering on /mnt/hda1/DSL instead of /media/hda1/knoppix. All directory references in that chapter should change accordingly.

3. **Get software**—After copying files to your new remastering (master and source) directories, you can get any additional software you need for the live CD. Instead of using apt-get to get packages from online repositories, if possible, I recommend that you use the MyDSL feature. To make that happen, I did the following:

   - **Open MyDSL**—Select MyDSL from the desktop. The MyDSL Extension Tool window appears.

   - **Choose application**—Choose the category and application you want. You are asked where to save the archive (tarred and gzipped) representing the application.

   - **Save archive**—To include the application on the live CD, save the archive representing that application in the master directory. For example, if you named your remastering directories as I suggested earlier, you could save the application archive to /mnt/hda1/DSL/master. Any archives saved to that directory will be unpacked when the new live CD is booted later. Although this slows down the boot process, it makes it much easier to add and remove applications during remastering.

NOTE

I selected Apps → gqview.dsl.info (for the slide show) to add to both puppetix images and Apps → openoffice-1.1.4.info (for the Impress presentations) to the puppetix-oo image.

4. **Configure desktop**—Instead of KDE, DSL uses Fluxbox as its default window manager. Although it doesn't have all the cool features of KDE, it runs efficiently and can still include colors, backgrounds, and other theme elements you choose. In general, system-wide Fluxbox settings are in /usr/share/fluxbox, while settings for individual users can go into /etc/skel/.fluxbox. I describe how Fluxbox was configured in PuppetiX a bit later.

5. **Modify boot files**—The GRUB boot loader was added to puppetix, replacing the isolinux boot loader usually used with DSL and Knoppix. Setting up the GRUB boot loader is described in Chapter 5, "Looking Inside Live CD Components," while the particular features used in this live CD are described later in this chapter.

6. **Making the ISO**—With the source and master directories as you would like them, you can follow the steps in Chapter 6 for making the compressed file system image and creating the final CD image. You will probably repeat those steps many times as you tune the live CD exactly as you want it.

The following sections describe the particular changes made in the process of creating the Puppetix live CD.

Setting Up the GRUB Boot Loader

Because the PuppetiX live CD is intended for the point-and-click crowd, it seemed best to start that approach from the boot loader. GRUB has a few nice features that make it a good choice for a presentation live CD:

- **Menu interface**—Boot labels appear on a menu that the user can select with up and down arrows. In this way, each bootable presentation can be launched without the end user needing to know what label name to type.

Advanced users who want to change or add options can edit (press E) the boot label they want before starting it up.

- **Splash screen**—The image on the splash screen can fill the screen. The menu appears in front of it. This enables you to use a larger image than you can with Isolinux.

Using GRUB, you can have as many presentations available from the boot screen as you want. Each presentation can be run with a different player or options that you define later.

To begin setting up the GRUB boot loader, I added a grub directory to the master/boot directory during remastering. On the resulting live CD, that directory will end up as the /cdrom/boot/grub directory. More important, however, when you make the ISO file system (mkisofs command), the El Torito boot image and related files will come from that directory.

The contents of the grub directory are fairly simple. By making the labels simple, you bypass extra help screens. The grub directory contains the following components:

- linux24—This is the 2.4 kernel copied from the isolinux directory from Damn Small Linux. That kernel is used for each bootable presentation in PuppetiX.
- minirt24.gz—Likewise, the initial RAM disk (minirt24.gz) was copied from the Damn Small Linux isolinux directory.
- stage2_eltorito—A stage 2 El Torito boot image is identified with the -b option of the mkisofs command when you build the ISO image. I got this image from the grub package that comes with Fedora Core. However, DSL has a grub package available from the MyDSL feature, which, I presume, would work as well.
- puppet.xpm.gz—The splash screen image is a gzipped image in XPM format (X PixMap image). I used an image of a giant puppet. The XPM image is 640×480 pixels and uses a 14-color palette. Chapter 5 includes a procedure for converting a digital image to this format.
- grub.conf—The grub configuration file (grub.conf) is where most of your customization goes for GRUB. With all the other files in place, you can begin editing the grub.conf file.

The following code example shows the contents of the grub.conf file in the PuppetiX boot/grub directory. I left out some comment lines to save space:

```
# grub.conf
#
```

```
default=0
timeout=10
splashimage=(cd)/boot/grub/puppet.xpm.gz
# color blue/green red/green

title Puppet Slide Show
    root (cd)
    kernel /boot/grub/linux24 ramdisk_size=100000 init=/etc/init lang=us
        apm=power-off vga=791 nomce noapic quiet BOOT_IMAGE=knoppix
        desktop=fluxbox puppet=slides
    initrd /boot/grub/minirt24.gz

title Puppet Presentation
    root (cd)
    kernel /boot/grub/linux24 ramdisk_size=100000 init=/etc/init lang=us
        apm=power-off vga=791 nomce noapic quiet BOOT_IMAGE=knoppix
        desktop=fluxbox puppet=impress
    initrd /boot/grub/minirt24.gz
```

For simplicity, this grub.conf file shows only two labels. For your presentation live CD, you might want to have multiple slide shows, presentations, or other content/players. Text that is highlighted in the example grub.conf file is of particular interest for this live CD.

The default=0 option sets the first boot label (title "Puppet Slide Show") as the default. After a timeout of 10 seconds (timeout=10), the default boot label boots automatically. You can see the seconds count down on the boot screen.

The image used on the splash screen (splashimage) is identified as being located on the CD image (cd) in the /boot/grub/ directory with the name puppet.xmp.gz. You need to give the full path to the image (a relative path such as boot/grub/puppet.xpm.gz is not supported).

The rest of the file is associated with the two boot labels. The title lines indicate the text that will appear on the splash screen menus that you use to select which presentation to boot (Puppet Slide Show or Puppet Presentation). For both, the target root device from which data will be read is a CD (cd). Both labels also use the exact kernel and initrd information that DSL uses in its default label in the Isolinux configuration file. In this case, however, two options were added.

Because the PuppetiX live CD was tuned for the Fluxbox window manager, that window manager is set explicitly on the kernel line (desktop=fluxbox). The puppet= option, however, eventually triggers the presentation to be run. The slide show of digital images is launched with `puppet=slides`, while the Impress presentation is launched with the `puppet=impress` option.

NOTE

I left a commented-out color line (color blue/green red/green) as a reminder that you can change the colors on the splash screen. The first set of colors indicates the foreground/background colors used for most text on the GRUB menu. The second set indicates the colors used for the high-lighted areas (from moving the arrow key to the label you want). Chapter 5 notes the colors you can use.

Starting the Presentation

Assuming that the kernel started up properly and mounted the initial RAM disk, control for booting up PuppetiX is passed off to the `init` process. As with other Knoppix-based live CD, DSL (and, hence, PuppetiX) boots up to runlevel 5, so the result of the boot process is a running desktop system. For that desktop system, we want to add our running presentation or slide show.

After a minimal X Window System display starts up, the window manager (in this case, Fluxbox) and any applications you want to run (such as launching a presentation) can be started from the `.xinitrc` file in the user's home directory. The default user that is created in DSL is appropriately named `dsl`. The `dsl` user's home directory (`/home/dsl`) is created at boot time by copying everything stored in the `/etc/skel` directory to that directory. That includes the `.xinitrc` file.

To start the presentation, I created a script called `mylaunch` and added it to the `/etc/skel/.xinitrc` file. The `mylaunch` script was added so that it would start after the X display was already running but just before Fluxbox started. Here are what the lines in the `.xinitrc` file look like, with the line I added highlighted:

```
case $DESKTOP in
  fluxbox )
    fluxter &>/dev/null &
    wmswallow -geometry 70x80 docked  docked.lua &
    /usr/local/bin/mylaunch
    exec fluxbox 2>/dev/null
  ;;
```

The `mylaunch` script is run here without an ampersand (&) at the end. That was done to prevent Fluxbox from starting up until the presentation is done running. (I tried it the other way, but Fluxbox kept opening any windows that were behind the presentation to add borders. They would come to the foreground and obscure the presentation.)

The `mylaunch` script was created to make the connection between what was entered at the boot prompt and which presentation is run. Here are the contents of the `mylaunch` script:

```
#!/bin/ash

# ================================================================
# text processing functions
# ================================================================

# egrep_o is a replacement for "egrep -o". It prints only the last
# matching text
# $1 = regular expression
#
egrep_o()
{
    cat | egrep "$1" | sed -r "s/.*($1).*/\\1/"
}

# look into cmdline and echo $1 back if $1 is set
# $1 = value name, case sensitive, for example livecd_subdir
# $2 = file to use instead /proc/cmdline, optional
#
cmdline_parameter()
{
    CMDLINE=/proc/cmdline
    if [ "$2" != "" ]; then CMDLINE="$2"; fi
    cat "$CMDLINE" | egrep_o "(^|[[:space:]]+)$1(\$|=|[[:space:]]+)" |
egrep_o "$1"
}
# ================================================================
# Presentations
# ================================================================

# Play slideshow
#
    if [ ! "`cmdline_parameter puppet=slides`" = "" ]; then
      /usr/bin/gqview -s -f /var/puppets/images/
    fi

# Play presentation
    if [ ! "`cmdline_parameter puppet=impress`" = "" ]; then
      /opt/openoffice-1.1.4/soffice -impress -show
/var/puppets/presentations/pp.sxi
    fi
```

The purpose of the `mylaunch` script is to read options set from the kernel boot line and then start up a presentation for any `puppet=` option that appears on that line. Those options are stored in `/proc/cmdline`. If you typed `cat /proc/cmdline`, you would see all the options from the label you booted.

The `mylaunch` script starts with several functions for reading values from `/proc/cmdline`. Those functions come from the `liblinuxlive` script that is part of the Linux Live CD project (www.linux-live.org). Then in the Presentations section of the script, the script currently looks for two options.

If `puppet-slides` was set, the `gqview` command runs a slide show mode (`-s`) in full-screen mode (`-f`) using all images placed in the `/var/puppets/images` directory. If `puppet=impress` is set, the `soffice` command is run in Impress mode (`-impress`) as a full-screen slide show (`-show`) to display the `pp.sxi` OpenOffice.org Impress presentation.

When the selected presentation is finished running, the Fluxbox window manager starts up. After that, you can begin using the desktop.

Because someone might want to run another presentation or slide show without having to reboot, the PuppetiX desktop has been modified to all users to run other presentations from the desktop or restart the original presentations. That desktop has also been tuned to include a different Fluxbox theme, to match the content of the PuppetiX live CD.

A Custom Fluxbox Theme

Instead of just exiting when the slide show or presentation is done or dropping you into a standard Damn Small Linux desktop, PuppetiX contains a custom desktop. Using a theme fashioned after the DSL Hat theme, the Puppet theme includes an appropriate background image and a menu that lets you launch any of your presentations from the desktop.

System-wide Fluxbox settings are stored in the `/usr/share/fluxbox` directory. Themes are in the `styles` subdirectory of that directory. By copying the default theme, you can create your own theme file and modify it as you like. In a theme file, you can change attributes that relate to toolbars, menus, windows, and fonts. You can even set the image used as the root window.

I created a style named `Puppet`, modified it to include attributes that worked for a presentation CD, and copied it to a file named `default` in the same directory. In particular, I added the `puppet.xpm` image to the `backgrounds` directory and this line to the `Puppet` theme file so it would be loaded each time the Fluxbox desktop started:

```
rootCommand:   xsri -scale-height=100 - scale-width=100
               /usr/share/fluxbox/backgrounds/puppet.xpm
```

The xsri command sets the X background to the image given to it. Figure 10-4 shows an example of the full PuppetiX desktop, incorporating the new background:

FIGURE 10-4 Set backgrounds and other Fluxbox attributes.

Other Fluxbox attributes set in PuppetiX are used to make the presentations and slide shows available from the desktop. To do that, entries for the two slide shows and presentations were added to the DSL menu that appears when you right-click on the desktop. The first change is to the etc/skel/.fluxbox/menu file that is copied to /home/dsl when PuppetiX starts up. A line indicting to include a mylaunch.menu file in the menu is added to the beginning of the menu file so it appears as follows:

```
Debian MENU
[begin] (DSL)
    [include](.fluxbox/mylaunch.menu)
    [include](.fluxbox/mydsl.menu)
    [submenu] (Apps) {}
        [submenu] (Editors) {}
    .
    .
    .
```

Next, a mylaunch.menu file was created in that same directory. That file contains the following:

```
[submenu] (Puppets) {}
   [submenu] (Puppet Slideshows) {}
      [exec] (Parade 2006) {/usr/bin/gqview -s -f /var/puppets/images}
   [end]
   [submenu] (Puppet Presentations) {}
      [exec] (Workshops 2006) {/opt/openoffice-1.1.4/soffice -impress \
               -show /var/puppets/presentations/pp.sxi}
   [end]
[end]
```

The `mylaunch.menu` file adds a submenu for Puppet Slideshows and one for Puppet Presentations. One entry exists on each submenu. The two entries align with the same slide show and presentation set up to launch from the boot prompt. The menu that results puts the Puppets menu at the top with two submenus, as shown in Figure 10-5.

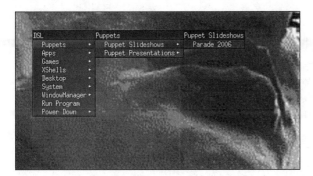

FIGURE 10-5
Restart any presentation from the DSL menu on the Fluxbox desktop.

Of course, just as with the boot labels, you can add as many menu items as you have presentations (or ways of running presentations).

Adding Content to the Live CD

Content was added to the live CD by copying files to `var/puppets` in your source remastering directory (for example, `/mnt/hda1/DSL/source/KNOPPIX/var/puppets`). Digital images of puppets ended up in the `/var/puppets/images` directory of the CD, and an Impress presentation went into the `/var/puppets/presentations` directory.

To be able to quickly create slide shows without creating multiple directories of images, I used the `-graft-points` option to the when creating the KNOPPIX image to insert into the live CD. Using `-graft-points`, you can graft a directory of files from your hard disk onto the live CD at any point in the live CD's file system that you choose.

The following is an example of the command I used to add images from the `/home/dsl/images` directory on my hard disk to the `/var/puppets` directory of the compressed KNOPPIX image for the live CD. I ran the following `mkisofs` command to produce the KNOPPIX image:

```
# mkisofs -R -U -V "My Knoppix File System"        \
    -publisher "John W. Jones"                      \
    -hide-rr-moved -cache-inodes -no-bak -pad \
    -graft-points /var/puppets/images/=/home/dsl/images/ \
    /mnt/hda1/DSL/source/KNOPPIX                    \
    | nice -5 /usr/bin/create_compressed_fs - 65536 >      \
    /mnt/hda1/DSL/master/KNOPPIX/KNOPPIX
```

Next, I ran the following to produce the final ISO image (called puppet-0.1.iso):

```
# cd /mnt/hda1/DSL/master
# mkisofs -R -b boot/grub/stage2_eltorito -no-emul-boot  \
    -boot-load-size 4 -boot-info-table \
    . > ../puppet-0.1.iso
```

You can also add multiple graft points to add images or other content from many directories to your live CD. With the small size of the operating system (50MB to about 150MB for the examples of PuppetiX) and large removable media (up to 8.4GB for a dual-layer DVD), you have the potential to create massive bootable slide shows using the live CD described here. Grafting enables you to store them separately and join them to the live CD only when you make the final ISO image.

SUMMARY

The PuppetiX live CD was created for this book to illustrate how to make a live CD that boots up directly to a slide show or presentation. Using the GRUB boot loader, a PuppetiX user can select from a menu of presentations. The operating system then boots up to a remastered Damn Small Linux that results in a full-screen display of the selected presentation.

By starting with a mini desktop distribution, such as Damn Small Linux, you can create this special-use type of live CD in a way that enables you to add lots of content. Using features such as MyDSL, you can add only those players you need (such as the gqview and OpenOffice.org Impress applications). The rest of the space on your live CD or DVD can be dedicated to holding the digital images, presentations, videos, or other content you want to display.

Because DSL is based on Knoppix, you can use many of the remastering techniques described in Chapter 6 to tailor the content of your live CD. You can also customize the Fluxbox desktop to include images, colors, and other desktop attributes to match the content you are displaying.

## CHAPTER 11

Customizing a Gaming Live Linux CD

If you are interested in computer games, no shortage of opportunities awaits you in Linux. Hundreds of pleasantly diverting games are available, with practically no restrictions on how you use them. Games that can take advantage of 3D hardware-accelerated video cards are also being produced for distribution as open-source games, to produce more eye-popping games.

After you create a gaming Linux live CD, you can hand your children a bootable CD that plays tons of games you've hand-picked for them. Or you might create a CD to carry around your favorite open-source games so you don't get bored when you're on the road. So much open-source software is available for gaming these days that most gaming live CD distributions have grown into DVD distributions.

This chapter takes several approaches to describing topics that you might find interesting when putting together your own gaming live CD or DVD:

- **Gaming live CDs**—A handful of Linux gaming live CDs already exist that you can try. With so much gaming software available, many of the most popular gaming live CDs have expanded to DVDs. DVD versions of Games Knoppix (http://games-knoppix.unix-ag.uni-kl.de) is 2.7GB; the SuperGamer gaming live CD (www.pclinuxos.com/forum/index.php?board=31.0) is about 3.7GB.

- **Free games**—Free and open-source games (distributed under the GPL or similar license) are quite plentiful for original games or clones of traditional computer games. You'll find no shortage of solitaire games, maze games, board games, and the like. In recent years, more complex action and strategy games have been created for free distribution.

If you want to put together a live CD that you can distribute freely, you can check out several lists of available applications. Later in this chapter, I take you through the selection of games that are included with the Linux Live Game Project live CD.

- **Commercial games and demos**—Many of the most popular computer games were, of course, created to sell commercially. Most commercial computer games were made for Microsoft Windows platforms, but some commercial games have been ported to Linux.

  Although it might not be legal to include most commercial Linux games on a live CD, in some cases you can get permission to include demos of those games on a Linux live CD. We describe some of the licensing issues surrounding redistributing commercial Linux games later in this chapter.

- **Classic commercial games**—You might be able to legally include on a live CD some classic commercial games that were created originally for PCs or game consoles. That's not to say that it's alright to just include a game on your live CD because a company isn't selling it anymore. Most companies don't simply relinquish their copyright because the game is no longer being marketed.

  However, in some cases, rights to classic games have been released into the public domain. In other cases, game console emulators are available in Linux, and you can purchase the games themselves to run on those emulators. In yet another case, parts of a commercial game might have been released into the public domain, while open-source clones of the parts that are still copyright protected might have been created so the whole game can be freely distributed. Doom is an example of such a game.

- **Video card support**—A big impediment to getting support for 3D gaming in Linux is getting drivers for video cards that support hardware acceleration. Closed-source drivers for Nvidia and ATI graphics cards are available for Linux, but restrictions govern redistributing those drivers and some difficulties inhibit getting those drivers to play nicely with open-source video drivers on the same machine. Later in this chapter, I describe ways to get drivers to play more advanced 3D graphics games.

To start, this chapter takes you through some of the available Linux live CDs. Then it describes open-source games that you can include on your own live CD so that you can freely distribute your CD. To demonstrate many of these games, the chapter includes a description of a Knoppix customization called the Linux Live Game Project (LLGP) live CD.

This chapter goes on to cover the issues that surround including software on your live CD that was or is still covered under licenses other than GPL types of licenses. These types of games include games that are sold commercially or that have other licensing impediments that you might or might not be able to work through.

FINDING LINUX GAMING LIVE CDS

Linux live CDs specializing in gaming applications range from pure open-source gaming CDs to those that include the capability to play commercial demos and 3D games. To use some of these live CDs, you need special graphics cards and lots of RAM to run effectively. The following sections contain examples of some live Linux gaming CDs and DVDs.

GamesKnoppix Live CD and DVD

The GamesKnoppix (http://games-knoppix.unix-ag.uni-kl.de) gaming live CD is available as both a live CD (700MB) and a DVD (2.7GB). Like many specialty Knoppix remasters, GamesKnoppix CD removes the OpenOffice.org suite (saving about 200MB alone) and a bunch of KDE applications to make room for lots of games.

Besides including many open-source games (described later in this chapter), the GamesKnoppix CD features demos of commercial games that run natively in Linux; you can try demos for games such as Marble Blast Gold and Think Tanks (www.garagegames.com), as well as Mutant Storm and Space Tripper (www.pom-pomgames.com). Be sure to have 3D graphics-accelerator hardware to run these games. (The demos aren't available on the DVD.)

To enable you to stretch outside the bounds of games that run natively in Linux, the GamesKnoppix DVD includes several computer and game console emulators. Select Emulators from the KDE menu to see what is available. If you can find game ROMs (games extracted from console game cartridges) or executables from supported computers, you can use the following emulators to run them:

- **Atari**—Commands are included to run emulators of Atari 800, Atari 800 XL, Atari 130 XE, and Atari 5200 games systems. Many options are available for running the Atari console emulator. To be able to use the emulator, you need to have game ROMs that were made to run on those consoles.

- **MAME**—The Multiple Arcade Machine Emulator (MAME) is probably the most popular game console emulator available for Linux. MAME has been tested to run hundreds of classic console games from the 1970s, 1980s, and 1990s. You need legal game ROMs to be able to use the emulator.

  Three game ROMs are said to be in the public domain (see www.mame-world.net/legal). Capcom and Taito have licensed some of their game ROMs to be sold, however, so you can get some to use legally for noncommercial purposes. Some are bundled with Hanaho's HotRod Joystick control panel (www.hanaho.com). StarROMs (www.starroms.com) offers a legal way to get ROM for some supported games.

- **DOSBox**—If you have old DOS games, you can use the dosbox command to run real- and protected-mode games created originally for the Disk Operating System (DOS).

- **Amiga**—For games that ran on Commodore Amiga 500, 1000, and 2000 computers, you can use the UAE Amiga emulator (uae command). Those machines were based on the Motorola 680x0 CPU chip.

- **Super Nintendo**—The zsnes utility (http://zsnes.com) is an emulator for playing games created for Super Nintendo systems.

The presence of game emulators is one feature that distinguishes GamesKnoppix from other gaming live CDs. However, if you don't have legal game ROMs (or if you're not willing to hunt them down), the emulators themselves are not that useful. However, this live CD has about 300 games to keep you busy. Check the Games-Knoppix Web site (http://games-knoppix.unix-ag.uni-kl.de/gamelist-4.0.2-0.3.txt) for a complete list of available games.

The interface for GamesKnoppix is the familiar and stable Knoppix 4.0.1 KDE desktop. Besides game emulators, you can try literally hundreds of games from the GamesKnoppix DVD. The Games menu has more than 50 arcade games and nearly 20 strategy games. There's even a Potato Guy game for kids. Figure 11-1 shows an example of GamesKnoppix displaying a billiards game (foobilliard), a space game (kasteroids), and a game for putting a face on a potato (Potato Guy).

PCLinuxOS SuperGamer

If you want to test the limits of your computer hardware for gaming, the SuperGamer live DVD (based on PCLinuxOS) has plenty of 3D accelerated games you can play. SuperGamer doesn't have a home page yet, but you can learn more about it from the

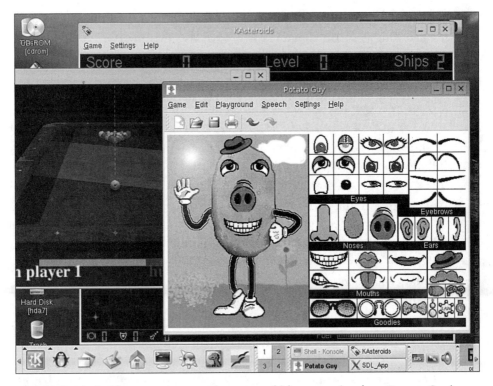

FIGURE 11-1 Play strategy, arcade, or even kids games (such as Potato Guy) with GamesKnoppix.

SuperGamer forum on the PCLinuxOS site (www.pclinuxos.com/forum/index.php?board=31.0).

To play 3D accelerated games, SuperGamer includes Nvidia drivers; an Nvidia card (at least an FX5500) is recommended to get the best performance from the 3D

NOTE

If you don't have an Nvidia card, you might encounter driver conflicts if you try to use 3D acceleration on other video cards. When I tried a machine with an old Intel i810, games requiring 3D acceleration failed to run (complaining that GLX was not available). I uninstalled Nvidia drivers and restarted the system. After that, I was able to run games requiring 3D acceleration using the proper i810 drivers. (It didn't run fast because it was an old machine with low RAM, but it did work.)

games. A lot of RAM is also required to run these games. Don't expect very good performance with less than about 512MB of RAM and a sub-1GHz processor.

The PCLinuxOS SuperGamer live DVD includes these playable demos and 3D games:

- **Doom and Quake**—Demos of the popular Doom 3 (www.doom3.com) and Quake 4 (www.quake4game.com) first-person shooter games are on the DVD.

- **Wolfenstein**—The Return to Castle Wolfenstein: Enemy Territory demo (http://games.activision.com/games/wolfenstein) is included on this DVD. In this game, you can save the world from Himmler and his evil occult army.

- **Neverball**—Roll a ball through an obstacle course in this combination puzzle and action game. You can learn more about it from the Icculus site (http://icculus.org/neverball). Neverputt, a miniature golf game based on the same technology, is also included here.

- **BZFlag**—Play against the computer or in teams over the Internet with this 3D tank battle game (www.bzflag.org).

- **PlanetPenguin Racer**—Help Tux race down the mountain on his belly in this 3D race-against-the-clock game (http://projects.planetpenguin.de/racer/).

- **UFO: Alien Invasion**—Fight against hostile aliens in this tactical battle game (www.ufoai.net).

- **America's Army**—This video game, sponsored by the U.S. Army, was designed to portray soldiers' experiences in different occupations in the army. The game includes training events that proceed to multiplayer operations. See www.americasarmy.com for more information.

Aside from the games, SuperGamer includes some multimedia applications for working with digital images (GQview, GIMP, XSane, and others), sound (Kaboodle, KsCD, and Xmms), and video (Realplayer, TVtime, and Xine). The Networking menu also has a good set of communications applications (file transfer, instant messaging, e-mail, and so on).

Figure 11-2 shows an example of the SuperGamer desktop, displaying the Battle of Wesnoth game and the XMMS media player.

FIGURE 11-2 SuperGamer contains a mix of 3D accelerated games and multi-media players.

RUNNING THE LINUX LIVE GAME PROJECT LIVE CD

As an example of a gaming live CD, I've included the Linux Live Game Project (LLGP) live CD (http://tuxgamers.altervista.org). This is a good representation of how Knoppix can be customized to meet a specific purpose. In this case, the purpose is gaming. The LLGP live CD also limited the games it added to free and open-source games, so there is no problem using or redistributing any of the games described here.

Literally hundreds of games are included on the LLGP live CD. Despite not including any commercial games or game demos, the live CD contains many fun and challenging games. To see the games included with the live CD, refer to the project's List of Games page (http://tuxgamers.altervista.org/List_of_games). To see all packages in the distribution, go to List_of_packages_on_LLGP_0.1pre0 from the home page. (If you do your own Knoppix or Debian remaster, you can refer to either of these lists as a reminder of packages you might want to include.)

To focus on games, LLGP developer Fabio Fabbri removed office and multimedia applications to make lots of room for games. He added multiple available LLGP backgrounds and a separate Games menu to the panel. He also put a Games Jukebox icon on the panel so you can select a random game to start. To speed up the boot process, kudzu hardware detection was completely removed, leaving all hardware detection done by hotplug and udev.

Although LLGP includes Nvidia drivers, they were included in a more thoughtful way than I have seen with other live CDs. For example, I tried LLGP on my old Intel i810 computer, and no apparent conflicts arose with Nvidia drivers. Typing glxinfo showed that direct rendering was on (Yes) and GLX extensions were enabled, so I could play games requiring DRI and GLX (albeit, rather slowly, given the slow processor and low RAM amounts). See the LLGP Nvidia discussion for more information (http://tuxgamers.altervista.org/LLGP_Nvidia_packages).

If you have questions about LLGP, you can go to the Tuxgamers forum area to ask questions or see what others are discussing about LLGP (http://tuxgamers.altervista.org/forum). English and Italian forums are available there.

Figure 11-3 shows the LLGP desktop with one of several LLGP backgrounds in use. In the lower-right corner, you can see the game selected today from the Games Jukebox icon. The complete Games menu (shown on the left) is displaying the Strategy games submenu. Other games shown on the screen include Xbill and KPoker.

The following sections contain descriptions of games that you can try out from the LLGP live CD. Because all these games are available from Debian/Knoppix repositories, you can use them in any Knoppix remaster you do yourself. Because they are open source, most other Linux distributions offer the games as well (if you prefer, for example, a Fedora, Gentoo, or Slackware remaster).

Adventure Games

Falcon's Eye is a graphical version of the popular NetHack game. With Falcon's Eye, instead of moving keyboard letters around ASCII grids, you see graphical characters and items appearing around a colorful grid. The purpose of the game is to travel through mazes to retrieve the Amulet of Yendor. Along the way, you encounter creatures and items that can help you on the quest.

Running Falcon's Eye requires Simple DirectMedia Layer software support (www.libsdl.org). Read about the game from the Falcon's Eye home page (http://users.tkk.fi/~jtpelto2/nethack.html). To install the game from Debian repositories, request the falconseye package.

FIGURE 11-3 Choose a random game or select from hundreds of games on the LLGP menu.

Arcade Games

Dozens of games appear on the Arcade submenu of the LLGP games menu. Some of the games are simple KDE games that will run in almost any working X desktop. Others games require SDL support to work. Table 11-1 shows information on games in the Arcade list so you can try them and decide whether you want them on your own live CD.

Some of the most entertaining games of those just mentioned are BZFlag and TuxRacer. You can play BZFlag against the computer or against others on the Internet. It contains a server component that lets you start your own BZFlag server that others can connect to. You move your tank around a landscape, destroying opponents and picking up flags. In capture-the-flag mode, you try to get the opponents' flags before they get yours.

TABLE 11-1 Arcade Games in LLGP

Game Name	Debian Package Names	Description
IMaze	`imaze-lesstif, imaze-sounds, imaze-xaw, imaze-xlabed, imazesvr`	Multiplayer network maze game.
Abuse	`abuse, abuse-frabs, abuse-sdl, abuse-sfx`	Fight your way out of a high-security underground prison, full of prisoners and guards who have been transformed into grotesque mutants by Abuse genetic sequence.
Amphetamine	`amphetamine, amphetamine-data`	Fight evil monsters with magic weapons in this jump and run game.
Armagetron	`armagetron, armagetron-com, armagetron-ser`	High-speed, 3D Tron-like game.
Atomic Tanks	`atanks, atanks-data`	Shoot missiles at tanks to destroy them.
Blob Wars: Episode I	`blobwars`	Rescue MIAs, collect keys and defeat enemies in this platform shooting game.
BomberClone	`bomberclone, bomber-clone-data`	Free clone of Bomberman game.
Bugsquish	`bugsquish`	Squash bugs before they drop on your arm and suck your blood.
Bumprace	`bumprace, bumprace-data`	Multilevel one- or two-player space race in which you avoid crashing into blocks.
BZflag	`bzflag, bzflag-server`	Multiperson, networked tank game.
Chromium	`chromium, chromium-data`	Arcade-style scrolling space game.

GAME NAME	DEBIAN PACKAGE NAMES	DESCRIPTION
Circus Linux	`circuslinux, cir-circuslinux-data`	Clowns try to pop balloons by launching each other from platforms.
Conquest	`conquest, conquest-data, conquest-gl, conquest-libs, conquest-server`	Multiplayer space adventure game.
Egoboo	`egoboo, egoboo-data`	Dungeon-crawling adventure in 3D that is similar to NetHack.
Frozen-Bubble	`frozen-bubble, frozen-bubble-data`	Pop bubbles by firing at groups of similar-colored bubbles.
Galaga GalagaHyperspace	`xgalaga`	X versions of Galaga space shooting game.
GL-117	`gl-117, gl-117-data`	Action flight simulator.
Heroes (SDL version)	`heroes-common, heroes-data, heroes-sdl, heroes-sound-effects, heroes-sound-tracks`	Avoid opponents and walls as you collect power-ups in this worm-style game.
Kasteroids	`kasteroids`	Avoid and destroy asteroids in this KDE version of the classic game.
KBounce	`kbounce`	KDE clone of Jeezball.
KFoulEggs	`kfouleggs`	KDE clone of PuyoPuyo game from Japan.
KGoldrunner	`kgoldrunner`	KDE clone of Loderunner arcade game.
KSirtet	`ksirtet`	KDE clone of Tetris and PuyoPuyo.
KSmilTris	`ksmiletris`	KDE clone of Tetris with smiley faces.

continues

TABLE 11-1 Continued

Game Name	Debian Package Names	Description
KSnakeRace	ksnake	KDE snake race.
KSpaceDuel	kspaceduel	KDE two-player space arcade game.
KTron	ktron	KDE clone of Tron game.
Kobo Deluxe	kobodeluxe	Space battle game.
Kolf	kolf	KDE miniature golf game.
LBreakout	lbreakout2	Clone of Breakout ball-and-paddle game.
Mad Bomber	madbomber	Catch bombs before they hit the ground in the Kaboom! clone.
Mangoquest	mangoquest, mangoquest-data	First-person maze game Blue Mango Quest.
Neverball Neverputt	neverball, neverdata	In Neverball, you tilt the floor to get the ball to its destination. Neverputt is a 3D golf game.
Nibbles	gnome-games, gnome-games-data	Worm game from GNOME desktop games.
Penguin Command	penguin-command	Defend cities by shooting missiles and smart bombs.
Pinball	pinball	Pinball machine emulator.
Powermanga	powermanga, powermanga-data, powermanga-base	Graphical, 3D shoot-'em-up game.
Race	race	3D overhead car-race game.
Robots	gnome-games, gnome-games-data, gnome-games-extra-data	GNOME robots game.

Game Name	Debian Package Names	Description
Slune	`slune`	Racing and 3D car-crash game.
Starfighter	`starfighter,` `starfighter-data`	Scrolling 2D shooting game.
SuperTux	`supertux, superdux-data`	Tux penguin in a 2D jump-and-run side-scrolling game.

TORCS	`torcs, torcs-data,`
	`torcs-data-cars-extra,`
	`torcs-data-tracks-oval,`
	`torcs-data-tracks-road`
		Car-racing simulator in 3D (OpenGL)

Thrust	`thrust`	Destroy nuclear reactors from space in this clone of classic Commodore 64 game.
Toppler	`toppler`	Nebulus game clone.
Trophy	`trophy, trophy-data`	Car-racing action game in 2D.
Tux: A Quest for Herring	`tux-aqfh`	Take Tux the penguin on a quest to find golden herring.
TuxRacer	`tuxracer, tuxracer-data,` `tuxracer-extras`	Race Tux the penguin down the hill on his belly.
TuxType	`tuxtype`	Learn to type from Tux the penguin.
TuxKart	`tuxkart, tuxkart-data,` `tuxkart-extras`	Tux 3D go-kart racing game.
Typespeed	`typespeed`	Type to cancel out words as they race across the page.
Wing	`wing, wing-data`	Galaga-style space shooting game.
XBill	`xbill`	Stop Windows viruses from infecting the computers.

continues

TABLE 11-1 Continued

GAME NAME	DEBIAN PACKAGE NAMES	DESCRIPTION

XBlast-TNT
XBlast-TNT-mini
	`xblast, xblast-data,`
	`xblast-sound, xblast-`
	`tnt, xblast-tnt-images,`
	`xblast-tnt-levels,`
	`xblast-tnt-mini,`
	`xblast-tnt-models,`
	`xblast-tnt-sound`
		Blast away opponents in this space shooting game.

XKoules	`koules`	X-based space action game.
Xscavenger	`xscavenger`	Platform, Loderunner-type game for X.
Xsoldier	`xsoldier`	X shoot-'em-up game.
Xboing	`xboing`	X-based block-out-style game.
Xbreaky	`xbreaky`	X-based break-out-style game.
Xracer	`xracer, xracer-tools`	X-based Wipeout clone racing game.
Xscorch	`xscorch`	Scorched Earth clone for X.
Zblast	`zblast-data, zblast-x11`	X-based shoot-'em-up space game.

TuxRacer is a 3D racing game. You steer Tux the penguin down the hill, going around flags and avoiding obstacles. Try to make it to the finish line first. Figure 11-4 shows an example of the TuxRacer game running from the LLGP live CD.

FIGURE 11-4 Pick up herring as you race Tux down snow-covered hills toward the finish line.

Board Games

Many of the board games available in open source are fashioned after real board games (backgammon, mahjongg, and chess, for example) and are packaged in KDE and GNOME games packages. Table 11-2 contains lists board games that are packaged with LLGP live CD.

Some of the board games just described include editors for creating design elements to go with the games. Atlantik Designer lets you design each estate on the Atlantik board, as well as name rents, property prices, and street names. Penguin Taipei-Editor lets you design tile combinations to play with the Ace of Penguins Taipei game.

TABLE 11-2 Board Games in LLGP

Game Name	Debian Package Names	Description
Ataxx	gnome-games, gnome-games-data	Flip disks to dominate the board.
Atlantik	atlantik, atlantikdesign	Monopoly-style KDE game that can be played over the network.
Five in a Row	g5	GTK-based five-in-a-row game.
Four in a Row	gnome-games, gnome-games-data	GNOME-based four-in-a-row game.
Gnome GYahtzee	gnome-games, gnome-games-data	Yahtzee game for GNOME.
Gnome Iagno	gnome-games, gnome-games-data	Iagno game for GNOME.
Gnome Lines	gnome-games, gnome-games-data	Match five balls of the same color in this GNOME game.
Gnome Mahjongg	gnome-games, gnome-games-data	Mahjongg tile game for GNOME.
KBackgammon	kdebackgammon	Backgammon board game for KDE.
KBlackBox	kblackbox	KDE blackbox board game in which you play hide-and-seek on a grid of boxes.
KMahjongg	kmahjongg	Mahjongg game for KDE.
KReversi	kreversi	Reversi game for KDE.
KWin4	kwin4	Connect Four clone for KDE.
Kenolaba	kenolaba	Enolaba board game for KDE.
Mahjongg	xmahjongg	X-based Mahjongg tile game.

GAME NAME	DEBIAN PACKAGE NAMES	DESCRIPTION
Penguin Taipei	`ace-of-penguins`	Match tiles to remove them from the board.
Shisen-Sho	`kshisen`	Match tiles to clear the board.

Figure 11-5 shows examples of several board games that come with LLGP. Those games include 5-in-a-Row, KReversi, GNOME Tali, and Shisen-Sho.

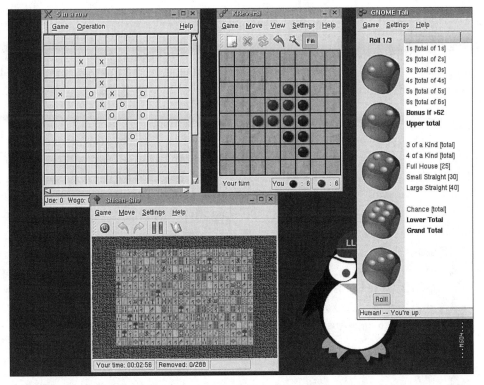

FIGURE 11-5 Add Yahtzee (GNOME Tali), 5-in-a-Row, KReversi, and Shisen-Sho board games to a live CD.

Card Games

Card games that come with LLGP are dominated by solitaire games, including include AisleRiot, FreeCell, and Gnome Solitaire. A few, however, can be played with others over the network (see Table 11-3).

Kids Games

The only game in the Kids Games category in LLGP is Potato Guy, in which you put a face, hands, hats, and other accessories on a potato. Although the game is not very complicated, it keeps younger kids amused for a long time.

Sports

The sports games included with LLGP are all 3D games that can test your hardware. Battleball (`battleball` package) is a soccer game played with tanks and helicopters. BilliardGL (`billiard-gl` package) is a 3D billiards game. CannonSmash (`csmash` package) is a table tennis game simulator. Foobilliard (`foobilliard` package) is another 3D billiards game.

Strategy

Some of the most challenging games available on LLGP are the strategy games. Freeciv (`freeciv-client`, `freeciv-data`, and `freeciv-server` packages) is a clone of the game Civilization, in which you build and maintain civilizations. Lincity (`lincity` package) is a similar game for building communities and city infrastructures.

Battle for Wesnoth (`wesnoth`, `wesnoth-data`, `wesnoth-editor`, `wesnoth-music`, and `wesnoth-server` packages) is a popular fantasy, turn-based strategy game. Scorched3D (`scorched3d`, `scorched3d-data`, and `scorched3d-doc` packages) is a tank game that is based on the classic DOS game Scorched Earth. Liquidwar (`liquidwar` and `liquidwar-data` packages) is a multiplayer war game.

Other Gaming Categories

Other categories of games included on the LLGP live CD include Puzzles, Tactics & Strategy, and Tetris-like games. You can try out games in those categories from the LLGP Games menu. Some fun games from those categories include SameGame (remove all the balls from the screen by clicking on matching colors), KBattleship (a clone of the Battleship board game), and KSokoban (a challenging Japanese game in which you try to push items around a warehouse without getting them stuck).

TABLE 11-3 Card Games in LLGP

GAME NAME	DEBIAN PACKAGE NAMES	DESCRIPTION
AisleRiot Solitaire	gnome-games, gnome-games-data	Solitaire card game
Blackjack	gnome-games, gnome-games-data	Blackjack card game
FreeCell Solitaire	gnome-games, gnome-games-data	FreeCell game played from sol engine
Gnome Blackjack	gnome-games, gnome-games-data	GNOME blackjack game
Gnome FreeCell	gnome-games, gnome-games-data	GNOME freecell game
Gnome Solitaire Games	gnome-games, gnome-games-data	Several solitaire games for GNOME
KPoker	kpoker	KDE poker game
Lieutenant Skat	lskat	Skat card game
Patience	kpat	KDE Patience solitaire game
Penguin Canfield	ace-of-penguins	Ace-of-Penguins version of canfield
Penguin Freecell	ace-of-penguins	Ace-of-Penguins version of freecell
Penguin Golf	ace-of-penguins	Ace-of-Penguins version of golf solitaire
Penguin Solitaire	ace-of-penguins	Ace-of-Penguins version of classic solitaire
Penguin Thornq	ace-of-penguins	Ace-of-Penguins version of thornq solitaire
PySol	pysol	Python-based solitaire game
XSkat	lskat	KDE Lieutenant Skat card game
XSkat via IRC	lskat	KDE Skat game to play online via IRC

COMMERCIAL GAMES LICENSES

By focusing on the LLGP live CD, which was built from Knoppix and from packages included in the Debian/Knoppix software repositories, I've managed to skirt some of the more complicated issues related to licensing. In fact, if you want to make sure that you can freely redistribute any live CD you build, you can stay clear of most patent and copyright infringement issues if you stick with software in repositories of established Linux distributions that carefully scrutinize licenses (Debian, Fedora, and Gentoo).

However, sometimes you might want to include games that are or were once covered under commercial or other non-GPL licenses. The general rule of thumb is that if a copyright owner of a piece of software has not released it into the public domain, you can't just assume that it is okay to use and redistribute the software. This is still true if the owner is no longer selling the product and even if the company no longer exists.

However, in some instances you might be able to include commercial gaming software on your personal, or even redistributed, live CD. Here are some examples:

- **Commercial demos**—A producer of commercial games for Linux might be happy to have you redistribute demos of its commercial games. Before doing so, however, you need to contact the producer to get written permission to do so. I've heard that GarageGames.com has given permission for some live CDs to redistribute its demos. Keep in mind that the demos you distribute probably include some sales materials.

- **Closed-source drivers**—To do high-quality 3D gaming on Nvidia and ATI cards, you need to include closed-source drivers from those manufacturers. In many cases, such drivers can be redistributed freely, in many people's opinions (see www.nvidia.com/object/nv_swlicense.html).

  However, open-source purists say that, when distributing closed-source drivers, you don't know how those drivers might be infecting your Linux kernel. In fact, depending how you configure those drivers, they can ruin your kernel's capability to use other video drivers. (Earlier I noted such a case that I had with my i810 motherboard conflicting with the Nvidia drivers.)

- **Commercial products released to the public**—Some games actually were released into the public domain some years after they stopped being viable products. If you want to include such gaming software on your live CD, however, you should make sure that the entire product is modifiable and can be freely redistributed.

An example of a slightly sticky case is the free release of the popular first-person shooter game Doom. Although the game was released to be fully redistributable, a clause remained related to the Doom shareware Wad: "You may not: modify, translate, disassemble, decompile, reverse engineer, or create derivative works based upon the Software."

Because the capability to change the code is an important element of software projects such as Fedora Linux, that project decided to replace the offending part (the Doom engine) with the Freedoom package. Freedoom was a Doom engine written completely from scratch, so it can be redistributed—and also modified—by those who receive it.

Another piece of gaming software that can be used to play games released to the public is ScummVM (www.scummvm.org). LucasArts originally created SCUMM to create many games, such as Monkey Island, Day of the Tentacle, and Legend of Kyrandia. ScummVM is released under the GPL and can play many games that originally ran on SCUMM. See the ScummVM compatibility list (www.scummvm.org/compatibility.php) for details.

Games in this category that will play on ScummVM that have been released into the public domain include Beneath a Steel Sky (made available as freeware in August 2003) and Flight of the Amazon Queen. These games are included on some games live CDs/DVDs, such as the GamesKnoppix DVD.

Some great places for investigating the licensing issues related to different gaming software include the mailing lists for Linux distributions that deal with what software to include or not include in their distributions. For example, the Fedora Extras mailing list has had good discussions on game-licensing issues (www.redhat.com/mailman/listinfo/fedora-extras-list).

CREATING A FEDORA GAMING LIVE CD

To illustrate how to put together your own Linux gaming live CD, the following procedure describes how to use Kadischi and the Fedora installer (anaconda) as the basis for the gaming CD. Because there are few games of interest in Fedora Core, you need to go to other repositories to get games for a Fedora gaming CD—in particular, the Fedora Extras repository.

You can use most of the information included in Chapter 7, "Building a Basic Fedora Live CD," for creating a live CD based on Fedora. However, instead of setting up a local repository of Fedora Core, the procedure draws completely from online repositories. Therefore, to get started, you can simply install the kadischi

RPM package (that comes on the DVD), make sure that you have enough work space in /tmp, and run a command similar to the following to get started:

```
# kadischi –graphical -f \
http://download.fedora.redhat.com/pub/fedora/linux/core/6/i386/os \
/tmp/fedora-live.iso
```

The command just shown should appear on one line (the backslashes are there to indicate that the line should continue). I have you use the --graphical option because selecting multiple repositories is not currently supported in text mode. The -f option causes any previous ISO image (fedora-live.iso) to be overwritten.

Step through the installation screens until you get the screen that lets you select multiple repositories. Select the check box next to Fedora Extras. If you like, you can also choose other third-party repositories and add them as well (in particular, rpm.livna.org).

Next, select the Customize Now option near the bottom of the screen and continue. The next screen that appears shows the available package groups from which to choose. Select Applications → Games and Entertainment. Then select Optional packages. The screen appears as shown in Figure 11-6.

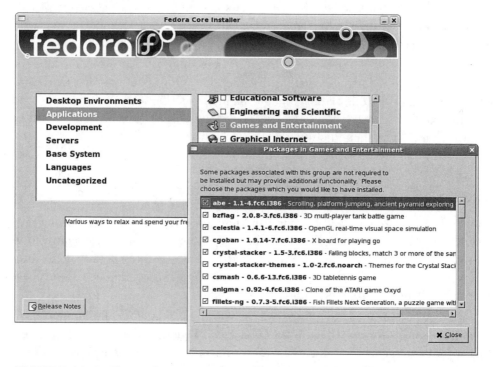

FIGURE 11-6 Choose from more that 60 gaming packages from Fedora Core and Fedora Extras.

Select the games packages you want to add to your live CD. Refer to descriptions of gaming packages earlier in this chapter to help choose which might be the most fun for you to include. After that, choose other packages from other categories to install. You will notice that there are many more interesting packages available that you get with a basic install of Fedora Core, because the listing contains packages from Fedora Core and Fedora Extras.

Continue through the installation procedure as described in Chapter 7. Use the procedures in that chapter to add your own splash screen or other custom settings as appropriate for a gaming live CD.

SUMMARY

Gaming live CDs can be just plain fun to put together and use. Hundreds, if not thousands, of free and open-source games are available to include on your Linux live CDs. Categories of games include adventure, arcade, board games, card games, sports, and strategy games.

A big issue with getting high-quality 3D games running well on Linux live CDs is the issue of supported 3D accelerated video cards. Nvidia and ATI release binary versions of their drivers, but those drivers can sometimes conflict with drivers for open-source hardware-accelerated video cards. Open-source purists also note that there's no way to know how those drivers might be causing conflicts in your Linux system kernel.

Outside the realm of open-source games, you might be able to include with your live CD some older commercial games that have been released as freeware. Games once sold commercially, including Doom and games such as Beneath the Steel Sky and Flight of the Amazon Queen, that run on the GPL-licensed ScummVM can also be included on a live CD.

The Fedora installer and tools from the Kadischi project are used to illustrate how to build a gaming live CD that is based on the Fedora Linux distribution. Using the latest Fedora anaconda installer, you can select packages from multiple online repositories to gain access to many more gaming and other software packages.

## CHAPTER 12

Customizing a Multimedia Live Linux CD

Creating, manipulating, and displaying multimedia content has long been a favorite pastime for PC users. Computers these days are just expected to enable you to play music, watch movies, and work with your digital images. Improvements in free and open-source multimedia applications make for a rich set of choices for someone putting together a Linux-based live CD that focuses on multimedia applications.

Multimedia live CDs covered in this chapter fall into two categories:

- **Multimedia players**—By specializing in only playing video, music, and slide shows, multimedia player live CDs can be trimmed to a very small size. Consuming only a few megabytes of disk space allows these players to run totally in RAM, while the CD or DVD drive can be used to hold music or movies.
- **Multimedia production tools**—For Web designers, musicians, graphic artists, and animators, live CDs provide a means of carrying tools to produce high-quality digital art. Many open-source tools are beginning to rival commercial offerings in areas of image manipulation (The GIMP) and 3D animation (Blender).

To illustrate multimedia players, I've added a description of GeeXboX to this chapter. Besides describing how to use GeeXboX as a multimedia player, I describe the GeeXboX Generator, which can be used to add content, codecs, and personal settings to a remastered ISO image of the GeeXboX multimedia player.

In the area of multimedia toolkits, I describe Dynebolic live CD. Dynebolic includes more than 100 open-source applications that can be used with a desktop system dedicated to producing and publishing multimedia content.

Whether you are interested in playing or producing multimedia content, one issue spans both arenas: getting legal codecs for audio and video content in Linux. So before we jump into some different types of multimedia live CDs, read the following sections to understand the issues related to the software you need to play your music and movies.

UNDERSTANDING MULTIMEDIA COPYRIGHT AND PATENT ISSUES

By licensing software under the GNU General Public License (see www.gnu.org/copyleft) and similar licenses, the free and open-source software movements have made freely distributed operating systems such as Linux possible. However, writing software from scratch and licensing that work under the GPL still might not make it possible to freely distribute that software. In no area of free software development are issues more contentious than in multimedia.

Problems related particularly to free distribution of audio and video codecs (coders/decoders) stem from several issues, including these:

- **Software patents**—Many of the audio and video standards that are used for creating and playing commercial music and video contain patented technology. Anyone writing music and video players is subject to claims from those royalty holders to pay for every player or encoder the software creator distributes.

- **Digital Millenium Copyright Act (DMCA)**—The DMCA is an act of the United States Congress in 1998 that made it illegal in the U.S. to create technology to circumvent copyright-protection measures.

The threat of software patent claims has been looming over the free and open-source software movement since people began distributing free software. To fight the long-term battle someday, major software vendors have been gathering patent portfolios relating to everything from database structures to how you click to buy something on the Internet. In the short term, however, some of the most litigious types of software components have been those related to multimedia.

In theory, you should understand the licensing arrangements associated with every piece of software that you use. In reality, most of us rely on the legal interpretations of the commercial software vendors or open-source software organizations that create and/or redistribute software for our consumption. So instead of giving you legal advice about what you can and cannot do with the software described in this book (which I am not qualified to do), I pass on the general interpretation of what is and is not considered to be freely distributable software for multimedia.

If you are creating video or audio content from scratch, you can use open-source audio and video codecs. Any content you create with these open-source multimedia players can be freely distributed along with the players and encoders themselves. You can even include these encoders and players in your own commercial products, as long as you adhere to the licensing associated with them (which generally requires that you make the source code available).

- **Audio (Ogg Vorbis and FLAC)**—The Xiph.Org Foundation (www.xiph.org) produces Ogg Vorbis as an efficient, high-quality competitor to MP3 audio encoding. Ogg is the media container and Vorbis is the audio codec. Ogg Vorbis is a nonproprietary, patent- and royalty-free audio format that can produce good-quality audio at high rates of compression.

  The Free Lossless Audio Codec (FLAC) is another audio format sponsored by Xiph.org (see http://flac.sourceforge.net). FLAC audio files are much larger than comparable Ogg Vorbis or MP3 files, but this format features some compression with no discernable loss of audio quality.

  Nearly every audio and video player available for Linux (ogg123, xmms, mplayer, xine, and others) supports Ogg Vorbis audio.

- **Video (Theora)**—Theora (www.theora.org) is the free video codec sponsored by Xiph.org. Theora was based on the VP3 codec from On2, which was released into the public domain several years ago (see www.theora.org/svn.html). Tools such as Cinelerra (http://cinelerra.org) and ffmpeg2theora (www.v2v.cc/~j/ffmpeg2theora) can be used to create Ogg Theora audio/video files. Open-source video players (including VLC player, Helix Player, Totem, and mplayer) can play Ogg Theora content.

As I noted earlier, playing your own multimedia content in Ogg Vorbis and Theora from live CD is not a problem. Playing commercial multimedia content, however, is an issue. This is where you need to do some digging. Every major Linux distribution includes software for playing commercial music CDs, but most don't include software for playing MP3 music files. Likewise, every major video format outside of Theora comes with some patent restrictions that prevent it from being freely distributed.

Playing commercial movies from DVDs is a different case. The encryption techniques used to produce and play commercial movies on DVD were kept as trade secrets and, therefore, were not patented or copyrighted. So when that encryption was broken with software refered to as DeCSS, there was nobody to claim a royalty for distributing the software to play commercial DVDs.

However, what makes the distribution of DeCSS illegal are the DMCA and various hacker laws around the world. The DMCA made it a felony in the U.S. to circumvent copyright protection, as DeCSS did. To my knowledge, there has been no legal action taken against anyone in the United States for using or distributing code that breaks DVD encryption. One of three creators of the DeCSS, Joon Lech Johansen, was tried several times in Norway under a criminal hacker law but was later acquitted (see http://en.wikipedia.org/wiki/DeCSS).

Because of licensing issues and other legal entanglements, most open-source DVD players use the libdvdcss library (http://developers.videolan.org/libdvdcss) for unscrambling and accessing commercial DVDs based on the Content Scrambling System (CSS). Despite the fact that CSS is not really a copy-protection system, but a means of keeping people from playing DVDs without licensed software, most major Linux distributions don't include libdvdcss in their distributions.

With all that said, software for playing just about every audio and video codec under the sun is available from unofficial sources to go with most Linux distributions. In some cases, private use of these codecs is permitted without paying royalties (assuming you are using GPL sofware and not stolen commercial software). The following are examples of repositories where you can get codecs you need for playing and encoding a variety of audio and video formats for your particular Linux distribution:

- **Debian/Knoppix/Ubuntu/Damn Small Linux, etc.**—The Debian Unofficial Packages site (www.debian-unofficial.org) contains software packages you can add to the Debian GNU/Linux distribution that have licensing issues that make them incompatible with the Debian project. It includes packages for playing MP3 audio (lame), commercial DVDs (libdvdcss), and MPEG-4 video (XviD). Some of these packages will work with Debian-based live CDs. Some live CDs have their own versions of these packages.

- **Fedora/Red Hat Enterpries Linux**—Using yum repositories available from rpm.livna.org, you can get video players such as mplayer and xine. Downloading players from that site also gives you the opportunity to get a variety of video and audio codecs for playing commercial audio and video content. (A new feature in Fedora Core 6 lets you include multiple software repositories when you use Kadischi to build a Fedora live CD.)

Before you include any contentious software on a live CD, particularly if you plan to redistribute that software to a larger audience, you need to check carefully into licensing and patent issues. For in-depth discussions of multimedia software issues as they relate to the Fedora Project, refer to the Fedora Project Forbidden Items page (http://fedoraproject.org/wiki/ForbiddenItems)

MULTIMEDIA PLAYER LIVE CD

For multimedia-player live CDs, you basically want to include player applications (music, video, and image players) and ways to get content. The other issue is hardware support. To get the most out of a multimedia player, you might want to include support for special video cards, sound cards, PCMCIA cards, and TV tuner cards.

Open-source music and image players are plentiful. Although there are also open-source video players, getting video the codecs you need to play certain kinds of video content can be more problematic (more on that later). As for how you get the content to play, a multimedia player needs to offer one or more of these ways of getting content:

- **On the live CD**—If you are remastering a live CD and you have space available, you can add as much content as you can fit on the live CD itself. You can then play the content without needing to access any medium other than the live CD itself.

  The eMoviX project, which is a spin-off of the MoviX project, is an example of a media player designed to let you add video to a live CD so that the video plays directly when you boot up. The GeeXboX project produces the GeeXboX Generator, which lets you add codecs and content to a personal GeeXboX live CD.

- **CDs or DVDs**—Because most commercial music and movies come on CDs and DVDs, respectively, any valid music or movie player needs to deal with that fact. Tiny media live CDs such as GeeXboX and MoviX run completely in RAM, so the CD or DVD drive is free for inserting the media you choose.

- **Hard disks or other storage media**—By detecting and automatically mounting hard-disk partitions, a media player live CD can let the users browse the computer's hard disk for the content they want to play. As long as the live CD includes support for file systems that are on the hard disk (in particular, NFTS support for most Windows systems), you can play any content you added from your computer's native operating system (usually Windows).

Most multimedia live CD include support to connect the live CD system to a LAN or the Internet. Support for wired Ethernet cards typically lets you configure your network connection (or do it automatically via DHCP). Wireless network support is less common but is available in some cases with PCMCIA cards. After that, you can use applications for grabbing content from the network. Those applications might include the following:

- **Network file systems**—If your LAN supports file-sharing applications such as Windows file sharing (Samba, SMB, or CIFS) or Linux file sharing

(NFS), you can mount shared remote folders or directories that contain content to play.

- **Network file transfer**—By connecting to FTP repositories, you can select content contained in those repositories.

- **Streaming content**—By including media players that can play streaming audio and video, you can play that type of content from your live CD.

The following sections contain descriptions of several multimedia player live CDs. Descriptions include information on the features each live CD supports and ways that you can add content. You'll also find descriptions of how to add codecs so you can play additional types of audio and video content.

Running GeeXboX Open Media Center

By being tuned purely for playing a wide range of audio and video content, the GeeXboX open media center can be a truly tiny Linux distribution. The GeeXboX 1.0 ISO image is only 6.8MB. When you consider the number of features it contains, the feat is quite amazing. Features include these:

- **Playing music CDs**—After GeeXboX loads into memory and starts running, you can insert a standard audio compact disc. You can use simple keyboard controls (basically, those included with mplayer) to jump to different tracks and adjust the volume.

- **Playing video DVDs**—Again, using mplayer, GeeXboX is capable of playing video DVDs in a variety of video and audio content. The version of GeeXboX you use must include the capability to decrypt CSS encryption, to be capable of playing most commercial movies delivered on DVD. (DeCSS and other legal issues surrounding playback of commercial DVDs and other video content are discussed earlier in this chapter.)

- **Playing SVCDs, VCDs, or XCDs**—VCDs and XCDs are both container formats for audio and video content. VCDs support MPEG1 streams, while MPEG2 supports MPEG2 streams. XCDs, on the other hand, can contain different types of video and audio content, including MPEG4, VP3, Divx, XVID, OGG, and others.

- **Playing files from hard disk**—GeeXboX automatically mounts partitions from the local hard disk on mount points on the /mnt directory, so any content stored on any supported file system on the local computer can be selected from the GeeXboX interface to play.

    Supported file systems include ext2, ext3, ReiserFS, ISO 9660, UDF, and VFAT. The NTFS and xBSD UFS file systems are supported read-only. File-sharing file systems that are supported include NFS, CIFS, and Samba (SMB).

- **Playing television**—Both analog TV cards and digital video broadcast (DVB) cards are supported, so you can watch television from GeeXboX.

Originally created to play DivX movies, GeeXboX now supports a variety of video formats, most of which are available via the included mplayer media player software. This content includes MPEG 1, MPEG 2, and MPEG 4 (DivX, XviD, H.264, and so on). You can also play RealMedia and Windows Media movies, as long as you have the proper codecs.

Supported streaming media content includes OggMedia and Matroska open-source container formats. A variety of codecs are supported within those container formats, including variable bit-rate audio (VBR), variable frame rates (VFR), advanced audio coding (AAC), Ogg (Theora and Ogg Vorbis), and Real Video 9 (RV9). Network streaming media from WebRadio and WebTV (via SHOUTcast) is also supported.

Using Multimedia Hardware

To display and play your multimedia output, you can use most standard video cards, monitors, and sound cards that Linux supports. Hardware that has been tested and found to work with GeeXboX is available from the supported hardware page (www.geexbox.org/en/hard.html).

TV Out is available with GeeXboX for those supported TV cards that include TV Out, although the default resolution is 800×600 and some cards support only 640×480. TV Out standards include NTSC, PAL, and SECAM. Many TV card remote controls also are supported by GeeXboX.

To provide network connectivity, GeeXboX supports a wide range of Ethernet cards and a smaller set of WiFi cards. In many cases, where DHCP service is available, the Ethernet cards automatically are configured.

Using GeeXboX Controls

No resources are wasted on the user interface with GeeXboX. Content can be selected and controlled from simple menus. All selections are done using keyboard keys. No mouse support exists.

Besides the menu interface, which can be traversed mostly by using arrow keys and pressing Enter, keyboard controls that mplayer uses can control content once it is playing. Figure 12-1 shows the menu interface that appears when you first start GeeXboX.

To select content to play, with the cursor (< >) on Open, select the right arrow key. Depending on what media are available on your computer, you can select to play a DVD, a VCD/XCD, or an audio CD. If you select Open File, you are presented with a list of mounted file systems from which you can select content.

FIGURE 12-1
Simple menu interfaces
keep system resource
use low with GeeXboX.

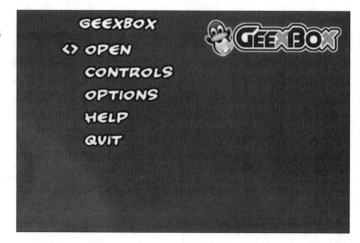

All partitions are mounted on the /mnt directory under names that relate to their partition numbers. For example, the first partition on the first IDE hard disk (/dev/hda1) would be mounted on /mnt/Disk 1 Part 1 directory. Use the right and left arrow keys to move up and down the directory structure to find the media files you want to play.

Before you select any content to play, only a few commands are available. Select M to show or hide the GeeXboX menu. Choose S to switch to TV Out. While you are playing audio or video content, you can use regular mplayer features to control playback. Table 12-1 details playback controls.

To choose other options for playback, select Options from the main GeeXboX menu. From the Options menu, you can do such things as adjust the aspect of the video playback, switch to TV Out, switch vertical sync, and set a sleep timer.

Normally, if you insert a DVD, it simply begins playing the movie. By selecting Autoplay Mode from the Options list, you can disable that feature. Then go to DVD settings and choose DVD Navigation Menu. The next time you open a DVD, you will be able to use the regular DVD navigation menu as you would on a standard DVD player. With the DVD navigation menu enabled, you can use the keys shown in Table 12-2 to get around.

Regenerating GeeXboX

The GeeXboX ISO Generator lets you rebuild GeeXboX using existing binaries so you can use GeeXbox exactly the way you want to. This software provides the means to include content, codecs, or settings in a way that completely personalizes your own version of GeeXboX completely personalized.

TABLE 12-1 Audio/Video Playback Controls

KEY	RESULT	KEY	RESULT
0 or *	Turn volume up	9 or /	Turn volume down
Right arrow	Go forward 10 seconds	Left arrow	Go back 10 seconds
Up arrow	Go forward 1 minute	Down arrow	Go back 1 minute
P or spacebar	Pause/unpause audio and video	M	Mute audio
1	Decrease contrast	2	Increase contrast
3	Decrease brightness	4	Increase brightness
5	Increase hue	7	Decrease saturation
8	Increase saturation	O	Onscreen display (on/off)
>	Go to next item in playlist	<	Go to previous item in playlist
F	Full-screen mode (on/off)	J	Turn subtitles on/off
Z	Delay subtitles (+0.1 second)	X	Reduces subtitle delay (–0.1 second)
Q or ESC	Quit	K	Halts

TABLE 12-2 DVD Menu Navigation

KEY	RESULT	KEY	RESULT
0	View DVD menu	Enter	Chooses the highlighted selection
2	Move cursor down	4	Moves cursor to the left
6	Move cursor to the right	8	Moves cursor up

You can regenerate GeeXboX on a Linux, Mac OSX, or Windows system. To get started regenerating your own personal GeeXboX, do the following:

1. **Download the GeeXboX ISO Generator**—Go to the GeeXboX download page (www.geexbox.org/en/downloads.html) and choose either the i386 or PowerPC version. Then select the nearest download site to download the geexbox-generator package to your hard disk. Or refer to Appendix A for information on using the geexbox-generator included on this book's accompanying CD.

2. **Unpack the** geexbox-generator **package**—Save the geexbox-generator package to a directory on a partition that contains enough space to do the regeneration that you want. The software itself requires only about 13MB of disk space, but if you are adding a movie to your regenerated GeeXboX ISO, that can take considerably more space. To unpack the package in Linux, type the following:

```
# tar xvfz geexbox-generator-*tar.gz
```

The archive is uncompressed and added to a geexbox-generator subdirectory (for example, geexbox-generator-1.0.i386).

3. **Start the GeeXboX Generator**—Go to the geexbox-generator* directory and launch one of the following commands, depending on which operating system you are using to regenerate the ISO:

```
# ./linux-i386-generator          # for Linux Systems
# generator.exe                   # for Windows Systems
# ./macosx-generator              # for Mac OS X Systems
```

Figure 12-2 shows the GeeXboX Generator window when it is run from a Linux system.

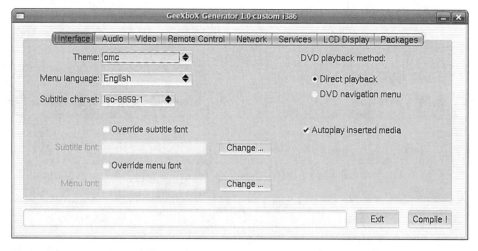

FIGURE 12-2 Tune different aspects of your personalized GeeXboX from the GeeXboX Generator.

4. **Begin modifying the ISO**—The GeeXboX Generator contains eight tabs of information that you can modify. You can change these settings from those tabs:

   - **Interface**—Choose from more than a dozen languages and character sets to use with your GeeXboX interface. If you add other themes (see the Packages tab), you can use that theme instead of the default omc theme. Likewise, you can install and change fonts to use on subtitles and menus.

     By default, DVDs begin playing immediately when you insert them and start direct playback. You can have GeeXboX wait before playing back media until you request it. You can also use the DVD navigation menu instead of direct playback.

   - **Audio**—GeeXboX uses the first ALSA sound card it finds (0) for playback. If you have multiple sound cards, you can select to have GeeXboX use a different one. Other audio selections let you change output from analog to SPDIF (and change associated settings) and select the number of channels (2 for stereo, 4 for surround, or 6 for 5.1 surround).

   - **Video**—The default screen resolution is 800×600. You can change to lower (640×480) or higher resolutions and a different number of bits representing colors (24, by default). You can also choose whether to show the bootsplash screen.

   - **Remote Control**—You can enable a variety of remote-control devices if you expect those devices to be on the computers that will run your personalized GeeXboX.

   - **Network**—GeeXboX autodetects available network cards. By default, it tries to connect to a DHCP server to get its network address and other needed information for GeeXboX to use the network. Select manual configuration to add your own IP address, subnet mask, gateway address, and DNS server IP address. WiFi settings are also supported but might require that you download a supported driver (see the Packages tab).

   - **Services**—By default, no network services are enabled on GeeXboX. However, you can enable network services, including a TELNET server, FTP server, or Web server. Likewise, you can enable a username and password for Windows file sharing or to enable SHOUTcast radio and TV playlists.

   - **LCD display**—The LCD display is not enabled by default. You can enable it on this tab and choose the monitor model you expect to use.

- **Packages**—The interesting stuff happens on the Packages tab. Some codecs that are needed to play back certain types of audio and video content cannot be freely distributed. However, from the Packages tab, the GeeXboX Generator provides a service that lets you download some of those codecs and add them to your personal GeeXboX ISO (be warned some restrictions might govern on their use).

If you have a DVB card or WiFi card, you can download the firmware needed to use those cards from the Packages tab. Other software your can download from this tab includes Themes, to use with GeeXboX and several Asian font sets.

Keep the GeeXboX Generator window open at this point while you consider some other features that you might want to change manually.

5. **Add content and other manual changes**—Any of the changes you just made using the GeeXboX Generator could also have been made manually from the shell. Read about manual changes you might consider in the README files located in the DOC directory from the `geexbox-generator` packages.

Open a shell and then, starting from the `geexbox-generator*` directory, change to the `iso/GEEXBOX` directory. At this point, you can:

- **Add content**—Copy any video or audio content you want to include on your personalized GeeXboX (either to that root directory or to create your own subdirectory).

- **Add codecs or firmware**—Any additional codecs or firmware you want on your ISO can be added to the `codecs` and `firmwares` directories, respectively. As a service, GeeXboX lets you download some of these components from www.geexbox.org/releases/extra-codecs-nonfree.tar.gz.

- **Change mplayer features**—From the `geexbox-generator*` directory, go to the directory containing mplayer configuration files:
```
# cd iso/GEEXBOX/etc/mplayer
# ls
codecs.conf  input.conf  mplayer.conf  no_nvidia_vidix
```
The `input.conf` and `mplayer.conf` files are where you can do most of your mplayer configuration. For example, in `input.conf`, you can change which keyboard keys are used to navigate your audio and video playback. In `mplayer.conf`, you can change such things as the video output (`vo=cvi-cix,vesa`) or various cache settings.

Change the setting associated with particular codecs in the `codecs.conf` file. If you have an NVIDIA card and want to enable the Vidix feature (to provide better performance on low-end hardware), simply remove the no_nvidia_vidix file.

- **Configure other features**—Do a quick check of the iso/GEEXBOX/etc directory to see whether you want to configure other features differently. In particular, check the etc/init.d directory to see the different services that can be started. Many of these services start if an existing configuration file is associated with it.

6. **Build the ISO**—Returning to the GeeXboX Generator, if you have made all your changes, select the Compile! button to build the new ISO image. When processing is done, the word "Done" appears in the GeeXboX generator window. The new ISO image will be in the geexbox-generator* directory. In my case, the file was named:

geexbox-1.0-custom-en.i386.iso

Burn the ISO to CD or try it using Qemu or VMware to see how it works!

Exploring Other Multimedia Center Live CDs

You can try other Linux-based multimedia live CDs as well. Because it is easy to add support for playing different content types, it's quite natural that many of them play video, audio, and digital images in various ways.

- **MoviX**—The MoviX project (http://source.net/projects/movix) is actually a set of three related projects. The first, named MoviX, is a reduced version of MoviX2 that can be used on computers with less than 128MB of RAM. MoviX2 is the full multimedia player that fits on a mini CD (about 50MB). It contains menus for selecting and playing video, music, images, and streaming audio content. Like GeeXboX, it can get that content from CDs, DVDs, VCDs, XCDs, hard disks, or network connections. Content can be played from the CD drive in which MoviX2 was booted because MoviX2 will run from RAM if at least 128MB is available.

  The eMoviX project contains tools for remastering MoviX to contain content you want to play. In the process of creating your own eMoviX ISO image, the video content is placed on the image in a way that it is automatically started when eMoviX boots up.

- **WOMP!**—Like GeeXboX and MoviX, WOMP! (http://womp.sourceforge.net) is a mini Linux distribution that can run entirely in RAM and lets you play a wide range of multimedia content. You can play audio, video, and slide shows. Depending on the options you select, the size of WOMP! ranges from 13MB to 30MB.

■ **LiMP**—The LiMP Linux Multimedia Player (http://limp-vkk-ver1.source-forge.net) live CD includes mplayer, XMMS, and OpenOffice.org components to play a range of content. From the LiMP menu, you can select to play video, audio, slide shows, or some games. There is also a way to play a slide show of help screens while running LiMP.

If you are interested in playing multimedia in Linux, another project that might interest you is MythTV (www.mythtv.org). Although MythTV was designed to install and run from hard disk, the project contains a front end that can run from a live CD. Using that live CD, you can play multimedia content from a MythTV server on your LAN and display that content on an inexpensive client PC. KnoppMyth (www.mysettopbox.tv/knoppmyth.html) is a live CD that can get you started installing Knoppix on a hard disk.

CREATING A MULTIMEDIA PRODUCTION LIVE CD

Today enough high-quality free and open-source software exists for producing and working with multimedia content that you could fill a live CD with it. As you might guess, someone has done just that. The Dynebolic live CD (http://dynebolic.org) contains hundreds of features aimed at helping "media activists, artists, and creatives."

Dynebolic is an excellent representation of providing a way to carry around a complete set of software tools needed to get a particular job done. To aid the graphic artist, Dynebolic includes tools for creating, manipulating, playing, and publishing images, video, music, Web sites, and other creative digital output.

Freedom of expression is at the core of Dynebolic (see the RASTA Software Digital Resistance page at http://rastasoft.org/resistance.txt). Although all software contained on the Dynebolic live CD is released freely under the GNU General Public License (GPL), you should review the particular components in Dynebolic live CD before deciding to redistribute it in any way. Of course, you should look carefully at any software you redistribute. But in the area of multimedia, some particularly contentions patent issues are related to royalties on codecs and video drivers.

Keeping the previous disclaimers in mind, Dynebolic offers a wonderful way to survey the landscape of multimedia software available in the free and open-source world. It also includes features to make this live CD a useful, portable toolkit for designers. Those features include the capability to back up data to a USB pen drive and options to boot as a networked thin client (to use Dynebolic to run on low-end machines and access resources from other computers on the network).

Understanding Dynebolic

The Dynebolic live CD was designed to run lean so that most resources can be directed toward running powerful multimedia applications. Dynebolic boots up directly (no login required) to a WindowMaker window manager without many frills. Emphasis is on ease of use, so access to available storage device and root privilege are immediately opened.

The WindowMaker window manager (www.windowmaker.info) incorporates small applications called docapps into its interface instead of end-to-end panels. For Dynabolic, docapps are added to the desktop to let you immediately open folders on different storage locations using the rox file manager. Locations include your home folder, hard-disk partitions, network shared folders, and any removable media (CDs, DVDs, floppy drives, and USB flash drives).

Hard-disk partitions and removable storage devices that have read/write capabilities (such as USB flash drives) are all mounted with read/write permissions. When you open a terminal window or storage device from the desktop, you do so as root user with the capability to effectively change any file or directory on the computer. Again, this reflects Dynebolic's intent to be as easy and open as possible.

The menus on the WindowMaker desktop are where you see what there really is to do with Dynebolic. Right-click the desktop to see the dyne:II menu, which includes categories of applications that include video, audio, image, text, Net, files, devel, xutils, and desktop applications. There are also selections for opening a terminal window (XTerm) and configuration window (Configure).

Figure 12-3 show some docapps (right) for opening disk partition and other storage media, as well as the dyne:II menu for selecting multimedia applications to run. Applications for configuring language, networks, modems, printers, screen resolution, sound cards, and WindowMaker itself are shown in the Configure folder.

To support lots of work going at the same time, the Dynebolic WindowMaker desktop is configured with six virtual desktops. Select the docapp from the upper-left corner of the screen to switch desktops.

Dynebolic also enables you to save the changes you made in a way that allows you to restore those changes later. The Nest (which you can create by selecting the Nest icon from the Configure window) lets you save your desktop settings and data to an archive on hard disk or USB key so that you can restore these later. (Chapter 2, "Playing with Live Linux CDs," contains descriptions for setting up a Nest.)

With Dynebolic booted, you have a lean desktop, access to all locally connected storage media, and basic tools for configuring the desktop and saving data and settings going forward. Now for the fun part: using the multimedia applications.

FIGURE 12-3 Open multimedia applications and disk partitions from the Dynebolic desktop.

Running Multimedia Applications

Whether you use Dynebolic or create a multimedia live CD yourself using your favorite Linux live CD platform, Dynebolic contains an excellent cross-section of free and open-source multimedia software for you to check out. So if you are a digital designer or just a multimedia enthusiast, Dynebolic gives you a good way to try out applications you might want to add to your own multimedia toolkit.

Because the charter for Dynebolic is not only to construct digital communication, but also to bring that communication to the world, Dynebolic includes software you can use to publish as well as create. You can use software such as icecast to broadcast audio on the Internet, using all open-source codecs (such as Ogg Vorbix and FLAC). You can use MP4Live to stream video to the Web.

The following sections describe the multimedia applications you can use from the Dynebolic Linux Live CD.

Using Video Applications

Open-source tools also exist for playing, recording, editing, and streaming video in Dynebolic. There are even tools for doing video visual effects.

To play video, Dynebolic includes mplayer (www.mplayerhq.hu) and Xine (http://xinehq.de) media players. Both players can play a wide range of video and audio content, depending on which codecs are included. Xine offers a panel for controlling video playback, as shown in Figure 12-4.

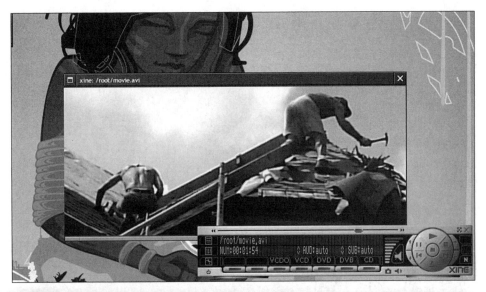

FIGURE 12-4 You can play DVDs, VCDs, CDs with a variety of supported video types from Xine media player.

For viewing television, Dynebolic includes xawtv (http://linux.bytesex.org/xawtv), which uses the video4linux interface. Dynebolic also includes the gmp4player MPEG4 player.

For recording video, Dynebolic includes the Kino DV recorder and editor (www.kinodv.org) from the desktop menu. Several different commands for recording video also come with Dynebolic, including `ffmpeg` (http://ffmpeg.mplayerhq.hu), `streamer`, and `mencoder`.

Video editors include Avidermux (www.avidemux.org), transcode and gtranscode (www.transcoding.org), and Cinelerra (http://heroinewarrior.com/cinelerra.php3). Figure 12-5 shows the Cinelerra video editor being used to edit a video.

To stream video to the Web, Dynebolic includes HasciiCam (http://ascii.dyne.org), which can stream live ASCII video from a Web cam to the Web. MP4Live can stream video4linux video and OSS audio output to the network.

Using Audio Applications

Besides audio players, recorders, editors, and streamers, Dynebolic includes some music applications for performing music. For playing audio, Dynebolic includes the popular Xmms audio player (www.xmms.org). The AmaroK music jukebox (http://amarok.kde.org) provides an interface for combining player and playlist features in the same window. Figure 12-6 shows the AmaroK audio player, displaying information about an artist as that artist's music plays.

FIGURE 12-5 You can edit video and audio content using Cinelerra.

FIGURE 12-6 View artist information as you play music from playlists and collections in AmaroK.

Open-source audio editors have become quite sophisticated in recent years. Dynebolic includes the Ardour multitrack studio (http://ardour.org), Audacity audio editor (http://audacity.sourceforge.net), and reZound sample editor (http://rezound. sourceforge.net). RoseGarden (www.rosegardenmusic.com) is a MIDI sequencer and music composite editor, while TimeMachine is a real-time audio recorder.

To let you stream audio to the Internet, Dynebolic includes the Icecast streaming audio server (www.icecast.org). It also includes the MuSE multiple streaming engine, which can be used to gather audio input, mix it, and deliver it to an Icecast server for delivery over the Internet.

Using Image-Manipulation Applications

Applications for working with images have become sophisticated enough in recent years to compete with commercial applications in features and quality. GIMP (www.gimp.org) is the most popular open-source program for image manipulation. Inkscape (www.inkscape.org) is a vector graphics editor that works toward SVG compliance.

Blender (www.blender3d.org) is a powerful application for doing 3D modeling. Blender can also do animation, rendering, and interactive playback. You can use this application to produce professional-quality commercial games and movies.

Several applications are available for browsing image files and converting images. GQview (http://gqview.sourceforge.net) lets you work with images and display them as slide shows (see Chapter 10, "Customizing a Presentation Live Linux CD," for a description of GQview). ImageMagick (www.imagemagick.org) is a good tool for converting images to different formats, sizes, colors, or other attributes.

Using Supporting Applications

Most of the other applications on Dynebolic are there to support the multimedia work you are doing on the live CD. To communicate with the Internet, Dynebolic includes Web browsers (Firefox and Links). E-mail applications include Thunderbird e-mail client and Mutt. File-sharing applications include bittorrent, Nicotine, and Gnutella.

Chat and instant-messaging clients include XChat IRC chat, Gaim instant messaging, and Irssi console IRC chat. To visit FTP repositories, Dynebolic includes the GFTp graphical FTP client and the NCFtp console FTP client.

File-sharing applications include Rox file browser, Samba file-sharing server, xFE file explorer, and Midnight Commander file explorer. Dynebolic also has tools for configuring network interfaces needed to browse network file-sharing resources.

SUMMARY

Many multimedia tools and players are available in the free and open-source world. Some live CD developers have created tiny Linux distributions that are dedicated to playing and displaying audio, video, and digital images. Those types of distributions include MoviX, GeeXboX, and LiMP.

An example of a live CD that focuses on creating a multimedia toolkits of open-source applications is Dynebolic. Using Dynebolic, you can create, edit, and publish audio, video, and digital images in a variety of formats. Dynebolic contains a lightweight window manager and many easy-to-use features to facilitate an efficient platform for running multimedia applications.

## CHAPTER 13

Customizing a Firewall Live Linux CD

Live Linux CDs make an excellent choice for a firewall, for a number of reasons. First, most firewall-specific distros require very little software, so they fit quite well on a single CD-ROM. Second, performance isn't much of a factor because, again, not a lot of software is involved in setting up a Linux-based firewall; the system shouldn't need to read from the CD-ROM very often, so it shouldn't take a performance hit in reading from CD-ROM instead of a hard disk.

Third, the software on the CD-ROM is write-only, so you don't have to worry about an intruder tampering with the software included with the live CD distro. Finally, you don't usually need to write data to disk with a firewall distro, so you can make use of a system that doesn't even *have* a hard drive.

Customizing a firewall CD can include putting new packages on the CD or just hard-wiring your configuration so that you don't need to read additional data off a hard drive, floppy, or USB flash drive.

In this chapter, we look at the Devil Linux distribution and how to use and customize it, and we briefly discuss some of the other options in the live CD firewall arena.

CHOOSING A FIREWALL COMPUTER AND LIVE CD

Let's start the chapter with hardware requirements and then look at how to select a firewall live CD.

If you're looking to set up a firewall for your home office or small business, a Linux live CD and an older PC with two network interface cards (NICs) will do just fine. Unless you'll be setting up a firewall and/or gateway for a fairly large network, a used Pentium or Pentium II computer with at least 32MB of RAM is usually sufficient to provide decent performance. For my home network, I use a Pentium III clocked at 350MHz, with 384MB of RAM and two 10/100 Ethernet cards.

This is probably overkill because the firewall serves only two users and a handful of computers, but it's the oldest machine I had lying around when it came time to set up a firewall.

After you select your hardware, it's time to choose the distro. You have the following options when it comes to using a live CD for your firewall:

- **General live CD**—Choose a general-purpose Linux live CD such as Knoppix and customize it to suit your needs.
- **Specialized firewall CD**—Grab a specialized live CD distro specifically tuned for use as a firewall.

If you're using a live CD for your desktop and you have only a single computer, you might want to just configure firewall rules in Knoppix (for example) and leave it at that. If you'll be setting up a dedicated firewall, though, you probably want to go ahead and use a distro that's specifically set up for the task.

I spent a fair amount of time considering the options and finally chose Devil Linux as the firewall of choice, for the following reasons:

- **Flexibility**—Devil Linux is very flexible. It can run off a live CD or a USB flash drive. The configuration can be stored on the CD, on a USB drive, or on a floppy disk. You don't need a hard drive in the system at all, although you can take advantage of the hard disk for storing data if it's present.
- **Customization**—Devil Linux also has a customizable build system, so you can easily create a custom Devil Linux disk that fits your needs. It's not too hard to customize a lot of distros, but the fact that Devil Linux is specifically designed to be customized makes it much more attractive.
- **Development community**—I also like the fact that Devil Linux seems to have an active development community. If you look on DistroWatch at some of the other firewall live CDs, you'll probably find that a lot of them haven't had a new release in a year or more. As we all know, things move pretty quickly in the Linux world, and any distro that doesn't keep up with kernel development and other software updates is not very attractive.
- **Security patches**—Devil Linux also uses the GRSecurity (www.grsecurity.net/) patches for the Linux 2.4.*x* series kernel, to prevent

buffer overflows and other attacks that take advantage of minor vulnerabilities to run arbitrary code. Because the firewall is your first line of defense, you want it to be as secure as possible.

- **Simple GUI tools**—I also like Devil Linux because I can use a simple GUI application, Firewall Builder, to create firewall rules to run with Devil Linux.

- **All open source**—Finally, Devil Linux is totally open source. Some of the nicer live CD firewall distros, such as Coyote Linux, include proprietary components that prevent modification or prevent use in commercial environments without licensing fees. Well, I don't want to waste my time and trouble learning a system that I can't use in a commercial environment down the road, if I so choose.

GETTING DEVIL LINUX

The first step, of course, is to get the Devil Linux ISO image and burn it to a CD. We've already covered burning ISO images to CD, so let's start with finding the right ISO image for you.

The latest release of Devil Linux, as of this writing, is 1.2.10, which was released in July 2006. The Devil Linux project offers three versions: one optimized for 486 and higher, one optimized for 586 and higher, and another for 686 and higher. There's no AMD64 version at this time, nor are there any versions for other processor architectures.

The i586 Devil Linux release (version 1.2.10) is included on the DVD that comes with this book. You can get the compressed tarball representing that release as described in Appendix A, "On the DVD."

If you would like a different, or later, version of Devil Linux, you can go to the downloads page on the Devil Linux Web site (www.devil-linux.org/downloads/index.php). There you'll see a number of mirrors. Choose the mirror closest to you or, if none of the other mirrors are near you, click the SourceForge link.

The different releases are obvious by the filenames, so pick the right version for your hardware and go ahead and download the files.

After you've downloaded the file or copied it from the DVD that comes with this book, you should have something like `devil-linux-1.2.10-i586-SMP.tar.bz2`.

Uncompress the tarball using this command:

```
# tar -jxvf devil-linux-1.2.10-i586-SMP.tar.bz2
```

This should give you a directory such as devil-linux-1.2.10-i586-SMP. In this directory, you'll find a sample configuration tarball (etc.tar.bz2), the ISO image for Devil Linux, scripts for creating new Devil Linux ISOs, and documentation.

> **NOTE**
>
> To use Devil Linux, you'll need to have at least a 486 or compatible CPU, 32MB of RAM, two or three Ethernet cards supported by Linux, and a device to store a configuration to. In this chapter, we assume that you have a hard disk attached to the computer—even a small one will do. You can also use a USB flash drive or floppy disk, if you still have any floppies!

BOOTING THE DEVIL LINUX LIVE CD

When you first boot Devil Linux, you'll see a menu with several options for screen resolution and the option to press F1 for help. If you don't enter one of the screen resolutions or boot parameters, or press F1, Devil Linux starts loading after 5 seconds by default.

As part of the boot process, Devil Linux looks for configuration files on other media—IDE and SCSI disks and CD-ROMs, floppy disks, and so forth. It looks for a file called etc.tar.bz2; if it finds this, it uses that configuration.

You can also pass the location of the configuration archive to Devil Linux using this syntax:

```
DL_config=/dev/ide/disc0/part1:myconfig.tar.bz2
```

So, to be clear, the complete command line includes the kernel name as well. This is taken as read in the Devil Linux documentation and is likely to confuse new Linux users. The entire command line would look like this:

```
boot: /boot/vmlinuz root=/dev/ram0 initrd=/boot/initrd.gz
  init=/linuxrc DL_config=/dev/ide/disc0/part1:myconfig.tar.bz2
```

That probably seems like a lot of typing, but remember that when you have your firewall set up, you shouldn't need to reboot very often.

This example would tell Devil Linux, "Look for the file myconfig.tar.bz2 on the first IDE disk (disc0) on the first partition (part1)."

> **NOTE**
>
> Yes, the syntax is a bit muddled—0 is the first disk, but 1 is the first partition. Not only is counting from 0 confusing, but it's also nonstandard because it's not applied across the board.

Finally, you can string more than one config location, if you need to, by separating them with commas, like so (make sure that the entire text of both lines is typed into one line):

```
DL_config=/dev/ide/disc0/part1:myconfig.tar.bz2,/dev/scsi/disc0/part1:sc
siconfig.tar.bz2
```

Note that there's no space between the comma and configuration locations.

If this is the first time you're booting Devil Linux, you can save the bit of time it takes to scan the drives by passing this option instead:

```
DL_config_no_scan
```

The initial scan can take quite a while (a couple minutes, so you probably want to use the DL_config_no_scan parameter if you already know that you don't have the configuration file.

If you don't pass the DL_config_no_scan parameter and there's no configuration file for Devil Linux to find, it will stop during boot-up with a prompt saying "Would you really like to load DL without configuration Media?" Go ahead and press y; Devil Linux then finishes booting.

Devil Linux also includes the memtest utility on the live CD, so if you're a bit concerned that a machine has bad RAM, you can type M at the boot prompt to boot Devil Linux into memtest.

Pressing F1 takes you to the help screen, and F10 returns you to the main menu.

When the CD finishes booting, it's time to log in.

LOGGING IN AND SETTING UP DEVIL LINUX

When Devil Linux boots up, you can log into the system as root with no password. Devil Linux has no regular user defined by default.

It's worth noting that Devil Linux can also make a passable rescue CD because it includes a fair number of standard utilities that you might need, including fdisk, fsck, chroot, and other standard GNU utilities that can help with rescuing a system.

The first thing you'll want to do is set up a file system to save your configuration on—assuming that you don't have a file system already available. You'll need to do this using the fdisk command, which is pretty simple.

If you've never used fdisk, the first thing to do is scan for devices. You can do this using this command:

```
# fdisk -l
```

This returns something like this:

```
Disk /dev/sdb: 203.9 GB, 203928109056 bytes
255 heads, 63 sectors/track, 24792 cylinders
Units = cylinders of 16065 * 512 = 8225280 bytes

   Device Boot      Start         End      Blocks   Id  System
/dev/sdb1                1       24792   199141708+  83  Linux
```

Or you might see a line like this:

```
Disk /dev/ide/host0/bus0/target0/lun0/disc: 60.0 GB, 60011642880 bytes
```

As you can see, in the first example, there's one SCSI disk on this system, and it already has a Linux partition. The second example looks a little more complicated, but it's not too hard to follow; the system has an IDE drive as the first device on the first IDE bus, which translates to /dev/hda. (SCSI disks are usually sd*n* and IDE disks are hd*n* where *n* is the letter for the device—a for the first one, b for the second one, and so on.)

If the disk doesn't have a partition or you just want to get rid of it and start fresh, run something like this:

```
# fdisk /dev/sdb
```

Replace /dev/sdb with the appropriate device. Note that you'll see an error message about lacking a file system if the disk has never been initialized. It's okay to ignore that.

To create a new partition, press n at the fdisk menu and follow the prompts. Note that you can see the fdisk help menu by pressing m; remember to write the changes to disk when you're finished with w, or press q to quit without saving.

When you've got that finished, run setup to enter the Devil Linux System Configurator menu. The main System Configurator screen is shown in Figure 13-1. Although most menus are self-explanatory, the following descriptions walk you through a few of the more important menus.

First I recommend that you set the root password (the LoginPW option); you don't want to have a firewall with a blank root password, right?

After that, it's time to move on to the basic configuration. Select the Basic option from the System Configurator menu shown in Figure 13-1. The Config Menu screen appears as shown in Figure 13-2.

In the basic configuration, you can configure the host name, time zone, keyboard layout, and so forth. Go ahead and set up the system the way you like it, and press Back when you're finished.

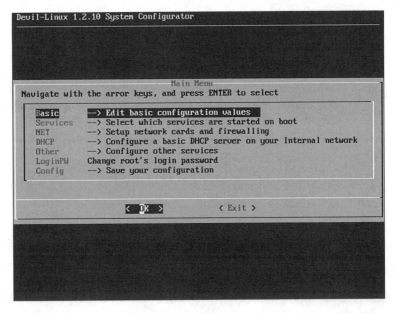

FIGURE 13-1 Choose firewall configuration options using the Devil Linux System Configurator.

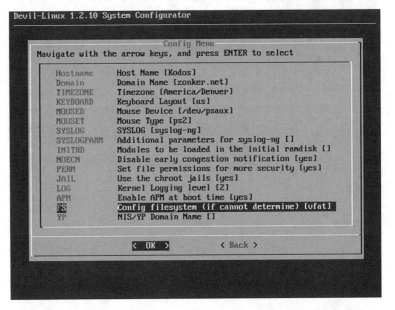

FIGURE 13-2 Change hostname, time zone, and other basic firewall settings using Devil Linux System Configurator Config Menu.

Most of the defaults in the basic configuration menu are probably safe to use. Be sure to change the host and domain names to reflect your network, though. As you can see in Figure 13-2, I've set the hostname (Kodos), domain name (zonker.net), and time-zone (America/Denver). You can also set the logging level, mouse device, and so forth.

The next step is to configure services. If you're just running a firewall, the default set of services will probably be fine. However, if you want to be able to run cron jobs, an SSH daemon, or other services, or maybe remove IPv6 support, you'll need to configure the services here. From the System Configurator main menu, select Services. Available services are listed as shown in Figure 13-3.

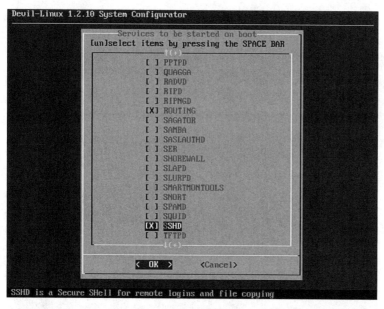

FIGURE 13-3 Turn on system services for your firewall from the System Configurator Services menu.

As you can see in Figure 13-3, there are quite a few available services to choose from. Very few, if any, additional services should be turned on for a firewall. I do recommend setting up SSHD, though, if you plan to administer the firewall remotely. My firewall doesn't even have a keyboard or monitor attached to it; I do all the administration via SSH after its set up.

You'll also need to set up your network devices, naturally. From the System Configurator main menu, select NET. The Networking Menu appears as shown in Figure 13-4.

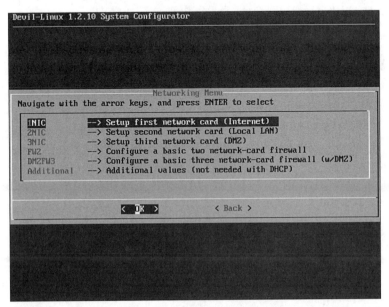

FIGURE 13-4 Configure network interfaces and settings from the System Configurator Networking Menu.

One of the reasons I like Devil Linux is that it's better suited to more complex network setups, such as three-NIC configurations that provide a DMZ, instead of the standard two-NIC configurations that provide only a single barrier between the LAN and the Internet.

As you can see on the Networking Menu in Figure 13-4, you have several options here. You can choose a two-card Local LAN configuration or a DMZ setup with three interfaces. You can set up the interface to each card individually.

As you can see, Devil Linux makes it easy to set up a basic firewall framework with the FW2 and DMZFW3 options. Unfortunately, it *doesn't* make it easy to set up the NICs. On systems I've tested, Devil Linux doesn't autodetect network cards, so you have to explicitly tell Devil Linux what modules to use for the cards.

Because users rarely know exactly what model network card they have, and because the name and model number of the card might or might not bear any resemblance to the actual module name, this can be a bit tricky. I recommend booting the computer using another live CD, such as Knoppix, and then seeing what module it uses to fire up the NICs. (Type `lsmod` and `lspci -v` to get information about your network interface cards.)

Go ahead and set up the NICs (remember, it's a pain the first time, but you shouldn't have to do it again) and then go back to the main configuration.

Now it's time to save your configuration and reboot. After you reboot, you should be ready to set up your firewall rules. You can save the configuration via the text menu or using the `save-config` command. You'll want to use the menu option for the first go and use the `save-config` option after configuring your firewall rules.

The configuration is saved under `etc.tar.bz2` on the hard drive or other media. This will come in handy later because you can do away with the need for a hard disk, floppy drive, or USB key by copying that to another system and creating a new CD-ROM with the configuration already available on it. Devil Linux includes `scp`, so you can just use `scp` to send the file to another machine.

However, Devil Linux might not mount the drive, so you'll need to mount it before you can copy the file. Assuming that your media is the first partition on the first IDE drive, for example, you would use this:

```
# mount -t ext3 /dev/hda1 /mnt
```

Then use `cd` to change to the `/mnt` directory and use `scp` to copy the file to another host:

```
# scp etc.tar.bz2 username@host:/home/username/
```

We return to that in a bit when we discuss making a custom CD. Now it's time to set up firewall rules.

SETTING UP FIREWALL RULES

You can set up your firewall rules in a couple ways with Devil Linux. The first way is to configure them manually using iptables rules. That's a fine option if you happen to be an expert at iptables, but most folks aren't.

The second option, and the one I recommend, is to use Firewall Builder, which is available at www.fwbuilder.org/. If you're using Linux, Firewall Builder is probably available with your distribution. If not, the project has packages available for Windows and Mac OS X, though these are not GPL'ed; the Linux version is freely available under the GPL.

Ubuntu and Debian users can grab Firewall Builder by running this:

```
# apt-get update
# apt-get install fwbuilder
```

This also grabs any dependencies you might need for Firewall Builder.

Firewall Builder has three templates that should get you started: a basic set of firewall rules that allows connections to the firewall only from the internal LAN and only via SSH, a more complex set of rules that also allows the firewall to serve as a DHCP and DNS server for the internal network, and a set of firewall rules with a DMZ for a machine with three interfaces.

The templates assume a couple things: first, that you want to use the 192.168.1.0 private subnet, and, second, that you're pulling your IP address on the Internet-facing interface using DHCP.

Firewall Builder is a bit too complex to cover in depth here, but it's not too difficult to use. You should be able to master it in an afternoon if you are at all familiar with networking. When you have your firewall configuration, you can use Firewall Builder to publish it to the firewall and then save the configuration.

CREATING A NEW CD

The Devil Linux distribution ships with a script called custom-cd. You might think that mastering a new CD would be a royal pain, but it's actually quite easy and takes only a few minutes, at worst. Note that you'll need to either be running as root or use sudo to run the script because you'll need to mount a directory for the ISO image while the new one is created.

Earlier in the chapter, we discussed saving the configuration to another machine so you could create a new Devil Linux CD with your custom configuration. We use that as an example of how to create new CDs. You can also use this process to add software or replace other configuration files or packages.

To start, you need to be in the Devil Linux directory, which should be something like /home/*username*/devil-linux-1.2.10-i586-SMP/. (This differs based on the version of Devil Linux that you are using.)

Now create a directory called new to hold any new files that need to be added to the ISO image. Note that you need to replicate the CD-ROM structure under the new directory, so if you want to add a file under, say, /home, you would add it under /new/home.

To replace the Devil Linux default configuration, place the etc.tar.bz2 file you created earlier under the new directory, and make sure you have a directory under /mnt (or anywhere, really, but /mnt is standard) for the script to mount the ISO image. I usually just use `devil`, which is what the script defaults to, but you have the option of giving it a different name if it suits you.

Now run `./custom-cd` as root, or `sudo ./custom-cd` if you use a distro such as Ubuntu that doesn't use the root account by default.

You'll see a series of prompts:

```
jzb@kang:~/local/devil-linux-1.2.10-i586-SMP$ sudo ./custom-cd
Enter location of existing CD drive or ISO image [./bootcd.iso] ->
Enter your new ISO image [./bootcdnew.iso] -> ./newboot.iso
Enter where to mount your CD/ISO [/mnt/devil] ->
Enter location of directory with new files [./new] ->
Enter temporary location to hold the files [./tmp11832] ->
```

Notice that I changed the name of the new ISO image to `newboot.iso` instead of `bootcdnew.iso` because I already had a `bootcdnew.iso`.

Then you'll see a bunch of status messages and a `mkisofs` message about the options used. You can safely ignore these. At the end, you should get a final message saying that the new ISO image has been created.

Depending on the speed of your machine, it can take 5 minutes, or it can take considerably longer. On my Athlon 64 3000+ with 2GB of RAM, it takes about 5 to 10 minutes to generate a new ISO image.

You definitely want to be sure that you've got the configuration that you want before you burn the ISO image to CD-R. Descriptions in Appendix B, "Building, Testing, and Burning ISOs," can help you use QEMU or VMware to test your Devil Linux ISO image. Refer to this appendix for information on burning the ISO image to CD.

OTHER FIREWALL DISTROS

As I mentioned at the beginning of this chapter, you might consider a number of other distros if Devil Linux doesn't meet your needs—or if you just want to sample other approaches to setting up a live CD firewall.

Coyote Linux (http://www.coyotelinux.com/) is a good solution if you need to run a firewall for only a small home network and you don't want to modify it or redistribute it. The licensing for Coyote means that it's not very flexible and it's not suitable for use in commercial environments. It *is*, however, a really easy-to-use firewall/router combo, so consider it if you're just looking for a quick "set it and forget it" solution for the home. I used Coyote (the floppy version) for more than a year, and it was dead easy to use.

The m0n0wall distribution (http://m0n0.ch/wall/) is another popular firewall solution that can run off a live CD with a floppy for the configuration. Like Devil Linux, it has a healthy development community and sees regular releases. However, m0n0wall is actually based on FreeBSD, so it doesn't quite qualify as a *Linux* live CD.

Another popular live CD firewall is the SmoothWall distribution. Unfortunately, at the time of this writing, it hasn't had a new stable release since September 2005, so I decided it wasn't suitable for coverage here. However, by the time this book is in your hands, a new release might be available. Check http://smoothwall.org/ for more on SmoothWall.

SUMMARY

As you can see, the live CD format is ideal for some firewalls and routers. Devil Linux, in particular, is great for any situation when it's necessary to customize the live CD.

In this chapter, we covered basic use of Devil Linux, configuration of a new firewall, and how to modify and update the Devil Linux live CD. Using the information in this chapter, you should have no problem building your own live CD based on Devil Linux.

Although Devil Linux isn't the only game in town, it is one of the most flexible and relatively easy to use. If you're fairly familiar with Linux, it will probably take you the better part of an afternoon to use Devil Linux to create a customized firewall CD.

## CHAPTER 14

Customizing a Cluster Live Linux CD

Imagine that you have an office full of computers that are used only from about 9 a.m. to 5 p.m. That's a lot of computer power going to waste, and there's an easy way to harness the horsepower of those computers the rest of the day using live CD clustering distributions.

If you're looking for a way to create a quick-and-dirty cluster, a live CD is definitely the way to go. You can pop a CD into each machine's drive and reboot, and use it for a few hours (or a few days, and make the most of a long holiday weekend!). When your computing task is finished, reboot the machine, pop out the CD, and you've got the PC's original operating system available, untouched by the cluster operating system.

For really hardcore computing tasks, you probably don't want to use a cluster live CD; if you're doing work for the Department of Defense doing battlefield simulations or something equally computationally intensive (not to mention high budget), you'll probably want to go ahead and install the operating system directly to the hard drive. In fact, in that sort of scenario, you'd probably be working with a vendor or IT department that would supply its own customized version of Linux.

This chapter discusses basic clustering concepts in general and looks at the options for live CD cluster distributions.

WHAT'S A CLUSTER?

Let's start this chapter by discussing what a cluster is and what you can accomplish with a live CD distro to be used for creating a cluster of computers.

The simplest definition of a cluster is two or more computers that are connected and that work together. Clustering is used for many different reasons. A cluster can provide high availability, load balancing, high-performance computing, and utility or "grid" computing facilities. Note that these functions are not exclusive, so a cluster can provide high performance *and* high availability, or high availability *and* load balancing.

High Availability (HA)

HA computing is used to provide redundancy. A single computer represents a single point of failure. Even if you have a server that has redundant power supplies, a RAID array with hot-swappable drives, and all the other goodies, it still represents a single point of failure (like if a junior admin accidentally disconnects the wrong network cable…).

An HA cluster can be as small as two systems, or nodes, or it can be much larger. One example might be a company that has two firewall systems—one that serves as the firewall, and another with the same configuration that stands by and listens for a "heartbeat" from the other server. If the first firewall system fails, the second system kicks in and provides the service until the master firewall comes back up.

Another example is an e-commerce company that has a master and slave MySQL cluster, where the slave is configured to mirror the first MySQL database and take over as the master MySQL server if the master fails.

Load Balancing

Sometimes a task is just too difficult for one server to take on, no matter how much horsepower that server has. Consider a popular site such as Slashdot; the traffic it handles is far too much to be handled by a single server.

A load-balancing cluster spreads the computing load across two or more computers. Sites such as Slashdot have several Web nodes and database nodes to handle requests. Usually a load-balanced cluster is also an HA cluster—that is, if one node in the cluster fails, the application that the cluster provides does not fail. It might take a performance hit, but it won't fail when one node drops out.

High-Performance Computing (HPC)

If you follow Linux much, you're probably well aware of the Top 500 list of supercomputing systems and the fact that more than two-thirds of the systems on the Top 500 run some version of Linux. These are systems that are built for raw computing performance to run simulations and other compute-intensive applications that simply wouldn't be practical to run on a single computer.

For example, oil companies use HPCs to analyze geographical data to try to determine where to drill for oil. HPCs are also used extensively for biological research and for rendering computer-generated effects for movies. If you've seen *Monsters Inc.* or *Toy Story*, you've seen what HPCs can do for the world of entertainment.

Grid Computing

Grid computing, also called "utility" computing, is similar to HPC and load balancing, but the difference is that grid computing often makes use of nondedicated machines. For instance, the SETI@home project uses a client on the computers of volunteers to search radio transmissions for signs of intelligent life in the universe. (We've ruled out Washington D.C., and have the rest of the universe to search!)

Now that we have our terminology straight, it's time to look at ParallelKnoppix.

PARALLELKNOPPIX

ParallelKnoppix, or PK, is a modified Knoppix live CD designed for use in creating HPC clusters. In this section, we look at how to start up PK on multiple nodes to run a cluster, and how to customize PK to add or remove applications. We also review some of the applications present on the live CD and when you might want to use PK.

Starting ParallelKnoppix

ParallelKnoppix is contained on the DVD that comes with this book. Refer to Appendix A, "On the DVD," to learn how to get and boot ParallelKnoppix. After it's booted, ParallelKnoppix appears as shown in Figure 14-1.

In Figure 14-1, you can see the PK boot screen. To start PK, just press Enter, unless you need to pass boot options to the kernel to get it to boot. For example, you might want to pass the acpi=no argument to the kernel if you have had problems getting PK (or other live CDs) to boot.

PK can also be used to run memtest to check the system memory. This is a good idea if you have any problems with the machine that you can't track down, such as programs crashing for no apparent reason.

After ParallelKnoppix has started, you might notice that it seems to be missing the menu bar. Actually, ParallelKnoppix has a taskbar, but it's hidden. Move the mouse to the bottom of the screen, and you'll see the taskbar after it unhides. In Figure 14-2, you can see the KDE taskbar, and PK's documentation in Konqueror.

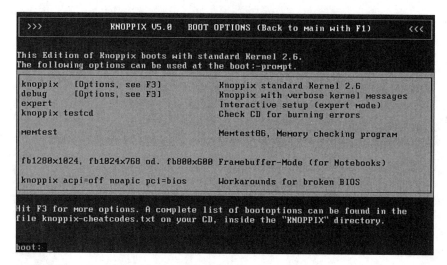

FIGURE 14-1 ParallelKnoppix boot options.

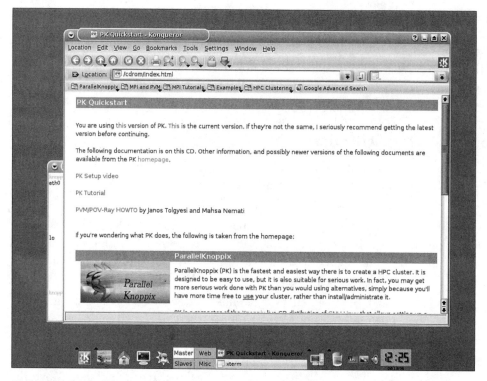

FIGURE 14-2 The ParallelKnoppix desktop with KDE taskbar and Konqueror.

If this behavior annoys you as much as it does me, you can just right-click the taskbar and select Configure Panel. Then you'll see the Configure KDE Panel dialog, and on the left side you'll see Hiding. Click that and deselect Hide Automatically under Hide Mode.

> ## NOTE
>
> ParallelKnoppix assumes that you'll be able to pull an IP address via DHCP. If you're not running DHCP on your network, you can open a terminal and use su - to switch to root. ParallelKnoppix has no root password, by default.
>
> Then run the following to set up your IP address:
>
> ```
> # ifconfig eth0 10.0.0.10 netmask 255.0.0.0 gw 10.0.0.1
> ```
>
> Of course, you'll want to change the values to reflect your network setup.

Setting Up Swap Space

If you're booting PK on a Linux machine, it can find and use the swap partition that's already available on the machine.

However, if you're using Windows, you won't have a swap file that PK can use. You'll want to create a swapfile that PK can use in the long run. If the system has a FAT file system, you can mount that and create a swapfile using dd. For example, to add a swapfile name swapfile.swp to a FAT partition located at /media/hda1, you could type the following:

```
# dd if=/dev/zero of=/media/hda1/swapfile.swp bs=1024 count=1024k
```

This will give you a 1GB swapfile; adjust the count to reduce or increase the size of the swap. Note that the general rule of thumb is to have twice the amount of system RAM—at least, that used to be the case before 1GB and more of RAM became common. If you're using swap enough to need *more* than 1GB of swap, you probably need more RAM than a bigger swapfile. Remember, accessing swap is much, much slower than accessing RAM.

Now you need to format the file as swap and tell the system to use it:

```
# cd /media/hda1
# mkswap swapfile.swp
# swapon swapfile.swp
```

That's all there is to it. When remastering the system, you might want to make sure that you set up the swapfile permanently in /etc/fstab. To do this, you add a line like this:

```
/dev/hda1/swapfile.swp    none    swap sw    0  0
```

Another alternative, if you're going to be using a machine as a cluster node on a regular basis, is to use something like the GParted live CD to reduce the Windows partition a bit and add a swap partition. Because most machines have fairly big drives, users shouldn't miss a 1GB partition for swap, and because PK automatically detects swap, it will make your life just that much easier—and isn't that what computers are all about?

Using Applications from the PK Live CD

The ParallelKnoppix CD comes with quite a bit of software that isn't necessarily related to clustering. You'll find a number of editors (including my favorite, vim), multimedia applications, Internet applications, games, and a lot more.

Games and whatnot probably won't be on your list of desired apps if you're actually being productive, but if you just happen to have the PK disc with you and want to kill some time, you can always turn a boring old Windows machine into a Knoppix desktop for a while.

But PK also comes with a number of useful applications for clustering. On the KDE menu, you'll find a ParallelKnoppix menu (catchy, huh?), and this includes a set of scripts for remastering ParallelKnoppix, setting up the cluster, saving your PK settings, and so forth. We cover the most important of these items individually.

If PK doesn't include an application you want, such as Firefox, you can add it to the system by remastering PK. We look at that a bit later in the chapter.

Saving Settings

One of the annoying things about a live CD distro is that all your hard work disappears into the ether if you reboot the machine—unless you have a way of saving your settings, at least. PK gives you a way to do this quickly and painlessly.

Go to the ParallelKnoppix menu and look for the Save PK Configuration menu. The Create PK configuration archive dialog appears as shown in Figure 14-3:

This dialog walks you through a series of options to save your personal configuration, network settings, printer settings, and whatnot. In Figure 14-3, I've asked PK to save my network settings, desktop files, and personal configuration. I don't worry about the X configuration because I may want to use the configuration on a machine with a different video card.

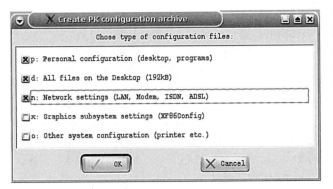

FIGURE 14-3
Save settings from the ParallelKnoppix Create PK configuration archive dialog.

First, the dialog asks what settings you want to save and then asks where you'd like to save the information. PK is a bit dumb here—note that in Figure 14-4 it shows an option to save the configuration to a floppy drive, whether or not one exists! Make sure you verify where you want the file saved to. After you have chosen what to save, the dialog asks you where you want to save the configuration files, as shown in Figure 14-4.

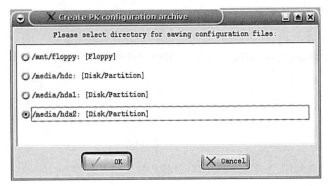

FIGURE 14-4
Selecting a partition to save the information.

Unfortunately, PK doesn't automatically detect the configuration on your hard drive—you have to specifically tell it to scan the disk for the configuration at boot time, like so:

```
boot: knoppix myconfig=scan
```

That sure beats reconfiguring PK every time you reboot!

Running ParallelKnoppix in Qemu

If you'd like to try ParallelKnoppix but you don't have two computers to spare, you can run PK under Qemu (http://fabrice.bellard.free.fr/qemu/). If you're using a recent Linux distro, odds are, your distro has a Qemu package available. Ubuntu users, for example, can install Qemu by running the following:

```
# apt-get update
# apt-get install qemu
```

This installs Qemu and any necessary dependencies. A version of Qemu is available for Windows as well. Descriptions of the Windows version of Qemu, as well as other Qemu options are described in Appendix B, "Building, Testing, and Burning ISOs." If you use Windows as your desktop, you can download the Windows installer and give that a shot instead.

To run ParallelKnoppix in Qemu, use this syntax:

```
# qemu -m mem -cdrom parallelknoppix-2006-06-19.iso
```

The -m option tells Qemu how much RAM to allocate for the virtual machine. You probably want to allocate at least 384MB of RAM, and more if your machine has enough RAM to spare. (If you're running on a machine with less than 512MB of RAM, running things under Qemu might not make sense.) The -cdrom option tells Qemu to use an ISO image to boot from.

Note that Qemu is *not* as high performance as VMware Player, Server, or Workstation. You might want to download VMware Server or Player if you want to play with ParallelKnoppix for any amount of time. VMware is also described in Appendix B.

MANAGING NODES AND STARTING YOUR CLUSTER

Okay, let's get to the fun part! Now it's time to start a new cluster. The first step is to boot what will be the master node. Of course, you will need at least two machines (even if they're virtual machines) and they should be on their own network. This is because PK uses DHCP to assign addresses to the slave nodes; if you've got a DHCP server running for the rest of your network, there can (and will) be confusion about assigning IP addresses.

If you're doing this on a home network with a cable modem or DSL modem that does DHCP, you can get away with just unplugging the cable modem from the network while you're working with PK—assuming that no one else in the household wants to get on the Internet. If you're going to be using ParallelKnoppix a lot, you might want to consider buying a spare switch to connect the cluster nodes when they're not connected to the main network.

Go to the ParallelKnoppix menu option on the KDE menu, and select Setup ParallelKnoppix. PK will launch the cluster configuration dialog.

Next, tell PK how many nodes, maximum, you want to allow in the cluster. I have about 12 computers on my home network at any given time, but I never use all of them simultaneously, so I usually say 10 here.

After you've selected the number of nodes, you have to choose the network card you want to use. This can be handy; if you have a system with two (or more) network cards, you can let it remain connected to your main network while keeping one interface on the LAN.

PK *should* autodetect the interface that you want to use here, so it's probably okay to accept the default. Next, PK asks if you want to provide any boot options. Again, unless there are any specific options, you can probably accept the default.

PK will also ask what network card(s) to support on the slave nodes. Just accept the default here, because we're going to boot from the PK disc and it should support just about any Linux-compatible network card without help from the master node.

NOTE

Technically, you can boot the slave nodes using PXE boot rather than using a PK disc—but, because many computers don't support PXE, I'm going to stick with the tried-and-true method of using a PK disc here. If your systems support PXE, you can try booting using PXE and let the systems boot entirely off of the master system.

Next, select media that can be read-write. Your master machine will need to have a hard disk with space it can write to, your slave nodes will not need a hard drive unless you would like them to have swap space (which is probably a good idea). This will be a working directory for all the nodes that will be shared via NFS. After this step, PK will be ready to accept compute nodes to the cluster.

Adding Nodes to the Cluster

Everything has been easy up until now, so you might think that configuring the slave nodes will be the difficult step, right? Nope. Configuring the slave nodes is a cakewalk.

After your master node is ready, it's time to boot the rest of the computers. Pop a PK disc into the slave node(s) and boot them up. If you have everything configured properly—the master node is running and waiting for slave nodes, and they're on a network separate from other DHCP servers—the remaining nodes should automatically configure themselves as slave nodes without any intervention on your part.

Re-run the StartHPC script, and it will add waiting nodes to the cluster. You'll see a dialog labeled tkping, and it will show green blocks for each node that's attached to the cluster, and red blocks for open slots in the cluster.

Testing the Cluster

Now it's time to make sure that your cluster is actually computing as one big computer. The first task that PK suggests is to run a POV-Ray job to see the cluster in action:

```
# cd /usr/share/doc/povray-3.5/examples/advanced/
# povray +N +NT2 mediasky.pov
```

This will fire up POV-Ray, and tell it to render the scene in mediasky.pov. Depending on how many nodes you have and how fast they are, this can be done in a minute or so or it may be done in a few seconds. With two compute nodes, it takes about 45 seconds in my test environment.

NOTE

POV-Ray, the Persistence of Vision Raytracer, is a program that creates 3D scenes and graphics. It's capable of some stunning images—but they can take a very long time to render using a single computer. Using PK, you can render images much, much faster.

Another way to monitor and manage your cluster is to use XPVM, which is a GUI manager for the Parallel Virtual Machine (PVM). PVM is the software that allows your cluster to be used as a single virtual machine. XPVM provides an easy-to-use interface for PVM.

Open a console on the master node and run xpvm. This fires up the XPVM interface, which shows all the attached nodes and their states.

To run a program across the nodes, click the Tasks button and select SPAWN. You'll see a dialog with a field labeled Command. Put the PVM-compatible command in the command field and click Start. (When you're starting out, you can probably just accept the defaults here.)

Note that programs have to be compiled with PVM in mind to be used with PVM/XPVM. For example, POV-Ray is designed to use PVM, but Firefox or the Gimp aren't—so they won't run under PVM.

To test XPVM, go ahead and do another POV-Ray test run using the following:

```
# cd /usr/share/doc/povray-3.5/examples/advanced/
# povray +N mediasky.pov
```

Note that you can take nodes out of use with PVM if you want to run a job with just a fraction of your compute cluster. Go to the Hosts menu and unselect any hosts that you don't want to use. (You can bring those nodes back online by reselecting them.)

That's really all there is to it. And you thought running a cluster would be hard!

REMASTERING PARALLELKNOPPIX

According to the PK notes, you need at least 2GB free to remaster PK to create a new disc. That's a very, very optimistic estimate, and I've found that you'll probably want to go with at least 4GB. Given today's humongous disk drives, it shouldn't be too difficult to scrape up a disk with at least that much space free for remastering.

NOTE

Here's one helpful hint: If the system you'll be remastering PK on is a system you use for day-to-day work, copy the files or packages you want to use to your file system before rebooting into PK. That way, you can just copy them over into the PK file system after rebooting instead of having to download them while running PK.

The version of ParallelKnoppix I have been testing had a slight error in the second script, the 2-StartCHROOT script, located in the `/home/knoppix/Desktop/ParallelKnoppix/Remastering` directory. On line 72, the path to `xterm` is listed as `/usr/bin/X11R6/xterm`. This is incorrect; it should be `/usr/bin/xterm`. Open the file in vi (or your preferred editor) and modify that line. After you modify the line, it should run fine. This might be fixed by the time this book is published, so give it a shot and see whether it works before modifying the script.

Start the process by going to the KDE menu → ParallelKnoppix → Remastering → 1-CopySourceForRemaster entry. Here you'll get a dialog similar to the one shown in Figure 14-5, asking where you want to save the source for remastering.

FIGURE 14-5

Select media to copy the ParallelKnoppix source to.

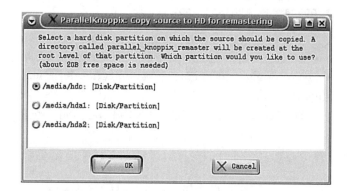

Again, be sure to check for free space. Remastering ParallelKnoppix can take more than an hour, and you don't want to get to the middle of the process and find out you've run out of room!

Now run the 2-StartCHROOT script, either from the command line or from the ParallelKnoppix menu, and you'll be dropped into the `chroot` environment and be able to make changes, including adding and removing packages using `dpkg`, or adding users, modifying the root password, and so forth. For instance, let's say you want to add Firefox. The best way to do that is to grab the official Firefox distribution from Mozilla.com and then copy it into the `chroot` system.

Figure 14-6 shows the Get into CHROOT Environment dialog. This lets you select which disk and partition to use for the CHROOT environment.

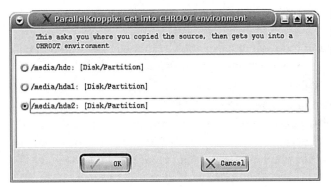

FIGURE 14-6
Select the partition for the chroot environment.

Now, when you're in the chroot environment, you're limited on what you can do, so it's best to copy it into the directory beforehand. Let's say you've selected the first partition on an IDE drive to copy the PK source to. This would be mounted as /media/hda1. You will find the PK source under /media/hda1/parallel_knoppix_remaster/source/KNOPPIX. When the chroot is started, this will be the root directory, and all the rest of the file system lives under here. If you want to copy a few files into /etc on PK, you copy them to /media/hda1/parallel_knoppix_remaster/source/KNOPPIX/etc, and so forth.

For instance, let's say you want to add the very latest version of a program to your PK system. You can copy a Debian package into the chroot file system and install it there, or compile the source, give the root user a password, or whatever you want to do.

When you're finished, you'll be able to create a new ISO image by going to the KDE menu → ParallelKnoppix → Remastering → 3MakeISO. This runs a script to create an ISO image out of the file system that PK created after copying the source from the original ISO to the file system.

As I mentioned earlier, PK will run under Qemu. PK offers to let you test out your shiny new ISO image under Qemu if you want, or you can just press Ctrl+C to exit and collect your ISO image to burn it to CD.

The ISO image can be found under /media/hda1/parallel_knoppix_remaster/ as parallelknoppixhomebrew-*XXXX-XX-XX*.iso, where *XXXX* is the year and *XX-XX* is the month and date.

SUMMARY

In this chapter, we looked at the ParallelKnoppix live CD that can be used to create HPC clusters. As you can see, PK is very versatile, easy to use, and probably one of the best cluster live CDs available.

Although you probably wouldn't want to use PK to break into the Top 500, it's definitely suitable for a number of other tasks when a temporary cluster will do. PK is also the best choice for a cluster CD because it's well maintained and development is steady; many of the other cluster CDs are out-of-date and don't seem to be well maintained.

With the remastering capabilities, PK can be almost anything—the only limit is your imagination.

Part IV

Appendices

On the DVD

A special live DVD included with this book features the contents of more than a dozen live Linux CDs. Those live CDs come in the following forms:

- **Directly bootable**—By adding a new boot screen, creating special boot options, and doing a bit of remastering, I've created a DVD that (from the boot prompt forward) lets you launch about a half dozen of the live CDs included on the DVD.

- **ISO images**—For all the live CDs included with this book, there is an ISO image included that you can burn to CD. If you have a blank or rewritable CD, you can burn any of those ISO images to CD and boot them separately.

Use any of the live CDs you fancy that boot directly from this DVD to see how they work. As for the ISOs included for the live CDs, you can burn them to CD or DVD (using tools such as cdrecord and K3b, described in Appendix B, "Building, Testing, and Burning ISOs"). In most cases, you should use the CDs you burn to build and remaster your own live Linux CDs.

NOTE

One item on the DVD that doesn't fall into either the boot directly or ISO image areas is the kadischi RPM package. Because the Kadischi project, which is used to create live CDs based on Fedora Linux, is still in early development, there is no official software package available for Kadischi.

For that reason, I created a kadischi RPM file for this book and placed it in the /RPMS directory on the DVD. Chapter 7, "Building a Basic Fedora Live CD," describes how to use this RPM.

BOOTING LIVE CDS FROM THE DVD

A handful of live CDs have been remastered to boot directly from the DVD that comes with this book. To try any of those live CDs, all you need is a PC (with a DVD drive) that you can reboot.

The default live CD on the DVD is Knoppix. So, to use Knoppix, you can simply press Enter at the boot prompt or wait for the timeout period (just a few seconds) and Knoppix will automatically boot. To boot any of the other live CDs available from the boot prompt, you need to type the label associated with that distribution.

Choosing Which Live CD to Boot

The live CDs that you can boot directly from the DVD include the following live Linux CD distributions:

- **Knoppix**—A desktop-style live Linux CD that is the world's most popular live CD

- **BackTrack**—The security-oriented live Linux CD based on the SLAX live CD

- **Gentoo Live CD**—An official live CD produced by the Gentoo project using the Catalyst Gentoo installer

- **Damn Small Linux**—A desktop-oriented mini Linux live CD distribution that fits on a bootable business card–size CD (about 50MB)

- **SLAX KillBill**—A SLAX-based live CD that features tools (such as wine and qemu) for testing and using applications created to run in Windows in a Linux system

- **Live Linux Gaming Project**—A Debian-based live CD that features dozens of open source games

These live CD distributions vary in size from about 50MB to nearly 700MB each.

Starting the DVD

To try out the Live Linux CDs DVD, use the following procedure:

1. Insert the DVD into your DVD drive.

2. Reboot the computer.

3. When you see the Live Linux CDs splash screen boot prompt, either press Enter (or wait for the timeout) to boot Knoppix or type one of the following boot labels listed in Table A-1.

TABLE A-1 Labels for Booting Different Live CDs from the DVD

Boot Label	Live CD Boots	Boot Label	Live CD Boots
knoppix	Knoppix	**dsl**	Damn Small Linux
llgp	Live Linux Gaming Project	**slax**	SLAX KillBill
back	BackTrack	**memtest**	Memtest 86 (to test RAM)
gentoo	Gentoo		

You can add boot options, if you like. Any boot options available from the live CD selected should be available by typing the options after the label noted earlier.

To exit most of the live CDs included, you can select a shutdown option from the desktop. Entering Ctrl+Alt+Delete or `init 0` (as root user) should work as well. Sometimes you can simply turn off the computer. However, you should unmount any file systems you have mounted before you just press the off switch.

Using Live CD ISOs from the DVD

I've included about a dozen different live CDs on the DVD that comes with this book to save you the trouble of hunting them down on the Internet. Every ISO image representing live CDs come directly from the projects that built them. So, you can go directly to each live CD's project site on the Internet to ask questions or find out more on how to use the CDs.

All the live CD ISO images are contained in the /distros directory at the top of the DVD. The following sections describe the contents of the /distros directory and where to find more information about each of the live Linux CDs contained in that directory. I suggest that you refer to each of the project sites directly to get later versions of those live CDs or if you have questions about how to obtain, use, or contribute to any of those projects.

NOTE

Many Linux live CD projects are maintained by individuals outside of their regular places of business. Most offer ways for you to contribute money or expertise to help advance the projects. I encourage you to donate whatever you can to the projects you like, to help those projects improve and grow.

To use any one of the live CDs that come with this book, do the following:

1. **Insert the DVD** into the DVD drive on your PC with any operating system running that includes CD-burning software. The operating system can be Windows or Linux. (As an alternative, you can boot the DVD itself and use Knoppix or one of the other live CDs to do this procedure.)

2. **Copy the ISO** for the live CD that you want to use to a folder on the hard disk. With an installed operating system running, copy the live CDs from the /distros directory. With a live CD running from the DVD, look in /cdrom/ distros. (If you have two CD/DVD drives, you can probably skip copying the ISO you want to hard disk and burn the ISO directly from your DVD to the writeable CD drive.

3. **Eject the DVD** and insert a blank or rewritable CD into the DVD/CD drive.

4. **Burn the ISO image** to CD, using a tool such as cdrecord or K3B.

5. **Try the live CD** by inserting the newly burned CD into any PC and rebooting it.

The following sections describe the live CDs that have ISO images included on the DVD.

About Knoppix

Knoppix is the premier desktop live Linux CD. The home page for Knoppix (in English) is www.knopper.net/knoppix/index-en.html. From there, you can get information on what Knoppix contains, how to use it, and how to download or purchase it.

The Knoppix.net site includes a great deal of information and an active community related to Knoppix. There you can find documentation, forums, and download information.

The ISO image for the English version of Knoppix 5.0.1 is included in the /distros directory on the DVD (KNOPPIX_V5.0.1CD-2006-06-01-EN.iso).

About MoviX2

MoviX2 is part of the MoviX project (http://sourceforge.net/projects/movix) and can be used to play movies, music, and images. You can get information about MoviX2, as well as the related eMoviX (for creating bootable movies), from that site. You can also find forums and screenshots and download information from that site.

The DVD that comes with this book includes a zipped archive of MoviX2 (movix-0.3.1rc2-iso.zip) that contains the MoviX2 ISO image (movix2-0.3.1rc2.iso) and some useful README files. Use the `unzip` command to unzip the archive. Then burn the ISO image to CD.

About BackTrack

Information about the BackTrack network security suite live CD is available from the Remote Exploit site (www.remote-exploit.org). Refer to that site for developer information, as well as news, tutorials, and ways of donating to the BackTrack project. BackTrack 1.0 (backtrack-v.1.0-260506.iso) is included in the /distros directory on the DVD.

About Devil Linux

Devil Linux (www.devil-linux.org) is a full-featured firewall live CD that includes many other useful server features as well. Go to the Devil Linux Web site for further information on Devil Linux, including documentation, news, product information, technical support, and download information.

The i586 version of Devil Linux is included in the /distros directory on the DVD (devil-linux-1.2.10-i586-SMP.tar.bz2). Devil Linux should not be burned directly to CD. Instead, you should create a custom version of Devil Linux using the instructions contained in Chapter 13, "Customizing a Firewall Live Linux CD."

About GeeXboX

GeeXboX (www.geexbox.org) is a tiny multimedia player live Linux CD, created particularly to play movie DVDs and music CDs. To use GeeXboX, burn the ISO image of GeeXboX version 1.0 (geexbox-1.0-en.i386.iso) from the /distros directory to a CD. The GeeXboX Generator (geexbox-generator-1.0.i386.tar.gz) is also included in the /distros directory. You can use GeeXboX Generator to create your own live CD that includes audio and/or video content you choose, as described in Chapter 12, "Customizing a Multimedia Live Linux CD."

About Gentoo Live CD

You can use the Gentoo Live CD included with this book as a basic Linux desktop system, but you can also use it to start a Gentoo installation. Visit the Gentoo site (www.gentoo.org) for general information about the Gentoo project.

The Gentoo site includes a tremendous amount of information. The Catalyst page (www.gentoo.org/proj/en/releng/catalyst) is a good place to start for information on building live CDs from scratch. To obtain a copy of any of the official Gentoo live/install CDs, refer to the "Where to Get Gentoo Linux" page (www.gentoo.org/main/en/where.xml).

The DVD that comes with this book includes Gentoo 2006.1 installer live CD (livecd-i686-installer-2006.1.iso) in the /distros directory.

About Damn Small Linux

Damn Small Linux is the most popular mini live Linux CD available today. The best place to start learning about Damn Small Linux is its Web site (www.damnsmall-linux.org). There you can find forums, user documentation, and information on obtaining copies of Damn Small Linux. Damn Small Linux version 3.0.1 (dsl-3.0.1.iso) is included in the /distros directory on the DVD that comes with this book.

About Live Linux Gaming Project

The Live Linux Gaming Project live CD (http://tuxgamers.altervista.org/Llgp.php) contains a good cross-section of open source games, running on a remastered Knoppix live CD. A prerelease version of the Live Linux Gaming Project live CD (llgp-0.1pre0.iso) is included in the /distros directory on the DVD that comes with this book.

About SLAX KillBill

The SLAX KillBill live CD is derived from the SLAX project (www.slax.org). You can download SLAX KillBill from the SLAX download page (www.slax.org/download.php). Refer to the basic SLAX documentation, screenshots, cheat codes, and modules for information on how those items apply to SLAX KillBill.

About ParallelKnoppix

Create HPC clusters with ParallelKnoppix (http://idea.uab.es/mcreel/Parallel-Knoppix). The ParallelKnoppix live CD is included in the /distros directory on the DVD that comes with this book (parallelknoppix-2006-06-19.iso).

About Ubuntu Live CD

As with the Gentoo live CD, the Ubuntu live CD is both a desktop-oriented live CD and an Ubuntu installer live CD. By default, Ubuntu boots to a GNOME desktop. After that, you make a selection from that desktop that lets you do a permanent install of Ubuntu to hard disk. The live CD contains enough software to do a basic Ubuntu installation, but allows you to connect to Ubuntu software repositories over the Internet to any available software you want.

The Ubuntu live CD included on the DVD that comes with this book is Ubuntu version 6.06.1 (ubuntu-6.06.1-desktop-i386.iso) and is located in the /distros directory.

About Presentation Live CD

The Presentation Live CD (called PuppetiX) included on the DVD that comes with this book is a remastered Damn Small Linux live CD made specifically for doing slideshows or OpenOffice.org Impress presentations.

Two versions of PuppetiX are contained on the DVD. The smaller version (puppetix-0.1.iso) is about 62MB and contains images and software needed to play a slideshow. The larger version (puppetix-oo-0.1.iso) is about 160MB and contains both a slideshow and a OpenOffice.org presentation (including the OpenOffice.org software needed to play the presentation).

Because this live CD has no official Web site, and no separate version of it exists outside of the DVD, there is no place to download later versions of the live CD. However, because you had the fortitude to make it this far in the book, if you are having trouble with the Presentation live CD, send me an e-mail and I'll try to help. My e-mail address is chris@linuxtoys.net.

Building, Testing, and Burning ISOs

When you have all the pieces of a live CD in place, you can gather those pieces into a bootable ISO image from Linux typically using the mkisofs command. That ISO image can then be shared from software repositories and run by either of these ways:

- **Starting the ISO image from an emulator**—A convenient way to try an ISO image is to run the ISO image from the local file system using a CPU emulator. Popular emulator software includes VMWare and Qemu. Because Qemu is available with most of the Linux distributions described in this book (and works well in most cases), this appendix primarily describes how to use Qemu to test the ISO images you build. A short description of how to get and use the VMWare Player is also included.

- **Burning the ISO image to bootable media**—Because the live Linux ISO image is intended to be bootable from a removable medium, the last step in producing a live Linux system is to burn that image to CD, DVD, or other removable boot medium. This appendix describes how to use tools such as the cdrecord command and K3b graphical utility to burn ISO images to CD or DVD.

Utilities for making ISO images (mkisofs command), testing ISO images before burning (qemu), and burning them to media (cdrecord and K3b) are noted in procedures throughout the book. However, because those utilities have more features than the few that are mentioned earlier, you can use this appendix as a reference for expanding ways of building, testing, and burning your ISO images.

BUILDING AN ISO IMAGE WITH MKISOFS

When you have finished customizing all the components of your live CD and gathered those components into a directory structure on your hard disk, the next step is to make that directory structure into a single image that you can later burn to CD or DVD. The mkisofs command is the tool most often used in Linux to do that job.

The mkisofs command converts a directory structure into an ISO 9660 filesystem image. For making bootable live Linux CDs/DVDs, mkisofs supports an extension of ISO 9660 referred to as El Torito.

NOTE

Refer to Chapter 4, "Understanding How Live Linux CDs Work," for information on what the El Torito specification is and how it is used to make bootable live Linux CDs.

Using mkisofs

The mkisofs command is noted in several places in this book as the last step in producing a live CD. The following command line shows many of the common options you might add to a mkisofs command when you produce a live Linux CD.

```
# mkisofs -R -b isolinux/isolinux.bin -c isolinux/boot.cat \
   -no-emul-boot -boot-load-size 8 -boot-info-table . > ../livecd.iso
```

In the example of mkisofs just shown, you are starting with the following assumptions:

- **Live CD directory structure**—The dot (.) indicates that the directory structure of your live CD starts at the current directory and its subdirectories. Unless told otherwise (and it's not in this example), all files and directories below that point go into the resulting live CD ISO image.

- **Isolinux files**—The Isolinux files (isolinux.bin and isolinux.cat) are in a subdirectory of the current directory named isolinux.

- **Live CD image**—The final live Linux CD ISO image files are named livecd.iso and are placed in the directory above the current directory (> ../livecd.iso).

The locations of those files just mentioned can vary, depending on your setup. Also, instead of directing the output of mkisofs to a file using the less-than character (>), you can use the -o file option to indicate the name and location of the resulting ISO image. You also have the option of piping the output of mkisofs directly to the cdrecord command. The method for doing that is described later in this section.

You need to supply the El Torito boot image (-b image option) or use the isolinux.bin boot image that comes with the isolinux software package (which most people do). If you are using the GRUB boot loader, an El Torito boot image comes with that package as well. The boot catalog (-c catalog) is produced during the mkisofs process.

Because the ISO 9660 images originally included only DOS-style file naming, extensions need to be added to allow such things as longer filenames, UNIX-style user and group information, symbolic links, block and character devices, and permission bits. The -R option generates System Use Sharing Protocol records (SUSP) and Rock Ridge Interchange Protocol (RR) records to add this information to files that need it on the live CD.

Instead of the -R option, you can use the -r option, which changes permission and ownership to be restrictive in a way that makes sense for a read-only file system. Ownership and group are assigned to the root user. If execute permission is assigned to a directory, to allow searching of that directory, the execute bit is assigned to all directories above that point as well.

The -no-emul-boot option prevents hard disk or floppy emulation from being used to create the boot image. The -boot-load-size 8 option tells mkisofs to load the image into eight 512-byte sectors. The -boot-info-table option instructs mkisofs to modify the boot file indicated by the -b option.

Including and Excluding Files from Your ISO

If you know that you want to exclude files from your ISO image that are contained in the directory structure you feed to mkisofs, you can do that with the -m glob option. In this case, glob is replaced by the wildcard-style pattern matching the file or directory you want to exclude. Here is an example:

```
# mkisofs -m '*.junk" -m core -m whatever > livecd.iso
```

In this example, all files ending with .junk would be excluded, as would all files named core or whatever. Instead of excluding files on the command line, you could add all the files you want excluded to a list and give that list to the mkisofs command using the -exclude-list option, as follows:

```
-exclude-list filename
```

Although it seems easiest to keep all the files for your live Linux CD in one directory structure, mkisofs enables you to merge files from multiple paths. Instead of just changing to the root of the master directory containing your complete live CD directory structure and identifying it with a dot (.) on the mkisofs command line, you could add multiple paths to the end of the mkisofs command line. Files from each of those paths would be added starting from the root of the live CD's file system. For example:

```
# mkisofs [options] /home/chris/master /home/chris/stuff > livecd.iso
```

Another way to add files to your live CD without having them exist in the live CD directory structure is to use the -graft-points option to graft files or directories into your live CD at other points in the file system than the root directory. For example, if you wanted to add photos from the /home/a/image directory to a directory called data/photos on the live CD, you could use mkisofs with the following option:

```
# mkisofs [options] -graft-points /data/photo=/home/a/image > livecd.iso
```

I have used this option myself to drop a changing set of images I download from my digital camera to a live CD without changing the structure of my live CD remastering directory. (See Chapter 10, "Customizing a Presentation Live Linux CD," for an example of how you can graft a directory of images into your live CD.)

Adding Information to the ISO Volume Header

You can add other interesting and useful options to the mkisofs command when you are making a live Linux CD. You might want to use a few of these options to add more information into the volume header for your live CD:

- -p "*preparer_id*"—Replace *preparer_id* with information about how to contact you (or the organization responsible for the live CD). You might use -p "www.example.com" or something similar for this option.

- -publisher "*name*"—You could identify the name of the publisher with this option. For example, you could use -p "Acme Widgets" as the value.

- -V "*Vol_ID*"—Replace *Vol_ID* with a volume name you want to assign to the volume. This name is important because it will be used as the name of the mount point for the live CD in many Linux systems. For example, you could use the option -V "LiveLinuxCD" so that when the resulting live CD is inserted into a running Linux system, it can be mounted automatically to the directory /media/LiveLinuxCD.

- -volset "*ID*"—Specify the volume set ID. Because you can enter up to 128 characters here, it provides space for a longer description of the volume set.

This is useful if you are creating a set of live CDs. The option might be set as in this example:

```
-volset "This is 1 of 5 live CDs showing live Linux solutions"
```

If you burn your ISO to CD using K3b, as described later in this chapter, you can see this information you added to the volume header. If you had used the options shown in the earlier examples, when you load the image to K3b for burning, the header information will appear as shown in Figure B-1.

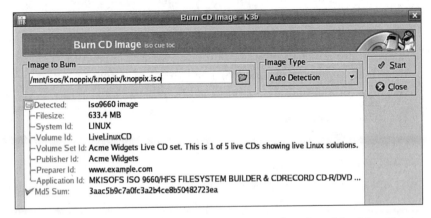

FIGURE B-1 Information added to a volume header with mkisofs appearing in K3b.

As you can see, the system automatically filled in the image type (Iso9660 image), the size of the image (633.4MB), and the system ID (LINUX). The system ID, volume ID, volume set ID, publisher ID, and preparer ID all came from the mkisofs options just described. The other information shown includes the application ID (indicating that mkisofs created the ISO) and the MD5SUM (which is checked on the fly when the ISO image is read by K3b).

If you are preparing a lot of live CDs—say, for your company or organization—you might want the same header information included in all the live CDs you produce. You can use a .mkisofsrc file to set these values. The mkisofs command checks the current directory, then your home directory, and then the directory where the mkisofs command is located to find a .mkisofsrc file.

This example of a .mkisofsrc file contains the tags that can be used instead of the mkisofs command-line options. To see how those tags can be used to provide the same information shown in Figure B-1, that information has been added to the tags as shown here:

```
PREP="www.example.com"
PUBL="Acme Widgets"
VOLI="LiveLinuxCD"
VOLS="Acme Widgets Live CD set. This is 1 of 5 live CDs showing live
      Linux solutions."
```

Other tags you can use in a .mkisofsrc file include APPI (to set an application identifier of up to 128 characters), COPY (to add up to 37 characters of copyright information), ABST (to identify a file on the disk containing an abstract with the disk's contents), BIBL (to add up to 37 characters of bibliographic information), and SYSI (to change the SYSI to something other than LINUX).

Here's one last, extraneous use of the mkisofs command that you might need to use. If you are going to pipe the output of mkisofs directly to cdrecord, some CD writers (and some writing modes) need to know beforehand the size of the ISO image. The form of that command would then be something like the following:

```
# mkisofs options | cdrecord options -
```

Along with the other mkisofs and cdrecord options you enter, you need to pass on the size of the image file to cdrecord using the tsize=#s option, where # is replaced by the number representing the size of the resulting ISO image. To get the number that cdrecord needs (the number of 2048-byte sectors), add the -print-size option to the mkisofs command line you are about to run. For example:

```
# mkisofs -R -b isolinux/isolinux.bin -c isolinux/boot.cat \
  -no-emul-boot -boot-load-size 8 -boot-info-table -print-size .
Using ".mkisofsrc"
Total extents scheduled to be written = 324323
```

Using this example, when you go to run cdrecord (or when you pipe the output of mkisofs to cdrecord), you can add the following value to the cdrecord command line:

```
tsize=324323s
```

Many other options are available with the mkisofs command. To read about those options, refer to the mkisofs man page (man mkisofs). Alternatively, you can run mkisofs with the -help option (mkisofs -help).

TESTING AN ISO IMAGE WITH QEMU

By emulating a PC processor and system components, the QEMU processor emulator (http://fabrice.bellard.free.fr/qemu) can boot up disk images so that you can work with an entire bootable operating system from a window on the Linux desktop.

The system being emulated is either a standard PC with an IDE bus or a PC with an ISA bus (by adding the -M isapc option).

QEMU can operate in user mode (allowing it to run processes created for one CPU type on a different CPU) or full system emulation (emulating the CPU and key peripherals). Often people use QEMU in user mode to run WINE, allowing them to install and run Windows applications, or DOSEMU, to run DOS applications. However, for the purposes of testing live CD ISO images, this book describes QEMU in full system emulation.

For the Linux distributions described in this book, prebuilt binaries are available for QEMU. With an Internet connection, you can install binary packages of QEMU from Debian/Knoppix, Fedora, and Gentoo, respectively, using the following commands:

```
# apt-get install qemu          Debian-based systems like Knoppix
# yum install qemu              Fedora-based systems
# emerge qemu                   Gentoo systems
```

If you prefer, you can also install QEMU from source code. QEMU source code is available from the QEMU download page (http://fabrice.bellard.free.fr/qemu/download.html). From that same page, versions of QEMU also exist for Windows and Mac OSX. (See the "Using QEMU in Windows" section later in this appendix.)

To enhance the performance of QEMU, you can add a kqemu accelerator module plug-in. Because it is available in binary form only (no source code available), it is not distributed with some Linux distribution. For Fedora 5, check http://fedoranews.org/tchung/qemu/ for information on the latest QEMU packages and the location of the kqemu plug-in RPM package. If you get the source code from the QEMU download page instead, you must follow additional instructions to install the kqemu module and create necessary device files.

NOTE

VMware Player is another technology you can use to test ISO images on your computer's desktop. See the sidebar "Testing ISO Images with VMware" for further information.

Starting with QEMU

With the qemu package installed, you run QEMU using the qemu command. Basic options to qemu can be quite simple. For example, to run an ISO image of Damn Small Linux 3.0.1, you could type the following:

```
# qemu -cdrom dsl-3.0.1.iso -boot d
```

The command just shown tells the qemu command to boot the file image named dsl-3.0.1.iso (from the current directory) and to boot it as an ISO 9660 CD image (-cdrom -boot d). If you already burned the image to CD, you can insert that CD into the drive and boot from it in QEMU using the following command line:

```
# qemu -cdrom /dev/cdrom -boot d
```

NOTE

Although we are focused on CD images for this book, QEMU can also boot from hard disk. For example, if you had Gentoo installed on a second hard disk (/dev/hdb) while you worked on Fedora from the first hard disk (/dev/hda), you could launch Gentoo on your desktop by typing something like the following:

```
# qemu -boot c /dev/hdb
```

The qemu command assumes you want to assign 128MB of your available memory as virtual RAM for qemu to run the live CD. If you have more available, you can tell qemu to use more memory with the -m ??? option (where *???* is replaced by the number of megabytes of RAM to use). For example, the following command boots an image called myliveCD.iso with 512MB of memory:

```
# qemu -cdrom myliveCD.iso -boot d -m 512
```

If the amount of memory you want is not available, qemu simply fails and notes the lack of memory.

Working with QEMU

Assuming that the live CD is working, you should see the boot prompt for the live CD image you just launched with qemu. Figure B-2 shows an example of a Fedora live CD being booted in the QEMU window from a Fedora (GNOME) desktop. The qemu command line appears in the terminal window at the top, while the QEMU window displays the live CD boot screen.

To start using the QEMU window, click inside that window and continue the boot process of the live CD as you would if you were booting from a physical CD. Just press Enter or type a boot label to begin testing your live CD.

You should learn several keystrokes to work with your QEMU window:

FIGURE B-2 Boot a live CD to a QEMU window on your desktop.

- **Switch mouse/keyboard**—Because QEMU takes control of your mouse and keyboard after you click in the QEMU window, to use other windows on your desktop again, press Ctrl+Alt. Click inside the QEMU window to return control to QEMU.

- **Full screen**—To view the QEMU window in full-screen mode, press Ctrl+Alt+f. Pressing that key sequence again returns the QEMU window to its original size.

- **Switch virtual consoles**—Within QEMU, you can switch among four different virtual consoles. Pressing Ctrl+Alt+1 always returns to the target system display (in other words, the system you are booting). Ctrl+Alt+2 lets you work from the QEMU monitor (more on that later). Ctrl+Alt+3 switches you to a serial port console (COM1). Ctrl+Alt+4 switches you to a parallel port console (LPT1).

You can use the QEMU monitor (Ctrl+Alt+2) as a way of sending commands directly to QEMU itself (rather than the system you are booting). Ideas for using the monitor (from QEMU documentation) include removing and inserting removable media (CDs, DVDs, or floppies), restoring the VM's state from a disk file (after freezing and unfreezing the virtual machine), and using an external debugger to inspect the virtual machine.

You can use a few commands with the QEMU monitor. With the monitor displayed (type Ctrl+Alt+2), you might want to try these commands:

- `help`—Lists commands that are available.
- `info ??`—Replace *??* with a component name to see additional information about that component. You can find out about VLANs associated with network devices (`network`), block devices (`block`), CPU registers (`registers`), command-line history (`history`), emulated PCI devices (`pci`), devices on a virtual USB hub (`usb`), and USB host devices (`usbhost`). You can also view the QEMU version number (`version`).
- `screendump file.ppm`—Captures the target system display (in other words, what you see when you type Ctrl+Alt+1) to a `ppm` file in the current directory. Replace `file.ppm` with the name you want to use.
- `eject device`—Ejects the medium associated with the device named. For example, replace *device* with `cdrom` to eject the live Linux running from your CD driver, or `fd` to eject your floppy disk.
- `savevm file`—Saves the entire virtual machine state to *file*.
- `loadvm file`—Restores the entire virtual machine state from *file*.
- `quit`—Closes the live CD and exits QEMU.

Other commands are available from the QEMU monitor as well. To find out about other commands, refer to the QEMU man page (`man qemu`) or the QEMU CPU emulator user documentation (http://fabrice.bellard.free.fr/qemu/qemu-doc.html).

Using QEMU in Windows

Imagine that you have a live CD ISO image that you have completed or downloaded. It's sitting on your Windows hard disk, and you'd like to be able to launch it from a running Windows system. The QEMU site references a QEMU on Windows page (www.h7.dion.ne.jp/~qemu-win) where you can download a binary that includes a small Linux from the QEMU `linux-test` package.

I used the following procedure to download QEMU to Windows so I could use it from a Windows desktop to test a Linux live CD. I did this procedure from Windows XP with an Internet connection:

1. Download the qemu-windows.zip file from www.h7.dion.ne.jp/~qemu-win using a Web browser (or other download tool) from Windows. (When I went to this Web site, the file was called qemu-0.8.2-windows.zip.)

2. Right-click the qemu Zip file and select Extract.

3. When prompted, select a folder to store the extracted qemu files.

4. Save the ISO file to an accessible folder on your Windows system. I saved it to a folder that was the parent to the folder where I saved qemu.

5. Run the qemu command to start the live CD. For my example, I opened a command prompt (DOS) window to the directory where I extracted qemu. Then I ran the following command to launch an ISO Damn Small Linux from the directory above the current directory:

```
# qemu.exe -L . -boot d -cdrom dsl-3.0.1.iso
```

Figure B-3 shows an example of the Damn Small Linux desktop displayed in a QEMU window on a Windows XP desktop:

FIGURE B-3 Use QEMU to test a Linux live CD in Windows XP.

TESTING ISO IMAGES WITH VMWARE PLAYER

The VMware Player (www.vmware.com/products/player) is a popular tool you can use instead of QEMU to test ISO images on your computer's desktop. The player, which is free to download, lets you start up a virtual machine to run a completely separate operating system from a window on your display. Because it can run in Windows, Linux, and other PC-based systems, you can test your ISO images without rebooting your operating system.

You can download the VMware Player from www.vmware.com/download/player. Because VMware Player is not open source software, it cannot be distributed with Linux distributions. Getting it to work can be a bit tricky. For Fedora Core, I used a description here to get it to work: http://tredosoft.com/node/9.

With VMware working, the next trick is to play the live CD within a virtual machine. A small piece of software from VMwarez.com can help you there (www.vmwarez.com/2006/02/livecd-player-virtual-machine.html). Any live CD you copy to the file livecd.iso in the directory where you unzip the Generic-LiveCD-Virtual-Machine software can be booted from that directory by typing:

```
# vmplayer vmwarez.com-Generic-LiveCD-Virtual-Machine.vmx
```

If you switch to another live CD (copy a new one to livecd.iso), be sure to set the VMware Player preferences (Select Player → Preferences) to power off the virtual machine on closing. Otherwise, closing the old CD will simply suspend it, so it is reopened the next time you start vmplayer. Figure B-4 shows the boot screen of a slide show live CD I made of a trip to DisneyWorld. It is running in a vmplayer window using the VMwarez.com software described previously.

BURNING ISO IMAGES WITH CDRECORD OR K3B

When you have a completed ISO image, you can use many tools for Linux and Windows for burning the ISO image to CD or DVD. This section covers two popular tools for burning images to CD and DVD that are available with every major Linux distribution: cdrecord and K3b.

Burning CDs and DVDs with cdrecord

The cdrecord command is an easy-to-use tool you can use to burn your ISO images to CD or DVD. By supporting the ATA Packet Interface (ATAPI) standard, cdrecord can work with IDE CD-ROM drives using SCSI commands that are transported over the IDE interface. To cdrecord, an IDE CD drive looks like a SCSI device. This works fine because all CD/DVD writes use SCSI commands to communicate.

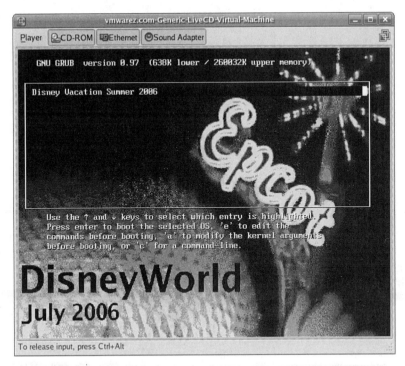

FIGURE B-4   Use VMware Player to boot live CDs on a Linux or Windows desktop.

Every major Linux distribution that I know of includes the cdrecord command. If you have a recent Linux distribution, it probably includes cdrecord 2.0 or later. Jörg Schilling created cdrecord, but several Linux distributions (including Red Hat Linux systems and SuSE) maintain their own versions of cdrecord.

Using default settings (set in the /etc/cdrecord.conf file), you aren't required to add a lot of options to cdrecord. The default drive is typically set to /dev/cdrom in that file. If a writeable CD or DVD drive is your first drive, and that drive is not being used currently to run a live CD, you might be able to burn an ISO image to CD or DVD with just one option: the name of the ISO. For example, if your ISO image were in the current directory and were named mylivecd.iso, you would insert a blank CD or DVD into the drive and type the following:

```
# cdrecord mylivecd.iso
```

With the example just shown, when cdrecord completes, you can eject the CD or DVD and you are done. If that doesn't work, or if you want a bit more control over the process, you can use one of many options to cdrecord.

You can get information about your writeable drives in several ways before proceeding. If you have multiple CD or DVD drives, you might need to indicate which one you want to write to. You can use a device name (such as /dev/cdrom) to indicate the drive or the SCSI device name. To determine the SCSI device name for your writeable CD and DVD drives, you can use the scanbus option, as follows:

```
# cdrecord -scanbus
Cdrecord-Clone 2.01-dvd (i686-pc-linux-gnu)
Copyright (C) 1995-2004 Jorg Schilling
scsidev: 'ATA'
devname: 'ATA'
scsibus: -2 target: -2 lun: -2
Linux sg driver version: 3.5.27
Using libscg version 'schily-0.8'.
scsibus1:
    1,0,0    100) 'LITE-ON ' 'DVDRW SOHW-1633S' 'BS0C' Removable CD-ROM
    1,1,0    101) *
    1,2,0    102) *
    1,3,0    103) *
    1,4,0    104) *
    1,5,0    105) *
    1,6,0    106) *
    1,7,0    107) *
```

In this example, only one CD/DVD writer is found, at the SCSI address 1,0,0. That indicates SCSI bus 1, target 0, and LUN 0. So using the dev= option, you can identify that device as either dev=1,0,0 or dev=/dev/cdrom on the cdrecord command line. The SCSI address form is preferred, for the simple reason that there is no guarantee that the Linux system you are using will use /dev/cdrom to access the CD drive you want.

To see a complete list of options, type cdrecord -help. To find the version number of cdrecord, use the -version option. For information on SCSI transport specifiers, use the dev=help option. You can use the driveropts and -checkdrive options to check for options that are specific to a drive. For example, to check options for the drive located at /dev/cdrom, type the following:

```
# cdrecord dev=/dev/cdrom driveropts=help -checkdrive
    .
    .
    .
Driver options:
burnfree       Prepare writer to use BURN-Free technology
noburnfree     Disable using BURN-Free technology
forcespeed     Tell the drive to force speed even for low quality media
```

When no speed option is given, cdrecord tries the maximum speed that it can detect is available for the drive and medium you are using. At times this value can be incorrect, or you might be getting write errors and want to change the speed yourself. In particular, I've noticed that the maximum speed for some DVDs is not detected properly; you might have to set the maximum writing speed yourself. To set the speed to the lowest possible value, use speed=0.

Other popular options to the cdrecord command include the verbose option (-v) and the eject option (-eject). If you are unfamiliar with the drive you are using, you can do a test run using the -dummy options. Using cdrecord with -dummy goes through all the motions requested on the cdrecord command line but doesn't turn on the laser and actually burn the disk. This command-line example includes several of the options just described:

```
# cdrecord dev=/dev/cdrom1 speed=4 -eject -dummy -v mylivecd.iso
```

In the example just shown, cdrecord uses the second CD drive (/dev/cdrom1) and a 4x speed (which is four times the audio speed). Verbose output is displayed as the recording progresses. When the entire image has been burned to CD/DVD, the disk is ejected.

You can choose from several writing modes. Most drives created after 1997 are compliant with the Multimedia Command set 2 (MMC-2) specification, so they should support at least one of the writing modes described. Consider these examples:

> **NOTE**
>
> In cases noted shortly, when you need to know the exact size of each track before you begin recording, you can determine that size when you run the mkisofs command to create your ISO image. Adding the -print-size option produces the information you need.

- **-sao**—The Session At Once (-sao) mode is available only with MMC drives that support this mode. To use this mode, cdrecord must know the exact size of each track. This mode is also sometimes called Disk At Once mode (so you can use -dao instead of -sao).
- **-tao**—The Track At Once writing mode is used by default with cdrecord. This mode is required if you are doing multisession recording.
- **-raw**—Some CD recorders that have bad firmware won't work in -sao or -tao modes. In those cases, you might need to use the -raw writing mode. When -raw is specified, it defaults to -raw96r. The -raw96r mode uses 2448-byte sector sizes (from 2352-byte sectors and 96 bytes of raw P-W subchannel data). Other raw modes include -raw16 (2368-byte sector size, from 2352-byte sectors plus 16 bytes of P-Q subchannel data) and -raw96p (same size as -raw96r, used only in a few CD recorders). Either -raw96r or -raw16 should be used in most cases when you want to write in raw mode.

If you are using a rewriteable CD medium (which is a good idea as you test your live CDs repeatedly), you can use a blank option with cdrecord to erase your CD before rerecording. To blank an entire disk, use blank=all, blank=disc, or blank=disk. For a quicker but less thorough way to erase your disk, you can just erase the PMA, TOC, and pregap using blank=fast or blank=minimal. Here's an example of a command for fully erasing the disk associated with /dev/cdrom:

```
# cdrecord dev=/dev/cdrom blank=all
```

Many more options available with the cdrecord command also might interest you. To learn more, refer to the cdrecord man page (type man cdrecord).

Burning CDs and DVDs with K3b

If you are more comfortable working from a GUI than from the command line, you might want to use several graphical CD/DVD writing tools available for Linux. The one described here is called K3b. If you are using Linux from a KDE desktop, it's possible that K3b is already installed. Often you can select it from the Multimedia submenu on the KDE menu or Sound & Video from the Applications menu in GNOME.

With K3b, most of the options described in the cdrecord section are available from selections in the window. The following procedure steps you through a simple CD-burning session with K3b:

1. Insert a blank CD or DVD medium into your writeable CD/DVD drive.

2. Open the K3b window (either from the Multimedia menu in KDE or the Sound & Video menu in GNOME).

3. Select Tools → Burn CD Image. (If you are burning a DVD image, select Burn DVD ISO Image instead.) A Burn CD Image pop-up window appears.

4. In Image to Burn, type in (or browse for) the ISO image you want to burn to disk. Figure B-5 shows the window after a live CD image named livecd.iso has been selected. Notice that the window shows information about the image. That information includes the type of image, its size, system and volume IDs, the application that created it (mkisofs), and the image's MD5SUM.

5. Change any settings you choose before you start the burn process. In particular, you might want to change the speed if you think it is not being autodetected properly. If you have multiple CD/DVD writers, you can choose which one to use. You can set the writing mode to DAO, TAO, or RAW. To do a test run first, you can select the Simulate option.

6. Select Start. K3b begins burning your ISO image to CD or DVD. You can watch the FIFO and Device buffers as the writing progresses. When it is done, a trumpet sounds and the CD ejects.

7. Select Show Debugging Output. You can see verbose output from the cdrecord command that was used to do the actual writing. At the end, the output show the full cdrecord command line that was used to write the ISO to CD or DVD.

8. If you changed any of the settings, you can select Save User Defaults. That way, you can bring back the same settings the next time you burn a CD/DVD.

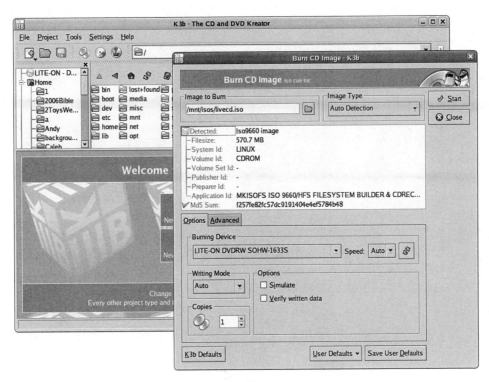

FIGURE B-5 Burn ISO images to CD or DVD using K3b.

Index

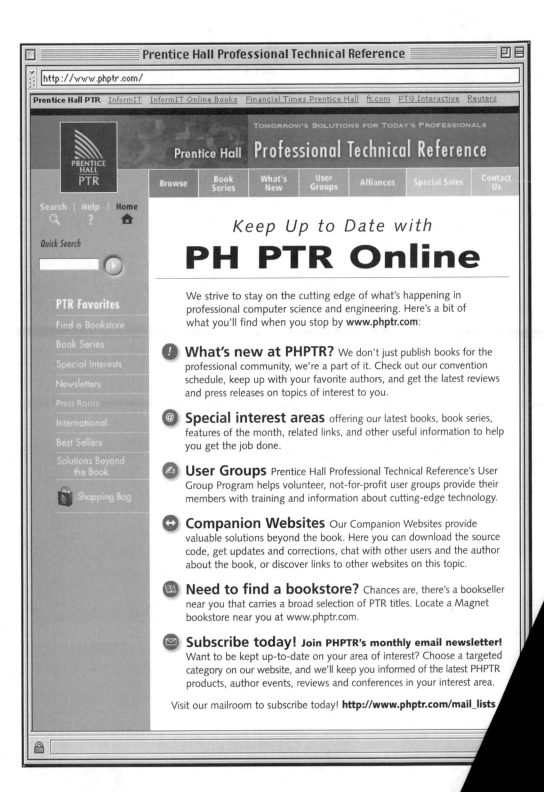